Breaking
the Real
Axis of Evil

Breaking the Real Axis of Evil

How to Oust the World's Last Dictators by 2025

Ambassador Mark Palmer

ROWMAN & LITTLEFIELD PUBLISHERS, INC.
Lanham • Boulder • New York • Oxford

ROWMAN & LITTLEFIELD PUBLISHERS, INC.

Published in the United States of America
by Rowman & Littlefield Publishers, Inc.
A wholly owned subsidary of The Rowman & Littlefield Publishing Group, Inc.
4501 Forbes Boulevard, Suite 200, Lanham, Maryland 20706
www.rowmanlittlefield.com

PO Box 317
Oxford
OX2 9RU, UK

British Library Cataloguing in Publication Information Available

Library of Congress Cataloging-in-Publication Data

Palmer, Mark, 1941–
  Breaking the real axis of evil : how to oust the world's last
dictators by 2025 / Ambassador Mark Palmer
    p. cm.
includes bibliographical references and index.
    1. Dictatorship. 2. Government, Resistance to. 3. Democratization.
4. Terrorism—Prevention. I. Title.
  JC495.P34 2003
  321.9—dc22   2003016010

ISBN 0-7425-3254-2 (cloth : alk. paper)
ISBN 0-7425-3255-0 (pbk. : alk. paper)

Printed in the United States of America

∞™ The paper used in this publication meets the minimum requirements of
American National Standard for Information Sciences—Permanence of Paper for
Printed Library Materials, ANSI/NISO Z39.48-1992.

To All Those with the Vision and Courage
to Oust Their Oppressors

Contents

Illustrations

Figures

Table

Acknowledgments

Peter Ackerman and Max Kampelman encouraged me to think through a strategy and tactics to achieve a 100 percent democratic world. Jack DuVall provided conceptual advice, critiqued the entire manuscript, and contributed to the sections on the use of nonviolent force. Kurt Bassuener and Eric Witte assisted across the board with ideas, research, and language. Kristin Guida and Charles Graybow worked on the profiles of the "The Forty-five Least Wanted." Dean Cowan used his considerable computer skills to create the manuscript. In the final stages, Carl Posey helped make the book more reader friendly.

Fellow American ambassadors Harry Barnes, Michael Armacost, Steve Bosworth, Howard Schaffer, Smith Hempstone, Win and Betty Lord, Roger Kirk, and others shared ideas and experience. Fellow democracy activists Ken Wollack, Michael Ledeen, John Sullivan, John Fox, Carl Gershman, Barbara Haig, Mark Plattner, Gene Sharp, Bob Helvey, Jennifer Windsor, Adrian Karatnycky, Stuart Auerbach, Walt Raymond, and many others shared experience and recommendations.

I am grateful to Jed Lyons and Jonathan Sisk of Rowman & Littlefield for deciding to publish my manifesto, and to Julie Kirsch for help with editing and proofing and production.

My parents, Capt. Robie Ellis Palmer (USN) and Katherine Hooker Palmer, came from Maine and Vermont. They instilled in me a fierce New England commitment to independent thinking and individual liberty. I recall my mother rising at a town meeting in the back of the hall in Westminster, Vermont, which my father was chairing, to proclaim loudly: "Robie, that's about the stupidest proposal I've ever heard you make." This attitude toward authority (and men) is the essence of democracy; I have found it in villages and cities across the globe.

On our first date, an Indian student was surprised to find that a young American diplomat's invitation to dinner meant sitting on the floor of a Tibetan monastery in New Delhi, eating and talking with the monks about Chinese oppression. Over the ensuing three decades of our marriage, Sushma has understood and shared my passion for dissidents and democrats, informed and shaped it, and played an immensely important role in conceiving and producing this book from its title to its conclusion.

Introduction

Standing before the British Parliament on 8 June 1982, President Ronald Reagan spoke about "our abhorrence of dictatorship in all its forms" and "the terrible inhumanities it has caused in our times." He called for all communist and other dictatorships to be put on the "ash heap of history" and expressed his ultimate Californian/American optimism that "with a global campaign for freedom . . . strong leadership, time and a little bit of hope, the forces of good ultimately rally and triumph over evil." Widespread skepticism greeted his predictions, but dictators across the globe have fallen since then, and entire regions have emerged as zones of peace and freedom.

I wrote the initial draft of President Reagan's speech, and my own conviction that all people want freedom and can achieve it was and is based on personal experience. On trips to the Soviet Union during the early 1960s, as a student majoring in Russian studies, I became convinced that Russian students wanted the same things I did. One girl told me, "I would cut off my right arm for a visit to Paris, London, and New York."

The importance of enunciating a vision became clear to me from Martin Luther King's "I have a dream" speech. I was one of hundreds of white northern students who traveled south in the early 1960s to stand with local blacks, to sit in, pray in, and march. This experience began to show me the power of nonviolent strategies against injustice.

I spent the summer of 1963 in a poor Mexican village with the Quakers, which also taught me a lot about oppression. Government officials or representatives of the Institutional Revolutionary Party (PRI)—the corrupt monopoly party in power since 1919—came heavily armed when they visited the village, because they knew that only intimidation and fear could preserve their hold on power. When that fear eroded, Mexicans threw off a one-party system and became vigorous supporters of democracy and human rights at home and across the globe as well.

My tenure as a U.S. Foreign Service officer from 1964 to 1990 in Moscow, Belgrade, and Budapest, and in the State Department itself, gave me a front-row seat, and I even became one of the minor actors, as the drama of the transition from frozen communism to full-scale democracy unfolded. From attending controversial plays and trying to encourage writers, directors, and actors at the Sovremennik and Taganka theaters as a junior political officer in Moscow in the early 1970s, to marching in the streets with the Hungarian democratic opposition in 1989 as the U.S. ambassador, I saw how dictators can be ousted by a determined opposition and the role outsiders can play—particularly in helping people gain confidence in themselves.

I was the chief speech writer for Henry Kissinger, Richard Nixon's secretary of state, accompanying him on his forays to dictatorships across the globe. I worked for six years inside Leonid Brezhnev's Soviet Union and Tito's Yugoslavia. I directed the State Department's Office of Strategic, Nuclear and Conventional Arms Control during the Carter administration, and when Ronald Reagan came to office, I became the deputy assistant secretary shaping U.S. relations with the Soviet Union and east central Europe.

It was in Moscow in 1985, preparing for President Reagan's first meeting with General Secretary Mikhail Gorbachev, that Secretary of State George Shultz taught me how to engage and educate dictators. In his talks with Foreign Minister Eduard Shevardnadze and General Secretary Gorbachev, he liked to stray from the standard agenda to explore the parameters of modern democratic society and market economics. At the time, I urged him to keep to the format. Then I watched as Ronald Reagan worked the same constructive ploy with Gorbachev in Geneva.

Having observed those two grand pros in action, when I took up the ambassador's post in Budapest in 1986, I applied Shultz's lesson to my dealings with Karoly Grosz, Hungary's last communist dictator. It was there that I fully understood—and employed—the axiom that, in the sea of tyranny, a democratic embassy must be an island of liberty and a steady, and not always subtle, proponent of change.

If anything, my views on the importance—and feasibility—of spreading democracy have hardened since I left the Foreign Service in 1990 and entered private enterprise. As one of the first American investors in eastern Europe following the fall of communism, I saw that stable democracies with market economies can emerge where none have existed before, and I saw again that outsiders have a key role to play. Together with our local partners, we created the first politically independent commercial television stations in eight countries and also built, at the site of Checkpoint Charlie, that symbol of communist oppression, cold war confrontation, and ultimate liberation a shining modern office complex, a fitting symbol of the successful transformation and opening of a closed society.

I helped conceive and create the Community of Democracies, which assembled representatives from 107 countries in Warsaw in June of 2000, and 110 countries in Seoul in November of 2002, and I serve on the boards of Freedom House, the Council for a Community of Democracies, and the Center for Communications, Health, and the Environment. All of which is to say that I have bet my career, my money, and much of my adult life on the possibility of a fully democratic world.

The alternative to that possibility seems to me bleak in the extreme. To see what dictatorships will bring to the twenty-first century, one has only to look at the century recently ended—by all accounts, the bloodiest in human history. Stalin, Hitler, Mao, and others committed the worst crimes against humanity in the short history of our species. On 24 June 2001, Pope John Paul II visited the woods outside Kiev where nearly 200,000 people had been killed on Joseph Stalin's orders and secretly buried in mass graves. A day later, he went to Babi Yar, also in Kiev, where another 200,000 bodies—Jews and other victims of the Hitler era—had been cached.[1] Within days, news came that Kosovars in the thousands had been secretly killed and secretly buried, on the orders of Serbian dictator Slobodan Milosevic.

I believe that the future does not have to mimic the past, that we have the means at our disposal to end dictatorships by 2025. As the last quarter century has seen the demise of dozens of dictators, it seems reasonable to strive over the next quarter century to "finish the job," to establish a "deadline for dictators."

This book is about the future, not the past.

It is about how the Arab world, described in a study by thirty leading Arabs as suffering three fundamental gaps—in freedom, women's rights, and knowledge—can join the democratic revolution. It is the only region without a single democratically elected leader, yet it is a region where public opinion polling shows strong support for democratic values and systems. I spent two years traveling in the Arab world trying to create the first politically independent television stations; it was crystal clear that the people wanted them but the dictators stood and stand in the way. On 21 October 2002 at a Freedom House ceremony to honor Saad Ibrahim, Egypt's leading democratic thinker and activist, I stood next to his wife as she read his inspiring call, written in a prison cell, for democracy in Egypt and throughout the Arab world. As 2003 opened and Saad was freed from prison, democracy came onto the Middle East's agenda in unprecedented fashion.

This book is also about China, which came so close to freedom in 1989, the same year the barbed wire was cut on the Hungarian border with Austria and the Berlin Wall came down. On 23 July 2002, I stood in front of the U.S. Capitol as chairman of the annual demonstration of Falun Gong—a movement based on ancient Chinese beliefs and practices that dictator Jiang Zemin's own people once estimated as having over seventy million followers. This movement is comparable to Gandhi's in its commitment to nonviolence as well as its skillful and courageous perseverance and power. The message at this demonstration was clear: the Chinese people demand, and will get, their human rights. But in the meantime, thousands of Falun Gong practitioners have been murdered by Jiang Zemin's regime.

Most of all, this book is about intervention. On the eve of receiving his Presidential Medal of Freedom in July 2002, legendary *New York Times* editor and columnist A. M. Rosenthal spoke to a gathering at Freedom House, recalling the 1964 Kitty Genovese murder in New York. More than thirty of Genovese's neighbors had watched as she was repeatedly stabbed and cried for help; no one intervened. Rosenthal asked, "When is it a sin not to intervene to help someone? When they are a hundred feet away? When they are further? When you can know they are being butchered, starved and oppressed but are not physically present?"

I answer that it is wrong to stand by and do nothing when people anywhere on Earth are being brutally treated by the despots who rule them. We know millions of North Koreans have starved because of Kim Jong Il. We know that the world's dictators are at the root of terrorism and war. We must act now. This is the story of the last forty-five dictators, the strategy and tactics to oust them, and the ways to empower the people of every nation to control their own destinies.

The Real Axis of Evil

*On one point we are all united: our abhorrence of dictatorship in all its forms.
. . . For the sake of peace and justice let us move toward a world in which all
people are at last free to determine their own destiny.*

—Ronald Reagan

In January 2002, when President George W. Bush gave his first State of the Union address, a new phrase entered the American vocabulary: axis of evil. The president used it to describe three nations that have been, at one time or another, deadly enemies of the United States: Iraq, Iran, and North Korea. None of the threesome much appreciated being identified in that way or, for that matter, with one another. And the world at large saw the freshly minted term as a careless lurch toward trouble. Such figures as French foreign minister Hubert Vedrine were inclined to describe it as "simplistic," as if such a coalition of evil were an impossibility in this new century.[1]

It seemed to me, however, that such coalitions were not just possible but exactly what was wrong with the world today. The difference was that I believed an axis of three fell woefully short of describing fully what is in fact a vast arc of tyranny, where a few dozen men hold a third of the planet's population under their thumbs.

This arc runs unbroken west from China and North Korea, through Kazakhstan, on to Syria and Algeria, and south to Angola. The map inside the front cover shows this arc appropriately in black. Asia has eight dictatorships: China, North Korea, Vietnam, Cambodia, Laos, Brunei, Bhutan, and Burma (Myanmar). Eleven dictatorships survive in sub-Saharan Africa: Angola, Burundi, Cameroon, Congo, Equatorial Guinea, Guinea, Liberia, Rwanda,

Swaziland, Togo, and Zimbabwe. And more than half of the world's forty-five dictatorships—twenty-three in all—are concentrated in and around the Middle East. Only three—Belarus, Cuba, and Haiti—lie outside this great desert where liberty is not allowed to grow.

In democracies, we sometimes equate dictatorship dismissively with tinplate tyrants and small men on horseback. But the important tyrants in our real axis of evil are nothing of the kind. The dictator of China controls something like a fifth of the planet's population, holds vast natural and industrial resources, and has a powerful, nuclear-armed military. Much of the world's petroleum—some 50 percent—is buried under the dictatorships of the Greater Middle East, where determined sponsorship of terrorists is sometimes coupled with a yen for chemical, biological, and nuclear weapons of mass destruction.

Although these dictators may differ in terms of religion, political ideology, ethnic background, and nationality, they nevertheless have much in common. They share, for example, a willingness to use such weapons as they have, whether machetes or canisters of lethal chemical agents, against all enemies, real and imagined, foreign and domestic. Under their stony gaze, millions upon millions have gone to their deaths, a great tide of refugees has swept across the planet, and promising nations have been driven into poverty, famine, and despair.

These despots care little for the welfare of their people. Saddam Hussein blamed the desperate circumstances of the Iraqi people on United Nations sanctions imposed in 1991, after a twenty-two-nation coalition drove his invading army from Kuwait. But all evidence indicates that Iraq's hardships have been overwhelmingly the result of his misrule. Having obtained permission to sell oil to buy food and other humanitarian necessities, the dictator spent the revenue on weaponry and an extraordinary number of palaces, many built during the sanctions regime.

Kurdish northern Iraq, under the protection of British and American aircraft, had to accommodate to the same sanctions as the rest of the nation. But there the oil for food program has been used as intended, and the standard of living has risen steadily. Infant mortality in the region has actually decreased.[2]

In Iran, Ayatollah Ali Khamenei systematically jails, tortures, and murders Iranians striving for democracy, in an effort to terrorize the people who must endure his unelected rule. He has continued Iran's close support of terrorism waged against democratic Israel. As the nation's elected parliamentary and government leaders lean toward more open relationships with the forces of peace and democracy in the world, Khamenei and his security apparatus go just the other way, embracing dictatorship wherever they find it.

In North Korea, Kim Jong Il continues in the terrible footsteps of his father, Kim Il Sung, who brought war to the peninsula in 1950.[3] Personally involved in acts of terrorism before his ascension to North Korea's communist throne, Kim Jong Il continues to nurture tensions between his nation and South Korea and, as his citizens starve by the hundreds of thousands, manages to sustain—and feed—a million-man army, the fourth-largest military force in the world. His interest in weapons of mass destruction is legendary, and his country leads the world in purveying nuclear-capable missiles to his fellow tyrants.[4]

Indeed, these dictators are quick to help one another, sometimes inadvertently. Saddam Hussein could not have meant to consolidate the hold of Ayatollah Ruhollah Khomeini when he invaded Iran in 1980, but that—and the deaths of hundreds of thousands—was one result.[5] The dictator of Iraq worked with Kim Jong Il, who, although widely seen as xenophobic, does business with Ayatollah Khamenei, Fidel Castro in Cuba, Robert Mugabe in Zimbabwe, and Aleksandr Lukashenko in Belarus, among others.

But these arrangements are almost trivial compared to the web spun by Jiang Zemin, the communist dictator of China. China—a longtime patron of the North Korean hermit state and a combatant in the war against South Korea in the 1950s—remains bound to the regime of Kim Jong Il. When China stages aggressive military exercises to pressure Taiwan, it apparently coordinates those actions with North Korean provocations in South Korean waters.[6] In recent years, Beijing has positioned itself as a supposed broker of peace on the Korean peninsula, but its motive may well be to scuttle, not promote, peace talks, delaying North Korea's democratization and modernization. Were North Koreans to bring down their communist dictator, China's communist dictatorship would also shudder. As a representative from a Chinese government-affiliated institute commented, "then the Korean Peninsula would be wholly controlled by the United States and its coterie. North Korea's existence protects China from American military domination."[7] While cooperation has been of mutual benefit to the dictators in Pyongyang and Beijing, it has done little for the North Korean and Chinese people. What were once billed as budding socialist utopias have become lands of repeated famine, brutal repression, and environmental devastation.

Even as controls seem to ease, China has scant interest in individual freedom for its people. In August 1999, for example, Jiang ordered the arrest of Rebiya Kader, one of China's shining stars in business. The crime? Kader, an ethnic Uighur in the western province of Xinjiang (also known as Chinese Turkestan), was trying to deliver a report on police harassment to visiting members of the U.S. Congressional Research Service.[8] The arrest was part of Jiang's continuing crackdown on the sizable Muslim minority in Xinjiang, which thus far has served only to feed separatist sentiment and the fantasies of radical militants. While indiscriminately targeting the "Islamic fundamentalist" and "terrorist"

Uighur population, Jiang supports leading state sponsors of terrorism. Through the sale of missile and other weapons technology, the political leverage of its permanent membership on the UN Security Council, political coordination, and economic aid, the dictator in Beijing has in recent years repeatedly come to the aid of Iran, Iraq, Libya, Syria, Sudan, Cuba, and North Korea—the seven state sponsors of terrorism listed by the U.S. State Department.[9] The first five of these states are listed for supporting terrorist organizations linked to Islamic fundamentalism, strange bedfellows for China's antireligious government. In June of 2000, for example, a member of the Chinese Communist Party Central Committee visited Baghdad on a mission to improve ties between the Chinese dictatorship and Saddam Hussein's party apparat. The Chinese delegate duly condemned UN sanctions against Iraq and anticipated a closer relationship between the countries' ruling parties. According to Beijing's *People's Daily*, Iraqi vice president Taha Yassin Ramadan responded in kind: "It conforms to the interests of the Iraqi government as well as the Arab Baath Socialist Party to develop relations with China."[10]

Although Iraq has been one of the prime beneficiaries of Beijing's eagerness to peddle military hardware to international pariahs, its deadly foe, Ayatollah Ali Khamenei of Iran, has also been welcomed by Beijing's proliferation bazaar. China has reportedly stepped up construction of an advanced air-defense system in Iran and resumed sales of nuclear and chemical weapons technology to the dictatorship.[11] Beyond the obvious security implications of such sales, Beijing's dealings strengthen Khamenei and other hardliners at the expense of the majority of the Iranian population, which favors a conciliatory approach to the democratic world.

On the terrible day of 11 September 2001, a Pakistani newspaper reported that a Chinese government delegation had just signed a memorandum of understanding on economic and technical cooperation with Afghanistan's Taliban regime.[12] Later reports revealed that two Chinese government companies had already been constructing a telecommunications system for the Taliban in Kabul.[13] This is the same Taliban regime that until its defeat hosted Osama bin Laden's training of China's Uighur extremists. An alleged senior Qaeda official told Britain's *Guardian* newspaper that China had paid large sums of money directly to Osama bin Laden for unexploded U.S. cruise missiles from Washington's August 1998 attempt to strike the terrorist mastermind at his training camps in Afghanistan.[14]

The first "Muslim nuclear bomb" and the missile technology to deliver it exist thanks to China's and North Korea's communist dictators aiding Pakistan's military dictators.

Beyond its support of dictator-state sponsors of terror and aspiring or actual nuclear-weapons states, Beijing lends its considerable diplomatic weight to any number of lesser tyrants. Jiang Zemin and Aleksandr Lukashenko of Belarus—the last dictator in Europe—have developed very close ties, twice in 2001 holding warm and fuzzy summits. At the first of these, Lukashenko demonstrated his usefulness to the Beijing regime by telling its tightly controlled Xinhua News Agency: "Belarus always supports China's constant position on the issues of human rights. I appreciate China's success at the recent UN human rights session. I congratulate you on your crushing the U.S. intention to put forward an anti-China motion."[15] The *People's Daily* reported that at the July summit in Minsk, "Jiang said China is thankful of the support from Belarus on issue [sic] of Taiwan, Tibet and human rights."[16] In return, less than two months before Lukashenko stole a rigged election, Jiang expressed his respect for Lukashenko's approach to Belarussian "internal and foreign policy." The *People's Daily* went on to report: "China supports the efforts of Belarus to oppose any foreign interference and to safeguard its national sovereignty and territorial integrity."[17]

As Zimbabwe has plunged into dictatorship under the misrule of Robert Mugabe, Beijing has stoked the fire. While Mugabe drives white farmers off their land, effectively emptying southern Africa's breadbasket, Beijing provides agricultural equipment for use on illegally seized farms.[18] Mugabe refers to China as "the number one friend of Zimbabwe," and Li Peng, of Tiananmen Square infamy, thanks the Mugabe regime for its "one-China" policy and support for China in international affairs.[19]

In June 2000, this same Li Peng took part in a fitting meeting with then-president of the Federal Republic of Yugoslavia, Slobodan Milosevic. The warm get-together between the Butcher of Beijing and the Butcher of Belgrade resulted in predictable pledges of mutual support in the face of criticism and pressure from democrats in Serbia, China, and the West. Li issued a pro forma condemnation of the NATO intervention in Kosovo. Milosevic, according to the *People's Daily*, paid homage to the Chinese regime. "China is the major force for advocating multi-polarity and fighting hegemony," he said. "Yugoslavia supports the Chinese central government's efforts to have Taiwan rejoin the motherland and upholds the one-China principle."[20]

Though Beijing is an important hub, not all dictator linkages intersect there. For years, Slobodan Milosevic's Yugoslavia joined Aleksandr Lukashenko's Belarussian regime in providing air-defense technology to Saddam Hussein's military. In a meeting with senior leaders of the Milosevic regime in July 2000, Saddam made the requisite condemnation of the NATO intervention in Kosovo.[21]

At a May 2001 meeting between Iran's Ayatollah Ali Khamenei and Cuban dictator Fidel Castro, Khamenei explained the mutual benefit of the relationship by saying, "Our resistance against the U.S. hegemony is based on

Islamic beliefs that Iran regards any resistance against arrogance in the world as a righteous move."[22] The Islamic Republic News Agency, a simple mouthpiece for Khamenei and other Iranian hardliners, further explained: "Iran and Cuba enjoy strong cordial relations and Cuba has always supported the Islamic Republic's stances at international scenes."[23]

In Africa, Muammar al-Qaddafi, the Libyan dictator, has supported nearly every tyrant on the continent. His government trained and befriended Liberian dictator Charles Taylor and his partner in crime Foday Sankoh, leader of the notorious Revolutionary United Front of Sierra Leone.[24] By financing slaughter in West Africa, Qaddafi opened up lucrative weapons-trafficking routes and gained profits from the diamonds mined by his protégés' child soldiers in Sierra Leone.[25] According to a *Washington Post* report, Osama bin Laden's Qaeda terrorist network has also tapped into Sierra Leone's blood-diamond wealth through Qaddafi and the West African branch of the dictators' club.[26]

Helped by such allies, Africa's dictators regularly send their thuggish armies across international borders with impunity, fueling genocidal conflicts that slaughtered well over one million people in 1994 alone. Robert Mugabe's brutal crackdown on democratic opposition forces in Zimbabwe was aided by political backing, oil on credit, and arms from Libya. Mugabe defied his own population by sending thousands of troops to support the Kinshasa dictatorship's side of Congo-Kinshasa's national nightmare. The British nongovernmental organization Global Witness issued a report exposing a deal between the Congolese regime and the Zimbabwean military that secured Zimbabwe's continued involvement in the futile war, promised tremendous wealth for the Mugabe regime, and would result in the total deforestation of part of the Congo the size of California.[27] While funding Mugabe's deeply unpopular war in the Congo and financing his party, the deal promised more trouble for Zimbabwe's opposition and devastation for the Congolese whose land would be ruined.

Non-African dictators also have a hand in prolonging the continent's remaining tyrannies. Kim Il Sung's North Korean regime provided training and equipment for Robert Mugabe's massacres in Matabeleland province in the 1980s, where he resorted to ethnic terror in a bid to consolidate his power.[28] And today, Kim Jong Il is perhaps the largest source of trainers for the African dictators' internal security forces.[29]

These men are epic pragmatists. The dictatorships of Saudi Arabia, the United Arab Emirates, and Pakistan were the only countries to recognize the recently toppled Taliban dictatorship as Afghanistan's legitimate government. They were likewise quick to withdraw their recognition when the West turned on the Taliban. Serbian president Slobodan Milosevic held secret meetings with his Croatian counterpart, Franjo Tudjman, while their nations ripped away at each other, acting out a hatred inflamed by the dictators' fascist rhetoric.[30] Tyrants survive with the help of their friends—and even, sometimes, of their enemies.

Curiously, these regimes have been able to trade on their worst qualities, parlaying modest improvements in human rights, for example, into a full partnership in world trade, or a promise of restraint in weapons sales into access to high technology. Democracies have always been willing to sit down with dictators to achieve some temporary, undemocratic end, always tricked by the illusion that the enemy of an enemy must be a friend.

The Future with Dictators

The Bush administration's idea of an axis of evil arose from the terrorist attacks of 11 September 2001 on New York and the Pentagon. In fact, such terror, appalling as it is, is really just one of a host of toxic weeds that bloom in the deep shade of dictatorship; famine, refugees, poverty, environmental degradation, corruption, war, genocide, and terrorism—all flourish there as well.

Let us begin with famine and proceed down this toxic list. Nobel laureate Professor Amartya Kumar Sen, of Cambridge University, shows the strong correlation between famine and autocratic rule. While natural factors no doubt play a role, the fact remains that governments accountable to their citizens cannot afford to blithely disregard their existential fates. The correlation between democracy and effective measures against famine is striking: Sen has found that famines in democracies with an independent press are exceedingly rare.[31]

Even in his native India, where poverty is rife and many are undernourished, famines have not occurred since independence. In contrast, China has suffered a number of particularly devastating famines since the communists took power in 1949, along with many prior to that. Political factors played a decisive role in each, either in actually creating the famine, as was the case with the lunacy of the "Great Leap Forward," or in exacerbating natural phenomena and allowing ideological factors to outweigh the fundamental responsibility of a government to assure the welfare of its citizens. The case of Ethiopia in the 1980s (and Soviet Ukraine in the 1930s) shows that food is often used as a weapon by dictatorships against their own people. And a lack of government, as in Somalia, makes a Kalashnikov, rather than a plow, the only assured meal ticket.

Professor John Norton Moore of the University of Virginia estimates that 77 percent of refugees flow from undemocratic countries.[32]

If one excludes democracies that are being attacked by undemocratic states, only 8 percent of refugees emanate from very liberally defined "electoral democracies." A spot check of the world's worst crises of refugees and internally displaced persons shows Afghans and Congolese topping the charts. With the tenuous beginnings of democracy in Kabul, already the displaced are returning.

While economic and political freedoms do not necessarily move in lockstep, a pronounced lack of one tends to affect the other over time. And these freedoms are mutually reinforcing, producing pronounced benefits where both political and economic freedoms are at high levels. Freedom House recently found that countries with the highest levels of democratic freedom produce 89 percent of the global economic output. On the other side of this spectrum, those countries with the least political freedom, which account for 36 percent of the world's population, produce only 6 percent of the world's wealth. Gwartney and Lawson's 1997 *Economic Freedom of the World*[33] convincingly illustrated a strong correlation between economic freedom and growth in real and per capita gross domestic product. In the quintile with the most economic freedom, the annual growth rate averaged 2.9 percent, while countries at the other end actually saw their economies contract on average 1.9 percent annually. In their 2000 report, economic freedom is also positively associated with life expectancy, crop yields, and even income equality. Prior studies, such as those conducted by the Heritage Foundation and the Fraser Institute in Canada, showed a linkage between absolutism and low economic growth. In the past few years, the World Bank has taken notice of these factors, though in my opinion not nearly enough. Where political power is concentrated, economic power tends to be as well, and vice versa.

That the communist system in eastern Europe and Eurasia produced massive ecological havoc is well known. An economic system unfettered by market input costs is sure to be inefficient in its use of resources. Such misdevelopment, with all its attendant hazards for the population, could only occur under a system where there was also no need to court public consent and information about the risks at hand was strictly controlled. Even now, since the breakup of the USSR and the introduction of a semblance of democracy to Russia, the Soviet mentality that environmental data is a threatening state secret remains, but it is being challenged. In democratic states, while there have also been numerous scandals, a democratically empowered population and relentless free press help keep corporate and governmental polluters in check.

While corruption is hardly the sole preserve of dictators and their supporting casts, there can be no doubt it is harder to accomplish in the clear light of day, where free media can expose it and the public can demand it be addressed. German nongovernmental organization Transparency International has shown a major positive correlation between reduced economic free-dom and increased corruption. Of the countries deemed least corrupt in Transparency International's index,[34] only Singapore is undemocratic. On the other end of the spectrum, Pakistan, ruled by its military, is regularly seen in these surveys to be among the most corrupt countries in the world.

Dictatorships also lead to increased warfare. Of the 353 wars between 1816 and 1991 that Professor Rudy J. Rummel, of the University of Hawaii, classi-fied as "major international wars," 100 percent involved nondemocracies as one or more of the belligerents; none occurred between two democratic states.[35] While democracies have often engaged in warfare with nondemo-cratic states, the potential for external aggression is magnified in societies that do not rely on popular support. In his study of twenty major wars since 1945, John Norton Moore found only one case of democratic aggression in war: the Anglo-French and Israeli attack on Egypt in the 1956 Suez War.[36] An over-whelming preponderance of wars between democracies and nondemocracies have come as a result of aggression by nondemocracies, either against demo-cratic belligerents or against others. Democracies, however, can rely on deep reservoirs of popular support when attacked and rarely lose their wars. It is also true that a band of Atlantic democracies mounted the most effective ex-ample of deterrence in human history through NATO during the cold war.

Dictators make war not only on those outside their boundaries but also on citizens of their own countries. In his 1994 book, *Death by Government*, Rum-mel coined the term "democide" to refer to governments killing their own cit-izens. In the twentieth century an estimated 169 *million* died at the hands, or through the malign neglect, of their governments. This is an estimated *two to four times* the number of combatants killed in wars over the same period. The number certainly has risen since. In addition, Rummel found that there was a direct correlation between the incidence of democide and nondemocratic government.[37] The biggest killers in racking up this sickening death toll have been totalitarian leaders, including Adolf Hitler, Joseph Stalin, Mao Zedong, Pol Pot, Kim Jong Il, Mengistu Haile Mariam, and Idi Amin. A lesser num-ber were murdered at the hands of authoritarian "kilokillers" such as Slobo-dan Milosevic, Charles Taylor, and the Argentine junta in the 1970s.

None of the seven countries on the State Department's list of countries that sponsor terror is democratically governed. Iran's president, Mohammad Khatami, has been twice more or less democratically elected, but the Guardian Council and security apparatus remain beyond his grasp. None of the other six countries have any semblance of democratic structures.

In contrast to this linkage of social ills and dictatorial government, a number of prominent scholars have demonstrated a strong relationship be-tween positive economic and social indicators and liberal democracy—that is, democracy shaped by free elections, rule of law, and other fundamentals. Democratic systems, however imperfect, demand that the government answer to its people.[38]

Thus, a war on terror is insufficient reason for a democracy to lie down with a dictator; so is a campaign for human rights, or an environmental accord, or a threatened economy. To my mind, democracies should deal with dictatorships primarily to bring them down. For with them gone—and only with them gone—their crop of horrors will wither and die.

At this juncture, some readers may shake their heads and say that I ignore the lessons of realpolitik—that democracies must now and then make hard choices among evils of varying degree. But I would argue that, in fact, political reality has shown us again and again that the problem is solved, not by picking a lesser vice over a greater one, but by removing the point at which those vices naturally concentrate—not entire nations, but the individual tyrants who control them. Indeed, my argument springs not from innocence but from long experience and deeply felt belief.

The destructive hand of tyranny defies description. Millions have died because the tyrants of Germany and Japan, the Soviet Union, China, North Korea, and Iraq believed the wars they ignited could be won if enough life and treasure were thrown into the cauldron. Without the Soviet dictators and their puppets there would not have been a cold war. Without a Cuban dictator the 1962 missile crisis would not have happened. Without a dictator in Iraq, there would have been no first or second Gulf War. Talking about such things, one begins to sound like an astronomer—millions of lives, trillions of dollars, entire civilizations uprooted from an ancient homeland.

Without dramatic change, our new century promises to be much worse. Dictators who a generation ago would have relied on machetes, Kalashnikovs, and land mines to maintain power have begun to creep upmarket, as their nations have matured technically. A chemical industry can also yield the lethal payloads of chemical weapons. Pharmaceutical research facilities are also farms for toxic bioforms. A nation capable of operating nuclear reactors and uranium reprocessing plants is well down the road to a nuclear bomb. The aircraft and rockets used to loft conventional weapons are readily converted to delivery platforms for weapons of mass destruction. It is not a question, for example, of whether Iran and North Korea will have nuclear weapons, but of when, or even whether they already do.

Nor are chemicals, germs, and fissionable atoms the only powerful weapons now coming within the dictators' grasp. There is also terror, raised to a grisly art by the advent of the suicide bomber.

All state sponsors of terror are dictatorships, and all receive the backing of other dictators. But dictatorships that are not on the State Department list also have become fertile incubators of terror. In states such as Saudi Arabia, Egypt, Algeria, Uzbekistan, and Pakistan, corrupt dictators have tried to stifle all legitimate dissent; in fact, they have merely driven it underground. Unemployment and poverty born of these regimes' misrule foster widespread frustration and a population rendered susceptible to the demagoguery of radical extremists. Discontent in Saudi Arabia and Egypt has intensified until it poses a danger to both regimes, and to the rest of the region and world as well. The Saudi and Mubarak regimes have responded by trying to co-opt the preachers of extremism, handing them the keys to important media outlets. The corrupt elites in both countries hope to save themselves by letting radicals rant about the evils of the West and garner more recruits. Western countries have worsened the situation by propping up these regimes, thereby associating themselves with corrupt and brutal practices. If these regimes are ever to give way to democrats (as opposed to radical extremist dictators), a major policy shift in the West will be necessary. Until then, tyranny will crank out more terrorism. As President Bush stated on 27 February 2003, "The world has a clear interest in the spread of democratic values, because stable and free nations do not breed the ideologies of murder."[39]

Countries such as Saudi Arabia and Algeria are also major suppliers of oil to the United States and other democracies. Their vast oil-producing infrastructure of wells, pipelines, shipping lanes, and refineries is vulnerable to terrorists seeking to undermine not only their governments but also the dependent American economy. In 2000, 27.8 percent of net imports of crude oil and petroleum products into the United States came from countries categorized by Freedom House as Not Free.[40] The actual exposure of the U.S. economy to brittle Not Free countries is even greater. For example, though the United States doesn't do business with Libya or Iran, fungible Libyan and Iranian oil exports nonetheless affect world oil prices, which in turn affect the U.S. economy.

Beyond the possibility of terrorist attacks on U.S.-supported oil-producing dictatorships like Saudi Arabia, civil war—notably in the dictatorships of Algeria and Angola—could result in sudden increases in the price of oil. A continuation of the current number of dictators will likely cause major instability in the oil markets.

Taking a pessimistic view, one may ponder the democratic texture of a world in which dictatorships, rather than fading, increase. The republics shaken out of the former Soviet Union like Ukraine and Russia itself are still in a state of fragile transition, as are Indonesia and Nigeria. Until these transitional democracies mature and stabilize, they risk turning away from the often daunting challenges of freedom to the relative simplicity of familiar dictatorial rule. One imagines Serbs again trying to create a Greater Serbia,

Russians trying to re-create the Soviet Union. In a world where dictatorships are on the rise, China might see greater chances of military success against Taiwan and perhaps even Siberia. Conflicts might erupt between dictators, setting up currents that would inevitably draw in the world's democracies.

Even without another global war, the further spread of tyranny would impose immense costs on the democratic world. Terrorists would have even more sanctuaries, supporters, and access to weapons of mass destruction. World trade would be shaken and economies deformed to pay the rising costs of more and more defense, rather than meeting such social imperatives as health care, education, and environmental protection. There would be less freedom in the world; democracies would decline to a kind of mirror image of their opposites.

A Democratic World

Happily, this dismal forecast seems to me to go wide of the mark. The tide seems to have set against tyranny. In 1972, there were only forty-three Free countries in the world; as of 2002 there were eighty-nine; together with the Partly Free countries they make up three-quarters of all nations. Moreover, many of the surviving dictatorships are held by men who have no obvious successors beyond a few spiritually stunted, middle-aged sons.

We have noted that dictators tend to foster similar regimes around them. Adolf Hitler supported his ideological soul mates in such countries as Italy, Hungary, Croatia, Slovakia, and occupied France. The Soviet Union insisted on a protective barrier of puppet communist dictatorships. Apartheid-era South Africa took pains to prop up the racist regime of Ian Smith in what is now Zimbabwe. But this is a sword that cuts two ways. In these nations, democratization in one had the effect of discrediting the shared ideology of undemocratic neighbors, further isolating and weakening the dictatorships that remained. As happened in central and eastern Europe in 1989, once the toppling begins, dictators tend to fall like dominoes. And now is the moment to start them falling.

Given the efflorescence of democracy around the world in the last quarter century, given the fact that many of the world's dictators are growing old, it seems to me that we have a unique opportunity—and an obligation—to wipe away the stain of tyranny everywhere on the planet. At the average rate of democratization seen between 1974 and the present—more than three dictatorships ended every year—the world would be free of tyrants in thirteen years. Even half the average rate would end tyranny by 2025.

A world without dictators would not be without competition and strain. But it might well be a world without wars between nations. Proof of this abounds in Europe. The border between France and Germany, once deadly enemies, no longer teems with troops and armor. The cold war division of Europe healed swiftly once the communist dictatorships were democratically transformed. Romania and Hungary seem to be solving the issue of the two million ethnic Hungarians living in the neighbor state. Two of the dictatorships remaining in Europe after 1989—those in Belgrade and Zagreb—were transient anomalies and are now history, and there is hope for full democracy in the region. Only Belarus remains under one man's rule, and that will almost certainly change in time. All of this is possible because democracies have peaceful mechanisms for working away at difficult ethnic, religious, and historical problems. Dictatorships have none.

This imagined dictator-free planet, on which no nation was led by all-powerful general secretaries, ayatollahs, kings, and bosses, would not be devoid of human rights abuses, nor would democracies abandon competition. Moving fully to democracy would not be the end of history, after all; these young democracies, being eminently human institutions, would now and then sputter and miss. But open societies end up with open borders and open minds. Even in its immature form, democracy offers a better world than the tyranny it displaces.

In that world, we see how seemingly insoluble problems can be thrashed out. A democratic China would pose no threat to Taiwan, whatever their final relationship. Arab democracies in the Middle East would be more tolerant of Israel and, even more important, of one another. Democracy could perhaps extinguish Africa's endless strife.

We know from the transition in central and eastern Europe that the security situation would be transformed. The defense budgets of the former dictatorships and their neighbors in Western Europe and the United States were cut in half or better. The threat posed by central and eastern European dictatorships evaporated. Hungary, Poland, the Czech Republic, and other former members of the Warsaw Pact have entered NATO, cooperating with other democracies around the world on security issues, the environment, and other challenges. Within these countries the threat to individuals has also eased. After a messy start, an economic transformation is under way that will eventually integrate these countries into the world's economy, with per capita incomes matching Western standards.

A transition of equally fundamental importance would take place if China, Vietnam, Iraq, Uzbekistan, Egypt, Congo, and Cuba joined the democratic world. Some will argue that the very process of change will be destabilizing: that China could descend into civil war and even break apart; that Mubarak-style dictatorship in Egypt would yield to an Islamic fundamentalist regime; and that Africans are simply incapable of democracy. We will argue against such concerns later. For the moment, let us consider what the world would look like if these remaining dictatorships successfully crossed the divide.

In Africa, a far greater barrier to development than the burden of foreign debt is the absolute corruption and incompetence of its dictators. The initial and necessary condition to correct this fundamental failing is good governance, which cannot flourish except in a democracy, with all that it brings: independent legal systems, a free and critical press, a voice for the people.

As figure 1.1 shows, the free nations produce 89 percent of the world's economic output; the dictatorships produce just 6 percent. Those demonstrating in Seattle, Quebec, and Washington against globalization, the World Bank, and multinational corporations are aiming at the wrong targets. They should be crusading against dictatorships, the real cause of fundamental backwardness and war. Such African democracies as Ghana, Botswana, and South Africa shine a light on what could be the future for the Congo, Liberia, and Angola. But the latter must be pushed into that light.

As leading Arab intellectuals themselves are beginning to argue, the Middle East is backward by so many social, educational, and economic criteria

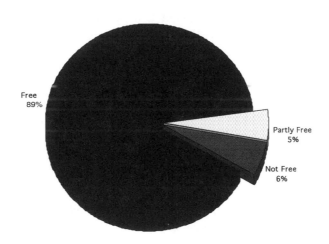

GDP Output by Free, Partly Free, Not Free

	GDP*	%
Free	$26,759,070,650,480	89
Partly Free	$1,467,413,737,800	5
Not Free	$1,671,285,457,000	6
Total*	$29,897,769,845,280	

World Bank Development Index 2002

Figure 1.1.   World economic output by Free, Partly Free, and Not Free countries.

precisely because of its dictators and a dearth of a civil society's institutions. Removing the bosses, generals, kings, and clerics from absolute power would unleash the immense talent and energy stored in these nations. Equally important, it would transform the security situation in a region where neighbor preys on neighbor. Most of the casualties in these conflicts have occurred in clashes between and within Muslim nations. The only security solution for the nations of the Middle East is to achieve democracy. This includes security for Israel, whose minister without portfolio and former fighter for human rights inside the Soviet Union, Natan Sharansky, sees "A direct correlation between the depth of democracy [in individual Arab states] and the warmth of our relations."[41]

We face a similar situation in South Asia. There will be no durable solution to the confrontation between India and Pakistan as long as Pakistan is ruled by generals with a vested interest in keeping the pot boiling. The defeat of the Taliban in Afghanistan creates new opportunities in that region only if the victors follow through and help reshape Afghanistan and Pakistan as democracies.

In Asia, the greatest danger is a China led by a communist dictator and the constant threat of military action against Taiwan. The vast country also extends its standard all the way to Indonesia.[42] A democratic China would be a peaceful partner for its neighbors and a magnet for democratic Taiwan.

The real impact of full democracy, however, is ultimately less geopolitical than personal, less a matter of nations than of the individual. Tyranny means that North Korean mothers must watch helplessly as their children starve to death in their arms, and then starve to death themselves—while food is produced in abundance across the barrier in democratic South Korea. Before India was a democracy, famines stalked the subcontinent with the regularity of the monsoon, but there has not been a single famine since the nation's independence in 1947. Under tyranny, Joseph Stalin and Mao Zedong each allowed twenty million of their subjects to starve to death, evoking a level of privation we can hardly comprehend; such atrocity is impossible where the citizens rule the land.

Tyranny ruins ordinary lives and creates extraordinary hardship and despair. And one of the curious byproducts of dictatorship is the persistent chauvinism against women. On a recent flight from Miami, a young Saudi woman and I struck up a conversation. She had just graduated from the University of Miami and I asked what she was going to do with her education. She replied, "Look across the aisle. Who do you think is sitting there and why?" It was her brother, sent from Saudia Arabia to ensure that she returned home. The Saudi woman bitterly explained that she would not be permitted to do anything with her education—she was going home to a sexist prison.

In Afghanistan, lawyer Nabila Ahmad spent five years almost entirely confined to her apartment in Kabul, prohibited from working by the enforced male chauvinism of Taliban rule. When she did venture out, the regime's religious police required that she wear a burqa to completely cover herself.[43] The Taliban's defeat now brings new hope to Afghanistan's women, many of whom are shedding their burqas, returning to work, and sending their daughters to school for the first time. Muslim women in democracies—where over half of all adherents of Islam now live—can pursue their faith but also work and fight openly for their rights.

Every year modern society loses some of its tolerance for tyranny. Today we have a unique opportunity to shrink this tolerance to zero. The dictators are growing old, their oppressed subjects restive. It is time for change. The democratizing impulse that swept the planet in the last quarter of the last century can finish the job in the first quarter of this one, if we will only encourage it.

Let us resolve, then, we citizens of democracies, to help eradicate those last forty-five tyrants by the year 2025. Let us consider now how we might proceed.

2

Ousting the Last Forty-Five

If you do not have a dream, you cannot get results.

—Oswaldo Paya, Varela Project, Cuba

The different perspective that political leaders bring to the management of world affairs is like the difference between the hedgehog and the fox: The hedgehog knows one big thing and the fox knows many little things.

—Isaiah Berlin

The one big thing we know is that the world's surviving tyrants are a vanishing race, driven to extinction by the palpable superiority of free democratic societies. And we have seen proof of this in just one generation.

From 1972 to 2002, the number of fully free countries more than doubled across the globe. In 2002 there were eighty-nine Free countries, which, together with the world's fifty-six Partly Free countries, make up over 75 percent of the world's countries and 65 percent of its population (see figure 2.1). From Portugal and Spain to Poland and Russia, from Chile to South Africa and on to the Philippines and Indonesia, a quiet, largely nonviolent, and unpredicted revolution swept across the planet. It is still gathering steam. During 2002, twenty-nine countries demonstrated forward progress in freedom, while eleven countries registered setbacks. Today the majority of the world's Muslims live in electoral democracies; even Iran's people, faced with determined and violent opposition, have repeatedly demonstrated at the ballot box and in the streets the universal desire for popular governance. Taiwan has proven that democracy can take root and thrive in a Chinese culture. Eastern Europe has thrown off half a century's communist conditioning.

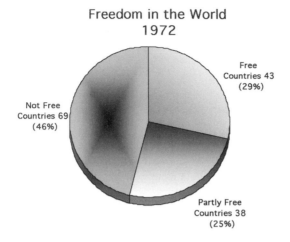

Freedom in the World
1972

Free
Countries 43
(29%)

Not Free
Countries 69
(46%)

Partly Free
Countries 38
(25%)

Freedom in the World
2002

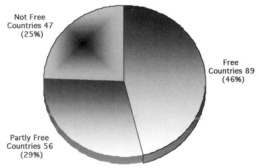

Not Free
Countries 47
(25%)

Free
Countries 89
(46%)

Partly Free
Countries 56
(29%)

Figure 2.1.   Number of Free, Partly Free, and Not Free countries (1972 versus 2002).

This progress over the last quarter century should give us confidence that we can finish the job by 2025. There is no reason the peoples of the dictatorships still standing should not join the majority who now exercise their right to elect their own leaders, read independent newspapers, join independent trade unions, and practice their faiths in peace and tolerance.

As of the end of 2002, there were just forty-seven Not Free countries in the world according to the "Freedom in the World" annual analysis of Freedom House, and just forty-five dictators—Lebanon is classified as Not Free because it is occupied by Syria and controlled by Syria's Bashar al-Assad, and Afghanistan is still classified as Not Free despite substantial progress because of continuing problems outside Kabul. President Hamid Karzai clearly is no dictator (see table 2.1).[1] Just forty-five men—and, notably, no women—are preventing more than two billion people from achieving their real potential! These few remaining dictators must go, to be replaced by the institutions provided for in the Universal Declaration of Human Rights—regular and free elections, a free press, trade unions, and an independent judiciary—which passed the UN General Assembly unopposed.[2] Now we must insist that the dictators honor their own commitment to the Universal Declaration. But that is only a beginning. We must then equip ourselves for what promises to be a difficult and often dangerous undertaking.

First, a new mind-set must be developed among people both inside and outside dictatorships, to accrete a critical mass of real belief that democracy can and will be achieved. The first strategic objective must be to strengthen this conviction, to take as a simple truth that history has demonstrated that it is on the side of freedom, that ordinary people have the power to get rid of their oppressors.

Second, democrats must be organized for function and continuity inside the dictatorship, within democracies, and in the links between those within and those helping from outside. One of the paradoxes we face is that dictators take their democratic opponents more seriously than do our "experts"; they know that eventually, if the democrats stay the course, the dictators will lose power.

Third, democrats must develop the political and economic tools and techniques for the nonviolent overthrow of their oppressors. The past quarter century abounds with examples: Indonesian students filling the streets against Suharto; the predominantly young people of Poland's Solidarity trade union movement who pushed out Wojciech Jaruzelski; the Hungarian students who got the barbed wire cut along the Austrian border; the young East Germans who ripped down the Berlin Wall. Lessons can be learned.

Removal of dictators is first and foremost a domestic political matter, undertaken by the people living under tyranny. Over the past quarter century we have seen repeated successes due overwhelmingly to a change in domestic consciousness, strategic organization, and coordinated, mostly nonviolent action. What is not always so clear is the critical part played by the international community. Indeed, it is remarkable that the relatively small efforts of outside democrats had such a significant impact. Imagine what outsiders could do with a creative strategy backed with money and determination.

What holds us back? Put bluntly, our partial paralysis arises from the fact that such fields as national security, international relations, diplomacy, intelligence, and even journalism are prisoners of the conventional wisdom of an earlier era. These fields are still dominated by a conceptual framework developed in a fundamentally different, even pre-twentieth-century, world. They have experienced less innovative shock than perhaps any other fields

Table 2.1. Combined Average Rating, Independent Countries, 2002–2003

Free 1.0	1.5	2.0	2.5
Andorra	Belize	Botswana	Benin
Australia	Bulgaria	Croatia	Bolivia
Austria	Cape Verde	Dominican Republic	Brazil
Bahamas	Chile	Guyana	El Salvador
Barbados	Costa Rica	Israel	Ghana
Belgium	Czech Republic	Korea, South	India
Canada	Estonia	Mexico	Jamaica
Cyprus (G)	Greece	Mongolia	Lesotho
Denmark	Grenada	Romania	Mali
Dominica	Hungary	Samoa	Namibia
Finland	Japan	Taiwan	Papua New Guinea
France	Latvia		Peru
Germany	Lithuania		Philippines
Iceland			
Ireland			
Italy			
Kiribati			
Liechtenstein			
Luxembourg			
Malta			
Marshall Islands			
Netherlands			
New Zealand			
Norway			
Portugal			
San Marino			

Slovenia
Spain
Sweden
Switzerland
Tuvalu
United Kingdom
United States
Uruguay

Partly Free

3.0	3.5	4.0	4.5	5.0	5.5
Albania	Fiji	Armenia	Comoros	Bahrain	Azerbaijan
Antigua and Barbuda	Indonesia	Bangladesh	Cote d'Ivoire	Central African Rep.	Jordan
Argentina	Madagascar	Bosnia-Herzegovina	Djibouti	Congo (Brazzaville)	
East Timor	Moldova	Burkina Faso	Gabon	Ethiopia	
Ecuador	Mozambique	Colombia	Guinea-Bissau	Malaysia	
Honduras	Paraguay	The Gambia	Kuwait	Mauritania	
Macedonia	Sri Lanka	Georgia	Nigeria	Morocco	
Nicaragua	Tanzania	Guatemala	Singapore	Russia	
Seychelles	Turkey	Kenya		Uganda	
Solomon Islands	Venezuela	Malawi			
Trinidad and Tobago		Nepal			
		Niger			
		Sierra Leone			
		Tonga			
		Ukraine			
		Zambia			

(continued)

Table 2.1. Combined Average Rating, Independent Countries, 2002–2003 *(continued)*

Not Free 5.5	6.0	6.5	7.0
Algeria	Afghanistan	China (PRC)	Burma
Angola	Belarus	Equatorial Guinea	Cuba
Bhutan	Cameroon	Eritrea	Iraq
Brunei	Congo (Kinshasa)	Laos	Korea, North
Burundi	Egypt	Liberia	Libya
Cambodia	Haiti	Somalia	Saudi Arabia
Chad	Iran	Uzbekistan	Sudan
Guinea	Qatar	Vietnam	Syria
Kazakhstan	Rwanda		Turkmenistan
Kyrgyz Republic	Zimbabwe		
Lebanon			
Maldives			
Oman			
Pakistan			
Swaziland			
Tajikistan			
Togo			
Tunisia			
United Arab Emirates			
Yemen			

of human endeavor, and this obsolescence shows. Radical change is long overdue. The basic actors they acknowledged were nation-states and national governments run overwhelmingly by dictators of one sort or another. Strength was defined first as military power, then by economic clout. Relations were between governments, run through foreign ministries. Good relations meant getting along with the people with whom you thought you had to get along. Stability received a high premium, but it was also defined as the opposite of change.

This mind-set is precisely why the most important developments affecting national and international security were and are nearly total surprises to foreign and defense ministries, intelligence services, academics, and the press. National security and foreign policy establishments in every established democracy were caught off balance by every single one of the many democratic/strategic developments of the past quarter century. Paradoxically, the dictators themselves were usually not surprised at all.

Of course it is not sufficient to proclaim democracy as a high ideal worthy of promulgation without honestly reckoning with difficult, immediate, real-world security threats. On the other hand, the experts too frequently invoke this "real world" to excuse chronic short-term thinking that insistently discounts the inherent value of democracy for the governed. But in the real real world, the spread of democracy remains humanity's most powerful currency and the surest way to ensure our own security. Simply put, our moral interest in democracy coincides completely with our interest in security and prosperity.

And yet, the democratizing changes of the past quarter century were not just unexpected; they were often resisted and impeded by democratic nations. Nor has much been learned from this experience. The conventional wisdom in Washington, Paris, Berlin, Tokyo, and elsewhere throughout the foreign national security community remains that in the Middle East, Africa, and much of Asia, dramatic progress toward democracy is simply not possible in the near to medium term. Indeed, this view holds that it would be destabilizing, counterproductive, and even against national interests to aggressively promote democracy in these regions. The dominant view is that we should focus on keeping the new democracies from backsliding, discouraging the world's existing crop of dictators from some of their more visible and egregious violations of human rights, and exceedingly gently urging very gradual movement toward democracy.

This misguided common wisdom repeatedly gave rise to many of the great blunders of the cold war and continues to this day. One classic example: The CIA helped overthrow the democratically elected leader of Iran in 1953, installing Shah Mohammad Reza Pahlavi as Washington's anticommunist dictator.[3] Like all of our dictator "allies," the shah was far more concerned with his own protection than the protection of U.S. interests, including during the oil crisis of 1973. U.S. opposition to Iranian democracy helped to create a virulently anti-American regime committed to terrorism. The denial of a democratic outlet for opposition to the shah's stifling regime became the decisive factor in bringing broad public support behind the 1979 revolution, which in turn was hijacked and turned into an Islamic fundamentalist dictatorship by Ayatollah Ruhollah Khomeini. Compounding their errors yet again, U.S. experts looked around for a counterweight to the dreadful new regime in Tehran. They found one in Iraq: Saddam Hussein.

By attempting to base U.S. security on tyranny in other parts of the world, the practitioners of foreign policy common wisdom not only failed but also undermined American credibility worldwide. We Americans talked a good game when it came to democracy and human rights, but to Iranians and Iraqis suffering under U.S.-supported dictators, we seemed timid hypocrites.

Today in Iran, a majority of the population is disillusioned with fundamentalism and supports democracy. Having twice voted overwhelmingly for the reformist President Mohammad Khatami, Iranians now openly protest his failure to stand up to the dictator Ali Khamenei. The United States now has a second chance to get it right, to actively encourage Iran's democrats as they attempt to prevail over the continuing dictatorship of the ayatollah. But we need to be clear about what and whom we are for, not just what we do not like.

Ambassadors often find themselves pinned between their nation's conventional wisdom and the political reality they—and often only they—can see firsthand. For example, arriving in Portugal in 1975, U.S. Ambassador Frank Carlucci perceived a real possibility for democracy despite the left-wing military, increasingly communist regime that had succeeded to power after four decades of Antonio de Oliveira Salazar's dictatorship. Henry Kissinger, then secretary of state, advised the ambassador to stay with the American agenda—that communist rule was a fact, and we should just concentrate on containing it. Carlucci nevertheless followed his instinct for democracy and worked with Portuguese democrats to insist upon elections and defeat the communists at the polls.[4]

I went through a similar situation in 1989 in Budapest, where I was U.S. ambassador. The embassy actively supported democratic change, so much so that Foreign Minister Gyula Horn complained to Secretary of State James Baker. I was recalled to Washington and urged to moderate this activity. During a subsequent visit by President George Bush in the summer of 1989, I arranged for him to meet with the country's leading democrats in my living room. Afterwards, Secretary Baker told me, "Mark, I know these are your friends, but they will never run this country." That was American conventional wisdom talking. The barbed wire had already come down along the Austrian border; four months later the Berlin Wall came down. My "friends" won the election shortly thereafter. One of them, Viktor Orban, later became prime minister of Hungary. In 1989, he was the head of Fidesz, the student movement that was at the forefront in ousting the communists, while being largely ignored by the West.

In 1999 Western diplomats, press, and experts seemed absolutely stunned by Indonesian students' success in bringing an end to the era of corrupt dictatorships of Suharto/Sukarno. And so it goes.

Power in the Modern World

Such fundamental changes in the global security situation are still only poorly understood by much of the foreign policy community in the democracies. In the absence of a fresh paradigm, these so-called experts fall back on conventional thinking. They believe, for example, that an increase in defense spending and the prospect of the proposed Star Wars defense system led to the "collapse" of the Soviet Union. This comforting resort to old thinking may relieve the experts of the work of understanding and predicting global change, but it ignores the other, political forces at work to bring the Soviet empire to abandon communism and start down the road to democracy.

One sees that same process at work in the CIA's study, published in December 2000, *Global Trends 2015: A Dialogue about the Future with Nongovernment Experts*, which is based on the "best" thinking of both outside and inside experts.[5] While this study at least allows for the *possibility* of democracy emerging in China, its dominant message is that things will stay pretty much the same in the parts of the world still run by dictatorships. It shows little understanding of the profound forces for change operating at the grassroots level. Worse, it provides no analytical basis for leadership toward democratization.

With regard to such countries as Saudi Arabia and Egypt, Washington and other Western capitals still support, sustain, and even praise dictators who are utterly corrupt. Yet the Saudi and Mubarak regimes are dedicated to little more than maintaining power and enriching themselves. Both have extinguished avenues of legitimate political dissent and opposition for years. As public frustration and poverty have increased, so has the radicalization of elements of Saudi and Egyptian society. The fundamentalist threat has become so clear that both governments have sought in recent years to placate the demagogues who distort Islam and thrive under repression. Both governments have turned over media assets to fanatical movements, perhaps hoping that anger vented at the United States will not be vented at home. We saw one result on September 11, 2001. That attack on the United States originated in Saudi Arabia and Egypt. Fifteen of the nineteen terrorists were Saudi nationals; their leader, Mohamed Atta, was Egyptian. Seven of the twenty-two men on the FBI's most wanted list are Egyptian nationals. The source of the money for the September 11 operation was Saudi.

Even as the ground sags beneath the hollow Saudi and Egyptian tyrants, the West has doggedly pursued a myopic policy of heaping more aid and political support on these teetering dictators. Both regimes are considered "strategic allies": Saudi Arabia primarily for its military bases, strategic location, and huge oil reserves; Egypt as a perceived pro-Western, "moderate" voice in the Arab world and home to the Suez Canal. It requires skill to fundamentally change policy toward key countries so as to encourage a phased process of change within them. Too-rapid change could have disastrous consequences. The situation in Saudi Arabia is so fragile that elections held tomorrow could yield a radical, anti-Western government and a throttling of the oil spigots. Egypt is a powder keg of thwarted expectations that could very well be detonated by a drastic reduction in Western aid. There, too, radical Islam is waiting in the wings.

Conversely, policy changes could as easily produce governments genuinely willing to join the modern world, much as the post-Taliban government in Afghanistan is trying to do. A difficult middle way will have to be found that puts world democracies in the corner of those Saudis who are fed up with dictatorship and corruption. A start could be made by increasing pressure on the Fahd regime to introduce democratic reforms and by working toward the rapid democratization of Iraq and Iran. These two are major oil producers and their increased production could reduce world dependence on Saudi oil. Their democratization would also change the psychological atmosphere in the region, emboldening Saudi Arabian reformers to work toward modern democracy. In any case, new approaches to the region are urgently needed, for the traditional policies only maintain an untenable status quo. Toward the end of 2002, the Bush administration began to show more interest in promoting democracy in the region, but still very timidly; the Europeans and other democracies are even more cautious.

There continues to be a particularly glaring failure to grasp the nature of power in the modern world. The shift in power over the past quarter century was due to a shift in the domestic political systems of dozens of countries from dictatorships to democracy. Hungary, Poland, and the Czech Republic, for example, have gone from membership in the Warsaw Pact to membership in NATO because they have become democratic states. At the same time, maintaining a strong defense among the democracies is an absolute precondition for peace and for ousting dictators. Thus, all who favor the spread of democracy should push for robust defense budgets. But the military balance has shifted mainly for political reasons, and such threats as that of Islamic extremism are primarily political and ideological. The German police reported about a group of Moroccans, Egyptians, Afghans, and a German they arrested on 3 July 2002, "The group strives for a worldwide holy state and does not accept the free democratic constitutional structure."[6] The other major security threat we face is a communist China. As Professor Ross Terrill has written, "The United States is needed as an adversary to shore up the legitimacy of the Communist party state."[7]

Given the evidence of recent history, it is breathtaking folly for the foreign policy community to persist in its belief that aggressively promoting democracy and human rights may sound nice in terms of "values" but is irrelevant to, and even conflicts with, the protection of "national interests" and "stability" and "security." It should be obvious that for China to become a democracy and for key nations in the Middle East to become democracies would have profound and beneficial impacts on global security and peace, just as the transformation in eastern and central Europe did. Evidently, it is not—except for some with direct experience. Poland's foreign minister, from "Young Europe," recently noted, "Democracy is the indispensable condition for peace in the Middle East."[8] Would that the "Old Europeans" would recognize this fact.

A better set of equations is:

- National security equals the spread and protection of democracy.
- Power varies with the strength of alliances among the democracies and inversely with the strength of dictators.

We in the democratic world need first of all to liberate ourselves from the conceptual baggage of the past. We need a new understanding of power, national interest, and national security in a world where a majority of nations are now democracies, a world with obvious potential for still further fundamental change, for the achievement of universal democracy. We need to recognize that the world is really divided not between cultures, religions, or economies but between democrats and dictators.

This is important for those living in the dictatorships, who must do the really heavy lifting. President Bill Clinton, just out of office, came to a Hong Kong awash with the issue of democracy and China and talked about the next fifty years without a word on the need for China to become a full-scale democracy. That was the wrong message to send those inside China who want to become like Taiwan and the advanced countries of the world and who look to the democratic world for leadership. President George W. Bush's speech at

Tsinghua University on 22 February 2002, was a considerable improvement. The president focused on the strength democracy gives the United States, praised some modest reforms in China's political system, such as secret ballots and competitive village-level elections, and said he looked forward to an expansion of democratic elections to the national level. But even President Bush failed to fully and frankly address China's future as a democracy and to lay out a program to help China get there.

Our lack of creativity and new thinking also leads us into fights among ourselves. When some particularly egregious atrocity or aggression by a dictator surfaces, all democrats want to respond. Many of the options we perceive as available to us are either insufficient or actually harmful to our larger interest in promoting openness and democratic change. Decision makers are presented with unappealing choices: military action, economic sanctions, isolation—or complete inaction. The military option obviously has limits against dictators armed with nuclear weapons. Economic sanctions have not brought democracy to Burma and Cuba. In Africa, we have done virtually nothing. Clearly, we need more than a bold, fresh vision and a new strategy; we also need a better set of tools. These are primarily the implements and tactics of nonviolent protest, strike actions and boycotts, and what used to be called passive resistance. The democracies need to be on the front lines, inside the dictatorships, heavily engaged in opening the country, helping the resistance, and confronting the dictator. Sometimes the tools of democratization will be drawn from military arsenals, to add elements of force to the nonviolent design. And we need scenarios of escalation to encourage dictators to leave or to drive them out.

Democracy Promotion: Number One National Security Priority

Imagine how much of a boost global democratization would receive if existing democracies finally stopped supporting "friendly" and tolerating "unfriendly" dictators. Then combine this new policy of nonsupport and nonacceptance with comprehensive efforts to aid and embolden indigenous democracy movements, and it becomes absolutely feasible to rid the world of its last dictators in a single generation.

The first step for the democrats outside dictatorships is to help encourage those inside; to enunciate a positive vision of a world without dictators, with all of its benefits for peace, prosperity, and freedom; and to establish a deadline for all the dictators to go. As noted earlier, the year 2025 is a reasonable outside date. The next step is to begin to build broad international consensus behind this vision—and this deadline—and to begin to develop the necessary organizational fabric, tools, and resources.

An essential part of this strategic paradigm shift is to elevate the promotion of democracy to the number one priority of national security, foreign policy, and international relations. Neither unlimited defense spending nor trade alone will as fundamentally alter the security and well-being of the democracies as having China, Pakistan, and the Arab world in the democratic camp.

Building consensus behind this strategy will require a massive amount of education, persuasion, leadership, and organization. Consensus will not come easily or quickly, but the effort must be started now.

There are some potent elements to work with. For the first time in history, in June 2000, the world's democracies gathered to discuss democracy and agreed to establish the Community of Democracies and work together as a caucus in the United Nations and other bodies. The core founding group of nations provides a solid basis for leadership, comprising the world's largest and oldest democracies in India and the United States, along with Poland, the Czech Republic, Portugal, South Korea, Mali, South Africa, Chile, and Mexico, among the youngest and most vigorously pro-democracy nations. All of them, the United States very much included, have some distance to go to fully adopt the strategy and tactics outlined in this book. To one degree or another, even these founding ten democracies are concerned about "interfering in the internal affairs of other nations." India, for example, has stated repeatedly as a central principle of its foreign policy that it will not try to influence another country's domestic affairs. Of course, it has interfered quite often in its neighbors' affairs. But it has failed to be a leader in openly promoting democracy. India reveres its own nonviolent resistance movement conceived and led by Mohandas K. Gandhi, who argued that injustice anywhere was a universal concern. "If any Englishman dedicated his life to securing the freedom of India, resisting tyranny and serving the land," he declared, "I should welcome that Englishman as an Indian."[9] Poland's Solidarity movement, the Czechs' Velvet Revolution, South Korea's Kim Dae Jung, and South Africa's Nelson Mandela share that view. They all understand, as do those Americans who were active in our own civil rights movement, that nonviolent conflict is, to use Gandhi's words once again, "A force more powerful." If one focus of our strategy is to back the nonviolent struggle of peoples to achieve their freedom, it will be possible to achieve a consensus among these ten core leaders of the Community of Democracies and eventually all democracies everywhere.

This is particularly true if experienced democratic politicians, not just career diplomats, are involved. In India for example, Prime Minister Atal Bihari Vajpayee is much more comfortable with India's leading role in the Community of Democracies than the Indian Foreign Service officers staffing the foreign ministry. The same phenomenon can be seen in Washington,

D.C., where members of Congress are nearly always ahead of career people in the State Department, the Pentagon, and the Central Intelligence Agency. Those closest to their own domestic democratic process are most likely to understand the desires of those in other countries struggling to construct similar systems. Elected politicians also are closer and more responsive to the nearly universal sympathy of their own constituents for ordinary people struggling in other lands. Diplomats are often closer and more responsive to other governments—some of them dictatorships. Democratic, elected politicians understand that a government is only legitimate if elected by the people. Diplomats tend to think a government is legitimate simply because it exists, even if it holds power against the clear will of its people.

The propelling force, therefore, must come from people who have been elected or those appointed by elected officials and from organizations outside government. Mobilizing democrats and democracies is in part the function of the nongovernmental organization (NGO) effort represented by the Forum on Democracy of the Community of Democracies and the World Movement for Democracy. These bring together the practitioners of nonviolent struggle from around the world with their NGO backers from the democracies. The first meeting of the World Movement was held in New Delhi in 1999 and was warmly welcomed and actively backed by India's leaders. The first meeting of the NGO Forum on Democracy was held in Warsaw in 2000, coterminous with the first meeting of democratic governments as the Community of Democracies. Among other things, it provided a platform for then Peruvian dissident Alejandro Toledo to seek support for the Peruvian resistance to President Alberto Fujimori. It is both instructive and characteristic that the U.S. State Department, responding to pressures from Fujimori, lobbied against Toledo's being invited to Warsaw and actually threatened Freedom House, the forum's U.S. organizer, with being cut off in the future.[10] As we all now know, Toledo and other democrats in Peru managed to oust Fujimori in a campaign of nonviolent conflict, and Toledo was elected president.

The Use of Force

Though internal nonviolent democratic change aided from the outside is clearly preferable to the use of force, it is not always up to the task. Sometimes it takes military force to oust a dictator and pave the way to democracy. In World War II, for example, the Allies defeated Nazi Germany and imperial Japan, then stayed on with a military presence to oversee the two countries' successful transitions to democracy. As Michael Ledeen of the American Enterprise Institute has said, "The best democracy program ever invented is the U.S. Army." Kosovo is another clear-cut case for the use of force. Because Slobodan Milosevic had committed atrocities on a massive scale in Croatia and Bosnia, there was little reason to believe that negotiating with him would bear fruit once he trained his sights on Kosovo in 1998. Milosevic pursued a classic "talk and fight" strategy, and delaying a military response progressively raised the costs and risks of the ever-more-necessary military intervention.

History suggests that military force is indispensable when a significant part of a society has heeded the nationalist call of a dictator bent on genocide or aggression against other states. World War II and the wars in the former Yugoslavia also suggest that, contrary to common wisdom, force should not always be considered a last resort. Delayed reaction can make intervention more difficult by giving the dictator time to consolidate power, further develop weapons of mass destruction, and cause more deadly havoc. The longer he is left in power, the greater will be the resentment among a victimized population, and the more it will cost to rebuild and rehabilitate the formerly fascist society. We see this again in Iraq, where the transition to democracy would have been far easier had the coalition carried on to Baghdad and ousted Saddam in 1991. The international mind-set of "force as a last resort" failed shamefully in Rwanda. Many millions died as a result, and the legacy of the 1994 genocide has made democracy immeasurably harder to achieve.

Most dictators are best removed by the people they have oppressed, applying the techniques of strategic nonviolent protest. And it is critical to their success that they remain nonviolent. But democratic leaders have not given much creative thought to how the forces on both sides of the divide might reinforce one another—how, for example, a small application of military force, or even a credible threat to use it, might break open a way for nonviolent protest to succeed. Nor has much thought been given to applying international law enforcement and/or military force very narrowly tailored to the task of ousting a dictator. Our new paradigm will not be complete until the interactions between these elements are better understood and more readily at hand.

Sanction Dictators, Not Peoples

A case in point is the way in which democracies have applied economic, military, and other sanctions. Sanctions have generally been imposed upon offending nations, causing extreme hardship for everyone except the individual—the dictator—who orchestrated the offense. Saddam Hussein reportedly quadrupled the already substantial number of his own palaces during the decade of sanctions against Iraq. Democrats and democratic governments now must rethink and transform their approach to sanctions. They need to ask two simple questions: first, what is our objective? and, second, what works? In other words, they must change the blunt instrument of sanctions into a smart weapon.

Dictators commit outrages against their own people and against other nations every day of every year that they are in power. They are systemic violators of international law. Occasionally, their violations rise to the attention of the rest of the world and there is a felt need to react, to punish. Broad sanctions are put into effect against an entire nation. But, more often than not, the sanctions imposed simply consolidate the dictator's hold on power, and they frequently create major rifts among democrats themselves, exposing their weaknesses and delaying the achievement of democracy.

Tyrants thrive in the environment of broad economic sanctions, as the Burmese colonels, Fidel Castro, Slobodan Milosevic, and many others have shown. In Iraq, Saddam Hussein continued to live in great luxury. An economy forced by sanctions to engage in smuggling and other forms of corruption fits right into the dictator's criminal mentality and methods. The sanctions specifically permitted sales of Iraqi oil to pay for food and medicine for the Iraqi people; Saddam diverted that revenue to his own personal and repressive uses then blamed the democratic world for the suffering of his subjects. The sanctions on Iraq also demonstrate the problem that inevitably arises as nations once united behind them begin to fall away. The democratic world (and the poor oppressed people) is then faced with an absolutely no-win situation. If the sanctions are diluted or lifted without remedial concessions from the dictator, the villain is handed a victory. Democrats look feckless. On the other hand, trying to keep the sanctions in place hurts the people while dividing the democratic sanctioners.

A new, better, and bolder approach would recognize one simple fact: until the dictator is ousted, there will be no end to the human rights violations and threats to peace; therefore, the objective of any sanctions must be the dictator's ouster. The strategy and tactics must be based on what has worked, not just made us feel good for having "done something." We must remember that ineffectual sanctions actually erode the prospect for democracy.

As William F. Schulz, executive director of Amnesty International USA, wrote: "When it comes to economic sanctions, the record of success is decidedly mixed. Economic sanctions alone rarely, if ever, topple a government and often lead to humanitarian catastrophes, but sanctions as part of a larger strategy, particularly sanctions targeted to affect the power brokers, may well have a salutary impact."[11]

In a general way, we know what works, what brings about the ouster of dictators and the introduction of democracy. It is for a significant portion of a population to decide "Enough is enough" and to begin to work peacefully but forcefully to remove the dictator. What works is for the democratic world to join the effort and support it openly, as we did (if belatedly) in Serbia, the Philippines, and Chile. Smart sanctions, to be effective, cannot be imposed by just a handful of individuals or by one or two governments or for one or two months or years. We need first to gather together all the power of all the democracies and democrats; unity guarantees success. We then need a new consensus about strategy and tactics among democratic activists within and outside dictatorships, among democratic governments, and with such big global actors as business and international organizations.

A central reason the world's democrats are divided is the failure to develop and enunciate a creative, forceful, and peaceful strategy to deal with the dictators. In the absence of such a strategy, democrats end up reacting piecemeal and most often injuring one another.

Calling for Departure

The most powerful single sanction is to call upon the dictators to resign. This must be done at the macro level. We have to set that fuse. The year 2025 should be made the absolute deadline for all dictators.

But departure deadlines must also be tailored for each dictator. Sometimes these deadlines are self-evident, as with upcoming elections. In all cases, democrats of the country concerned should be the ones to set the deadline, with outside democrats acting in solidarity behind them.

In response to particularly outrageous actions by dictators, democrats inside and outside should make very loud, persistent, and pressing calls for the dictator's resignation or ouster. After all, in a democracy, if a leader fails to perform, calls for his resignation now or ouster at the next election are the norm. Democratically elected presidents and prime ministers rarely stay in power for more than a term or two. Dictators typically stay for decades; most want never to give up power. The people must trim the tyrants' wings.

Blood does not run in the streets of a dictator's capital unless incendiary language is used to justify the violence. Indeed, all events are defined and interpreted by those who live them—otherwise they cannot be recognized or remembered. In that sense, the American poet Adrienne Rich was absolutely right when she said that "language is as real, as tangible, in our lives as streets, pipelines, telephone switchboards, microwaves, radioactivity, cloning laboratories, nuclear power stations."[12] If ideas are power, then words are weapons. Dictators understand this. It is time for democrats to understand it too.

When the media baron Rupert Murdoch was angling to have the Chinese government permit his satellite television channels to be carried in that country, he agreed to leave certain Western news channels out of the package deferring to our host's views about what may be broadcast in countries in which we are guests."[13] But it was not the people of China Murdoch felt would be disconcerted by seeing uncensored news from the West, it was the communist dictatorship in Beijing. Yet Murdoch, hiding behind the fiction that a "country" and its dictators are interchangeable terms, was able to evade the reality of what he was doing: kow-towing to tyrants. The result is an endless number of cases from the democratic press and governments of "China believes," "Iraq believes," "Egypt believes." In one recent example, the Shanghai correspondent of the New York Times wrote 15 July 2002, upon completing a 2½-year stint there, "Most Chinese . . . continue to support the party as a unifying force and a check against the 'luan' or chaos that all Chinese deeply fear."

Democracy poses no danger to Chinese shopkeepers or peasants—it is only dangerous to the Chinese politburo. The danger that democracy poses to dictatorships arises from democracy's higher legitimacy as a basis for political power: leaders not selected by the people have no choice but to oppose and denigrate the idea of asking the people for a mandate to rule. Although the cold war with the Soviet Union is over, the struggle between the remaining communist and other dictatorships and the natural desire of people to rule themselves is not. To have any resemblance to the truth, the language we use to describe the Chinese regime—the world's largest remaining communist state—has to remind us of that fact continually. Even the word "communist" is no longer used by polite society in the democratic world to describe the system in China, North Korea, Vietnam, Laos, and Cuba, despite the fact that the communist dictators themselves still use it daily. In February 2003, new Chinese general secretary Hu Jintao said to the visiting Fidel Castro, "As socialist countries led by communist parties, China and Cuba share the same ideals and faith."[14]

We timidly prefer "authoritarian" to "dictator."

When the Chinese Communist Party began to use the word "cult" to describe the Falun Gong, the spiritual movement it has ruthlessly suppressed, Western networks and newspapers quickly picked up and began recirculating the term, thereby unfairly anathematizing the movement in the minds of millions. More recently the communists have begun calling Christian denominations that refuse to accept government control, and therefore must operate underground, "cults" as well.

In one respect, it is not surprising that those who edit and frame the news in Western countries adopt the doublespeak of dictators. They are parroting diplomats, who have long resorted to verbal conceits and euphemisms to lubricate contact with hostile powers. But while the ostensible diplomatic purpose is to avoid confrontation, the result since the rise of the global media has been to spawn a whole language of accommodation. Addressing and resolving problems with dictators does not require words like "highly intelligent," "perceptive," and "my friend"—terms used by France's President Jacques Chirac to describe Robert Mugabe in March 2001.[15]

People who live under such governments are under no illusions about their condition: they are not free, and nothing can disguise that fact. But unless that truth is reinforced by at least verbal solidarity from the world community, the lie that democracy is not essential to human welfare is reinforced. In every instance in which a popular movement has eventually overthrown an oppressive government in the last half century, the support and encouragement of people and governments elsewhere in the world has been important in sustaining the movement through long years of opposition. But when Iraqis see French diplomats referring to Saddam Hussein as if he were a civilized partner in bilateral relations, or when the Union Oil Company is unwilling to criticize Burma's military junta with which it does business—when there is a failure by leaders and organizations in democratic countries to condemn governments that have contempt for individual liberty and human rights—the people subjected to those rulers are not encouraged to develop a strategy and muster the spirit for resistance that change requires. Conversely, as columnist Jackson Diehl noted, "The more the United States offers honest support to a suffering public against a totalitarian regime, and the more that regime squeals in protest, the more the prestige and influence of the United States will grow."[16]

Language affirming a future of freedom is just as important as an honest vocabulary about the misdeeds of dictators. But when our leaders finally do stand up to be counted as democrats, the media usually fail to appreciate the power of words. In March 2000, Madeleine Albright became the first U.S. secretary of state to address the UN Human Rights Commission, and she named names, mentioning China as one of the governments that did not respect basic rights. But the *Washington Post* dismissed her appearance as "merely symbolic."[17] It badly missed the mark. If symbols were without force, there would be no Statue of Liberty in New York's harbor, and the Chinese students who defied tyranny in Beijing would not have erected a copy of that statue in Tiananmen Square.

Those who have been jailed by dictators could teach lessons in language to those who have only had to negotiate with them across polished mahogany tables. In his memoir of the Balkan wars, U.S. ambassador Richard Holbrooke described Slobodan Milosevic, the Serbian president, as urbane and charming, but he and his fellow Western diplomats spent several years trying and ultimately failing to contain the dictator's Balkan atrocities.[18] Srdja Popovic, one of the leaders of Otpor, the nonviolent Serbian student movement, called Milosevic "a preacher of death," and he and his fellow dissidents organized and resisted until they got rid of him.

In the benighted attempt to quell instability in regions strewn with ruthless regimes but perceived as strategically useful to the United States, the masters of American foreign policy have often ignored the domestic crimes of their regional partners. Instead of encouraging and channeling assistance to independent unions, underground media, or nonviolent movements in such countries in Asia and the Middle East, the State Department confines itself to hand-wringing about their lack of respect for human rights. By contrast, the regimes themselves speak more clearly about the political challenges they face. When faced with the largest publicly expressed opposition in communist China's history, Deng Xiaoping said on 9 June 1989 that the Tiananmen protesters wanted "to overthrow the Party, state and socialist system and to replace it with a pro-Western bourgeois republic."[19] That may have somewhat misstated the student protesters' agenda, but it did not mince words.

We refuse to state clearly what we actually want. We do not tell China, Saudi Arabia, and the others that we want political parties, free elections, independent trade unions, and politically independent commercial television, radio, and newspapers. Instead we most often use broad euphemisms like "respect for human rights" or focus on an individual case of abuse. We do not say that the dictator must leave power; we talk about reform. We do not say that we support movements using nonviolent strategy and tactics to oust the dictators and bring about democracy. We should speak our mind, calling the world's remaining dictators what they are: preachers of death, enemies of freedom, and history's failures.

And we should not be shy about the uses of ridicule. Georgie Anne Geyer, writing in the *Washington Times* in January 2002, notes Fidel Castro's reaction to her book about him.[20] What bothered Castro the most was a caption she wrote under a photo of him without a shirt: "A flaccid Fidel Castro plays table tennis." He didn't like "flaccid," which in Spanish connotes physical, moral, and—above all—sexual weakness. "Quite by accident, I had hit upon the major weak spot of any dictator, caudillo, strongman, vozhd, fuehrer, Duce, general-purpose demagogue or homegrown charismatic leader: his overwhelming, preening ego. And when writers dare even to approach that ego, interestingly enough, it is then that we get responses infinitely sharper and more outraged than any criticisms we might make of these men's policies, their stupidity or their savagery. For essentially, they are political prima donnas and will often go to any length to keep their personal lives, their true political personalities—and, yes, even the weight they have taken on around the midsection—far from public view."

Of course there is nothing irrational in such concerns. Dictators know well that their power is based on fear. Undermine that fear through ridicule and exposure and their days are numbered. Developing the inside information about each dictator and widely disseminating it ought to be a high priority for democrats and their governments. "Disrespecting" dictators in ways that other governments are particularly well positioned to do is very effective.

Enforcing the Departure

We need to develop sanctions aimed directly and forcefully at the dictator himself. These should include targeting and eventually seizing his assets and those of his pillars of support. The democracies have some initial experience with this in places like Serbia, where the assets of Milosevic and his business and other supporters were identified and frozen. The dictator of Zimbabwe may be similarly vulnerable. As one expert reported: "With real estate probably the easiest asset to trace, financial investigators think it highly likely that members of Zanu-PF, Mugabe's party, have used proceeds from 20 years' access to the national treasury to buy houses and other real estate in the UK, the U.S. and elsewhere. . . . A United Nations' report of November 13, 2001, found that senior army officials, close Mugabe allies have made personal fortunes from the war in the Congo from timber, copper, and diamonds. . . . Members of the armed forces are touring Harare buying houses and commercial property with bundles of cash amassed in the Congo. . . . Tracing money is the challenge. . . . In the case of Nigeria's late dictator Sani Abacha, $1.6 billion was traced by international investigators through London, and Swiss financial institutions. . . . An array of senior figures in Zanu-PF and their families—led by Mr. Mugabe's wife, Grace—shuttle back and forth to London and New York on shopping expeditions. For this reason, in some circles Air Zimbabwe's six planes are known as 'Zanu-PF taxi service,' with planes commandeered for semi-official business at a few hours' notice. Clamping down on that could hit senior figures where it hurts: The comfort zone. It also penalizes those members of the hierarchy whose children are educated abroad. Both Mr. Mnangagwa (architect of the commercial activities of Zanu-PF and Speaker of Parliament) and Justice Minister Chinamasa, to name but two, have children in college or school in the United States."[21] Thus, smart sanctions against Mugabe would include identifying and freezing the overseas assets of the dictator and his cronies, including the military, and banning travel by the leaders, their cronies, and their families. Impoverish, immobilize—and oust.

As we develop the process of international review and judicial action through special tribunals, dictators must be made to understand that if they do not respect international law, which provides for free elections and free media, they will be prosecuted in The Hague. *Dictatorship itself must be recognized as a crime against humanity.* Subpoenas will be issued. Whether or not they appear, dictators will be tried and convicted. They will then either appear for sentencing or an international warrant will be issued for their arrest. Even in those few cases where extraction may not be practical or the international will is lacking to pursue still more forceful means, an internationally convicted dictator loses legitimacy, is seen to be vulnerable, and ultimately will be ousted. But we need to generate the international will to take more forceful means as well.

Such sanctions need a better set of teeth. We must also develop the means to physically bring dictators to justice wherever and whenever possible. In certain circumstances, this may be easier than at first appears the case. Obviously, a dictator traveling abroad could be taken into custody if the will is there. But even inside a country, with sufficient orchestration by a skillful set of local democrats and ambassadors, peaceful extraction might be doable. Moving up a notch, a multinational special forces unit, operating to implement the order of a legitimate tribunal and supported by intelligence agencies, would be able to identify the location of the dictator and bring him to justice, perhaps with the cooperation of local security forces reluctant to share his fate. And if all else fails, more forceful and direct methods could be applied. Precision-guided munitions now offer new possibilities for avoiding innocent casualties while ending the life of a tyrant. The death of a man who murders others, keeps his nation in poverty and bondage, and threatens the security of his neighbors is morally and politically justified; would anyone today blink at killing Hitler? One doubts it.

Another powerful sanction is for democrats inside the dictatorship and in solidarity with their democratic supporters worldwide—governmental and individual—to call for and launch a nonviolent campaign leading to the dictator's ouster.

Part of this requires the generation of very much larger resources to assist those inside working for democracy. Again, this must be done at the macro level by building democratic institutions and budgets and developing programs for every one of the forty-five dictators. In response to a particularly egregious action by a dictator, specific additional actions can be developed and funded.

Almost unlimited effective sanctions are available to democrats if we put our minds and wallets to work. One of the best is to show solidarity on the ground. Pope John Paul II's visits to communist Poland had electrifying and fundamental effects. We should flood dictatorships with democrats of all sizes and shapes. For democratic leaders to go to China, North Korea, Burma, Saudi

Arabia, Iran, Rwanda, and Cuba and publicly and privately call for democracy and free elections is powerful stuff. Parliamentarians and business leaders can do the same thing, to the same good effect, although it carries some risks. As noted earlier, it cost two Czech democrats six weeks in a Cuban jail in 2001 but raised European awareness and support and showed Cuban democrats they are not alone.

We need to paint on this much larger and bolder canvas in looking at sanctions. We should organize a global Students for Democracy whose members could train in the techniques of nonviolence, then go to China and other dictatorships to work beside the local democrats. Not everyone will welcome this idea. But it worked in our South, and it will work elsewhere. Yes, there are sacrifices. Local people know the risks far better than we do. There are also great rewards. Those willing should be helped to proceed.

Such activities have already sprung up. For example, thirty-three people from Australia, Europe, and North America went to China in November 2001 to show solidarity with their Chinese Falun Gong colleagues by demonstrating their peaceful, spiritual exercises in Tiananmen Square. Over a hundred foreign supporters had demonstrated in China by the summer of 2002. Unlike their Chinese colleagues, who have been jailed by the tens of thousands and murdered by the thousands, the foreigners were released within days. This will not always happen, but it makes a critical point: in promoting freedom, outsiders tend to be at less risk but to have greater public impact than local insiders. (Some in the Falun Gong give me credit for initially suggesting these solidarity trips; this underlines the value of sharing experience across movements and time.)

New Basis for Unity: Business Community for Democracy

As noted earlier, for sanctions to work, we must unite the democrats. A key to this is organization. One important first step was creating the Community of Democracies, which can provide a new architecture for the twenty-first century. With democrats working together in international bodies like the United Nations, we can bring the weight and legitimacy of the international community and international law behind specific actions. Organization on the nongovernmental side is equally important. The World Movement for Democracy and the Community of Democracies' NGO Forum on Democracy are also good starts.

There is also much we must *not* do, lest the cause be weakened or derailed. We democrats are divided about sanctions along a number of different lines. For example, democratic activists inside and outside dictatorships believe investors and businesspeople do not care about democracy and human rights and even support dictators, supposedly finding them easier to deal with than democrats. These activists push for broad economic sanctions. But traditional diplomats and practitioners of Realpolitik and many business leaders believe the pursuit of democracy is about values and is unrealistic, destabilizing, and even counter-productive. They push for strengthening relations with the governments of dictators.

In my judgment, both are wrong. To the democratic and human rights activists, I say that we should be isolating the dictators, not isolating and penalizing entire nations, which is the effect of sweeping economic and some other isolating sanctions. I have long been convinced that Castro would have been ousted years ago by his own people if the United States had pursued an aggressive policy of opening the country and supporting internal change. Similarly, in Burma we should be aggressively targeting the military dictators from within, not unintentionally cooperating with them in walling off the country.

But the traditional diplomats and practitioners of bilateral relations are also wrong. National interest and international security require that we oust, not get along with, the dictators. Even viewed from the standpoint of bilateral relations, everything becomes easier when the dictator is gone. This is most particularly the case for investors and businessmen who need the predictability and transparency of a legitimate legal system, respect for private property rights, and the ability to fend off corruption—none of which exists in dictatorships.

So democrats need to come together and strike a larger deal among ourselves. It must be based on a new confidence that we are all working for the same objective: to oust the dictators and build democracies. Here are the elements of such a deal: We agree that the sanctions should be focused on the dictators and not on the nation as a whole. We agree on a range of specific political sanctions as outlined in this book. We agree on economic sanctions that directly hurt the dictator and his pillars of support. And we agree that more broadly based economic sanctions like total bans on investment and trade for an entire nation should almost never be applied, although targeted sanctions on a specific company or industry that is sustaining a dictator would be permitted. Each of us must agree to do his part. It is not enough for businesspeople to argue (rightly) that business is inherently helpful to the process of development, modernization, and reform. They must also agree to actively and explicitly support democracy and the ouster of the dictator. This means using their resources and in-country representatives to help the democrats.

To help shape this common approach, the business community needs a new vehicle. I propose that the major multinational corporations and their associations establish the Business Community for Democracy as a partner for the governments' Community of Democracies and the NGO Forum on Democracy. This new institution, made up of the world's largest and most successful corporations, would agree that democracy, including the rule of law, is required for proper functioning and success of business. Each of its member firms would agree to support nonviolent groups and movements in all forty-five dictatorships to achieve democracy by 2025. It would create a Global Democracy Fund of $10 billion to fund democracy groups in the forty-five dictatorships and democracy and human rights groups outside who can help them. Member firms would agree not to engage in corrupt practices and specifically not to offer financial support in any form to dictators or their families; they would also cooperate in tracking and exposing dictators' corruption and assets and in seizing these assets when called upon to do so by international legal institutions. Member firms would hire democrats inside the forty-five dictatorships and provide democracy training for their local staff. And they would work to persuade the business community in the forty-five dictatorships to oust the dictators and establish free-market and democratic political institutions. Local businesspeople in a dictatorship are almost by definition in league with the dictator, and they are key to his survival; but many harbor a desire to become more legitimate and to preserve and extend their gains through a less arbitrary, more law-based system.

Democracy and human rights activists must do their part as well. They need to do more than write and meet and criticize. They must focus on ousting all dictators and instituting democracy, not just dramatizing the dictators' violations of human rights. They must not be afraid of seeming "political," which seems to mean differentiating between dictatorships and democracies. Most democracy and human rights organizations are more comfortable working on and in countries already in transition or already democratic. Many activists spend more effort attacking their own democratic governments and business leaders than on the serious culprits, the dictators themselves. Too few activists are willing to get on the front lines, where they can help organize strategic nonviolent actions and get the job done. Amnesty International USA's William Schulz notes, "A new realism . . . would view human rights as more than the release of prisoners of conscience or an end to torture but as a comprehensive effort to shape democratic communities of rights that will be peaceful neighbors, fair trading partners, and collaborators in the effort to preserve a green planet."[22]

Perhaps most important, the United States must lead the way to smarter sanctions. Such leadership could dramatically increase the willingness of the European Union, Japan, India, and other leading democratic nations to join in ousting dictators. To date, these countries have been divided and in part paralyzed over "engagement" versus "containment/isolation." But a far more powerful approach is to do both: engage with the people/nation and isolate/contain/oust the dictators. Of course, a consensus on paper is not sufficient. Parties on both sides of this divide need to take concrete actions across the entire range of new sanctions and programs proposed in this book.

Reaching agreement among the leading democracies and democrats on this new approach will breathe new life into the democratic revolution across the globe. It will deny the dictators the ability they now have to play one democratic nation or group off against another, as China, Cuba, Sudan, Libya, and others did so well in the UN Human Rights Commission in 2001 and 2002, even putting in one of their own, Libya, to chair the commission in 2003.

The goal is to help oppressed people summon the courage and unity to oust dictators. This task is immeasurably eased by increasing all forms of presence of, and contacts with, the democratic world. Sanctions that reduce student exchanges, professional cooperation, and other "opening" programs are the opposite of what is needed. When dictators do something particularly visible and egregious, democratic governments correctly feel the need to strike back. But the best response is in fact to *increase*, not decrease, contacts and programs with the people in dictatorships. Overall, we should be vastly expanding these programs inside all forty-five dictatorships. Opening up these countries is one of the most powerful "sanctions" in the democratic arsenal.

3

Communities of Democracies and Democrats

I believe this is a fight for freedom. And I want to make it a fight for justice, too—justice not only to punish the guilty, but justice to bring . . . [the] values of democracy and freedom to people around the world.

—Prime Minister Tony Blair
After the terrorist attacks of 11 September 2001

During World War II and its immediate aftermath, an entirely new architecture of international institutions and alliances was created in recognition of the new realities. In his recent book *After Victory*, Professor John Ikenberry of Georgetown University recounts this massive effort of creation and its enduring, largely positive legacy. From the United Nations to the European Community, from the North Atlantic Treaty Organization (NATO) to the World Bank and the International Monetary Fund, a host of organizations of a type not seen before sprang up. At the same time, the democracies openly interfered in the internal affairs of Germany, Italy, and Japan to recast them in a democratic form. Rarely had vision flowed so successfully into action.

At the outset of this new millennium, we are once again "after victory." The fall of the Berlin Wall and all that ensued is as great a victory for humanity as the outcome of World War II. Now, as before, we need to create new structures to take advantage of the new realities. We need new institutions and alliances that recognize the fact that democrats have achieved what amounts to victory in over half the countries of the world. Furthermore, it is clear that a much wider democratic world can now be achieved. Indeed, these new international structures should not only serve the needs of the existing democracies but also aim at extending the democratic horizon.

If democracies can view increasing (and deepening) their ranks as a real common interest, with tangible as well as intangible benefits, they need to make common cause and seriously refocus and coordinate policies. Otherwise, dictatorships, rogue states, extremists, and terrorists will continue to dominate and drive the international agenda, to the exclusion of more constructive pursuits.

At the heart of the new institutions and new alliances must be the democracies and democrats. This is not to replace the existing institutions—importantly including the United Nations—but to ensure that they work the way they should.

The New Architecture of International Power

Following World War II, the democracies of Europe and America discovered how powerful they could be when they pulled together—and we formed NATO. Now we need to apply that same power to the pursuit of a fully free world. We need to create a global democratic alliance.

As noted previously, the seeds of such an alliance were sown with the first meeting of the Community of Democracies (CD) in Warsaw in June 2000. With representatives of 107 countries in attendance, 70 at the level of foreign minister, a founding document was approved that, in its way, is even more important than the North Atlantic Treaty. A second meeting took place in Seoul, 10–12 November 2002, with 110 governments participating and endorsing an action plan to preserve political freedom in their own countries and spread it to their neighbors and around the globe. The third ministerial meeting will be held in Chile. But the very existence of the Community of Democracies is the best-kept secret in foreign affairs. As columnist Jackson Diehl noted, "Outside of Seoul, where it was held, the Community of Democracies Ministerial meeting received almost no attention."[1]

The CD is still a work in progress, but it holds many possibilities. Its central purpose should be (although it is not there yet) to develop, adopt, and pursue a grand strategy to unseat the remaining dictators. It should set the goal of "all out and universal democracy by 2025" and adopt an action program to achieve that aim. The *Wall Street Journal* reported from the Warsaw Ministerial, "Mark Palmer is urging the world's democracies . . . to drive the globe's remaining dictators—including the criminal rulers of Cuba, Sudan, Burma, and North Korea—from power. Interestingly, the world's democracies seem to be listening. Mr. Palmer was one of the architects of the first global conference held to promote worldwide democracy. . . . The pro-democracy forces have momentum on their side."[2] The Community of Democracies launched in Warsaw should be a core organization for achieving democracy. How can it proceed?

Freedom Caucuses

The Warsaw founding document and the Seoul action plan provide for caucuses of the democracies within UN, regional, and other international bodies. Now it needs the kind of support described by *New York Times* columnist William Safire: "A more creative reaction to the domination of the United Nations by dictatorships, oligarchies, and rogue nations, would be to breathe life into . . . the Community of Democracies" and its caucuses.[3] An adequately supported Community of Democracies will be able to make the democratic agenda the agenda of the UN and other bodies, as well as to focus resources on countries that are still not free and on those still in transition. A particularly appalling and compelling example of the need for CD solidarity and action is the UN Commission on Human Rights in Geneva. It is supposed to be the number one body in the world to promote human rights. On the basis of the regional caucus system within the United Nations and a flaccid new African Union literally bought and paid for by the Libyan dictator, the African caucus in 2002 selected Libya, one of the world's nine worst violators of human rights, to chair the UN Human Rights Commission. And on 20 January 2003, the members of the commission went along in a secret ballot, with only three states out of fifty-three members having the principle to vote against the move and seventeen abstaining, including all seven members of the European Union.

Global Security Alliance and Coalitions of the Willing

While nonviolent overthrow of dictators is usually preferable to external intervention or internal violent revolution, it occasionally is necessary to use force (and of course the capacity to use force yields enormous leverage). When doing so, democracies should plan to eliminate the source of the problem—the dictator and his ruling system—and plan for the aftermath. There at present is no global democratic security structure or alliance. I believe there needs to be. NATO, the most successful alliance in human history, has had to go "out of area" a number of times since the end of the cold war, though mostly in Europe but more recently in Afghanistan.

It is becoming increasingly apparent that there are contingencies in which assets from these democracies may need to be deployed far afield, well beyond the scope of their original charters or mandates. The United Nations, while it has global coverage, has a crippling flaw: dictatorships have full membership status, are treated as equals, and have representation at the top. China regularly deflects even the most trivial condemnations of other dictatorships, usually on the basis of "interference in internal affairs." Russia, while a tenuous democracy, maintains relationships with a host of brutal dictatorships. Because of these obstacles, it is undesirable for democracies to rely on the UN Security Council alone as the ultimate legitimizer of international action. A broader, not merely North Atlantic, forum for security is desirable.

I believe the Community of Democracies and an expanding NATO should take this vital role. The Community of Democracies would have its own security council, allowing democracies to form "coalitions of the willing" that address contingencies including, but certainly not limited to, interventions abroad. The community can also provide a forum for the coordination of targeted sanctions and even the disposition of the deposed; those who leave power peacefully may need a safe haven, for example. As noted earlier, the Community of Democracies members would also pool their strength in the UN and other international bodies.

The mobile force approved at the NATO summit in Prague in November 2002 can become a building block for a new *Global Force for Democracy*—a global NATO. Asian, Latin American, and other democratic nations can make their own contributions to this force. NATO itself is now operating in Afghanistan. It should gradually expand its geographic mandate and membership. There has been consideration of its use as a buffer between Israel and Palestine. NATO could develop "Partnerships for Peace" with the nations of the Middle East and beyond as it did in central and eastern Europe, with nations qualifying for full NATO membership as they become full democracies.

Again as columnist Jackson Diehl pointed out, "The plan adopted at Seoul is aimed in part at building regional alliances of democracies that can reinforce one another and pressure their neighbors for change."[4] One of the fathers of the Helsinki process, Ambassador Max Kampelman, and I and others are working on ways to organize a Helsinki-like process for the Middle East and possibly Asia and Africa as well. With the CD regional nations at the core and working closely with nonregional democracies and nations such as the United States, the European Union, the Organization for Security and Cooperation in Europe, and the UN Development Programme, there is the potential to negotiate an "ought" document and then to proceed to bring the "is" closer to the "ought" in the Middle East, Asia, and Africa. The three baskets of Helsinki (political/security, economic, and human rights) can provide a framework for these regions as well.

The scenario in which the democracies of the world have the greatest latitude—and therefore the greatest responsibility—to help establish democratic structures and governance is in postdictatorship and/or postconflict situations, especially where they have intervened militarily. The immediate postconflict period is always very delicate, but it affords great possibilities to set a country in the right direction. In no other situation do democracies have greater pull or less excuse for getting it wrong. A recent example of this is Afghanistan, where an interim government cobbled together at a conference hosted by Germany in Bonn has evolved through a constitutional convention and plans an election in 2004. The surrounding dictatorships—China, Iran, the Central Asian states, Pakistan—along with still not fully democratic Russia cannot help feeling nervous about the example being set by Afghanistan.

Protectorates are the most involved of these possible relationships. In cases of total state collapse or civil war, these way stations to full sovereignty and democracy are often necessary. Some of these missions, like the continuing one in Bosnia, have shown a lack of vision and decisiveness on the part of the peace-implementing democracies. An unwillingness to tackle pivotal problems, such as the continued liberty of indicted war criminals and continued obstruction of refugee return by corrupt ethnofascist elites, prolongs the necessity of the custodial relationship while simultaneously devaluing the credibility of the protecting powers. The goal has to be the establishment of democratic and legal structures that will put the country on the path to sustained democratic practice and prosperity. This process necessitates local participation by principled actors, not obstruction by spoilers. Often those who wish to maintain their own corrupt power use the language of democracy to attack necessary (and usually overdue) international efforts to build genuine democracy. Without personal security and rule of law, democracy is a fiction, especially in places like Bosnia.

I believe the democracies of the world, under the aegis of the Community of Democracies *and* the nongovernmental organizations (NGOs) in the Forum of the CD and the World Movement for Democracy, need to meet and come up with a comprehensive template for what must happen to plant democracy after a dictatorial government has been ousted by international intervention. Doing this, by both examining lessons learned and gathering a roster of specialized talent, would help ensure that the opportunities to build viable democracies are not missed. The results of such a meeting (and the follow-up and constant contact thereafter) could be applied to future international postconflict missions. By making such preparations, democracies could get ahead of the curve and be able to react with dispatch when such situations arise. We cannot afford again to be caught essentially flat-footed, as we have been in Afghanistan (and, most recently, Iraq).

International Criminal Tribunals

The United States is certainly one of the premier nations in the world that believes in the rule of law, and we led the way in creating the International Criminal Tribunal for the former Yugoslavia at The Hague and the International Criminal Tribunal for Rwanda. These demonstrate the central role such tribunals can play in ousting dictators for violating international law—of which they are all guilty. Why then are so many in Washington so heavily opposed to the establishment of an International Criminal Court (ICC)? It is clearly because of concern that governments not committed to the rule of law would have judges on the court, could destroy the court's integrity, and could end up trying the United States and American soldiers for alleged crimes committed in the course of promoting democracy and peace. One way to address this dilemma is for the United States to try to convince other members of the CD that judges on the ICC should only come from countries that do respect the rule of law—namely, the world's democracies. In the meantime, we also could continue to use ad hoc tribunals and even cooperate with other democracies in bringing to the existing ICC cases that are clearly in our interest.

Bringing criminal cases against dictators is a very powerful tool, but it must be used. Former U.S. ambassador at large for war crimes David Scheffer noted, "Throughout the Clinton Administration, I waged an often lonely campaign to compile the criminal record against the Iraqi regime and to seek indictments of Iraqi officials. By the end of 2000 our investigating team had amassed millions of pages of documents . . . demonstrating Iraqi crimes against humanity. Yet no Iraqi official has ever been indicted for some of the worst crimes of the 20th century. My own efforts to obtain UN Security Council approval for an ad hoc international criminal tribunal encountered one obstacle after another in foreign capitals, in New York and even within the Clinton Administration. The usual excuse was that we needed Hussein's cooperation (with inspections and sanctions) which a criminal indictment might discourage."[5] If such an indictment of Saddam Hussein had proceeded, we might not have been faced with the option of using force.

The Yugoslavia and Rwanda tribunals provide some experience and precedents. These bodies represent current international law, with mandates to cover crimes committed in given countries in defined periods of time. There are also possibilities, likely to be applied in the cases of Sierra Leone and East

Timor, of hybrid tribunals, which would have elements of international participation and also of local elements. These give the added benefits of local public legitimacy and increased local judicial capacity once the international role is reduced or curtailed.

There are numerous examples of countries that have moved beyond Not Free status and have instituted judicial review of crimes committed under the previous regime. Usually, these reviews are best done in countries that are unimpeachably democratic and achieved power nonviolently, as with the cases in Germany of those tried for crimes committed under the German Democratic Republic. However, even Partly Free countries such as Ethiopia, whose current rulers defeated the Derg regime by force, have applied reasonable legal standards for crimes committed under the Mengistu regime. In most cases, the crimes committed by dictatorships are against their own citizens, and it would be preferable, when practical, to have local rule of law (augmented as needed by international democratic expertise and monitoring) address these transgressions.

International Parliamentary Cooperation

Like the ICC, the International Parliamentary Union (IPU) is tainted by the participation of dictatorships. As exemplified by the fact that dictator Fidel Castro hosted the IPU's 2001 meeting in Havana, many of its "parliamentarians" are not freely elected and are not parliamentarians by any serious definition of the term. They represent the interests and dictates of some of the world's forty-five dictators and not those of a constituency of free voters. As a result, American legislators and other democratic parliamentarians have shown extremely little interest in the IPU.

In fact, bringing together the world's democratically elected parliamentarians would be an immensely important and useful achievement. Freely elected parliamentarians, certainly more than most foreign ministry bureaucrats, understand from their own experience the difference between democracy and dictatorship. The U.S. Congress has historically been ahead of the executive branch, and well ahead of the State Department, in recognizing the value of promoting democracy abroad. Democratic parliamentarians in general not only are much more supportive of the establishment of democracy worldwide but also are able to generate the resources required to promote it.

And on democracy, they are able to work across party lines. When San Francisco liberal Nancy Pelosi took over leadership of the House Democrats, Orange County conservative Republican representative Chris Cox proclaimed, "It's good news for people living under repressive regimes around the world." As one observer commented, "For more than a decade, Cox and Pelosi have constituted a two-person Congressional freedom squad . . . tough on dictatorships everywhere."[6]

They also make excellent ambassadors for democracy. In that capacity, Senator Paul Laxalt did much to help oust Philippine dictator Ferdinand Marcos, and Senator Ted Kennedy kept pressure on Chile's Augusto Pinochet. British members of Parliament have been strongly outspoken on the Burmese dictatorship. Kim Dae Jung, former member of the Korean parliament and recently president of his country, understands that penetrating North Korea, dealing directly with its dictator, fielding people-to-people programs, and in general opening up that iceberg is an important part of the path to unification, democracy, and peace. This is not to endorse every word President Kim has uttered or every step he has or has not taken (he was too reluctant to talk about the need to introduce democracy in the North)—but he definitely worked to open North Korea, a far better method than "containment," broad economic sanctions, or "malign neglect."

Monarchs for Democracy

Another project for the Community of Democracies is to establish a special working group of monarchs for democracy. Seven of the world's dictators are ruling monarchs, and there are a number of kings running Partly Free countries as well. The basic approach would be to have some of the community's constitutional monarchs, led by King Juan Carlos of Spain, work with the still ruling monarchs to help them through the transition to constitutional monarchy. They could be assisted by interested democracies with no monarchical history but with experience in transitions to democracy. We address this initiative in greater detail in chapter 9.

The Nongovernmental Dimension

It is also important to create a new alliance among the world's democrats outside government. This includes those still suffering under dictators and those outside who can help. Here, too, important seeds have been sown that require nurturing.

The World Movement for Democracy, launched in 1999, originally sprang from a conference organized by the U.S. National Endowment for Democracy in cooperation with the Confederation of Indian Industry and the Centre for

Policy Research, based in New Delhi, capital of the world's largest democracy. The meeting brought together over four hundred democratic activists and practitioners from around the world to network with one another. The conference ended with the foundation of the World Movement as a "pro-active network of democrats," which would meet at least once every two years. Gathering momentum, a second session in São Paulo, Brazil, in 2001 held practical workshops on the lessons learned from helping develop the still fragile democracy in transition countries and, to a useful but lesser extent, on how to break through in dictatorships. A third session was scheduled for 2003 in South Africa.

Another useful seed is the NGO Forum on Democracy of the Community of Democracies, which takes place at the same time as meetings of the ministerial-level Community of Democracies. The forum provides an opportunity for democrats struggling against dictators to be heard by the democratic governments. Exchange of ideas and tactics among struggling democratic activists has proven fruitful in the past, and it is heartening for participants to know that there are others the world over who fight similar battles. In addition, it is important that these democrats be heard by representatives of democracies. In the Internet age, regular communication between activists and democracies is more feasible, and less detectable by dictators, than ever before.

The Stakes

The cost of democrats' failure to maintain a common front against tyrants has been high in the past decade. Former *Financial Times* columnist Edward Mortimer some years ago wrote that the true architects of the new world order were not men such as George Bush, who coined the term, but dictators like Slobodan Milosevic and Saddam Hussein, who by forcing the world to respond to them essentially controlled the international agenda.

Serbian dictator Slobodan Milosevic was very skillful in dividing the West and the rest of the democratic world, exploiting and widening existing divisions. This helped insulate his regime from truly decisive pressure during the war in Croatia, later in Bosnia, still later in the post-Dayton era, during the war in Kosovo and the NATO intervention, and since. Repeatedly, democracies presented different policies to Milosevic, opening themselves to manipulation and giving Milosevic room to maneuver.

This lack of solidarity, both among democracies and among Yugoslav democrats, helped keep Milosevic in power, permitting bloodshed and repression. In this case, the lack of American leadership was crippling. Because the United States was unwilling to lead its allies in stopping the Bosnian Serb "ethnic cleansing" campaign, directed from Belgrade, it allowed fundamentalist Islamists to be the only external aid for the beleaguered Bosnian government. Once the United States finally did get involved, it made the mistake of basing its Balkan policy on dictatorial "partners," Milosevic and his Croatian counterpart Franjo Tudjman, both of whom repressed domestic political enemies and connived to carve up Bosnia. After Dayton, Italy and Greece, by buying into the Serbian telecommunications monopoly, gave Milosevic the funds he needed to pay pensions immediately before the 1997 elections. As the Kosovo crisis mounted, European countries were unwilling to use sanctions to pressure Milosevic. The democracies also failed to press Russia to show its democratic credentials by breaking its links with a dictator. The interrelated Balkans crises of the 1990s show in horrifying detail what can happen when democracies fail to make common cause in opposing dictators.

Saddam Hussein became quite adept at exploiting and exacerbating policy differences among democracies. France dropped out of the 1991 Gulf War coalition, preferring to aim for commercial advantage in Saddam's controlled economy. The United States, lacking a targeted policy to promote change in Iraq, relied instead on sanctions. Until recently, there had been no serious thinking, much less consensus, on how to bring Iraq out of dictatorship and into the international community. Iraqis have been subjected to this most repressive of regimes for far too long precisely because the democracies had not devised and agreed upon a coherent plan to oust Saddam and establish an Iraqi democracy that can set a positive example for the Middle East.

The fact that these failures of cohesion occurred simultaneously with an unprecedented expansion in the democratic world is alarming and, in my opinion, damning. The Community of Democracies, still in its infancy, can provide a framework to remedy these deficiencies in the democratic world's solidarity and help build both a common front and—most important—a common *strategy* with which to advance democracy where it has yet to take root. This is the final democratic frontier—the opening of closed societies.

Opening Closed Societies

The sovereignty of states must no longer be used as a shield for gross violations of human rights.

—UN Secretary General Kofi Annan

"Knowledge of the outside world as a basis for comparison is essential to the creation of pressure from within for change." Thus wrote an experienced Russian democrat, Leonid Romankov.[1] An East German engineer friend put it in blunter terms: "We East Germans learned via foreign television, radio, and from visiting West Germans what you could buy with the Deutschmark. We wanted to have the same cars, clothes, and opportunities for travel as those in the West, and this drove people into the streets." The trouble is that, if democracy is to prevail, such knowledge cannot simply leak into the world's closed societies. It must be pumped in.

What tools are available or could be developed to help with this information flow? What resources are required to provide these tools? And what gives people the courage to take to the streets, to feel that they can face down a regime that has not shunned violence and other tools of repression?

Though there has been considerable evolution in the two decades since President Ronald Reagan's speech to the British Houses of Parliament about the need to promote democracy, established democracies have not yet made the promotion of freedom a fundamental priority in their foreign policies, especially where the hardest-case dictators are concerned. A landmark study released in 2002 by Theodore Piccone and Robert Herman examines the foreign policy of the forty leading democracies. "It concludes that, while the international community has helped advance the cause of democracy and human freedom around the world, democratic states have largely failed to incorporate the defense and promotion of democracy as a central element of their foreign policies. Nonetheless, in more places than not, the gap between rhetoric and reality is closing."[2] This is absolutely essential if we wish to assure that corrupt, brittle dictatorships, like those in the Persian Gulf, do not give way to governments riding a virulent anti-Western view to temporary popularity. For the purposes of this book, I will focus on the United States, although I believe that structural reforms along the lines of those outlined here are equally applicable, and even more needed, in other established democracies.

Presidential Leadership

The U.S. government, despite the efforts of a number of talented professionals and some notable successes in helping democrats abroad, has yet to develop a serious structure to oust dictators and promote democracy overseas. To maximize our ability to help struggling democrats and avoid scattering our shot, the U.S. government needs to develop in the immediate term a solid and well-funded democracy portfolio in its foreign policy apparatus. Other democracies need to do the same, and there needs to be a coordinated effort, as outlined earlier, to make sure each dictatorship faces a cohesive democratic community with strong leadership.

To begin with, the president himself needs to show that the expansion of democratic rule in the world is a standing commitment that transcends domestic political differences and his own administration. Without this kind of backing, the dictators of the world will rightly believe that they can evade American policies they do not like by simply going to the top. This is especially true in the present climate, in which coalition sometimes trumps principle. A presidential-level initiative would send the signal that the United States is finally getting serious about promoting democracy, not just to countries that are "enemies," but also to those falsely termed "allies" that are under despotic rule. Only when the signal comes from the president of the United States, followed by concrete action in the policy realm, will the fact sink in with dictators worldwide that business as usual is truly a thing of the past.

A White House conference on democracy that includes the important players in the executive and legislative branches and the leaders of the community of nongovernmental organizations (NGOs) such as Freedom House, Amnesty International, and the National Endowment for Democracy and its affiliated core institutes, would be the ideal platform to announce this new initiative. Special effort should be made to include major business and foundation figures as well. Our considerable philanthropic and business communities' capacity has not been directed strongly enough toward ousting dictators and the promotion of democracy abroad, despite the fact that business would be a major beneficiary of a democratic world. This needs to change.

One proof of seriousness would be a substantial increase in the budget for democracy promotion. In a 26 March 2002 letter to members of Congress and Secretary of State Colin Powell, fifty-two leaders of democracy and human rights organizations called for an increase to at least $1 billion from the current level of $700 million. As they stated, "Substantially increased funding is essential not only in critical regions such as the Middle East, South and Central Asia, but elsewhere across the world, where civil society has taken up the democratic challenge and/or where nascent democratic regimes remain fragile. . . . Any effective long-term strategy to combat terrorism and other extremist violence must place democratic governance, accountability, transparency, rule of law, human rights, a robust civil society, civil education and regular competitive elections at its core."

In one of his 2001 departure valedictories, then U.S. assistant secretary of state for democracy, human rights and labor Harold Koh described four categories of countries: closed societies, countries in the early stage of transition, backsliding countries, and new democracies that had stabilized. He argued that funding should be concentrated on the second and third categories, that it was difficult to spend money effectively on closed societies. Professor Koh was reflecting a widely held perception—one that misses the mark, in my view. While early-transition and backsliding countries deserve significant attention and stable democracies should not receive such assistance, dollar for dollar, money spent on and in closed societies to oust dictators contributes more to human freedom and our own national security. It is profoundly wrong that closed societies receive probably 10 percent of the overall funding and effort when they are 90 percent of the problem. While ousting the last forty-five dictators does not all come down to money, they will go sooner and more peacefully if global funding directed at them—public and private—is materially increased.

This will require some structural adjustments. As an integral part of the new presidential initiative, a senior-level presidential appointee needs to be solely tasked with America's promotion of democracy abroad. This central national interest requires a new position, deputy secretary of state for democracy, that would make the incumbent one of the two principal deputies to the secretary of state. While housed within the State Department, the seat of American foreign policy, the deputy secretary with the president's mandate should have the authority to oversee democracy efforts throughout the U.S. government, including oversight of Defense Department and Central Intelligence Agency (CIA) relationships as they affect democracy. With presidential imprimatur and a dedicated budget and staff of his or her own, the deputy secretary for democracy should be able to overcome the typical bureaucratic resistance. When stymied by diplomats suffering from "clientitis" and other inevitable bureaucratic obstructions, the deputy secretary needs to have access to the president. In addition, there should be a full directorate within the National Security Council (NSC) staff for democracy to ensure clout and coordination of the effort vis-à-vis the Defense Department, the CIA, and others.

Two new bureaus headed by assistant secretaries should be created and report to the deputy secretary. An assistant secretary for democratic transitions would be charged with helping consolidate democracy in countries in transition, the Partly Free countries. This is where the lion's share of democracy assistance has been focused since the end of the cold war, and it remains important. Democracy does not root itself firmly with the mere ouster of the dictator, and many a promising transition has gone astray as new democracies revert to undemocratic, or at best tenuously democratic, rule. The capacities to address these countries' needs are fairly well developed and are heavily concentrated in the nongovernmental sector, particularly in the National Endowment for Democracy and its core institutes, as well as in NGOs like Freedom House and the Open Society Institute (OSI). The assistant secretary for countries in transition would focus primarily on assisting these organizations and augmenting them as needed. In addition, this assistant secretary would have responsibility to coordinate with democracy-promotion officers (many more are needed) in American embassies in these countries to tailor policy responses and push for them within an inevitably sticky bureaucracy in Washington.

A second assistant secretary would be responsible for countries under dictatorship. The strategy and tactics to oust dictators are different from those required to build democracy. The task here is to get help to those brave activists working to bring down the most repressive regimes, now numbering forty-five. This position also requires highly developed political skills, so that the assistant secretary can work with the Congress, all aspects of the American bureaucracy, the media, NGOs, the policy community, and diplomatic allies to accomplish the formidable tasks at hand. To achieve results, she or he will need real power and considerable resources. Given the importance of the task, presidential backing, and Congress's track record of supporting efforts to promote democracy in such places as Serbia and elsewhere, acquiring these should not be overly difficult. American leadership in democracy promotion and consolidation is as important to U.S. interests as "hard power."

The assistant secretary for ousting dictators would have primary responsibility for developing an annually revised "democracy action program" for each country, working with the relevant regional bureau and agencies. The regional bureaus are a particular impediment. The power in the State Department traditionally has been and remains with them, and they are the great protectors of "good bilateral relations." So the deputy secretary for democracy and the assistant secretary for ousting dictators need to be in the chain of command on all issues affecting the Last Forty-five. With the backing of the president and the secretary of state, they also must be able to keep the Pentagon's short-term tactical military desire to build up dictators and warlords from turning into strategy and curb the CIA's similar proclivities.

The United States need not act alone in democracy promotion abroad. The German *Stiftungen*, or political party foundations, were pioneering in their assistance to democracy advocates in Spain and Portugal, both of which had their transitions to democratic rule in the 1970s. The Stiftungen's efforts served as the inspiration for the National Endowment for Democracy in the United States and other democracy foundations in Europe, Canada, and beyond.

Still, there is no substitute for American diplomatic and political leadership in building coalitions of the willing to help citizens successfully confront their dictators. The advent of the Community of Democracies and its NGO counterparts, the Community's Forum for Democracy and the World Movement for Democracy, creates a useful umbrella structure for such coalitions, helping collect the necessary talent and resources to mount a strong campaign. But we should be opportunistic in putting together coalitions of willing governments and NGOs where they are ready to join together. There is ample skill and audacity at the operational level in new democracies, as one can see most recently with Serbia's Otpor (Resistance) youth movement activists advising colleagues in the Zubr movement in Belarus. The leadership factor remains a sine qua non. While there will be cases where other democracies take a leading role, no other country on Earth has the panoply of resources, publicly funded institutes, and NGOs devoted to helping spread and deepen democracy. If the United States does not prove its commitment to democracy by visibly being in the front rank of concerned democracies, local democratic leaders (and dictators) will draw the conclusion that we do not wish democrats to succeed. This is both tragic and very dangerous.

"Coalitions of coalitions" not only provide critical strategic depth to democratization campaigns, they also serve as a vital coordination mechanism. Democratic governments need to coordinate their efforts with one another as well as with the NGO world. NGOs also need to coordinate their activities and have proven themselves up to the task in a number of important instances. The U.S. government, at least, has some experience of openness to the NGO sector, as do the Nordic and British governments, recognizing that these groups can do things governments cannot and have access to information often far superior to their own. This level of cooperation, while sporadic and imperfect, is unfortunately not yet the norm for other established democracies. Considering the number of skilled nongovernmental actors in the democratic world, most with far more experience on the subject than their counterparts in government, who are consumed with bilateral relations and other fixations, this failure to cooperate represents a major squandering of a potentially crucial resource. The rotation system in the diplomatic corps and throughout the bureaucracy seriously undercuts effectiveness and continuity and is part of the justification for a permanent unit and cadre of democracy specialists within the U.S. Department of State and other foreign ministries.

Integrated coalitions of governmental actors and their nongovernmental counterparts should be organized first along geographical, then along sectoral, lines. For example, to assist democratic activists in Belarus, governmental representatives from the United States, Canada, the European Union and its member states, and neighboring democracies like Poland and Lithuania would coordinate with the NGOs from these countries and, of course, from Belarus. Then, they would organize under coordinators for media, election monitoring, political organizing, and the like. In this way, the coalition of coalitions for Belarus could effectively coordinate their efforts. Vital information would effectively and expeditiously travel from those who had it to those who could use it. The pool of talent and resources would be formidable and could be directed where it would most likely do the greatest good in the effort to oust the dictator. The ability to take advantage of rapid turns of events would be increased considerably. In a word, the coordination of democratization efforts greatly increases the likelihood of their success. Another big advantage of coalitions and a variety of NGO actors is the multiplier effect. In addition, the plurality of channels of support would make it much harder for the dictator to shut off support both cross-border and in-country. The truism applies: it is much easier to shut off one valve than ten or a hundred.

Strategy

With a strongly backed and articulated commitment to helping bring the Last Forty-five out of the dictatorial abyss, and an overall structure in place to help facilitate this, the focus must turn to strategy.

Often, to quote a famous blues song, local democrats have "been down so long it looks like up" to them. Their perspective on their struggle, through no fault of their own, is truncated. In 1986 I saw Hungarian democrats unable to think tactically much beyond getting their passports returned. Democratic assistance operators often have to help extend the horizons of indigenous civic activists beyond their immediate, often dire, situation. (Not infrequently, however, it is the outsiders who have their horizons of possibility expanded by indigenous democrats.) We must persuade them that they can actually prevail over their oppressors, that democracy waits at the end of dictatorship's drab rainbow. Encouraging local democratic activists and the international community to believe they *can* win is perhaps the most important factor of assistance and is an absolute prerequisite to developing successful democratization strategies. After the myopia of oppression has been corrected, we need to ask them what they need to achieve their goals—and help them.

In fact, promoters of foreign democracy, including government officials, NGO actors, and contractors, have often had a tin ear for the concerns of those who must bear the brunt of the struggle, the indigenous civic activists. A notable exception is George Soros, who deserves a Nobel Prize for his pioneering efforts to promote civil society and democratic governance in Eastern Europe and points beyond. His Open Society Institute has been quite successful in giving indigenous talent the lead in its efforts. Soros's view is that democracy promoters must "think like venture capitalists." That is, they must allow the locals to run the operation, with guidance from without only as needed. A seasoned democracy promoter should know what general strategies have worked and needs to impart the benefits of this experience to local activists. But external actors (and funders) must also realize that they cannot possibly be versed in the minutiae of the local situation and should assist the locals to craft a coherent strategy for their specific scenario. In other words, the democracy promoter must respect his local partners by deferring to them on matters where they are better versed. The fight for democracy cannot be successfully directed from without—only assisted and advised.

Special care should be taken for external actors not to fixate upon an individual as the embodiment of the democratic struggle. Often, the anointed are not what they seem. Of course, individuals can be important symbols. In Burma, for instance, Daw Aung San Suu Kyi has great symbolic and political value, not least because she was elected then deposed by military rule. But placing democracy on the shoulders of one favorite gives the dictatorship a single target; eliminate the figurehead, and the opposition wilts. In most cases, a broad front is needed to mobilize a critical mass of society to confront the dictator and his support system. Overall strategy must be cognizant of this, and promoters of democracy should make it clear to "prima donnas" that international support is to the movement to rid the country of the dictator and not to promote preening and internecine posturing.

Funding and Local Presence

While resources committed without a coherent strategy cannot be fully effective, a good strategy denied adequate funding, especially at critical junctures, is doomed to failure. All too often, funding is unavailable when it is needed, and unique windows of opportunity are missed. As John Fox (an experienced democratic activist in the government and former director of the Open Society Institute's Washington operation) recently told me, "Getting $100,000 support in four weeks is worth more than $1,000,000 in a year."[3] Activists on the ground need to be able to seize opportunities on the ground as they arise, without delays or funding bottlenecks. The United States and other established democracies that wish to assist democratic struggles effectively need new, streamlined procedures to allow quick turnaround for aid requests. Preferably, the deputy secretary for democracy would have signing authority for quick response. Furthermore, ambassadors and their embassy democracy officers abroad should have discretionary funding under a reasonable threshold. The prime necessity is that the local democrats' prioritization of needs is accepted rather than having to fit our bureaucratic template. Working in this way, Soros's Open Society Fund has left an indelible institutional footprint upon large swaths of the world.

In the midst of the 1996–1997 demonstrations, one of Soros's Serb partners, Veran Matic, and his team recognized that if local elections were validated, the municipal assets and control of local radio frequencies would largely come under opposition (if not always independent) control. Matic rapidly devised a plan for an Internet- and satellite-connected radio network covering most of Serbia; Soros pledged $200,000 (one quarter of the total); and together with Matic on a lightning visit to Washington, John Fox challenged the U.S. government to match that amount. Thanks to this funding and matches obtained from the British and Dutch (and robust European diplomatic support when Milosevic tried to shut down the network), ultimately a thirty-six-station ANEM radio network was launched in less than six months. There was no U.S. government democracy program in Serbia at that time, Richard Holbrooke was still having high-profile Sunday brunches with Milosevic as the supposed guarantor of regional stability, and media support from the U.S. government consisted of endless journalists' training sessions mostly unconnected to the real situation of media on the ground.

A manifestation of the bureaucratic tail wagging the dog is the problem regularly encountered when local democrats need funds to finance their demonstrations and campaigns. To mount a serious campaign requires more than the omnipresent out-of-country trainings, though these have proven helpful in a number of cases. The real name of the game is on-the-ground impact: visible nonviolent action by citizens confronting the regime. This requires cold hard cash to purchase cell phones, computers, and printing presses; rent office space; pay for transportation; rent audio equipment, public-address systems, and vans; and provide what we might call walking-around money.

An important factor in ensuring that taxpayer dollars (or euros, or yen) go toward the intended goal of forcing out dictators is an on-the-ground presence, created partly through active NGOs and embassies. Like forward observers, these eyes and ears not only help target funds and coordinate strategies but also serve as critical governors on how assistance is used. Often, seed money given by NGOs can be followed by a more sustained effort by governments, once they are convinced the prospects are good. The Open Society Institute worked in this way a number of times in Eastern Europe. Unfortunately, embassies and the U.S. Agency for International Development (USAID) are often the most resistant to real support for pushing out the dictator.

Another apprehension we must overcome is the reluctance to aid political parties. Aside from some assistance given by Swedish and other party foundations, direct assistance to democratic parties is sorely lacking. While such aid is not always appropriate (what form of assistance is?), a consensus appears to have taken root that it is never appropriate, a conclusion that is clearly not true. Rigidly assuming that party assistance is a bad idea without looking at the situation at hand is yet another case of bureaucratic concerns trumping effectiveness. Encouraging coalitions of parties is generally a good idea, but such encouragement should spring from an assessment that this offers the most effective adversary for the regime in question. The decision to assist political parties should not be evaluated in terms of whether the assistance crosses an imaginary line of internal interference. Where political parties constitute the best-organized opposition to dictatorship, democracies must be able to assist them. "Civil society" is all very well, but at the end of the day democracies need organized, disciplined political parties, trade unions, and independent media. Therefore helping these key forces get started during the "ousting of dictators" phase is important for the longer term as well as critical to the ousting itself. Of course, both sides of this transaction need to understand that once the dictator has been ousted, there can no longer be a privileged relationship.

In the democracy-support world, too much of the funding stays with the aid-granting countries or with their hired consultants. This is particularly pronounced in the case of contracted organizations, which live and die on the basis of USAID grants and the like. This reality, in most instances, reduces the value received for each dollar of assistance in two important ways. First, many of the consultants, particularly those on short-term contracts, approach a situation with a "one size fits all" mentality and do not get a proper feel for the situation they have been detailed to help. Second, the opportunity cost of such an approach is quite high, especially when one considers how far the dollar stretches in most of the world. Very little of the money allocated to assist foreign democratic activists is directly available to meet *their* priorities. While the current approach may look cleaner on the ledger in terms of accountability, it has proven a crippling impediment to assisting democrats abroad in an effective fashion.

For these reasons, we must see a radical departure from present practice. USAID embraced democracy-oriented work only reluctantly when it became a focus in the 1980s; since then the agency has tried to brand much of its normal development work as "democracy" projects, so as to tap into that till. The $700 million figure for democracy promotion cited earlier is very broadly defined. USAID has undertaken innovative and effective projects in some regions and has developed some first-class experts. But it is largely absent on the front line of the Last Forty-five, in part because USAID has no missions resident in many of these countries. Therefore, the leadership and management of the U.S. government's support to democrats in dictatorships must come from elsewhere. Only through an entirely new, specifically designed and outfitted operation can the job be done properly. The current Bush administration has recognized that it was necessary to establish an organization outside USAID to manage the new Millenium Challenge Account bonus programs for countries demonstrating good governance, respect for human rights, and market economies. A comparable U.S. Center to Oust Dictators is needed. It could be a U.S. partner for the International Dictatorship-to-Democracy Center proposed in this book, and it might well precede it as it will undoubtedly take time to persuade other democracies.

The Nongovernmental Democracy Promotion Institutions

Nongovernmental actors in the world of democracy promotion have a long and distinguished history. First lady Eleanor Roosevelt and former GOP presidential challenger Wendell Wilkie collaborated in establishing Freedom House, an organization to help fight dictatorships both fascist and communist, in 1941. The League of Women Voters and other civic organizations were deeply involved in helping plant democracy in postwar Germany, Italy, and Japan. The German party foundations (Stiftungen) undertook groundbreaking work in supporting democrats while Spain and Portugal were under Franco and Salazar, helping pave the way for democracy in both. International labor has a long and distinguished history of supporting democracy, rule of law, and human rights in general and has been particularly responsive to the needs of union members abroad and their priorities. AFL-CIO chief Lane Kirkland was the most consistent American supporter of democracy during the late cold war, when many distinguished Americans were apt to turn a blind eye to the depredations of "friendly" undemocratic states, like apartheid-era South Africa or Chile under Pinochet. As mentioned earlier, George Soros's Open Society Institute led the way in eastern and central Europe from the late 1980s on and provided vital assistance when and where it was most needed.

As foreshadowed in President Reagan's democracy speech in Westminster, the National Endowment for Democracy was launched in 1983. There had long been support among forward-looking members of both major parties, our trade unions, and the business community for a democracy-promotion organization. Finally the stars were properly aligned and the endowment came into being, along with its four core institutes: the National Democratic Institute for International Affairs, the International Republican Institute, the Center for International Private Enterprise, and the American Center for International Labor Solidarity (affiliated respectively with the Democratic and Republican Parties, the U.S. Chamber of Commerce, and the AFL-CIO). They have been major players in worldwide democracy promotion ever since. While its support base in Congress was initially touch-and-go, it is now on a solid foundation. Funded through an annual congressional allocation, the National Endowment for Democracy grants funds to the four core organizations, funds its own efforts, and is able to give grants to organizations abroad in line with its mission.

But it is still flawed. The endowment's family of organizations has a pronounced tilt toward countries in transition—those countries that are in the gray zone between the overthrow of dictatorship and the firm rooting of democracy. In the aftermath of 1989 and 1991, it is easy to understand. One need only look at countries teetering on the brink of failed governance, like Ukraine. But the larger challenges are the Not Free countries. While the endowment and others support distinguished intellectuals, journals, and so forth in these countries, they give material support to few movements engaged in an organized campaign directed at regime change. Too often, the endowment has been unwilling to take the lead in large-scale programs to oust dictators. In Serbia, for example, it refused the State Department's urgent request to channel the initial $10 million in post–Kosovo war democracy assistance through the endowment. The Democratic and Republican core institutes did make vital contributions to the opposition and independent civic organizations like Otpor through training, polling, and other means. The International Republican Institute's support of village-level elections in China is also on the cutting edge and is an innovative way to promote democracy in that crucial country. However, more such efforts are needed in all dictatorships. The independent democracy organizations too often have to swim upstream against USAID, the State Department, and the endowment. It was advocacy NGOs, led by the Open Society Institute, that were not dependent on the

U.S. government that pushed Congress for Serbia democracy aid and pressed the implementation in a way that could directly benefit the indigenous NGOs, media, and political parties. The dependence of the democracy-building organizations in fact makes them quite cautious, and they too often go against their better instincts to preserve relationships with their executive-branch paymasters.

Whenever suitable direct footholds can be found, they should be used. In any case, much can be done even without a formal presence. For example, much of the U.S. support for Serbian democrats was based in neighboring Hungary. Expertise in promoting democracy in the most repressed societies is in short supply, and the more experience generated, the better. Developing the capacity for this line of work while maintaining efforts in transitioning countries will require significantly more public funding.

The most recent public funding level (privately raised funds augment this only modestly) for the National Endowment for Democracy, roughly $37 million, is a pittance when one considers that this is supposed to cover the entire world.[4] Even this figure includes some wishful thinking, because most of it is devoted to operations in countries that are Partly Free, according to the Freedom House yardstick. When reflecting on the fact that this global figure is less than the cost of a single modern jet fighter, one cannot feel that we have our priorities right.

The goal should be to have a presence and program in each one of the Last Forty-five dictatorships through party institutes, groups like the Asia Society and the Asia Foundation, Freedom House, and other entities. Given the funds available, the organizations willing to pursue work in these riskier countries have to perform a sort of triage. Prospective efforts are better candidates for NGO funds if they are likely to be followed by U.S. government funding, which takes some time to come through. Were NGO funds more plentiful, organizations like Freedom House and the party, union, and business institutes could be more avant-garde and flexible, able to initiate and follow up on their own projects without having to rely on USAID. Fewer countries and opportunities would fall through the cracks. These NGO funds are particularly useful for rapid response to emerging crises or opportunities, where USAID's long lead times prevent it from being effective. This was not the intent in the creation of the endowment family. These organizations were supposed to be able to undertake their efforts without relying on branches of the U.S. government. The founders wanted the money and programs to be rooted in our own organic democratic institutions, not in a federal bureaucracy. The present arrangement particularly hampers efforts directed against dictatorships.

Congress is the one body that has fairly consistently tried to force the pace. It needs to be brought even more into the process and work closely with the new democracy leaders in the State Department and the National Security Council.

The timely application of assistance can head off more violent confrontations. In Serbia, the United States and its NATO allies used massive amounts of force to curtail dictator Slobodan Milosevic's ethnic cleansing of Kosovo. Allowing the situation to degenerate to this stage cost billions of dollars and thousands of Albanian and Serbian lives. Prior to the bombing, there were months of demonstrations against Milosevic, and Serbian democrats cried out in vain for more assistance. Had there been a harder focus on assisting Serbian democrats in ousting Milosevic, including training civic activists in strategic nonviolence, the bombing might not have been necessary. It is a sad irony that many of those who frown on allocating public funds for the promotion of democracy abroad are the same individuals who are most vocal opponents of using the U.S. military when neglect leads to the use of force. To prevent further waste of human lives and treasure, we must invest a great deal more in the front end of this equation, giving assistance when and where it is needed.

Since the foundation of the National Endowment for Democracy, democracy-promotion institutes, some affiliated with political parties, have been established in Great Britain, the Netherlands, Sweden, Austria, Spain, France, Canada, and Australia. A number of other countries, including recently democratized Taiwan, Japan, Ireland, Portugal, and Italy, are considering establishing similar institutions. These organizations have differences and specialties. The party foundations tend to promote their visions: social democracy, Christian democracy, liberalism, green, and so forth. Some of the European party foundations have a focus on consolidating democracy in Europe. The British Westminster Foundation for Democracy, in addition to addressing former communist states in Europe and Eurasia, also deals with Anglophone Africa. The French Fondation Jean-Jaurès, tied to the Socialist Party and inspired by the German foundations, focuses primarily on countries in East-Central Europe and Francophone Africa. Considering the task at hand, the efforts of all groups that exist, and then some, are required. The National Endowment for Democracy has called summits of democracy-promotion organizations in the past, and this sort of endeavor—in person when required and constantly via the Internet—should become more aggressive and focused on the Last Forty-five. The World Movement for Democracy website (www.wmd.org/) facilitates contacts among these foundations, the NGO world, and the frontline fighters for democracy and is updated regularly.

Many of the younger democracies are best at communicating with and helping those still under dictators. There is a rich lode of experience and creativity among Poles, Czechs, Slovaks, Hungarians, Spaniards, Portuguese, Chileans, Mexicans, South Koreans, Taiwanese, South Africans, and others.

Many of these countries do not have sufficient budgetary resources to be major power players in other aspects of international relations but could have a significant impact in democracy promotion, as it is relatively inexpensive. They should provide a modicum of democracy resources, including some funding. These new, young democracies have talent in abundance. They should set up democracy institutes and coordinate with others to maximize efficiency and impact, looking for their comparative advantages. The existing institutes in the richer democracies already rely to a considerable extent on talent from these countries and should do so even more as they add capacity. South Koreans provide a particularly intriguing case in point, given the situation with North Korea and the past West–East German dynamic.

Outsiders' Toolbox for Promoting Democracy in Dictatorships

Outside democrats have a rich toolbox to apply in opening closed societies. Many of these tools have worked in eastern Europe and elsewhere, but I also provide some fresh ideas here for ousting and opening the remaining dictatorships.

Election Monitoring

As in the Philippines and Chile, election monitoring can play a major role in building public momentum for ousting a dictator who thinks he can snooker his public by holding a pro forma election; a monitored election can turn his own ploy back on him. Since the 1980s, a veritable flowering of election monitoring has occurred. The Organization for Security Cooperation in Europe, through its Office for Democratic Initiatives and Human Rights, has organized scores of monitoring missions in transition member countries, training cadres of experienced young people who have monitored and administered elections. Many of these persons hail from countries that have recently undergone (often incomplete) democratic transitions and work for democracy NGOs. They know all the tricks of the trade and make particularly effective election monitors. Some have argued that monitoring elections certain to be rigged—as is regularly the case in Central Asia—legitimizes the pro forma, rubber-stamp elections, and it is true that, in some cases, mounting a mission does more harm than good. But more often than not, international monitoring of a flawed process, with honest, vocal, and detailed reporting of why it is not "free and fair," can be of great use in spotlighting the dictatorship. Indeed, dictators are often surprised, even when they believe they have a lock on the process; in a monitored election, they cannot know the outcome in advance. Even horribly skewed elections, when brought to the world's attention, give nascent oppositions some space to organize. Knowing that the democratic world knows they exist can give them the courage to persevere through the continued repression and develop new strategies to unbalance the regime— and eventually win.

In October of 1998, as chairman of the International Republication Institute's Election Observation Mission to Azerbaijan, I was able to see this happen on the ground. Our group of eighteen joined teams from the Organization for Security and Cooperation in Europe and Office of Democratic Institutions and Human Rights in Europe, the Council of Europe, and the National Democratic Institute. The election we were to monitor was almost certainly going to go to President Gaidar Aliyev, a smooth, menacing, manipulative figure who has not quite shed his experience as a career KGB officer and Soviet Politburo member. His country skates on the edge of being labeled Not Free by Freedom House. I remembered him well and not fondly from my days in the former Soviet Union.

Aliyev did what he could to wring from us a positive assessment prior to the election, even offering us the use of his personal helicopter for observing the elections. We declined. He had also recruited and paid for the travel of another group of Americans supposedly representing the Republican Party, no doubt hoping they would whitewash the conduct of the elections and offset our findings. (When we discovered this ploy, we vigorously intervened to neutralize this group.)

We ended our observations on October 11 in an urban voting station, where we saw election officials stuffing ballot boxes in plain sight. When the election officials realized that we knew what they had done, they vigorously shook the ballot boxes, trying to dislodge the wads of ballots they had inserted. But even this extraordinary effort failed, as numerous ballots still came out in wads. Our IRI colleagues and other international observer groups also witnessed ballot stuffing. In a press conference the next day we reported that "the elections fell short of international norms because of a variety of pre-election and election day problems, including the tardiness of [press and elections] reforms, the use of state resources for campaigning by the ruling regime, a skewed election commission, continued limits on political freedom, and the stuffing of ballots." We met with key opposition democrats both before and after the elections. The process did not make Azerbaijan free. But it focused international attention on Aliyev's abuses, made the point that the country was hardly a democracy, and most importantly gave heart to local democrats to continue their struggle for real elections.

Exchanges

Among the classic and best tools for opening closed countries are exchanges, which are possible at some level or in some form in all dictatorships. Student and young-professional exchanges are particularly important, as the minds of young people are more open and the young are overwhelmingly the ones with enough courage, idealism, and drive for a better life to go into the dictator's dangerous streets. There is no way to measure precisely the democratic influence of the hundreds of thousands of Chinese students, some of them children and grandchildren of China's elite, who have studied in the United States and other democratic countries and the unfortunately far smaller number of American and other students from democracies who have studied in China. But the democratic influence on the students who rose up across China in 1989 is clear (witness the student-built Statue of Liberty in Tiananmen Square). They remain the vanguard in the ongoing process of modernization within China. The democracy that will eventually overtake China will have been influenced by the experiences of Chinese students studying abroad and foreign students and teachers in China.

Professional exchanges are also crucial. In Eastern Europe, it was no coincidence that many of the dissident and postcommunist democratic leaders came from scientific fields. These professions were the most insulated from ideological corruption and frequently allowed for travel and contact with fellow scientists in the outside world. Free-spirited citizens of dictatorships often gravitate to these professions for these reasons.

A case in point is Pavol Demes, currently a grants officer for the German Marshall Fund. A biologist by training, Demes made his first trip to the United States on a scientific exchange program. While he was in Alabama, the Velvet Revolution occurred in his native Czechoslovakia. With one of his hosts, Ann Gardner, he helped establish a pioneering program to get American college graduates to work as English language instructors in Czechoslovakia. He later served in the federal Czechoslovak government. Once Czechoslovakia was sundered by the premiers of the two republics, Demes served as Slovak president Michal Kovac's foreign policy adviser. Kovac became a leader of the opposition to the eastward-looking, populist, and increasingly authoritarian premier, Vladimir Meciar. Demes was one of the main organizers of the OK '98 campaign to organize electoral opposition to oust Meciar. The lessons of this campaign were shared with democratic oppositions in Croatia and Serbia and offer a model for others.

Universities and Academic Institutions

Lectures by visiting professors can have enormous positive impact. Even conferences in safe locations, beyond the reach of the regime, can help. But there is no substitute for brave professionals willing to spend time in situ, available to answer questions and observe how their students live. The relationships—even networks—forged in such exchanges have proven valuable in the past for democratic activists abroad. Both faculty-to-faculty and student-to-student connections helped support the Alternative Academic Education Network in Serbia, founded in 1998 to circumvent the Milosevic regime's politicization of higher education.

A "global civic education initiative" was launched in Seoul 9–12 November 2002 by the NGO Forum of the Community of Democracies and supported by the 110 governments present. It is designed to ensure the teaching of the fundamentals of democratic governance in all primary and secondary schools worldwide.

President George W. Bush announced in 2002 that the United States would rejoin the United Nations Educational, Scientific and Cultural Organization (UNESCO) after an eighteen-year absence. The United States now hopes UNESCO will use its education programs to promote respect for democracy and to eliminate hateful propaganda from textbooks.

Young Judges and Lawyers

There is an endless array of fields in which dialogue and exposure to democratic thinking can be critical. The American Bar Association's Central and East European Law Initiative has conducted training for judges, lawyers, and average citizens in a gamut of countries in formerly socialist Europe and Eurasia. "Street law" programs, designed with local democracy activists, can inform citizens of their rights under their own legal code; such rights are typically unknown to many, leaving an already corrupt system open to further abuse. A program of this type was conducted in Croatia and other countries, helping with breakthroughs to democracy.

Military, Intelligence, and Law Enforcement Cadres

Dictators rely on the threat and use of force and on the willingness of their police, military, and other security elements to apply that force as reliably as the proverbial junkyard dog, on command. But, in one instance after another, the refusal of these forces to act against their fellow citizens has proved a decisive point at which dictatorships swung toward democracy. Making the military see that it is right to disobey orders that are morally wrong requires the very careful, balanced presentation of benefits and penalties.

In the narrow military and law-enforcement universe, such disobedience goes very much against the grain of sworn loyalties. Even soldiers from established democracies may balk at training foreign colleagues to go against orders in the name of such "unsoldierly" issues as human rights, democracy, and civilian control. But training that is devoid of democratic content—training of the type the United States provided such units as El Salvador's Altacatl Battalion and Indonesia's Kopassus—hands dictators brutal and efficient instruments to use against the democrats at home. As Secretary of State Colin Powell, a former general, stated in testimony before the Senate Foreign Relations Committee on 5 February 2002, we need to train other militaries how to reach, and operate in a, democracy.

A few experienced military men have begun applying their insights and experience to the ousting of dictators. One such is former army colonel Bob Helvey, today one of the world's leading experts and trainers in the use of nonviolent force to bring about the downfall of dictators. His skills need to be replicated throughout the armed and security forces of democratic states. Often, the desired result may arise just from the fact that professionals admire one another as professionals, even when they stand on opposing sides of the democratic divide.

We face similar dangers and opportunities with the CIA, the Federal Bureau of Investigation, the Drug Enforcement Agency, and other U.S. security agencies' relationships with their counterparts in dictatorships. In an era of heightened and legitimate concern over terrorism, these agencies must learn that among the root causes of some terrorism is repression by dictators. Reinforcing the wrong kind of behavior by these security services can increase terrorism against the United States. Instead, they must be split off from the terrorist-generating dictator and made to side with their own people.

First, the dictator's security forces must be exposed to their counterparts from democratic countries. They must see and, where possible, experience other ways of operating, of relating to the people, the law, governance, and local and national security. They must be trained out of the belief that they will go down with their dictator. Indeed, the major carrot we can offer is the assurance of a future under a democratic system. We can help introduce them to local democrats, so that the security forces can hear assurances from them. The corresponding stick is personal responsibility for their actions. Members of the forces must be made to understand that they are individually known and that they will pay for continuing to violate human rights and impeding the transition to democracy. It must be made particularly plain that opening fire on demonstrators will be considered murder and those involved will be tried and sentenced when democracy inevitably arrives. It is instructive how fast many of these men and women have abandoned sinking dictators' ships once the process begins. The abandonment of Milosevic by the Yugoslav police and army in 2000 is a recent example of this happy phenomenon.

Visits

Properly orchestrated visits by well-known figures, including current or former officials, can be powerful tools. The visit of two leading Czech democrats to Cuba to meet with Cuban democrats in 2001, while it landed the Czechs in jail, raised the morale of Cubans, focused world attention on the continuing repression, and removed a bit of the distance between Europe and the United States over how to handle Castro. But visits must not end up doing more to legitimize the dictator and his regime than to legitimize the people and their true representatives. Such visitors or delegations should always meet with the members of the opposition and common citizens and make clear that they take seriously human rights, press freedom, and other internationally recognized fundamental rights.

The visit to Cuba by Mexican president Vicente Fox on 3–4 February 2002, demonstrated both what should and should not be done. Fox was the first Mexican president to meet with Cuban dissident leaders. In a statement issued after the meeting, he stated that "I expressed my hope that Cuba can move toward the standards on human rights and democracy that, day by day, help make things more secure not only in Latin America but in the rest of the world . . . [and that he was] always ready to hear all the voices of Cuban society. . . . President Castro accepted it as a right that we have and he accepted that I have a very strong commitment with human rights and with democracy." Elizardo Sanchez, president of the Cuban Commission on Human Rights and National Reconciliation, commented, "The government tries to treat us as if we do not exist. The visit with President Fox demonstrates that we are here and it gives us a voice."

On the negative side of the equation, Fox took a friendly walk with Castro through the streets of Havana and issued his statement about democracy after leaving Cuba. Fox's foreign minister stated that Mexico would not join in sponsoring the annual human rights resolution criticizing Castro's repression at the UN Human Rights Commission in Geneva (in the end Mexico supported the resolution). Former president Jimmy Carter's visit to Cuba in 2002 brought the message of democracy even more forcefully and directly to the Cuban people. Unfortunately, he also was gentle with Castro.

While the Fox and Carter visits had their positive aspects, others have sent a profoundly deflating and negative message to the brave democrats trying to oust their oppressors. In an unfortunately common pattern, U.S. special envoy Richard Holbrooke repeatedly visited Belgrade to see Milosevic and did not hold talks with the opposition. Holbrooke made it appear that only Milosevic was important, giving only a desultory wave of the hand to an admittedly disparate opposition desperately trying to work together. It is impossible, of course, to be certain what would have happened had the United States been more supportive of the very active Serbian opposition in 1996 and 1997. But the United States clearly put too much trust in Milosevic after Dayton and later had to scramble to develop the solid democratization policies that should have been in place long before.

The world's democracies should design a schedule for repeated visits at the highest levels to the remaining dictatorships to carry the message of democratic change. The main purpose is not to see the dictator but to encourage the long-suffering people by showing them that they are not alone and to encourage them to take their destiny in their own hands.

Conferences

Dictatorships thrive on hosting conferences with foreign participation and often succeed in using them to enhance their legitimacy. But conferences can be another means inside a dictatorship to put pressure on the dictator and to make common cause with the local democrats. Let me cite one example. In September 1986, a Soviet-American conference was held in Jurmala, Latvia, then occupied by the Soviet Union. The conference was attended by 2,000 Latvians and Russians; some 220 private Americans, including some Latvian-American activists; and several U.S. government officials. Many hours of the discussions were broadcast for three days on local Latvian television and to a lesser extent throughout the Soviet Union. As Philip Taubman reported in the *New York Times* on 9 September 1986, "The vigorous, often sharp exchange of views, including hours of American critiques of Soviet domestic and foreign policies, was a sign of expanding opportunities for Soviet citizens to hear strong criticism of their Government." Crowds of people without tickets gathered outside the conference site as well, wrote Taubman, "Mark Palmer, Ambassador-designate to Hungary and until recently the State Department's top Soviet specialist, signed autographs like a movie star for dozens of Russians and Latvians, who showered him with questions about the United States."

Often at these conferences there is much too great a reluctance to offend the "hosts." But the real hosts are the enslaved people of the country, and it is hardly offending them to stand up for their rights.

Of course it may not always be possible to hold conferences on certain subjects in closed societies. An alternative is to hold them outside and beam their proceedings and conclusions into the country. For example as a follow-up to President Reagan's 1982 address in London on promoting democracy and peace, we organized a series of conferences. One brought together elected leaders from around the world to discuss promoting free elections; another addressed democratization in communist countries; and a third, hosted by the chief justice of the Supreme Court for colleagues from abroad, looked at promoting the rule of law.

There is no reason why we should not keep using that model. Three subjects cry out for White House conferences in the next twelve months: democratization of China, bringing democracy to the Greater Middle East, and democracy development in Africa. They too could appropriately be a follow-up to a presidential speech on democracy and could be broadcast back into all these key regions.

A Free Press, Posters, Buttons, and the Means to Produce Them

In this digital age, it is sometimes easy to forget that a free press still refers, first and foremost, to a printing press dedicated to publishing truths about the world and especially about governments. For those who work for democracy inside a dictatorship, nothing is more liberating or more powerful than independent publication of uncorrupted news and a spectrum of opinion. As often as not, the democratic wave that has swept the planet in the last quarter century was whipped up by the turning of small presses underground. In many countries, the government controls commercial publishing houses and what they print, a monopoly that can be chipped away by an underground alternative.

At relatively little cost, democratic governments and institutions could provide crucial financial and technical assistance to build a free press in dictatorships. Few things do more for the democratic cause—and spirits—than the arrival from outside of portable printing equipment. Now, as before, samizdat (self-publishing) is often the first crucial step toward freedom, and every dictator knows it.

In closed societies, the written word acquires special, almost magical, power. There is a huge thirst not only for books from abroad on almost every subject but also for materials from within. Making available the means to print underground is an enormous help, as is pressuring a dictatorship to allow a printing press to be controlled by independents. With the political support of the U.S. embassy to change the law barring an independent press, Freedom House is bringing into Kyrgyzstan the first non-state-controlled printing press. And as we witnessed in Yugoslavia in 2000, a single slogan stuck on walls across the country—*Gotov Je!* "He is finished!"—played a central role in ending Milosevic's rule and freeing the people of Serbia to rejoin Europe as a democratic, modern nation. The locally designed posters and slogans were a concrete example of the impact of outside assistance within a strategic program directed by local actors. Considerable financing and marketing advice came from abroad, talent and courage from within.

Language and Other Presence Programs

One of the key ingredients to opening up a closed society is foreign-language training. Without English or another world language, it is harder to make the comparisons Romankov calls for in the quote at the beginning of this chapter and to learn what modern society is all about. As the U.S. ambassador to then-communist Hungary, I persuaded first the Hungarian communist leaders and, on his first day on the job, Peace Corps Director Paul Coverdell, that a Peace Corps program in Hungary to provide English teachers could be great— the first in any communist country. In one of the fastest bureaucratic acts I have ever seen, Coverdell met with President Bush the same day and secured approval.

The democratic nations need to review all programs from language to food assistance that would involve a large presence and focus them on the Last Forty-five. For the Peace Corps to devote half or more of its programs and resources to these countries would have dramatic impact. In Cuba, for example, it would give the lie to the dictator's claims that the United States is opposed to the Cuban people rather than opposed to dictatorship. We give food assistance to North Korea; how can it be used to help open the most closed country in the world? We should creatively rethink limits on many of these programs. For example, why couldn't the Peace Corps teach civics classes as well as English? Why do we have to live forever with old taboos about it not engaging in "political" projects, when learning about democratic governance is a precondition for solving the rest of the development problems in countries served by the Peace Corps? Mary McGrory reminds us that "John Kennedy's original intention was that the volunteers serve as ambassadors for peace."[5] The connection between peace and democracy is now well established.

Movies, Radio, and Television

Ben Kingsley's portrayal of Gandhi is a compelling example of the power of movies to educate and to inspire, and it has been amazing to see the impact of this one film on a host of democracy activists the world over. The PBS television series A Force More Powerful and Bringing Down a Dictator also are having a powerful impact on those still suffering under dictators. To date, versions of the films in Spanish, French, Arabic, Russian, Chinese, Farsi, and Serbo-Croatian have been created and broadcast by satellite to Cuba, Iran, the entire Arabic-speaking world with special attention to Iraq, and other countries. Imagine a family in Saudi Arabia watching Baywatch, being beamed down from a Lebanese satellite channel, with an attractive female lifeguard rescuing a drowning man. While it may convince some devout Muslims of the decadence of the West, *Baywatch* is among the most-watched shows in Saudi Arabia and sends a clear message about equality for women. Taiwanese soap operas are now purchased and watched on the China mainland on local channels.

The end of the cold war is no reason for democracy to lose its voice. Democrats in eastern Europe give Radio Free Europe, Radio Liberty, the BBC, Deutsche Welle, Voice of America (VOA), and other democratic radio stations a great deal of credit for providing knowledge of the outside world. The radio and television efforts focused on the remaining forty-five dictatorships are chronically underfunded and technologically antiquated. We need a whole new effort directed at the three key regions of dictatorships: Africa, the Greater Middle East, and Asia. Within each region there needs to be a much more intensive look at individual countries.

In the poorest of the world's dictatorships, a majority of the population does not have access to a television set. In these societies, radio has a broader and more effective reach and needs to be supported. Publicly funded broadcasting services remain very important in a world laden with dictatorships. Their continued operation, including expansion in areas they do not sufficiently cover, will also be a critical factor in efforts by democracies to help those living under tyranny. These broadcasters are particularly effective when they use local stringers, or at least young announcers and journalists who are not far removed from their homelands. The popular music and news radio station that VOA launched in 2002 in and for the Arab world was reportedly an immediate hit, particularly among Arab youth. But this is not a substitute for freedom radios like Radio Azadi, which broadcasts to Iran. As columnist Jackson Diehl noted, "Every day, student leaders would call by cell phone from the roiling campuses to the radio's headquarters in Prague and narrate the latest developments live. Each night the radio would broadcast a roundtable discussion, patching together students and journalists in Tehran with exiled opposition leaders." That this station was taken off the air and replaced by popular music and news is a grand gift to Iran's mullah dictator. We need both kinds of radio for every Not Free country.[6]

For these hardest of the hard cases, shortwave and other transmissions from abroad will continue to be vital. The Office of Transition Initiatives, a branch of the USAID, funds Shortwave Radio Africa (SWRA), which broadcasts nightly to Zimbabwe. As reported in the *Guardian* in January 2002, "SWRA, which has been on the air for a month, has angered the Zimbabwean ruling party by giving the opposition a platform and providing a credible alternative to the endless diet of propaganda and falsehoods on state radio. . . . SW

Radio Africa is headed by Gerry Jackson, who was sacked by the Zimbabwe Broadcasting Corporation five years ago for broadcasting telephone calls describing police brutality."

This is precisely the sort of broadcasting assistance needed for closed dictatorships: stations run by professional journalists from the country in question, who know firsthand their audience and the repression they experience. For example, when the Milosevic regime managed to gain influence over the only independent national television station, Studio B, Serbs lost their only truly independent national television news source. Luckily, there remained a network of independently operated local radio and television stations throughout Serbia, the Association of Independent Electronic Broadcasters. The cornerstone of news generation was Radio B-92. When it was seized by the authorities in 1999, the station's original staff began operation as Radio B-292 on a different frequency. The station provided news programming to network affiliates throughout Serbia and was valued as an independent source by the population as the Milosevic regime tightened its control in the year following the NATO air campaign. B-292, along with the youth group Otpor, helped keep the flame of resistance alive in the worst days of repression, the spring and summer of 2000, making it possible to mobilize the democratic opposition.[7] Radio Free Europe and other foreign broadcasters like Deutsche Welle relied heavily upon local stringers for reporting, and their reports were rebroadcast into Serbia by these services, greatly increasing the credibility of the reporting with the target audience.

Without diminishing the key role radio has played in propelling the modern wave of democratization, it is clear that in this century a key medium must be television. As I know intimately—having developed eight independent commercial television stations in central and eastern Europe, helped in starting Taiwan's first non-KMT station, and tried in the Middle East for several years—nothing carries more influence and information than live images of the world, inside the dictatorship and out.

While democratic governments today are paying more attention to this option than in the past, they lack an understanding of the costs involved in building a popular, competitive TV channel from scratch. The U.S. government at one point earmarked $2 million to $3 million to help establish an Iraqi opposition channel. This was a laudable goal, as Iraq's people had been under one of the world's vilest regimes. However, the sum allotted would not even buy the necessary broadcasting equipment, studio facilities, and technicians for a skeletal TV operation, much less pay for journalistic talent and the production costs of news and entertainment programming. Without a critical mass of programming, a new channel will not build and sustain viewership.

Still, the potential for satellite and, where possible, in-country television is enormous. Editorially independent news would hold up a critical mirror to the stodgy "official versions"—the familiar clips of the maximum leader meeting a parade of underlings, sycophants, or official delegations from "friendly" governments. There is a hungry market for truth in countries where it is denied and hidden.

Entertainment programming is equally important, though it is rarely seen as such by policymakers. Programs on government-run television are usually dismal affairs, rarely if ever insulated from political content and low in production values. Government broadcasters occasionally supplement this dreary diet with foreign programs, most of them quite antiquated. When the viewers are given another choice, they invariably look elsewhere to be informed and entertained. Belarus is a case in point. The national television channel rarely misses an opportunity to showcase Aleksandr Lukashenko and offers little in the way of entertaining fare. So most Belarusians watch Russian channels, available throughout the country, for their entertainment. Russian channels, somewhat more independent than those in Belarus, also are an important source of less-biased news coverage for the Belarusian public.

While foreign-produced programming can be a draw, a successful channel will run a solid complement of shows (sitcoms, dramas, made-for-TV films, documentaries) designed for a specific audience. Fresh programming and unfiltered and credible news are the sine qua nons of a vital channel. Once on solid footing, such a channel will effectively break the government's information monopoly helping create more articulated pressure from below.

There are a few priorities in broadcasting into dictatorships. There should be a channel devoted to providing unbiased news and entertainment throughout the Arab world. China and Chinese communities in Asia (in Malaysia, Singapore, Indonesia, and elsewhere) need to have a channel broadcast for them in Cantonese and Mandarin. In Africa, a number of smaller, more regional channels would be most effective. Particular strategically important and/or single-language countries merit their own channels—for example Iran and Pakistan. The aim in all cases would be to give the maximum number of citizens in these countries access to news and entertainment geared to them.

Such television channels are most needed in the world's remaining dictatorships. No single democratic government is likely to, or should, provide the full costs of establishing such channels where they are sustainable and likely to do the most good. All democratic peoples have a vested interest in bringing their brethren living under tyranny into the fold.

The world's democracies must band together and contribute to an independently managed pool, which would be used to establish politically independent, locally run, commercial television broadcasters. The Independent Radio and Television Fund also would support radio broadcasts to countries poor in television sets. The member countries of the Organization for Economic Cooperation and Development should take the lead by making contributions proportional to their relative gross domestic product, and democracies of lesser means should be encouraged to make small contributions as a gesture of democratic solidarity. The fund, which should total at least $1 billion—and really needs twice that— should be self-perpetuating, as the aim is to create television and radio stations that can support themselves in their markets. With this initial capital, the fund's managers could begin identifying promising markets for independent commercial TV and radio and then summon the necessary local talent, including expatriate professional broadcast journalists and managers from the country in question.

Internet

The spread of the Internet throughout the forty-five dictatorships offers a whole new set of opportunities. Overcoming controls placed by the dictators will be a struggle, though democratic embassies and businesses from abroad can provide islands of unfiltered access. Even with government controls, the Internet opens much of the rest of the world to people who are otherwise repressed and isolated. Through aggressive, creative evasion of these controls, a virtual democracy can be created on the Internet. Websites, Internet postings, chat rooms, reports on atrocities, calls for nonviolent actions, polls, virtual elections, identification of individual oppressors, ridicule of dictators, attacks on corruption—the range is limited only by the access of citizens to the Internet and printers. The ability to communicate and interact locally, regionally, nationally, and internationally is extraordinary. The Internet is a force multiplier for democrats and an expense multiplier for dictators who wish to keep all such contacts under close surveillance.

In a Chinese case that demonstrates both the peril and the power of the Internet, Reporters without Borders (RWB), in its press release of 6 August 2002, called for the release of cyberdissident Li Dawei, who had just been sentenced to eleven years' imprisonment for having downloaded and printed out pro-democracy texts from the Internet. "Arrests, blocked sites, self-censorship, torture, police surveillance and closure of cyber-cafés, the Chinese State now has a repressive arsenal that testifies to its hostility toward freedom of expression on the Internet," RWB reported. It continued: "A former policeman, Li Dawei was accused of having downloaded more than 500 texts from Chinese democracy sites based abroad, especially www.89-64.com, and having edited them into a number of unpublished books. He was also said to have been in contact with 'reactionary' organizations based abroad. . . . At least 20 cyber-dissidents are currently detained in China, including Huang Qi, a web site creator, who was arrested on June 3, 2000 and is still held without having been tried. Yang Zili and three animators of the www.lib.126.com site have been held without trial since March 2001." But Chinese democrats continue in ever increasing numbers to use their Internet space.

RWB also reported, on 7 August 2002, that the government of communist Vietnam had that same day "suspended TTVNonline.com, named best Internet site for Vietnam's young people in 2001. Other official sources, quoted by Agence France-Presse, said it was discussion of issues on the site, such as territorial concessions to China in 1999, political reforms and corruption within the communist party, that prompted the ire of the government. The authorities have attempted to impose strict control over the Internet since its introduction in Vietnam in 1997. There are currently more than 4,000 Internet cafes in the country allowing access to the worldwide web for nearly 600,000 Vietnamese."

The collectives of chat rooms and e-mail give people courage, as they see they are not alone. In that atmosphere democrats can plan, initiate, coordinate, and manage actions, while governments struggle to construct countermeasures. Internet skills are readily taught, and should be, by the outside democracies. Few undertakings are more cost effective than "training the trainers" for Internet organizing. The main impediment to Internet organizing for civic activists is the fact that governments control telecommunications access in many of the forty-five remaining dictatorships. But even these impediments can be overcome. In Serbia, for example, a "mirror site" in the Netherlands helped keep Radio B-92's content available on the Internet. In most cases, the Internet can be of great use both to activists on the ground and to diasporas and virtual communities of concerned NGO leaders.

Private Initiatives

George Soros and his Open Society Institute (OSI) and its brave partners in every region of dictatorships offer a model of how private initiatives should operate. The OSI has done more in more countries than anyone else and has taken the risks governments have unfortunately not had the fortitude to take. But in general the foundation world and individual philanthropists have been timid and uninterested. Democracy seems to fall into an ideological chasm in the foundation world. The liberal foundations shy away from "democratization" because they think it is a code word for imperialism; the right leaning foundations take a Realpolitik view that democratization is nice but not necessarily essential to American economic or security interests.

They all need a new conceptual and programmatic framework—one this book attempts to provide.

It has been very difficult to raise private funds to support the China Democracy Party, Falun Gong, Burmese democrats, women in Islamic countries, efforts to support nonviolent conflict, and a host of other worthy programs. This is particularly sad, as entrepreneurial skills of private individuals and organizations are almost always greater than those of governments. The private sector's willingness to do the unorthodox, to push the envelope, is much greater, and there is a greater instinctive understanding of what private individuals and groups are going through, how they might best be helped. Investor Peter Ackerman, the driving force behind education and training in the strategy and tactics of nonviolent conflict is a case in point. His efforts have included books and the PBS film series *A Force More Powerful* and *Bringing Down a Dictator*. If more incentives are needed, we should note that entrepreneurs are also certain to benefit from the rule of law and reduced corruption that attend democracy. A senior and prominent American captain of industry with White House backing needs to step forward and lead an aggressive effort to generate private support for democratic assistance abroad.

5

Democracy Development Plans and Action Programs

Democracy is the absolute value that makes for human dignity, as well as the only road to sustained economic development and social justice.

—President Kim Dae Jung

For decades economic development planning and programs have been considered routine for economically underdeveloped nations. Planning and programs for the breakthrough to self-sustaining economic growth goes back to at least the 1950s. It is intrusive and yet widely accepted by the governments of the nations concerned, international institutions, and donor nations.

Nothing comparable exists for the *politically* underdeveloped nations (mostly the same countries)—those still ruled by a single man and consequently denied progress in a broad range of social and economic sectors. One of the main reasons there has been conspicuously less "bang for the buck" with development projects has been the mismanagement and corruption inherent in dictatorships. There are no political or democracy-development plans for these nations—that is, plans worked out between international institutions and donor nations and the various governmental and nongovernmental bodies of the individual nations.

Fortunately, growing awareness of the relationship between economic and political development is creating new momentum behind linking aid to democracy-development efforts. In a landmark speech to the United Nations Financing for Development Conference in Monterrey, Mexico, on 22 March 2002, President George W. Bush stated, "Developed nations have a duty not only to share our wealth, but also to encourage sources that produce wealth: economic freedom, political liberty, the rule of law and human rights." In announcing a new Millennium Challenge Account with a 50 percent increase in core development assistance, President Bush said, "We must tie greater aid to political and legal and economic reforms. . . . By taking the side of liberty and good government, we will liberate millions from poverty's prison." This same approach, on paper at least, is at the core of the new African Union and its New Economic Partnership for Africa's Development, which is supposed to reward democratic practice with increased aid and investment. By pledging to conduct democratic elections and respect the rule of law—and to intervene when member states violate human rights—Africa's leaders affirm that they should attract more than $60 billion annually in new trade and investment from the developed democracies.

But as Freedom House executive director Jennifer Windsor pointed out in a *New York Times* op-ed piece on 19 July 2002: "While hopes are high for the new organization, the promise of a regional union for better development through democracy could rapidly become a charade. For example, Col. Muammar el-Qaddafi, Libya's sole ruler for more than 30 years, and Daniel arap Moi, who has thwarted any democratic reform in Kenya for two decades, have joined the steering committee of the New Economic Partnership." And in the United States there also has been erosion before the president's new policy is put into practice, a policy that would fundamentally change the way America spends its development aid. As Jennifer Windsor notes, "Some [in the administration] want to weaken the democracy and human rights criteria." This is coming from the Treasury and Commerce Departments and even some in the U.S. Agency for International Development (USAID), the State Department, the World Bank, the International Monetary Fund (IMF), and other multilateral institutions. While the need for good governance and citizen participation has gained credence, the word "democracy" has still largely been avoided. Even pro-democracy World Bank officials say that they do not have a mandate to act to promote democracy.

Some United Nations bodies also are making conceptual strides forward, particularly the UN Development Programme (UNDP). In *Human Development Report 2002: Deepening Democracy in a Fragmented World*, UNDP administrator Mark Malloch Brown argues that "politics is as important to successful development as economics; and successful human development is best achieved through strong and deep forms of democratic governance at all levels of society. . . . That assertion remains controversial." Unfortunately, this report devotes most of its pages to existing democracies and countries already in transition; it is starkly and cravenly almost silent on the Last Forty-five. A UNDP 2002 report on the Arab world's democracy deficits broke new ground but remains at the level of analysis and generalized recommendations.

Another conceptual gain yet to be made hard political reality is that increasingly the United States and regional bodies are insisting upon new, written commitments to democracy. As Jackson Diehl pointed out in the 18 March 2002 *Washington Post:* "The declaration of strategic partnership that Secretary of State Powell and Uzbek Foreign Minister Adulaziz Kamilov signed—a 20-page agreement—is quite remarkable in its detail. The accord gives Karimov what he wants—a vague U.S. pledge to support Uzbekistan against 'any external threat,' along with promises of military training and hardware. But in exchange, the Uzbek ruler committed himself, in writing, to a long list of political and economic reforms. These include 'establishing a multiparty system,' 'ensuring free and fair elections' and 'ensuring independence of the media.' There are also promises to reform the judiciary and carry out the free-market economic program that the World Bank and International Monetary Fund have been unsuccessfully pressing on Uzbekistan for years." The Organization of American States (OAS) has taken a similar position in its Inter-American Democratic Charter, adopted on 11 September 2001, which commits the OAS to protect democracy throughout the Americas and contains a detailed program to accomplish this task.

Now we must move from declaration to decisive action. It is not enough to state what components of democracy must be achieved. We need to develop concrete action plans and programs to get there.

Therefore, as an integral part of the strategy to achieve a democratic world by 2025, three-, five-, ten-, and if necessary twenty-year political development plans should be created and implemented for each of the forty-five dictatorships. Obviously, one size will not fit all; there will be innumerable variations along the way. Ideally, momentum will build in these societies, accelerating the pace of change. But with or without such momentum, the goal is the same. Each national plan must be designed to achieve the full set of institutions and rights set forth in the Universal Declaration of Human Rights: free elections; independent press, judiciary, and trade unions; and equality for all, regardless of gender, race, religious faith, or ethnic origin.[1] While the path to freedom will vary from country to country, there is a menu of principles, stages, and steps that can help in the consideration and drafting of national political development plans.

In the area of principles, beyond specifying the goal, there should be agreement on the means. The plan should specify that violent means are acceptable neither from the standing government nor from those struggling for freedom. It should likewise be made explicit that the government recognizes the right of the opposition to implement the plan and that no violence can be used against democrats who are proceeding peacefully. As for the democracy movements themselves, they must follow Gandhi's pledge to avoid the use of violence even in pursuit of a just cause.

Another key area for agreement about means is national dialogue with the participation of all elements of society. This should work toward the national roundtables that played such a key role in the strikingly peaceful transitions to democracy achieved in central Europe in the late 1980s.

Dictatorships vary. The royal variety, where the country is in essence a family concern, might be swayed by the graduated approach outlined below. Already in the Persian Gulf, the Bahraini, Qatari, and Omani monarchs have made moves toward constitutional monarchy. While wholly insufficient, these are at least positive steps. Some monarchs are genuinely popular. One would think they would be even more likely to agree upon a specific, staged process. Personalistic and other dictators, especially those who violently seized power and hold it through massive repression, will not be easy to pressure into working within the context of democracy plans and programs. But such dictators have frequently miscalculated in the past and agreed to elections and other elements of the process I propose, believing they could control the situation and stay in power. Even a flat refusal has its uses. It tells the world that these despots rejected a gradual and peaceful shift to democratic rule. It would illuminate the fear such rulers have of their own people, further undermine their legitimacy, and encourage the people to oust them.

Stages of Democratic Growth

The following is a list of possible steps, grouped in three stages. Not every country will go through them all, or in this order. Some will leapfrog or bypass some stages; others may well regress. Still, putting the necessary progression down in this fashion reveals the magnitude of such transformations. Most important, it provides a concrete agenda for action with clear benchmarks.

Stage 1: Initial Steps

The initial steps are modest enough that dictators can hardly say no.

- Civil society groups established in such functional areas as environment, health, business, women's affairs.
- Multicandidate, nonparty elections at the local level.
- Professional development of legislatures at all levels.
- Independent trade unions in nonstrategic industries.
- Professional development of the judiciary.
- Development of business law and other less sensitive legal fields (for example, tenancy, civil and criminal cases without political significance)

and the evenhanded application of law in these fields, including exposure and prosecution of corruption.

- Free media on nonsensitive subjects, such as health and the environment.
- Openness to international contacts and exchanges; permitting international bodies and other governments and nongovernmental organizations (NGOs) to function.
- Open access to the Internet.

Stage 2: Halfway House

The next stage could see further development in each of these areas.

- Civil society groups in such areas as election monitoring, human rights, political parties, and religious groups.
- Multicandidate, multiparty elections at local and provincial levels for executive and legislative offices, and at national level just for legislature.
- Legislative checks on the executive branch in specified fields.
- Broadened trade union activity in all but most sensitive industries; local but not national strikes permissible.
- An independent judiciary at local and provincial levels.
- Development of the law in such sensitive areas as the right of civil society institutions to function and peaceful assembly.
- Roundtable that brings together government and independent civic representatives on subjects such as the environment, health, and social issues, with unrestricted coverage in independent media.
- Demonstrations and public gatherings approved without unreasonable restriction on such nonstrategic civic matters as environmental protection and social policies.
- Independent local and provincial print and electronic media and independent *national* print media.
- Openness to direct assistance in democracy development by international bodies, other governments, and NGOs and cessation of jamming and other barriers to the free flow of information.

Stage 3: The Real Thing

This stage establishes full democratic institutions and governance.

- Civil society groups with the full range of opportunities to pursue their goals.
- Multicandidate elections for president or "main man" monitored by international and local teams, and the incumbent's agreement to abide by their results; term limits for president.

- Roundtable on the full spectrum of public issues, without restriction.
- Ability to demonstrate on any topic, without restriction.
- Legislatures with the full range of rights and the ability to balance the executive branch, even in sensitive areas like internal security.
- Independent trade unions in all industries with the right to conduct nationwide strikes.
- Independent national radio and television and an end to the government's electronic-media monopoly.
- Independent judiciary at the national level.
- Enforced rule of law across the whole range of political rights.

As we think about how these phases may be made to happen, however, we have to wonder whether these plans make it look too easy. Who will be there to help in the international community, and who is in the opposition inside? We can hardly expect dictators to cooperate in their own overthrow. Perhaps it would be better just to pour into the streets with torches and banners.

Who Will Conduct: The International Dictatorship-to-Democracy Center

At present, there is no international locus for democracy planning, and in some respects international expertise is also lacking. As noted earlier, the vast majority of democracy work is focused on countries already in transition, already Partly Free as opposed to Not Free, to use the Freedom House categories. Various international bodies are active in the democracy/human rights field including the UNDP and the UN Human Rights Commission. The World Bank has begun to recognize that the major hindrance to economic development in Africa, the Middle East, and other areas of dictatorships is lack of "good governance"; accordingly, it has increased its civil society building efforts, although without saying explicitly that good governance necessarily requires full-scale democracy.

But no international body is really dedicated to the problem of dictatorship and dealing with it in the comprehensive manner proposed in this book. Even within democratic governments, NGOs in the democracies, and academia, there has been relatively little reflection on the process of ousting dictators and the need for plans and action. Still, there are definite stirrings.

UN Secretary General Kofi Annan reportedly has considered creating a democracy office within the UN Secretariat. The UN Human Rights Commission in 1999 passed a resolution on democracy. A majority of the world's nations gathered in Warsaw under the aegis of the Community of Democracies in June

2000 and again in Seoul in November 2002 agreed that the promotion of democracy is vital. The events of 11 September 2001 reinforced that. Perhaps the ground is now fertile to create a new *International Dictatorship-to-Democracy Center* tasked with moving these forty-five dictatorships to democracy through implementing five- and ten-year development programs and assisting indigenous democratic leaders. The Community of Democracies could play a leading role in establishing such a center.

The center would endorse the staged outline set forth above and build its work around getting dictators to accept these conditions, helping local democrats exploit these new opportunities, and making sure that democracies do their utmost to maintain pressure and that the dictatorships comply.

Today, there is no center that brings together the best, most successful practitioners with those in the Last Forty-five. The International Dictatorship-to-Democracy Center should train the leaders of nonviolent resistance, giving them the strategic and tactical tools they will need to pressure and eventually replace their regimes and sustain their new democracy. The center would also help train democratic activists from around the world to maneuver effectively on the uneven playing field dictators create. Perhaps most important, the center would help democrats see the importance of unity in confronting the dictator, as well as other "front-end" preelection skills. Diplomats from democratic nations also should spend a few weeks at this center to get better grounded in how to work with civic activists before they go to their embassies. Staff from ministries also would benefit from such training.

The center could have the sort of loose relationship to the United Nations that the World Bank does: endorsed by, but autonomous of, the UN. This would give the center the legitimacy of a UN body, while minimizing interference from the dictatorships within the UN. Moreover, such a center would probably be able to start more quickly and function more nimbly outside a formal UN context. Its leadership and staff would be experienced democrats. A founding president of the International Dictatorship-to-Democracy Center might be someone like former Polish foreign minister Bronislaw Geremek, who helped oust the communist dictatorship in Poland. The center's staff would also include younger people with practical experience in ousting dictators: younger Filipinos, Peruvians, Serbs, Czechs, Hungarians, Malians, and so forth.

Of course, we can expect little cooperation from dictators during the planning process unless the international community and key nations make it a priority. But there are useful precedents for such cooperation. The international community, the World Bank, the IMF, and individual governments are very much involved in planning and implementing market-based economies within numerous dictatorships. In the course of doing so, they also promote such key democratic qualities as private enterprise, rule of law, and opposition to corruption. When efforts of this type have produced meager or mixed results, it has been because they were building on a foundation that was inimical to democratic concepts.

A second precedent is the process launched by the Conference on Security and Cooperation in Europe (CSCE) in Helsinki. The talks, which began in 1972, were viewed by the Soviets as a way to recognize the governments in Soviet-dominated central and eastern Europe as legitimate, post–World War II borders as set, and to achieve a nonagression pact.[2] The Soviets also sought economic benefits. But in addition to these political and economic "baskets," CSCE had a third basket of issues, pressed by some in the West, devoted to political freedoms. When this third basket was being negotiated with the Soviet leadership, numerous foreign participants and observers, including Secretary of State Henry Kissinger, did not take the exercise seriously, thinking it was window dressing and not worth the expenditure of any capital. General Secretary Leonid Brezhnev and his people knew better. They fought long and hard against these initiatives but ultimately gave in, trying to make them just another document to be signed, then ignored and violated. Among the other key documents the Soviets and their Warsaw Pact subjects were persuaded to sign in 1975 were the International Covenant on Civil and Political Rights and the International Covenant on Social and Cultural Rights. History shows that the resulting Helsinki monitoring groups inside the Soviet Union and other communist dictatorships were an important element in cracking those "invulnerable" regimes apart.

Democrats in eastern Europe and the Soviet Union used the signatures of their leaders on human rights documents as a springboard to expose the illegitimacy and abject hypocrisy of their regimes. This legacy still resonates with those working internally in dictatorships in Belarus, Central Asia, and the Caucasus to encourage democracy, in part because the Organization for Security and Cooperation in Europe includes these countries and is applying the CSCE document to them. The example of Czechoslovakia's Charter 77 is instructive.

On 7 January 1977, Czech playwrights Pavel Landovsky and Vaclav Havel and author Ludvik Vaculik were arrested late at night en route to the Czechoslovak Federal Assembly in Prague carrying a three-page document titled "Charter 77."[3] The charter noted that the government had signed the International Covenant on Civil and Political Rights and the International Covenant on Social and Cultural Rights in 1975 and that they became binding as of March 1976. While welcoming what were in effect constitutional changes, the charter noted that the "basic rights in our country exist, regrettably, on paper only." The document went on to list the deviations from the basic rights that existed in communist, post-"normalization" Czechoslovakia. As Havel biographer John Keane described it, "The Charter's allegations were serious. The Czechoslovak Socialist Republic, supposedly on the road to a free and classless society, was in effect a lawless Leviathan, whose subjects were permanently held hostage by an unchecked Party-state apparatus." Charter 77 made clear it was not a revolutionary organization but was to act as "a free, informal, open community of people of different convictions, different faiths and different professions united by the will to strive, individually and collectively, for the respect of civic and human rights in our own country and throughout the world." The launch of Charter 77, signed by 243 citizens and coordinated by Havel and a few others, was timed for maximum impact, at the beginning of the UN's Year of Political Prisoners and before an upcoming conference in Belgrade on implementation of Helsinki obligations. Charter 77 became a hot topic in the West and began to percolate through Czechoslovakia—in large measure because of the Communist Party's full-court press against it and the priceless free publicity it provided.

The charter, Havel's follow-up treatise on "living in truth," entitled "The Power of the Powerless," and other civic actions in eastern Europe based on the platform of the Helsinki Final Act were mutually supporting. Polish dissident and Solidarity leader Zbigniew Bujak later wrote about the impact on their struggle of Havel's "Power of the Powerless." "This essay reached us in the Ursus [tractor] factory in 1979 at a point when we felt we were at the end of the road. Inspired by KOR [the Polish Workers' Defense Committee], we had been speaking on the shop floor, talking to people, participating in public meetings, trying to speak the truth about the factory, the country, and politics. There came a moment when people thought we were crazy. Why were we doing this? Why were we taking such risks? Not seeing any immediate and tangible results, we began to doubt the purposefulness of what we were doing. Shouldn't we be coming up with other methods, other ways? Then came the essay from Havel. Reading it gave us the theoretical underpinnings for our activity. It maintained our spirits; we did not give up, and a year later—in August 1980—it became clear that the party apparatus and the factory management were afraid of us. We mattered. . . . When I look at the victories of Solidarity, and of Charter 77, I see in them an astonishing fulfillment of the prophecies and knowledge contained in Havel's essay."[4] By putting their regimes on the spot—and themselves on the line—Czech, Polish, Russian, Hungarian, East German, and other dissidents helped build the critical mass over time to defeat their oppressive regimes. We propose just such a Helsinki-like process for the Middle East, Asia, and Africa.

It is well to remember that dictators are vulnerable to the perceptions of others. They like the veneer of acceptance and legitimacy conferred by membership in the UN and other international bodies, especially those concerned with money. And they need good relations with the world's leading nations, which are all democracies. But as dictators dissemble, stall, and manipulate, buying time for their regimes, they also afford democracies the enormous leverage of trade and investment opportunities—enough leverage, sometimes, to make dictators think about accommodation with their democrats.

Why Engage?

Of course, it is critical that democrats not let the dictator buy too much time. Each national plan should specify deadlines for each of the three stages, and this approach will need to be integrated with roles for governments, international financial institutions, and NGOs. Every deadline missed because the dictator refused cooperation should carry graduated sanctions targeted on the dictator and his clique, not on his people. Total refusal to cooperate at the outset should trigger a criminal process in The Hague or a special tribunal for the dictator and his removal, as should refusal to carry all the way through to full democracy in a reasonable period of time.

It is a legitimate question whether any of this planning/implementation process is needed, or indeed whether it might even prove counterproductive. After all, the remarkable progress in ousting dictators over the past quarter century was substantially achieved without this particular process by the international community and was always a surprise. The elaborate, escalating plans are intrusive and expensive and are sinks for political energy. Also, they may be subject to manipulation by the dictator. Efforts to implement such plans might create new tensions or, alternatively, discourage democrats from moving. History suggests that local democrats will eventually succeed. Why not just encourage them to go into the streets and oust the dictator through direct action?

There are compelling strategic reasons to pursue democracy-development plans. These plans are a logical next step beyond the numerous documents of principle that dictators have signed, such as the Universal Declaration of Human Rights, the UN Charter, and the new Helsinki-like process and documents we propose. They move from mere words to the fight for freedom.

Such plans will help build consensus across the wide divide within and between democratic governments and democrats inside dictatorships. For example, there are many who argue that Arab countries will need a very long time to modernize and become democratic and that precipitous action could be "destabilizing" and result in even worse governments. Without some action soon however, those worse governments, all antidemocratic, will almost certainly follow the current crop of dictators. A more legitimate, democratic process must be set in train to change that line of succession. Surely this is the lesson of the shah of Iran, where our failure to understand how vulnerable he was and our unwillingness to get behind moderate Iranian democrats left the door open for Khomeini and his successor Khamenei.

Another reason to engage in political development plans and programs is to change the content and focus of our dealing with the dictatorships. In a way, we are now playing their game by constraining discussion to episodes and individual outrages. This is to be chronically focused on effect rather than on cause. We ask the dictators to let someone out of jail when we should be compelling them through the stages of democratic development to full democracy.

Finally, and most important, the democracy plans and deadlines embolden and empower local democrats, thus providing a specific mandate and legitimacy for the coming struggle. The very premise of such planning is that at the end of the day, the dictator will go. This challenge to the legitimacy of the dictator is the central reason to engage in this exercise.

If the dictator stonewalls and refuses to work within the plan, the plan makes it more difficult for apologists in the democratic world, particularly in foreign ministries and even human rights organizations, to trumpet periodic releases of prisoners or government pronouncements as "progress."

Rather than discourage or delay the final day of reckoning, democracy plans should accelerate the departure of the dictator. If enough national unity and momentum are achieved before the plan's end date, that date should be brought forward. Most breakthroughs to democracy have occurred when a critical mass is achieved, and then events move very rapidly. Starting down that road in the manner recommended here should help hasten the achievement of that critical mass. In this sense, premature plan fulfillment will be all to the good.

As noted earlier in this chapter, U.S. Secretary of State Colin Powell recently concluded a twenty-page agreement with the Karimov dictatorship in Uzbekistan, detailing a host of specific democratic institutions that must be built. Now we must follow through with a specific democracy-development program and timetable for Uzbekistan actually to build them. It is heartening to think that Karimov, a man of the old Soviet school, may have underestimated the power of such agreements just as Leonid Brezhnev did at Helsinki twenty-eight years ago.

Embassies as Freedom Houses, Ambassadors as Freedom Fighters

We will defend the peace by fighting terrorists and tyrants. . . . We will ex-
tend the peace by encouraging free and open societies on every continent.

—The National Security Strategy of the United States

The shrinking global sea of tyranny is dotted with islands of freedom. These are the embassies of the democratic world. There are at least a handful, and sometimes as many as a hundred, embassies of democratic nations present inside North Korea, Cuba, Saudi Arabia, China, and the rest of the Last Forty-five. Some embassies play pivotal roles in helping nonviolent resistance movements establish democracy within individual countries, sometimes through the prominent visitors they encourage. There are wonderful stories of courage and commitment by diplomats and visitors from many countries, including former communist and other dictatorships, working to assist those still suffering under repression.

The Czech ambassador to Cuba in the early 1990s, Peter Pribick, had previously worked at Radio Free Europe and was well known for his role in encouraging freedom. His assignment to Havana was a clear signal that the Czech Republic, which itself had just emerged from communist dictatorship, wanted to support democracy's emergence in Cuba. He quickly established relations with Cuban dissidents and began to assist them in a variety of ways. One day after several dissidents had visited the embassy, Mrs. Pribick's car was hit by another vehicle in a manner that appeared intentional and intended to intimidate. (This is a tactic all-too-familiar to those of us who served in Western embassies in the Soviet Union—three KGB goons threatened my wife in front of me in 1971 and my colleagues' wives had the windshields of their cars smashed with sledge-hammers while they were inside.) Both Pribicks persevered in helping Cuban democrats.[1]

In this ongoing effort, one supported by Freedom House, two prominent Czechs—Ivan Pilip, former finance minister, and Jan Bubenik, a student spokesman during the 1989 Velvet Revolution—traveled to Cuba early in 2001 to meet and share experiences with Cuban democrats. They were arrested and incarcerated by Castro's security services for just under a month. Bubenik, 32, has worked for both the National Democratic Institute and the International Republican Institute on civil society-building projects in Bulgaria, South Africa, and Zimbabwe. Their willingness to take such risks showed how far Cuba remains from democracy. In November 2001, Olivier Dupuis, a member of the European Parliament representing an Italian constituency, and four European democracy activists from the Transnational Radical Party were arrested and tried in Laos for commemorating a students' democracy protest two years before, thereby damaging "the country's stability and security." Once convicted of "propaganda against the Lao People's Democratic Republic," fined, and given suspended two-year sentences, they were ordered deported.[2] The fact that one of these democracy activists, Nikolai Kramov, is Russian illustrates the commitment of many citizens of newly democratized countries to promoting this universal value further.

Such stories abound. Some concern American ambassadors. But, given the magnitude of opportunity for embassies to serve democracy, not much of the real potential for action has been tapped. Even relatively active promoters of democracy, such as Sweden, Great Britain, and the United States, realize barely 10 percent of what they could achieve, and the rest of the democracies realize barely 5 percent of their potential. In fact, it could be argued that, on balance, embassies of the democracies do more to keep dictators in power than to oust them.

Extraordinary Opportunity for Creativity

Of course ambassadors and their embassies are inhibited by tradition and practice, and of course the situations on the ground inside dictatorships present formidable challenges. Still, when the world's democracies decide that creating universal democracy by supporting fellow democrats is the best insurance of peace, security, and prosperity—and therefore make this a fundamental objective for their embassies—they will find an abundance of extraordinary opportunities.

Washington Post columnist and former diplomat Colbert King has urged that the United States and other democracies act consistent with their values when working in dictatorships and countries where oppression is the accepted norm. In his 2 February 2002 column, King assailed the apologia of those who say they need to act according to conditions abroad—the "when in Rome, do as the Romans do" approach. This attitude is particularly prevalent when dealing with "allies" like Saudi Arabia. King quotes retired Foreign Service officer and U.S. Army colonel Gerald Rose's reaction to this mind-set: "Having been posted to South Africa during 1983–87, I can attest that the U.S. Embassy personnel did not 'Do as the Romans.' We represented American values. We were an Equal Opportunity Employer in South Africa and no function we held was racially segregated. We flouted the system in place. . . . No, we should not act like the Romans—we should act like Americans." Our representatives should represent the values we hold dear. They should act like democrats.

The Arrival

When a new ambassador from a democratic nation arrives in a dictatorship, the tradition is that the ambassador presents his credentials to the government—to a regime that is entirely lacking in legitimacy and is violating international law and the rights of its own people. A democracy-centered diplomacy can identify ways for the new ambassador symbolically first to "present her credentials" to the country's legitimate representatives: its people and those struggling to achieve freedom for them. The specifics will vary from country to country, but here are some possibilities.

Prior to meeting the representatives of the dictators or the dictator himself, the ambassador can meet with the democrats. The more public and visible the meeting, the greater the impact. In Burma, for example, a newly arrived ambassador might call first on Aung San Suu Kyi at her home, where she was under house arrest until May 2002, to underscore our belief that she is the elected and legitimate head of the government. In Pinochet's Chile, American ambassador Harry Barnes early on met publicly with a number of political opposition figures, including Christian Democratic leader Gabriel Valdes. Ambassador Barnes told me, "I decided to use my credentials speech itself to highlight democracy as it was my first public appearance and I could say it publicly to Pinochet." In Budapest, early in my time as ambassador I met in the main dining room of the very visible Gellert Hotel with Janos Kis and Laszlo Rajk, two of the leading democratic dissidents in Hungary in 1986. (I now regret that this meeting took place *after* I presented my official credentials—it should have been before.) I told Kis and Rajk I considered that I was accredited to them and to the Hungarian people and asked what I could do to help. Their request—restoration of their passports—was exceedingly modest, and we immediately satisfied it. We then began a dialogue about much larger objectives.

In most countries, there are places that are identified with the freedom struggle and, of course, places identified with repression and subjugation. New ambassadors should publicly associate themselves with those local landmarks of freedom soon after they arrive. In Beijing, the ambassador could make a statement to the local and international press and lay a wreath with an appropriate ribbon at the location of the former Democracy Wall or at the bridge where thousands of students and workers were murdered by the ironically titled Peoples' Liberation Army in 1989 as they walked toward Tiananmen Square. Or an early event may allow the ambassador to make clear where his nation and other democracies stand. Within a month of his arrival in Chile, Ambassador Harry Barnes attended a candlelight vigil in the cathedral and joined in a procession for Human Rights Day, organized by the Catholic Vicarate of Solidarity to give moral support to those imprisoned, killed, or exiled by the Pinochet regime.

The ambassador's statement at a place or event should make clear and explicit what the ambassador's government has instructed her to do. It should first express respect and deep affection for the local people. The ambassador should then emphasize her intention to strengthen direct ties and forms of cooperation between the two peoples.

She should announce her government's intent to help the (Chinese, Cuban, Saudi) people in their desire to gain control over their own destiny through the full achievement of democratic rights and institutions. These three elements—affection for the people, people-to-people cooperation, and empowering the people—are key components of invaluable embassy involvement.

Local Personality and Voice of the People

Ambassadors and their governments need to understand that ambassadors themselves can become local personalities and surrogate voices for a people temporarily denied their own leaders and spokespersons. For example, as the *New York Times* wrote, U.S. ambassador to Kenya Smith Hempstone's "real contribution has been as an advocate of change. In an address in May 1990 [a few months after his arrival], he said that 'U.S. economic assistance should go to nations that nourish democratic institutions, defend human rights and practice multi-party politics.' Mr. Hempstone's comments gave life to an opposition movement which at the time was not more than a few individuals." Defending Hempstone's role in a private message to a timorous State Department, Hempstone's career Foreign Service officer deputy wrote: "Among the

Kenyan population at large, there can be no doubt that Hempstone is also a powerful symbol. He is probably the most popular foreigner in Kenya. Many of us in the embassy often receive unsolicited comments from Kenyans from all walks of life about his role and the hope he brings to those genuinely concerned about the future of their country."[3]

My own experience as the U.S. ambassador to Hungary echoes this. At the time, *Washington Post* columnist Mary McGrory wrote, "Palmer, a youthful live-wire type who operates out of a building that looks like the campaign headquarters of a maverick, is something of a cult figure. He represents the democratic government that Hungarians can almost taste for themselves."[4] Two years after I left Budapest a Hungarian newspaper poll found that I was one of the ten most popular people in Hungary. Every American ambassador, every ambassador from a democracy, should compete to become one of the most popular people among the long-suffering citizens in every one of the Last Forty-five.

This role within the peculiar circumstances of dictatorships requires serious attention in selecting ambassadors. Just as someone running for office in a democracy should be speaking to the local people, so should ambassadors be selected in part for their ability to appeal to North Koreans, Burmese, or Saudis and not just to their dictators. This appeal can come in many guises. For example, a Chinese American ambassador to Beijing definitely would emphasize the extraordinarily close ties between the people of the two countries. A Muslim Indian ambassador to Pakistan or Iran could have a similar effect.

Selection of ambassadors can be used to make a variety of fundamental points. Who and what ambassadors are makes a strong statement about the democracy and its priorities. For example, the selection of former *Time* magazine editor Henry Grunwald, an Austrian Jewish refugee who fled the Anschluss, to be American ambassador in Vienna sent the right message in a country that is still coming to grips with its wartime past.[5] Perhaps the principal barrier to progress in some Islamic societies is male chauvinism. A decision through dialogue in the Community of Democracies to send only women ambassadors to repressive, chauvinistic countries like Saudi Arabia for a period of years would definitely encourage Saudi women in their struggle to achieve their rights. The American role here is crucial. While many cynics hold the view that sending a woman as ambassador to an Islamic state would dull influence, this most assuredly has not been the case with the United States. Wendy Chamberlin, the U.S. ambassador in Pakistan on 11 September 2001, played a key role in pressuring Pakistan's dictator, General Pervez Musharraf, to change course. Whoever the United States sends must be treated with the respect governments accord to representatives of a great power. Pandering to the prejudices of dictators is the last thing the world's most powerful democracy should do; it sends the worst possible message to both the regime and the people who look to us for encouragement and assistance.

A sign should be posted in front of all of our embassies in countries where women are oppressed with the bumper sticker "Equal rights for women is the radical notion that women are people."

Ambassadors into the Streets

Once ambassadors and embassies realize that they can be local political actors, they will find hundreds of ways to express their affection for the local people, promote people-to-people cooperation, and support democrats. These can range from the sublime to what some would call the ridiculous or at least the lighthearted, and *definitely* not traditionally diplomatic.

If the ambassadors and staff of the democracies represented in China, for example, began to do Falun Gong's very easy and easily identifiable exercises in public parks in Beijing, in cities where they have consulates, and on trips to other cities throughout the country, it would be of enormous value. Such a protracted and coordinated demonstration would show both the people and the communist regime that Western criticism of the repression of Falun Gong and other religions, including Protestants, Catholics, Buddhists, and Muslims, was not merely pro forma. Most powerful of all would be for democracies' ambassadors and their staffs to march to Tiananmen Square, flags held high, to do the exercises with the Falun Gong practitioners who attempt to do so virtually every week and are beaten and dragged away to prisons and labor camps. If enough ambassadors and other diplomats from enough countries joined together, the communist regime might have to rethink its repression.

This tactic has already been employed, terrifying a regime that thrives on fear and political control. On 20 November 2001, thirty-five Western protesters converged on Tiananmen Square and unfurled a banner with Falun Gong's motto, "Truth, Benevolence, Forbearance," and chanted a Falun Gong mantra. The reaction by police was swift and violent. They surrounded the protesters with police vans and forced them inside, hitting a number in the process. One protester broke free and ran toward Chinese spectators at the scene, shouting in Mandarin, "Falun Gong is good," before being tackled and arrested by police. As the following day's *Washington Post* recounted the event, it noted that "police used less force than they have against Chinese members of the Buddhist-like group, refraining from drawing their batons, for example." The protesters were promptly deported from China, but their mission was successful by any measure. The event drew a great deal of press attention and gave great encouragement to millions of Falun Gong practitioners. Four months later, on Valentine's Day 2002, a slightly larger protest with forty foreigners from ten countries—Germany, Canada, Britain, Finland, Belgium, Switzerland, Sweden, Poland, the United States, and France—held another protest. All were arrested and expelled, and seven journalists who covered the event were detained and questioned. Again, the event made the lead page of the *Washington Post's* World News section, and news spread throughout China.

For the initial meeting of the Community of Democracies, my wife and I developed large, campaign-style buttons with messages that said "Diplomats for Democracy by 2025," "All Dictators Out by 2025," and "Women and Men Equal by 2025." Secretary of State Madeleine Albright wore these buttons as she moved through the meeting and when she spoke. For the ambassadors and lower-level diplomats from democracies to wear such buttons as they meet with representatives of the dictatorship—and, even more important, as they meet with the people of the country—would be a powerful statement. Messages could be tailored to local circumstances. Throughout the Middle East "Women and Men Equal by 2025" would work. In Africa "Development Requires Democracy" also is broadly applicable. And a message like "Free Elections/Free Press by 2025" works universally. Just as Soviet dictators could not really object to my distribution of "Freedom Now" buttons in the 1960s, present-day dictators will have a hard time objecting to democratic ambassadors wearing buttons saying "Diplomats for Democracy by 2025" and "All Dictators Out by 2025."

This raises a basic question. Won't the dictators eject from the country any ambassador or lower-level diplomat who pursues these recommendations and close any embassy that tries to become a Freedom House? The dictator will do precisely this if he can get away with it. Historically, dictators have declared some diplomats persona non grata for "interfering in their internal affairs." Saudi Arabia's dictator demanded the recall of U.S. ambassador Hume Horan within a few months of his arrival because his fluent Arabic had allowed him to penetrate beneath the surface of Saudi society, to see what actually was going on—something the Saudi dictator found threatening. The U.S. government cravenly acquiesced. When Kenya's dictator, Daniel arap Moi, repeatedly tried to force Ambassador Hempstone to leave, his own resistance and congressional backing were enough to keep the State Department and the White House from caving in. My freedom-fighting boss in Belgrade in the 1970s, Ambassador Laurence Silberman, faced down communist dictator Josip Broz Tito's concerted efforts to force him to leave.

So it depends upon the democracies more than the dictators whether we can keep in place effective freedom fighter ambassadors. If the larger democracies or simply enough democracies band together to pursue this route, the dictators will have a much harder time of it. They cannot very easily close down a swath of embassies representing the entire democratic world, say from the United States, the United Kingdom, Germany, India, Japan, and another one hundred countries. No doubt they would try to develop countermeasures. But the initiative would no longer be theirs, and their weakness and fear would be on display for their own people, and the world, to see.

My experience in Hungary indicates that people living under dictators understand this dynamic, even if they are sometimes afraid to talk openly about it. They do not consider it interference in *their* internal affairs when foreign diplomats and others clearly admire them as a people and want to help them gain control over their lives and government. They welcome the breath of fresh air from the modern, democratic world. Hungarians in all walks of life encouraged me to play an active role in their society in a host of different ways. They even selected me to chair the Miss Hungary contest live on national television. I was invited to join them in the streets to march for freedom in March 1989, and the reaction was enormously positive when I did so along with many of my embassy staff. As Ambassador Barnes told me, "The important thing is to be clearly interested in, supportive of, the agents of democratic change and to be seen as such." But foreign democrats should be just as fiercely committed to *noninterference* in internal affairs of countries once they become democracies as they are fiercely committed to *interfere* on the side of the oppressed inside dictatorships. This is not to say that democracies should not hold one another to common standards of democratic behavior. The Community of Democracies is committed to this principle.

Dictators and their ambassadors and embassies often "interfere" in the domestic affairs of democracies—a fact well worth recalling in response to their predictable cries of outrage and in persuading the too-timid foreign ministries of democracies to act forcefully in support of democrats within dictatorships. The Saudi ambassador to the United Kingdom wrote a poem called "The Martyrs" praising suicide bombers and had it printed in the London-based *Al Hayat* newspaper on 13 April 2002. His embassy and Saudi embassies throughout Europe, North America, the Middle East, Africa, and Asia establish, fund, and run madrassas—schools that teach locals hatred for, and often violence, against non-Muslims in those countries.

The Chinese embassy in Washington, D.C., and its consulates are actively engaged in physical attacks on, and bugging, surveillance, and intimidation of, American citizens. They have been so flagrant that Congress in July 2002 passed legislation to address the problem, and lawsuits were filed by American individuals and groups in 2002 against the Chinese embassy. Many Washington lobbyists are paid large sums each year by the Burmese Arab, Liberian, and other Asian and African dictatorships' embassies to influence American public opinion and the Congress in ways that are frequently far from transparent.

Vital Communication Links

Embassies can be vital communication links for those living in closed societies—both for getting information out and for getting information in. There is a long and honorable tradition dating back at least to the 1950s and 1960s of British, American, and other diplomats sneaking out underground manuscripts from Russian and other writers in the Soviet Union.

Diplomats from democratic countries should no longer consider that they are risking their careers by such acts. It should be the established policy of all democratic governments to encourage the free flow of such information. Equally important, embassies provide vital coverage of developments *inside* closed societies. Very often diplomats are the best-informed foreign observers; sometimes they are the only continuing foreign presence able to obtain and get out information about repression and resistance. Foreign journalists are not even present in most dictatorships. Where they are, their access is often severely restricted. Embassies' reports, to the maximum extent possible, should be made public and broadcast back into these closed societies. While the communications revolution has reduced their grasp, autocracies still attempt to control what people read, see, and hear. Methods to subvert this control in new ways are necessarily part of a democratic ambassador's toolkit. Democrats under repression should never remain unheard.

Embassies can help in numerous ways to bring light and hard information into closed societies. Diplomats should spend less time inside their embassies meeting with other diplomats and government officials/representatives of the dictators than is traditional. They need to be out, including outside the capital city, most of the time with the agents of democratic change in all their many forms. Universities and students should be a primary objective, but writers, professors, environmentalists, feminists, religious believers—any potential or actual groups forming civil society—need to be on an ambassador's dance card.

In a closed society, it can be electrifying to meet with free people, with people from another and more advanced and exciting world. People from the old Soviet Union can often still recall the first foreigner they ever met and how hungry they were to ask questions and learn. In a place like Burma or North Korea or Zimbabwe, nothing helps raise democrats' expectations more than seeing that they are not alone, that others care enough to meet them and spread their views.

Information can get out by other means as well. Many democratic nations' embassies have culture centers, libraries, or other places inside dictatorships that local people can visit. More should be created. We should provide democracy libraries and collections for embassies and for distribution throughout the country. In addition to the basic texts of democracy, there should be handbooks on nonviolent means to oust dictators and establish democratic governance. Videos like the movie *Gandhi* and the series *A Force More Powerful* and *Bringing Down a Dictator* should be readily available.

We need to take full advantage of electronic means as well. Embassies can become, in part, free cybercafés with Internet access unencumbered by political censorship, and the democracy libraries should be available on the Internet.

We also should consider the feasibility of electronic news boards across the top of well-located embassy buildings. There is a fine precedent for this. The German publisher Axel Springer put such an electronic news board on top of his tall building in West Berlin so that East Germans could look across the Berlin Wall and read the news. A large screen in front of embassies with democracy news and messages also could have a dramatic effect.

Ambassadors and also prime ministers and presidents from the democracies should give weekly "fireside" chats on radio and the Internet or hold Saturday morning radio talk shows; wherever possible, they should broadcast via satellite and other independent television. Perhaps these sessions could be called "The Democracy Hour" and run at the same time each week. Given the number of dictatorships and languages involved, as well as the number of democracies, perhaps the task could be divided. The British prime minister might talk to the Chinese one week, while the French president spoke to Rwandans and the Spanish prime minister to the Cubans, and the next week another mix. The content, continuity, consistent advice, and solidarity of such weekly talks could have an incalculable impact. Just as Britons and Americans waited each week for Prime Minister Winston Churchill and President Franklin D. Roosevelt to lift their spirits during World War II, so could the people struggling against dictatorship after dictatorship awaken and arise to the words of proven democrats like Kim Dae Jung from South Korea, Vicente Fox from Mexico, and Vaclav Havel from the Czech Republic. With roughly one hundred democracies, some new and others long established, there is an ample supply of potential speakers for the forty-five dictatorships.

Embassies as Campaign Headquarters

The democracies' embassies must reorganize internally and between themselves to focus on their most important goal, helping the local people gain control over their own destinies. Typical embassies currently have separate political, economic, commercial, military, intelligence, consular, aid, and other sections. No one of them has knowledge of nonviolent strategy, organization, and tactics to oust dictators and bring in democracy, but all of them have important resources and connections to bring to the struggle. There is also no organizational structure within embassies to focus on helping local democrats achieve their goal.

Ambassadors should consider themselves chief democracy officers. Many ambassadors tend to relegate dealing with democrats to more junior officers to preserve the ambassador's relationship with the dictator. This is a mistake. An ambassador's influence with a dictator is actually enhanced by direct contact with his opposition.

Dealing Directly with Dictators

The world's dictators vary in ideology, age, and time in power, but they share certain common traits. Occidental Oil Company founder Armand Hammer, that great scoundrel but astute observer of communist bosses and Middle Eastern potentates, once remarked to me that "dictatorships are like pyramids—everyone is afraid of the person next above him, and no one can make any decisions except the man at the top. The dictator in turn does not trust anyone below him including his own closest aides, family, and people." Hammer knew whereof he spoke, having had personal contact with Lenin, Stalin, King Idris, Qaddafi, King Hussein, and many others. Dictators are paranoid, and, as Henry Kissinger once remarked, "Even paranoids have enemies." They are not just afraid of losing power, they are afraid of losing their lives; they worry not just about being overthrown but also about being assassinated—with good reason. Many worry particularly about what will happen to them in their old age, how to hold on to their ill-gotten gains, how to take care of their families and political cronies, and how to ensure that history will view them well. For all their willingness to inflict cruelty, backwardness, and death on millions of their citizens, for all of their fundamental criminal conduct, they are also human beings, with at least some of what this implies.

Understanding the context within which dictators operate is of basic importance. From the outside they may appear invulnerable and permanent; from their perspective they are under fundamental and constant threat. Both increasing that threat *and* helping them see a peaceful way out are critical. I agree with the world's leading authority on nonviolent strategy and tactics, Gene Sharp, that "resistance movements cannot rely on negotiation with dictators to bring about democracy."[6] The major effort must be to push them out.

Waltzing a Dictator on the Danube

At the same time, I have come to understand that dialogues with dictators can be useful and should be tried. They can combine elements of pressure and promise. A year after I arrived in Budapest, Janos Kadar, the dictator in power since the slaughter of 1956, gave way to a somewhat younger, though still hard-nosed, dictator, General Secretary Karoly Grosz. Others in the communist leadership included Prime Minister Miklos Nemeth, Foreign Minister Gyula Horn, and economic czar Rezo Nyers. Over my four years in Budapest, I spent a substantial amount of time with these men. I did what George Shultz had taught me in Moscow several years earlier. I talked about the nature of modern economies and what was required to attract foreign investment. I also talked at length with them about democracy and about the democrats in Hungary whom they were oppressing, democrats they knew I saw at least as often as I saw them. I not only spent time in their offices in official meetings, but I also ate with them and played tennis and drank and talked with them afterwards.

I took Grosz on an extended trip around the United States in July 1988, beginning with Chicago and McDonalds, Los Angeles and Disneyland, Boston and a visit with Gov. Michael Dukakis, then running for president. The tour ended in the Oval Office with Ronald Reagan. "The President, who repeatedly extolled the virtues of free enterprise and political freedom during his visit to Moscow in May, also took the occasion to instruct Mr. Grosz on the importance of these values," reported the *New York Times*. "'I hope you'll remember what you've seen here about the strength to be found in a society that is free, in a society that is committed to upholding fundamental human rights and open to diverse opinion and talent.' In his reply to the President, Mr. Grosz seemed to agree, saying: 'Hungary has to face enormous tasks today. It will reorganize its economy. This can only be done, we are aware, if the people, if the citizens, will enjoy more rights, more freedoms. Therefore we are modernizing our political system and our political practice.' A senior administration official [yours truly], briefing reporters about the visit, said Hungary had made considerable progress on human rights. But he pointed out that some Hungarians are still denied passports, and that American diplomats are 'not always happy' with how the Hungarian police deal with demonstrations. Grosz later answered a question by saying that he could 'envisage any sort of a system' in Hungary, including a 'multi-party system.'"

Grosz had hardly been to the West prior to this trip. He told me that it was a real eye-opener. He was by no means converted to democracy or a free market. But he seemed impressed by our power, our dynamism, our wealth, our middle class. He visited an aunt in Los Angeles and was able to see how ordinary Americans live. Grosz knew the Soviet Union firsthand; I think he began to understand better that he was standing in quicksand. His will to fight was sapped. He and I developed a relationship that I believe played a modest but helpful role in assuring a peaceful transition when sufficient pressure had been mounted.

Indeed, even as Foreign Minister Gyula Horn asked Secretary of State James Baker to reprimand me and rein me in, Grosz shared with me his fears about being lynched and appealed for my help. While I reassured him that we were opposed to violence, I declined to intervene with Fidesz—the youth group led by Viktor Orban, later prime minister of Hungary—to stop demonstrations and pressures. I put Fidesz in the most prominent position during President George Bush's 1989 visit to Hungary—the first by any American president. The communist leaders and I were close enough that I could talk with them about whether the most repulsive organization in the country, the Munkas Orseg (Workers Militia) would issue bullets to its cadre for a major demonstration in March 1989. I noted that some of the members of the Workers Militia were known to be anti-Semitic (some hard-liners believed the democratic opposition in Hungary was led by Jews) and that they were not experienced in handling large, although peaceful, demonstrations. I pointed out to them that if the militia opened fire, they could kill, among others, the U.S. ambassador and many other Americans and foreigners, for I and part of the embassy staff would be marching. I also met with the leader of the Workers Militia himself just before the demonstration to urge moderation and to make the point that he would be held personally responsible for any shooting.

I was also able to have serious talks with the leaders about opening their border with Austria, about allowing the young East Germans camped out in Budapest and elsewhere in Hungary to travel through Austria to West Germany. And I was able to talk with them about their own futures in a democratic Hungary, persuading them that they could do well as long as they did not use force to stop the transition and cooperated in roundtable talks with the democrats. For example, the head of propaganda for the Hungarian Communist Party and I talked about his going into capitalist marketing—which he did even before the collapse. Many communists have done well under democracy. Some have been elected to political office, some have made more or less legitimate money in business. Most have not ended up being lynched, as they feared. Karoly Grosz retired to his native city in eastern Hungary and died quietly several years later.

Three-Dimensional Dialogue

While I am not trying to assert that every dictator is eager today to engage in this sort of dialogue, I do believe that every ambassador from every democratic country and every democratic leader who meets with dictators should try to develop a relationship and try to pursue a dialogue focused on democracy and the idea that the dictator would give up power.

What Works in the Twenty-first Century

There has been a tendency to focus on individual human rights violations, on getting a particular person out of jail, on stopping some particular campaign of oppression. But in a sense, this plays to the dictators' strengths. Romanian communist dictator Nicolae Ceausescu, with whom then Under Secretary Eagleburger and I negotiated in the 1980s, loved to let out a few Jewish and German-origin Romanians, even selling some to the Israeli and German governments, who paid a price per head. Ceausescu also was paid in plaudits from the West. The USSR's Leonid Brezhnev would agree after repeated discussions to let out a few dissidents, take credit for their release, and then put others in jail. Jiang Zemin has proven himself adept at this game in more recent years. When we talk to dictators, we should raise and press specific human rights cases. But we need to explicitly press all the dictators for the entire set of institutions that make up democracy: competing political parties, independent trade unions, free media, and an independent judiciary. The rule of thumb: Talk about twenty-first-century societies and the free market and free political infrastructure they require. With a majority of the Last Forty-five we still are not engaged in making these points.

Dictators Can Benefit from Democracy

Talk with the dictator about his own personal situation, his family, his future as he grows older, his image in history is key. The dictator needs to be persuaded that democrats inside and outside the country are reasonable and willing to work with him if he will work with them. He needs to be shown the growing number of cases where former leading figures in dictatorships have become respected participants in the democratic life of the country. Mikhail Gorbachev, for example, enjoys a good life, has his institute, and travels and speaks constantly, and his popularity at home is again on the rise. He has also become an outspoken democrat and a sharp critic of Vladimir Putin's efforts to muzzle Russian independent television. Poland's Aleksander Kwasniewski, and Hungary's Gyula Horn are among the many leading figures in communist parties who have transformed themselves and their parties and won legitimate elections to become presidents and prime ministers, and of course leave office again when their terms were up.

Kenneth Kaunda, Zambia's former dictator, may epitomize the benefits of life after dictatorship. In January 2002, the *New York Times* correspondent Rachel Swarns well captured this dynamic. "Kaunda is one of those rarities in African politics: a man who led his nation to independence, ruled with an iron fist and then gracefully accepted defeat at the ballot box." Swarns wrote: "'Look at me now,' Kaunda said, laughing, 'You are watching a relaxed old man. I'm very happy with what I'm doing. . . . I'm running a foundation now, fighting H.I.V./AIDS to the best of my ability. . . . Long ago, I learned one of the great forgotten truths of African politics: being out of power does not necessarily mean losing your voice. I have a duty to come and point out things. I have been pointing them out to great crowds, sometimes to wild cheers, sometimes to deafening silence. I'm not sure I have brought joy to many a heart in authority.'" And Swarns cited the editor of an independent Zambian paper as noting that "Kaunda's standing has risen tremendously."[7]

One of the ironies is that former dictators sometimes become beneficiaries of democracy and are some of its most powerful voices. They now have a vested interest in it, to sustain their voice and to protect their own skins.

The democracies need to give fresh thought to packages of incentives for dictators to leave office. Perhaps the democracies should set up and fund an institute on Lake Geneva or the Spanish coast where former dictators could be in residence, write (or rewrite) their memoirs, and plan their election campaigns. Perhaps there should be an Islamic Center for Democracy in East Jerusalem where former Muslim dictators could reside, pray, reflect on the future, and pronounce their views. Perhaps democracies and the United Nations, should guarantee the physical safety of any dictator and his family willing to leave office peacefully.

To meet this need, Cullen Murphy in the New Yorker proposed the creation of "the Last Resort"—the purchase of a remote island under UN auspices. Tyrants could check in at the Last Resort at any time in their careers (the earlier the better) and could bring with them as much money as they wished, no questions asked. Their persons and their fortunes would be off-limits to law enforcement agencies. The accommodations at their disposal, for which they would pay a high monthly rent, would be luxurious. The United Nations would widely publicize all these positive features of life. Less attention would be paid to the fact that the "guests" would never be allowed to leave the island. And given the guests' background and proclivities, the New Yorker notes, the social dynamics of the establishment would almost certainly be problematic—feuds, a black market, occasional bloodshed.[8]

In late 2002 and early 2003 there was a flurry of reports of Arab efforts to persuade Saddam Hussein to go into exile to avoid war, including a report that the foreign minister of Qatar, Sheik Hamad bin Jassim bin Jabr al-Thani, met with Hussein in Baghdad.[9]

Alternative Is Hanging or Jail

But this dialogue with a dictator also needs to address, with at least equal force, the negative outcomes awaiting him if he refuses to cooperate. The least of these is that history will remember the dictator for holding back his nation from joining the ever-widening membership of the Community of Democracies, from becoming a modern, civilized nation. The more direct negative consequences also need to be discussed: Deng Xiaoping states in *The Tiananmen Papers* "We will be put under house arrest"[10]; or as Karoly Grosz said to me, pointing out his office window, "They will hang me from that lamppost." Both were quite right, in principle. Resistance and continued refusal to let democracy come to his country will mean a dictator is in direct violation of international law, that the Hague Court or special tribunal for dictators will issue a subpoena, and that if he does not appear he will be tried in absentia, convicted, and ultimately apprehended and jailed. He needs to be made to focus on this set of alternatives: Will it be Milosevic or Horn—jail or redemption?

Of course, such dialogues will not always work, but they will never work without the application of some real muscle. Ambassador Smith Hempstone had it right. The average ambassador might have had a meeting with Moi once during his three-year tour in Nairobi. But, writes Hempstone, because he was the envoy of the United States "and perhaps because Moi and I had a personal liking for each other, at least at the start of my tour, I saw him more than forty times during my thirty-nine months in Nairobi. I was never denied access to him, even when our relations were most strained, and only once or twice was my request for a meeting delayed." Hempstone used this extraordinary access to try out many of the elements described in this chapter. He talked with Moi face-to-face at length about democracy, most often without the foreign ministry present. He was able to get Moi to reverse himself on multiparty politics and actually to hold elections, which could have resulted in Moi's ouster on Hempstone's watch if Kenya's democrats had held together, as they finally did in 2002. Hempstone found that "Moi, his political arteries clogged with the cholesterol of old age, paranoia, and inadequacy, understood and preferred the old ways to the new, repression to reconciliation."[11] But Hempstone and Kenyan democrats forced his hand to permit elections.

The real purpose of dialogue is not so much the conversion of dictators as moving them in the right direction—toward elections, away from firing on demonstrators. Ambassadors Michael Armacost and Steve Bosworth and envoy Senator Paul Laxalt never persuaded Ferdinand Marcos that he should reform his ways. But they did turn him toward leaving the Philippines peacefully. While in power, Gorbachev was never persuaded to support the development of democracy in eastern Europe or Russia—he just did not prevent it.

Of course, the ambassador cannot do it all, nor should she. Embassies need committed staff. Each embassy should have at least one democracy officer who is extensively trained in nonviolent strategy and tactics and how outsiders can help. The Foreign Service should establish a new specialty within the political officer cone, or career path, for political officers. Just as we have Arab, Russian, and Latin American specialists, we could develop a generation of officers skilled at helping to oust dictators. The ambassador should head a democracy working group that includes all sections of the embassy. There should be an annual democracy action program.

In embassies with larger staffs, new external and internal sections could be formed in place of the standard separate political, economic, and other sections. The internal section would have political, economic, aid, and other relevant officers assigned to it and would focus on bringing democracy and other internal progress. Every section of the embassy has its own particular constituencies that are critical to the ouster of the dictator. The democratic embassies' own intelligence and police personnel have relations with the local security services, the military attachés have relations with the local military, the commercial attaché with local business leaders, and so forth.

Where religion plays a pivotal role, it is worth considering the creation of religion attachés. In a significant number of dictatorships religious institutions and leaders are among the most important, influential, independent voices for change. This is true from Cuba through Africa and the Middle East and on through Asia. Sometimes religious voices are raised in favor of democracy and toleration. Sometimes, in part in reaction to repression, they have become the agents of violence and new oppression. It is critical that the forces of religious moderation eventually predominate. The secular nature and traditions of many career diplomats can make them poor interlocutors with Islamic leaders and believers in the Middle East and with Catholic, Protestant, Falun Gong, and others in China. Yet in many cases, a central task is to help educate religious groups about the wisdom of separating church and state, and in other circumstances, to help religious groups achieve their rights through nonviolent means.

Ambassadors and embassies should seek every opportunity to showcase and legitimize the democrats. One way is to go to their trials. On 16 January 2002, the embassies of Sweden, Norway, Holland, Switzerland, the United Kingdom, Belgium, Germany, Spain, Canada, and the United States had diplomats present at the trial in Cairo of leading democrat Saad Ibrahim. His release later in the year was directly related to these shows of solidarity by democratic governments and nongovernmental organizations (NGOs) like Freedom House, which was the first to visit Ibrahim in jail and awarded him a medal in 2002.

Another way to showcase the democrats is to invite them to embassy events along with the dictator's representatives. National days are a splendid opportunity to bring about this mix. Ambassador Hempstone describes a Fourth of July bash where "cabinet ministers and dissidents laughed and joked together, judges chatted amiably with those they had sent to jail, and the late-stayers ended up dancing on the lawn."[12] But smaller events, lunches, and dinners are also good. In most situations the dictator and his people have never met the democrats. While familiarity can breed contempt, it also can produce a healthy respect for the democrats' determination, as Gandhi did with the British overlords. It also gives the democrats an opportunity to take a personal measure of the dictator and his regime.

One objective is to push for dialogue, then for informal and, later, formal roundtables involving the democrats and the old regime. This is a classic way of persuading a dictator that he has a future, provided he goes peacefully. It was used in Poland and Hungary in 1989, among other places. The more such mixing can be created de facto, the easier it is to move down this road.

For a moment, I would like to speak directly to diplomats, to offer a few guidelines for those taking up their first posting in dictatorships.

Build Consensus at Home.   Before going to post, build consensus with various branches of your own government, including the legislature and the NGO sector. The backing arranged at the outset makes an enormous difference in your mandate and ability to press forward once at post. Remember, the central task is to bring about a fully functioning democracy, meaning that sooner or later the dictator must go. Having built a consensus (coalition) before going to post, keep it alive not only by staying in touch from abroad but also by reporting back in person periodically.

Proclaim Your Country's Position.   Immediately upon arrival, make clear that you view your accreditation to be to the people of the country, not just to the dictator's government. If the government stalls the accreditation process, do not make yourself invisible to the society at large. Traditionally, new ambassadors have acted upon the principle that they could not be active until their presentation of credentials; this formality should not apply in the Last Forty-five, whose dictators are illegitimate. Your country's outlook and disposition toward promoting democracy can be seen in your meetings with leading democrats, public association with freedom/democracy places and events, and early public statements and interviews.

Plan with Local Civic Actors.   Simply meeting with democracy activists is critical, but it is not enough. You need to listen to the indigenous actors about what you, your government, and other democracies can do for them, as well as where they see room for action. A systematic, flexible plan to help build a broad democratic consensus should be developed.

Work with the Regime.   Apply carrots and sticks to the regime in line with the tenets of the above plan, exploiting opportunities and pressing when necessary to keep a liberalization process going, providing more room for democrats. Recognize that the most important moment in the democratic breakthrough is likely to come when the military and police can be persuaded not to use force against their own people. As you work on these security forces, keep differentiating between the dictator and everyone else.

Generate Resources.   In accordance with the general plan discussed with democratic actors, work to get resources necessary to support nonviolent change. This includes communicating to your capital which of its policies have a positive or negative impact on the country to which you are posted.

Create International Democratic Coalitions.   Meet with ambassadors from other democratic countries (the Community of Democracies and various subsets thereof) at least once a month in a democracy action group to discuss the situation and coordinate efforts to assist the democratic forces in establishing popular rule.

Ambassadors in Action

To demonstrate how these principles can be applied, I have taken as paradigms two very different men. The first, professional diplomat Harry G. Barnes Jr., was U.S. ambassador to Chile from 1985 to 1988. The second, career journalist Smith Hempstone, a self-styled "rogue ambassador," served in Kenya from 1989 to 1992. Between them, these two men showed what can be done for democracy in the shadow of two dictators who, while also very different kinds of men, shared the belief that only they should rule, forever.

Barnes in Chile: The Career Diplomat

Harry G. Barnes Jr., arrived in Santiago de Chile in 1985, a dozen years after the September 1973 military coup that deposed the socialist regime of Salvador Allende Goshens, who died, probably by his own hand, in the siege of La Moneda, Chile's presidential palace. The junta that seized power was led by Gen. Augusto Pinochet, commander of the army and a longtime enemy of communism. He quickly consolidated his success by sweeping up all enemies, real and imagined, from the leftist ranks. Until then, Chile, one of Latin America's oldest democracies, had been immune from the regional disease of military coups. While most of the nation's twelve million citizens welcomed the end of Allende's socialist experiment and its flirtations with Cuba and the Soviet Union, they also expected a quick return to civilian rule.[13]

But the Pinochet-led junta, like all juntas everywhere, was not prepared to give up power after all. Much remained to be done in the way of erasing two years of socialism and rebuilding the economy, and it would take a strong hand. The ensuing war on communism was broad and brutal, marked by unspeakable torture, exiles, overseas assassinations, and several thousand "disappeared," or *desaparecidos*. Presiding over this nightmare of suppression was a newly created secret police entity, DINA (Dirección de Inteligencia Nacional). In 1974, Pinochet had himself named Chile's chief executive.

Thereafter, for something over a decade, repression waxed and waned in Chile, and the people bent under the heavy hand of their dictator. There was opposition, but so intimidated and ideologically mixed that it could not coalesce. A few bombs from splinter extremists on the left made hardly a dent in the regime. But then, at about the time Barnes took up his post in Santiago, the opposition had begun to show faint signs of life.

Through much of the early years of the Pinochet regime, the U.S. government had done nothing to promote the restoration of Chile's venerable democracy. In the cold war context, the end of Allende looked like the end of Cuban and Soviet penetrations into South America. Richard Nixon and his secretary of state, Henry Kissinger, had rewarded the coup with economic and military aid and had said little about its human rights transgressions. Indeed, the widely held view persists to the present day that the Central Intelligence Agency engineered Allende's overthrow, when, in fact, they merely let it happen. Still, as George Shultz, who would become secretary of state under Ronald Reagan, observed, "The United States was almost universally blamed for bringing [Pinochet] to power and helping him stay there."

The administration of Gerald Ford likewise did little to steer Chile back toward democracy, although it had numerous means, including leverage at the Paris Club of creditors and such institutions as the World Bank and the International Monetary Fund. Applying that leverage, Kissinger objected, would inject politics into the international financial institutions. Indeed, the U.S. administration rather liked the liberalizing, tight-money policies adopted by Chile's economic leaders. The U.S. Senate, where Edward Kennedy and others opposed the coddling of this new Latin dictator, was less impressed and cut military assistance to Chile.

At an Organization of American States 1976 summit in Santiago, Kissinger delivered what he later called a major speech on human rights and voted for a resolution censuring Chile for human rights violations. But he had neutralized his speech by reassuring General Pinochet offstage and suggesting that perhaps Chile should make some sort of gesture toward democracy. All this deepened the opposition's malaise. "Kissinger gave the image of very favorable treatment toward the regime," remarked Patricio Aylwin, then leader of the Christian Democrats (and later president), "and upon his return [to Washington] openly made very favorable declarations."[14]

The election of Jimmy Carter to the American presidency was watched very closely in Chile, for the candidate's pronouncements in favor of human rights offered hope to the scattered and beleaguered opposition, while sparking unease within the junta. This new emphasis achieved some real results, but there was no deflecting the policy dissonance within the Department of State between an emphasis on human rights and cold war diplomacy as usual—and, curiously, little emphasis on the core issue: a return to democracy.

By January of 1978, Pinochet had become sufficiently confident to hold a referendum on his rule. On the ballot: "I support President Pinochet in the defense of the dignity of Chile and reaffirm the legitimacy of the government." Citizens could vote yes by checking a glyph of Chile's lone-star flag. Unmarked ballots counted as yes votes. The inevitable triumph led Pinochet to declare, "Today there is a new Chile!"

He then ordered the drafting of a new constitution for this new Chile, allowing aides to pare a proposed sixteen-year presidential term down to two eight-year terms, with a plebiscite to be held in 1988. A constitutional plebiscite on 11 September 1980—the seventh anniversary of the coup—won with two-thirds of the vote. The democratic opposition dismissed the constitution as window dressing; like Pinochet, they were unaware that the mandated 1988 ballot would prove a portal back to democracy.

The first term of President Ronald Reagan restored a strong anticommunist note to American foreign policy. "Pinochet made everyone uneasy," recalled George Shultz, "but he was on our side." The new U.S. ambassador, James Theberge, came to Chile from a post in Nicaragua, then ruled by Anastasio Somoza. Against the mood of Congress, the Reagan administration tried to lift restrictions on military aid to Chile, the junta ruling Argentina, and other enemies of communism in the region.

By 1982, however, Chile's model economy had run aground on bad loans, dislocations among banks and creditors, and a reluctance to let the currency float. The downturn caused the regime to throttle the economy, which awakened Chile's dormant labor movement. There had been some progress here, helped along by the AFL-CIO in the United States, which had threatened to boycott Chilean products after a 1978 work action at the Chiquicamata copper mine was violently suppressed. The regime relented, allowing limited elections and a right to strike for up to sixty days. But death remained in the air. In 1982, Tucapel Jimenez, an aggressive union leader, was murdered after a vocal attack on the Pinochet regime.

The following year, Rodolfo Seguel, who had led copper workers in a 1981 strike that lasted fifty-nine days, became head of the National Workers Committee, and called for a nationwide general strike. Then, realizing how ferocious the regime would be in suppressing a strike, he called it a national protest day, set for 11 May. On that day, Chileans proclaimed with banging pots and pans, horns, and such other means as they could find that, in Seguel's words, "the dictator was a dictator, that it was a dictatorship, that we needed a change." Chile's national police, the carabineros, teargassed the happy crowds. But they, having finally broken their silence, could no longer be contained. Sensing this, as well as the rising tensions caused by the country's continued economic slide, the regime cracked down, proclaiming a state of siege. Chile's tenuous hold on the prospect of democracy weakened visibly.[15]

Shultz Shifts Gears with Barnes

In that context, Secretary of State Shultz decided that it was time for a new ambassador—indeed, for a new kind of ambassador—to take up the post in Santiago, and he selected Harry Barnes, who had served as ambassador to New Delhi. Barnes was a mild-mannered, soft-spoken career diplomat who would, in a quiet way, do much to help Chile regain democracy.

Known for his facility with languages, Barnes spoke Hindi and had put it to use traveling throughout India to be in contact with a full spectrum of people; the Indian government had made its unease about this known. "To me, their discomfort was a sterling recommendation for Barnes, a wizard at languages, to go to Chile," wrote Shultz. "He would similarly immerse himself in Chilean life and culture in his new post." Barnes selected George F. Jones, a Latin American specialist then finishing a tour in Costa Rica, as his deputy chief of mission.

Shultz made additional personnel changes in the State Department that helped facilitate moving Chile and other countries in the hemisphere toward democratic governance. Elliott Abrams, who had been serving as assistant secretary of state for human rights, became assistant secretary for inter-American affairs, replacing Langhorne Motley; Richard Schifter filled Abrams's previous position. These two would work together with Shultz to push for a policy dedicated to returning Chile to the democratic fold. Mike Durkee was head of the Office of Southern Cone Affairs at the time and was remembered by Jones as "an absolute tower of strength."

While intensively learning Spanish in Washington prior to deploying, Barnes worked to get solid policy guidance and backing. Barnes felt he had a clear mission to "a) push for an early return to democracy; b) promote full respect for human rights; and c) support the free market approach." Shultz felt that such an agenda would bring results and that "Chile did not need much in the way of lessons on democracy. The ideas and traditions were already built into Chilean society." Beyond gaining direct backing at State, Barnes used his time in Washington to build a network of support from NGOs and

Congress, which had had such a crucial, and historically more progressive and consistent, role in U.S. policy toward Chile.

Barnes arrived at his post in November 1985, well after his deputy, who had already assessed the contemporary Chilean political landscape. What Jones found was hardly encouraging. The opposition had managed to unite in a broad coalition—the National Accord for the Transition to Full Democracy—including the previously existing Democratic Alliance and two rightist parties, one of them former Interior Minister Jarpa's Union of Independent Democrats. The accord developed a detailed agenda for rapid transition to democratic rule, under the encouragement of the new Roman Catholic cardinal, Juan Francisco Fresno. The accord included calls for full respect of human and civic rights, legalization of political parties, and elections for the presidency and congress. Pinochet and his regime ignored the accord. When Pinochet summoned Cardinal Fresno on Christmas Eve, 1985, he rebuffed any attempt by the cardinal to discuss the plan. "It would be better if we just turned the page," he told the cleric before leading him to the door and to waiting cameras. This response sent the opposition into a funk of hopelessness. In the meantime, the hard left outside the accord had turned to violence, which brought out the worst in the junta and hurt the democrats who were attempting nonviolent change. One diplomat pegged the perverse cycle as a "nice, symbiotic relationship." Indeed, dictatorships, terrorism, and religious extremism feed on one another.

"The United States," Barnes reported to Shultz soon after arriving in Chile, "is genuinely real to many Chileans, partly because of the democratic example and link to Chile's past practices, partly because of the number of influential Chileans educated in the U.S., and partly because of our common economic philosophy. Whatever the reasons, we are seen as a model with inherent power: what we think, what we say, and what we do count a great deal in hemispheric and world affairs." When Barnes presented his credentials to Pinochet, he referred to Winston Churchill: "In our country . . . we have concluded that the ills of democracy can best be cured by more democracy." Pinochet was deeply insulted by the remark, and the Chilean foreign ministry refused to arrange the traditional calls of a new ambassador on senior officials for Ambassador Barnes for some time thereafter.

Barnes then began meeting very publicly with a number of political opposition figures, including Christian Democratic leader Gabriel Valdes. The Valdes meeting apparently riled the regime even more deeply. Soon thereafter, on 10 December 1985, the Catholic Vicarate of Solidarity, which worked to give moral support to the regime's victims and their families, held a candlelight vigil in the cathedral for Human Rights Day. Barnes attended and joined in the procession, much to the chagrin of the Chilean government. "Outrage! Fury! Incomprehension! That the American ambassador would associate himself with these communists in the Catholic Church," was Jones's assessment of the reaction. Shultz noted that one pro-government newspaper ran a cartoon "showing Barnes with a candle in his hand and next to him a terrorist wearing a ski mask with a bomb in his hand. The government of Chile wanted to equate advocacy of human rights with terrorism." But Barnes had it right. Within a month of his arrival, he had publicly shown solidarity with the Chilean people. The change was noticed on the ground, where it counted most.

The U.S. Congress continued its advocacy of human rights and democracy in Chile. In January 1986, Senator Edward Kennedy, long a critic of the Pinochet regime, visited Chile as part of a Latin American tour. The regime initially strongly opposed the trip, but the United States convinced the Chileans to allow it. To punish him for his years of criticism, the Chilean government arranged a "rowdy" reception for Kennedy upon his arrival at the Santiago airport; several opposition figures who had come to meet the senator were beaten. Once clear of the airport rent-a-crowd, however, democracy and human rights advocates in Santiago enthusiastically received the senator.

Washington had meanwhile turned its back on several other dictators. In February 1986, both the Marcos dictatorship in the Philippines and that of Jean-Claude "Baby Doc" Duvalier in Haiti were ended; the United States drew the line, ending their rule and provided a peaceful way out for the dictators. Even White House chief of staff Donald Regan, who fought to the bitter end against Shultz on the issue of supporting democracy in the Philippines, put the Pinochet regime on edge. When asked if the United States was seeking to depose the Pinochet regime, he replied "No, not at the moment"— hardly reassuring to Pinochet. Shultz recalls fighting early in 1986 an "unpublicized but tough fight within the administration to develop a dramatically different position toward Chile." For the first time, in March 1986, the United States sponsored a resolution in the UN Human Rights Commission taking Chile to task for its human rights practices. The resolution called on the Pinochet regime to stop its use of torture and other abuses of human rights and to adopt democratic institutions. After a history of American avoidance of such public condemnations in favor of "quiet diplomacy," the move made a strong impression in Chile, both among the government and the democratic forces. In Shultz's words, "The Reagan administration was now clearly supporting both a prompt return to democracy and greater respect for basic human rights. Chileans took comfort in U.S. solidarity with their democratic cause. So, while the Pinochet government and its supporters felt our pronouncements and actions—concrete or symbolic—constituted 'interference' in their internal affairs, the democratic elements viewed them as gestures of support and respect for what mattered. Interference, such as that implied when a country joins the United Nations and thereby accepts the Universal Declaration of Human Rights, was just right."

Later that year, a Chilean army patrol intercepted two teenagers on suspicion of having participated in antigovernment demonstrations in Santiago. They doused the pair with gasoline and set them alight. Rodrigo Rojas de Negri, a sixteen-year-old Chilean with permanent residency in the United States, died of his burns. Carmen Gloria Quintana, a Chilean, was severely burned but survived, thanks in large part to U.S. embassy involvement in finding medical care for her.

Ambassador Barnes and his wife, Betsey, returned to Santiago for Rojas's funeral, at the invitation of the Chilean Commission for Human Rights. Several other diplomats also attended. The ambassador and his wife, along with other diplomats, were photographed with the family next to Rojas's casket, which was positioned before floral wreaths set against drapes. "As the pictures were being taken," Barnes relates, "(and unbeknownst to those who were being photographed) the drapes were opened to reveal banners with the emblems of the two major terrorist groups." The pro-Pinochet press ran the photos on the front page the next day, along with "government sponsored comments that the U.S., through the presence of its ambassador, was supportive of terrorism." The police charged and teargassed the large demonstration outside the funeral, teargassing the ambassador and others in the process.

A few days later, the Chilean chargé d'affaires in Washington was told by Assistant Secretary Elliott Abrams, "the GOC [Government of Chile] had to be aware that breaking up a funeral procession had political repercussions. He observed that it would be hard to persuade people in the United States that it was right to use water cannon against people because they were carrying placards or because of a small amount of pushing or shouting." But Senator Jesse Helms went so far as to visit Chile, meeting with Pinochet and other government officials; he only met with Barnes some five days after his arrival to berate him "in the most contemptuous manner" for "planting the American flag in the midst of communists." In Jones's view, the senator "believed that Pinochet had done a service to mankind in getting rid of Allende. . . . For the minor defect of not holding elections, he was being pilloried by the U.S. Government." Helms reserved special vitriol for Barnes, whom, according to Jones, he saw as "a left-wing ambassador who . . . was trying to undermine this noble government." Upon his return, Helms tried without success to have Barnes recalled. Instead, Barnes received the unreserved backing of both Secretary of State Shultz and President Reagan, as well as many members of Congress.

By 1986, the Chilean economy was recovering and was in far better structural condition than that of any of its neighbors. At this point, a new World Bank structural adjustment loan was under consideration, but unlike in the past, political considerations—namely, a notable lack of progress toward democracy, as well as the investigation of the Rojas case—were part of the equation. Then events began to push the other way. Cuban arms caches were found on the northern coast. On 7 September there was an unsuccessful, but well-planned and incredibly close, attempt to kill Pinochet while on the road to his ranch. A communist revolutionary group claimed responsibility for the attack. Emboldened by this manifestation of a real enemy, the regime reimposed a state of siege. In response, the State Department issued a statement expressing concern about "sweeping powers of censorship, repression and forced resettlement, without any recourse to judicial review." President Reagan also sent a note to Pinochet voicing distress over the assassination attempt and the new repressive measures. In November, the structural adjustment loan sharpened the rift between the State Department and others in the administration. State had wanted to torpedo the $250 million World Bank loan with a no vote since July but was overruled by the White House, which allowed only an abstention. Shultz had wanted to send a clear message to Chile about the continued lack of progress toward democracy. However, he could take comfort in preempting President Reagan's notion of inviting Pinochet to Washington to discuss the loan. Shultz was repulsed by the very idea and reportedly told the president, "You cannot invite that man. He has blood all over his hands."

Supporting Chilean Democrats

In Chile, the disparate nature of the democratic parties was cause for concern for the U.S. embassy, which believed the fast-approaching 1988 plebiscite provided a crucial opportunity. "As October 1988 came closer," says Jones, "it became evident that there was a potential for forcing Pinochet to do something. . . . Our policy . . . in Chile, in 1986–88, was to encourage the opposition to participate in the plebiscite and to make every effort they could possibly make to win it. We devoted some resources to helping them win it, both through direct grants from AID [the U.S. Agency for International Development] and grants coming from the National Endowment for Democracy to the National Democratic Institute."

Getting the opposition political parties to believe in a fair ballot was a challenge. "When we pointed out to the opposition" that the plebiscite was a chance to hoist Pinochet by his own petard, "many of the opposition leaders said, 'You've got to be kidding. You think Pinochet is going to let us win this plebiscite? You don't know this man. We've lived with him all these years. He had outmaneuvered, manipulated, tricked the United States Government, every United States Ambassador, all of us, the Cardinal. Look how he embarrassed the Cardinal. The Cardinal went to see him and he brushed him off. There is absolutely no way. What you're suggesting is ridiculous. We will boycott this plebiscite. It is a sham and a hoax.'" Thus, overcoming this reluctance to get voters to even register for the poll, much less mount a serious campaign, became a focal point for the U.S. embassy.

Intriguingly, contacts with some junta members showed some promise for change as the plebiscite drew near. In mid-1986, Deputy Assistant Secretary of State Robert Gelbard met with the heads of the air force and the carabineros, the national police, who told him that the promulgation of election-related laws would help prevent further demonstrations. These laws, most importantly those governing voter registration and political parties, had not yet been enacted, but they expected Pinochet to assent to them within the coming months. Gelbard related his view that the regime's unwillingness to allow moderate democratic parties to compete in a democratic framework ceded the field of active opposition to the hard left, and "communist strength will grow unless real transition to democracy takes place." The non-army junta members, rather than handpicked civilian officials of the regime, opened up contacts with the opposition. However, the officers complained that the uncoordinated nature of the opposition made it difficult to hold a functional dialogue on the upcoming plebiscite, which some junta members wanted to transform into an outright election.

Some opposition figures also wanted to press for an open election, rather than an up-or-down vote on Pinochet, but efforts to select a single candidate came to naught. In October 1986, the Pinochet regime authorized the interior minister to meet with members of the opposition to discuss laws needed to conduct the plebiscite, but the full spectrum of opposition parties boycotted the meeting as a "trap" that would "legitimize [Pinochet's] framework." This move embarassed the junta members who were pushing Pinochet to hold such talks, and they were none too pleased. Air force general Fernando Matthei opined that Pinochet's successes against the opposition were mostly attributable to the "opposition's stupidities." Unless the opposition parties could unite behind the common purpose of returning the country to democratic rule, he saw little hope of moving Pinochet.

In 1987, the regime implemented the laws allowing registration of political parties and voters. The opposition now faced a choice of whether to use the plebiscite, about which they were rationally dubious, or continue to try to agitate outside the system, which had thus far yielded nil. Practically, this would entail parties registering themselves and encouraging voters to register as well. The malaise and indecision of the opposition continued to frustrate junta members who wanted to use the plebiscite as a lever to press for competitive elections.

Pope John Paul II visited Chile in April 1987, and his message of nonviolence and tolerance was later deemed to have helped create an environment conducive to change. By July, a shift began to take place, with the election of Patricio Aylwin as head of the Christian Democratic Party. In contrast to his predecessor, Gabriel Valdes, who believed there was little to be gained by participating in the vote, Aylwin was willing to take the risk, believing there was little to lose. Before being elected, he had noted to Barnes that the "social mobilization" efforts of his party and the rest of the opposition had proven ineffective and it was time to try something new. "His approach is to press the campaign for voter registration so that the military, when they see five million people registered will agree to an open election. If that fails, the opposition can still mobilize to denounce manipulation or fraud, and finally to organize for massive 'no' votes." The situation remained unclear through the rest of the year, however, with the new legal structures for elections in place but offset by closure of newspapers and the arrest of two members of the Vicarate of Solidarity, along with continued reports of torture.

The United States abstained in the UN General Assembly's annual vote on Chile, signaling its disapproval of continued repression. The United States also denied most-favored-nation trading status for the increasingly export-driven Chilean economy. President Reagan and Shultz issued a statement of support for democracy in Chile, buoying the Chilean democrats with such a public display of support. Senator Tom Harkin successfully put forward a proposal that the National Endowment for Democracy be given $1 million to support voter registration and civic education in Chile. In short, the United States through its embassy and overall policy made clear that the return to democracy in Chile was the central objective. However, according to Barnes, the opposition was still not completely committed to the plebiscite, and the progressive members of the junta felt their efforts to convince Pinochet to allow competitive elections, or even to stand as a civilian president rather than a member of the uniformed military, had reached a dead end. A great deal had to change if the plebiscite were to become a wedge for change.

Carl Gershman, president of the National Endowment for Democracy, visited Chile in January pursuant to the assistance package approved by Congress the month before. USAID was also implementing projects to promote voter registration. Large segments of the Chilean electorate were suspicious of the Socialists, and the Socialist Party's leader, Ricardo Lagos, worked hard to overcome these suspicions. The American embassy, with the exception of radicals of both left and right, had maintained relations with the entire political spectrum, including Lagos and his followers. In an effort to portray his moderate wing of the party as a solidly democratic and pro-free-enterprise party, Lagos formed the Party for Democracy, which, after a rigorous process requiring a petition with thousands of signatures, was legalized. In the meantime, activists established a "Command for the 'No'" campaign, with Patricio Aylwin as its spokesman, and established the Committee for Free Elections, which was to observe the registration and voting process. The Catholic Church, particularly through Bishop Carlos Gonzalez, who served as head of the bishops' conference, took an active role in encouraging Chileans to register for the upcoming poll. Democracy activists built up the church-affiliated Crusade for Citizen Participation, or Participa, to address this need. Monica Jimenez, the head of Participa, had been invited to the United States by the State Department to study past methods of voter mobilization, as practiced by labor or the League of Women Voters. Participa managed to register four million voters, using both blanket and targeted efforts. For example, Jimenez targeted the difficult-to-register youth demographic through "rock concerts, where prohibited music was played. We didn't charge admission, but to get in you had to bring your voter registration card. That motivated young people to get registered." But fear on the part of potential voters remained a considerable factor. Fear-mongering pro-regime papers depicted Lagos and Aylwin together with Allende. The regime also had innate advantages in mobilizing for the "Yes" campaign, namely, the entire state apparatus.

Lagos, who was a vocal and visible figure, presented a major target for the regime, which wanted to promote the view that he represented a return to the socialist chaos of the Allende era. Recognizing the difficulty this presented, Lagos made clear his view that Aylwin should lead, not merely be the spokesman for, the "No" campaign. In addition, Lagos worked to dispel perceptions that there was any connection between the "No" campaign and the extreme left. The major communist guerilla wing was opposed to the plebiscite, so imputing a connection became quite difficult for the regime. Lagos also visited the United States to reassure investors and others that the plebiscite did not threaten the successful economic reforms of the Pinochet era.

In the run-up to the plebiscite, Ambassador Barnes and his staff continued their intensive contacts with the political opposition, the government, human rights groups, the Roman Catholic Church, and the media. Part of this effort aimed at forestalling the Pinochet regime's attempts to stack the deck in its favor. And there was real concern that Pinochet would reject the result if it were a "no." Other junta members conveyed that Pinochet had mooted the idea of "doing everything over again" if he lost. As the plebiscite drew closer, the Vicarate of Solidarity came under threat of having its confidential human rights records seized by the regime, which would place a great many people at risk of persecution, arrest, or worse. Bishop Sergio Valech, the vicarate's head, invited Ambassador Barnes to see him, noting that he would have media there to assure the meeting was public. Sure enough, the meeting was shown on the television news, and the pressure on the vicarate eased.

Secretary of State Shultz thought this was a vital duty for a U.S. ambassador and that this "message of solidarity . . . was as important as some of the more tangible help we . . . provided" in helping Chile's democratic forces. "In a police state, such actions by our ambassador and by Chileans seeking democracy were not trivial," Shultz later wrote. When approached by the Chilean government for support on yet another World Bank structural adjustment loan, the U.S. Treasury Department asked for a document describing "the steps taken by the [Government of Chile] on human rights." The Reagan administration was now more unified behind the policy pioneered by Shultz, Barnes, and Abrams.

Prevote television advertisements illustrated the different approaches taken by the "Yes" and "No" campaigns. Even though they were only allowed fifteen-minute, late-night pitches, the "war of the spots" was seen by an overwhelming majority of the Chilean public. The "No" campaign used a theme song of "Happiness is on the way" and was positive in content. Designed by local advertising experts, their spots were, in Jones's words, "brilliant 15-minute political programs . . . very reassuring, very moderate. Nothing to give ammunition to those who claimed that the opposition were a bunch of fire-breathing radicals who would destroy Chile." In contrast, the "Yes" campaign stressed the dire consequences of a "No" victory, connecting the "No" campaign with the Allende period in a vivid and grave fashion. The regime decided to allow those exiled to return prior to the election, deftly exploiting the return of Communist Party leader Volodia Teitelboim. The mainstay of the regime's campaign was fear; it was almost exclusively backward looking.

The weekend before the 5 October vote the head of the Civic Crusade, Monica Jimenez, met with Ambassador Barnes at the urging of Patricio Aylwin. The civic forces had learned from a military source that plans had been drawn up to put down anti-Pinochet demonstrations on election night. The "No" campaign had already devoted a great deal of energy to forestalling communist provocations, and the new warning led Barnes to believe that anti-Pinochet demonstrations would be staged as a pretext for a crackdown. The Chilean chargé was called for consultations at the State Department, and informed of deep U.S. concern over any efforts to derail the vote. Ambassador Barnes met with air force commander Matthei and carabineros commander Stange, who told him that Pinochet had again brought up the possibility of intervening in the plebiscite if he was losing. The two told Barnes that they would argue the next day against any interference in the poll. On Monday, 4 October, the State Department spokesman confirmed at the daily press briefing that Chile had been called for discussions, and expressed concern about the conduct of the next day's vote. According to Jimenez, the U.S. government informed the Chilean foreign ministry that tampering with, or derailing of, the voting process would lead to U.S. refusal to recognize the official result.

The Plebiscite

The plebiscite the next day was a resounding defeat for Pinochet, with 53 percent voting no and 44 percent voting yes, according to the preliminary count by the Committee for Free Elections, which conducted a parallel vote count that evening. International observers present to monitor the conduct of the vote noted that it was orderly. The carabineros were ordered to allow celebrations of an anticipated "No" victory to get out of control so as to provide a pretext for a crackdown, but the men refused to comply. For some hours, the regime's official media hedged on giving any tally, showing American sitcoms after the interior minister told viewers the "Yes" vote was ahead with a minute number of ballots counted. On the Catholic university's TV station, former interior minister Sergio Onofre Jarpa appeared on a talk show with Patricio Aylwin and calmly "set the tone that the world was not going to come to an end if the 'No' won," which both acknowledged looked likely.

In the early morning, the junta was to meet at the presidential palace, La Moneda. Television cameras staked out La Moneda and stopped air force general Matthei on his way into the building, asking how things were proceeding. Matthei calmly delivered the coup de grâce to Pinochet on national TV: "It appears that the 'No' has won." According to Jones, "once Matthei said that on camera, of course he did that very deliberately, and he did it going into the meeting with Pinochet knowing that whatever happened inside, Pinochet's hands were going to be tied by what Matthei said outside." Initially, Pinochet urged his fellow junta members to impose martial law. That failing, he presented junta members with a draft decree granting him emergency powers; Matthei tore it up. At this point, Pinochet relented, "threw up his arms and said in effect it was all over." The interior minister reappeared on television, hours after he last appeared, and began to read off the results. Final results showed a 54 percent–44 percent victory for the "No" vote. The following morning, a million people celebrated their victory in downtown Santiago.

Pinochet had not given his last gasp; violence against opponents continued at some level. But these appeared to be the rearguard actions of a defeated dictator, brought down by the will of the people. Liberalization of the judiciary and media soon followed the plebiscite. One year later, Patricio Aylwin was elected president in the first free elections in two decades; he was inaugurated on 11 March 1990. Chile had restored itself to democracy. Despite difficulties presented by Pinochet's remaining commander in chief of the military and senator for life, concessions he demanded to step down, Chile has proven the resilience of its democracy and is now a much more open society. With democracy much more firmly established, the Chilean government and judiciary have increasingly leapfrogged some of the compromises deemed necessary over a decade ago. When Pinochet was detained in Britain, the question of crimes committed by his regime, for which he had arranged amnesty, came to the fore again in Chile, reopening old wounds and testing the resilience of democracy. However, Chile passed this test, and the Chilean judiciary even found legal avenues to prosecute those who had committed some of the worst crimes on behalf of the regime.

The hand of the American ambassador and his embassy was everywhere apparent in this transition, although the decision, as always, came from the people, not the representatives of a foreign power. Jones believed the U.S. role was *vital, though not sufficient,* to bring about the return of democracy. Holding the plebiscite gave the local democrats a foundation on which to build a coordinated campaign. Members of the U.S. Congress and civil society actors were the first to express solidarity with Chileans oppressed by the Pinochet regime. By the second Reagan term, according to Barnes, "the U.S. attitude became less patient and more critical." As he engaged the opposition, Barnes "never went so far as to side openly with the democratic opposition, but objectively its words and actions created a space and encouragement for the "No" campaign. . . . Everyone knew where the U.S. stood." Barnes noted that prior actions of other American actors magnified the new U.S. policy's impact and that "the coordination between the State Department and the embassy, the maintenance of close links with a number of key members of Congress, and the assistance provided by NGOs" were particularly important. Jones felt the impact was significant in that "although certainly a lot of Chilean effort was essential in getting rid of Pinochet, another essential element was pressure by the United States. We said OKAY—it is your decision to hold the plebiscite . . . it didn't come from us, but your constitution provided for this plebiscite, then let's see how you hold it and respect the decision that comes out." He felt that had the "buddy-buddy" approach toward Pinochet on display in the first Reagan term continued, there might not have been a free vote in 1988. He also saw international attention to the election, including international monitoring, as of great importance. "Had the eyes of the world not been on Chile and had there not been international observers for the plebiscite, then I think that Pinochet in any number of ways would have gotten away with it." In Harry Barnes's view, two lessons to take away from the experience in Chile were that "overall U.S. impact on Chilean behavior was marginal . . . but marginal does not necessarily mean insignificant." By helping Chilean democratic forces to marshal the population and overcome their fear that the plebiscite was a trap, the United States helped them turn the trap around on Pinochet, ending his strongman reign.

The efforts of Ambassador Barnes, Deputy Chief of Mission Jones, and the rest of the embassy staff, while they occurred in a country where the United States had perhaps disproportionate influence, show what determined diplomats can do to assist democrats. Dictators have a difficult time controlling a message sent publicly and visibly. The actions and words of diplomats also can have a decisive, indeed life-or-death, impact on tempering the actions of elements within dictatorships. Barnes says that ambassadors should "not hide out" when waiting for their accreditation when sent to post and should do what they can to meet the broadest cross section of society possible. Barnes's experience also demonstrates the value of deliberate and careful preparation for a mission in an undemocratic country.

Too often, American ambassadors operate not as representatives of the United States but of the State Department bureaucracy, which prefers the warmth of bilateral relations. State has been a reluctant convert, at best, to the idea that democracy is a national security interest. Congress as a body rather consistently has been ahead of the executive branch on democracy promotion, though it is fair to say that in the post-cold-war era requisite financial wherewithal to effect change is lacking. Coordination with Congress is crucial for a protracted effort to help bring about democratic change. When faced with obstacles not only in Chile but also with the hard right in Washington, Barnes was able to count on strong support from his superiors at State, congressional members and staff, and even the president himself. Making such backing clear on the ground further enhanced the ambassador's powers to conduct public diplomacy.

Coordination among international actors can also be critical. In Chile, Barnes helped create a "Western Hemisphere democracy group," which regularly included his counterparts from Argentina, Brazil, and Costa Rica. "We exchanged information and discussed how we (and our governments) might be more effective in promoting greater respect for human rights and democracy." He also found the French ambassador a well-informed, strong advocate of democracy and human rights. It is significant that other democratic governments represented in Chile did not visibly involve themselves in similar coordination activities. The advent of the Community of Democracies should lead to the practice of coordinating democratization assistance and policy.

Democratic, open societies underestimate not only the impact of their official pronouncements and policies in repressed societies but also the import of cultural, "soft" power. Union leader Rodolfo Seguel noted the inspirational effect of Sir Richard Attenborough's film *Gandhi*, released in Chile in 1983, at the same time that copper miners' strikes were signaling deep dissatisfaction with the Pinochet regime. "We all saw it at least twice. We had to, to really get it into ourselves." The powerful nonviolent message clearly resonated with him and the miners, and Seguel saw Polish Solidarity leader Lech Walesa in a continuum following from Mohandas Gandhi: "Both men took up struggles without violence that produced better results than armed confrontation."[16]

The cross-pollination effect of nonviolent democratic success in overthrowing tyranny is immeasurable in its power and builds on its successes. Immediately following the overthrow of Slobodan Milosevic in Serbia in 2000, Zimbabwean and Ivorian demonstrators drew the parallels between their dictators, Robert Mugabe and Robert Guei, and Milosevic. Early democratic demonstrators in Serbia, soon after the rout of the Iraqi army from Kuwait, chanted "Slobo, you are Saddam!" a comparison that was borne out in fact, insofar as Belgrade and Baghdad cooperated extensively on skirting sanctions and military cooperation.[17] After the People Power revolution in the Philippines in 1986, a diplomat posted to East Berlin noted a strong interest on the part of East Germans in how the Filipinos managed to nonviolently oppose a regime that had employed violence against the highest levels of the opposition. Without a doubt, the spread of democracy to neighboring states kept Chilean democracy activists confident that history and time were on their side. A leading democracy today, Chile will host the 2005 Ministerial Meeting of the Community of Democracies as one of its ten convening nations.

Hempstone in Kenya: The Rogue Ambassador

A sharp contrast to Harry Barnes, Smith Hempstone was a swashbuckling former journalist, as comfortable as Ernest Hemingway had been in the beautiful, troubled land of Kenya, where he served from 1989 to 1992, and as unlikely to genuflect to the nation's omnipotent dictator, Daniel arap Moi. Hempstone titled his memoir *Rogue Ambassador*, and with his permission I have drawn from it liberally by way of showing what American ambassadors are supposed to do when posted to a dictatorship.[18]

The dictator, Hempstone reported, greeted his nomination with "scarcely concealed satisfaction. I was a conservative, knew Kenya (and hence must be an admirer of Moi), and had a reputation as a Cold Warrior. And, as a political appointee, presumably I had the ear of President Bush. The Kenyans believed, in short, that they had drawn a patsy, that I would be as mindlessly supportive of Moi as was British High Commissioner Sir John Johnson, a man who preferred order to freedom. Moi and his minions believed that the boat with Washington would not be rocked, that I would amuse myself by hunting, fishing, playing bridge and golf, sunning on the beach, and gawking at the wild animals, with never a troubling word about human rights or democracy. That, after all, was how ambassadors were supposed to comport themselves. It was a classic case of mistaken identity. For the moment, however, it was my intention to try to co-opt Moi. I needed to gain such a position of influence that through him rather than against him I might persuade him, in his own interest as well as Kenya's, to lead the country in a more liberal tack. This, I reasoned, might save the country from . . . explosion. . . . A decent regard for other people's lives demands finding an evolutionary rather than a revolutionary solution to Africa's political problems."

Thus Smith Hempstone neatly defines the conceptual limits a typical ambassador brings to his job, even an ambassador interested in encouraging change—which many are not. At the outset, he thought Moi could be co-opted and reformed, and he thought the only alternative was violence. He specifically said that he did not want to "oust" Moi. As I argue in this book, it is important to work with the dictators but critical to recognize that they are no fools and will do everything possible to hold on to power. Ultimately they must be pushed out. And there is frequently an alternative to violence: a comprehensive strategy to lift the local population's expectations and help them with nonviolent tactics to confront and oust the dictator, using maximum leverage from the democracies.

But, even with these initial limits, Smith Hempstone's own love for Kenyans, his democratic instincts, his understanding that the State Department had changed course, and his firsthand experience with the dictator led him to launch an extraordinary and splendid fight for freedom, one which almost certainly would have led to Moi's ouster had it enjoyed sufficient support from others and had Kenyan democrats hung together.

Hempstone came to realize that "I was the spokesman not just of George Bush but also of George Washington and Thomas Jefferson, of James Madison and James Monroe, of Woodrow Wilson and Franklin Roosevelt. If I did not speak up for American ideas and ideals, if I did not champion democracy, who would? This was the new diplomacy as opposed to the traditional."

What he was up against became clear very soon after his arrival in December 1989. As Kenyan Anglican bishop Alexander Muge said to him, "Moi's cabinet is composed of some people who can be described as professional murderers." Moi's own qualification for this label was made clear on Hempstone's watch in February 2000, when Moi's foreign minister Robert Ouko was murdered. Following a visit to Washington that month in which Moi was received only by an assistant secretary at the State Department, Moi apparently grew suspicious that Foreign Minister Ouko had been received at higher levels in secret; perhaps he had secret discussions about replacing Moi. "Moi is said to have personally beaten Ouko, demanding to know what Bush and [Secretary of State James] Baker had said to him in Washington . . . [and] having allegedly beaten Ouko unconscious" and allegedly ordered that he be tortured. The next day Ouko was allegedly shot twice in the head in Moi's office. Whatever the truth about whether Moi beat and murdered Ouko, as Hempstone notes, "this is what a great many Kenyans believe happened." Moi dismissed the investigative commission looking into the Ouko killing before it could render a verdict and eventually rehired the minister suspected by Scotland Yard of doing the actual shooting.

The BBC reported on 31 July 2001, that Moi was suing Ambassador Hempstone for defamation over his book's account of Robert Ouko's death. Moi denied any involvement in the killing. The BBC notes laconically that Ouko's body was found "having been shot, dowsed with petrol and set alight."

It is good to note at this point that many of the dictators now in power have either murdered people themselves or personally ordered the murder of individuals and groups. There is a tendency to depersonalize this fact, to allege that a "regime," a "government," a "system" is responsible for these acts. We have a hard time dealing with the fact that someone the president of the United States and his ambassador may work with, invite to the White House, shake hands with, even praise, is a murderer, quite often a mass murderer. But that is the reality.

Just as Hempstone was arriving in Nairobi, the U.S. ambassador in neighboring Tanzania, Donald K. Petterson, a career officer, cabled Secretary of State Baker suggesting it was time to develop with our Western allies an African policy that more explicitly and broadly tied development aid to movement toward democracy. "In principle I had no problem with the Petterson cable," Hempstone responded. "While the Cold War had compelled the U.S. to support some extremely unsavory characters in Africa and elsewhere, the Russians, as Petterson pointed out, apparently were out of the game. Under these altered circumstances there was no reason for the U.S., as the sole remaining superpower, to support tyrants. Now, if ever there was one, was the time to push democracy abroad. Having said that, I did feel that the supporters of such a policy were gravely underestimating the difficulties of implementing such a blanket policy in Africa."

In the first quarter of 1990, President Bush and Secretary Baker made it clear on several occasions that it was U.S. policy to support the expansion of democracy in Africa. Thus, at a mid-April State Department conference on democracy, the forty U.S. ambassadors in Africa could only "vie with one another in the fervency of their support and belief in democratization. This took up so much time that the devil's advocate [Hempstone], who was scheduled to speak last, had little time to enumerate the difficulties each ambassador would surely face in implementing this policy. I didn't mind much, since my heart was on the other side of the issue. In any case, having heartily endorsed the new policy, most of the ambassadors returned to their posts and observed a discreet silence when the issue of expanding democracy came up. As for me, I returned to Kenya resolved to implement President Bush's policy with all the vigor and determination I could muster."

Making Waves

On 3 May, Hempstone had his chance to make a statement at "a most revolutionary forum, the Rotary Club of Nairobi. The early part of my speech was pretty routine stuff about American trade and investment in Kenya. . . . I got into the meat of the thing toward the end of my speech when I told the Rotarians that 'a strong political tide is flowing in our Congress, which controls the purse strings, to concentrate our economic assistance on those of the world's nations that nourish democratic institutions, defend human rights, and practice multiparty politics.' . . . None of this struck me as particularly inflammatory, but 'U.S. Mounts Pressure for Multi-Parties' headlined the next morning's 'Nation,' Kenya's largest and most responsible daily. 'Don't dictate to us,' huffed Kolonzo Musyoka, then organizing secretary of the Kenya African National Union (KANU). . . . Burudi Nabwera, minister of state in the Office of the President (and a former ambassador to the U.S.), ordered the provincial administrations to monitor my movements outside of Nairobi. Elijah Mwangale, the minister of livestock development and the most ardent of the Moi toadies—in a speech at the coast, he asserted that even the fish in the sea bowed down before the president—accused me of financially supporting the Kenyan dissidents. The foreign office told me, only three days before it was due to happen, that Moi would not open the U.S. trade fair. . . . The intensity of the reaction unquestionably was fueled by a coincidence: my Rotary Club speech was delivered the same day that two former Kikuyu cabinet ministers, Kenneth Matiba and Charles Rubia, announced the formation of a movement (not a political party, which would have been illegal) called the Forum for the Restoration of Democracy, known by its acronym FORD. They called for the repeal of Article 2(a) of the Constitution, establishing KANU as the only legal political party (Moi put this through in 1982), demanded new elections—those of 1988 had been blatantly corrupt even by Kenyan standards—and a limit on presidential tenure to two four-year terms. Moi immediately denounced Matiba and Rubia as traitors 'in the pay of foreign powers.' There was no collusion between myself and the leaders of FORD. . . . I had had about four hours' notice of the initiative."

This left Hempstone with a problem. While he was expected to encourage the expansion of democracy, it was also American policy that he should do what he could to encourage the sale of American goods in Kenya. In a back-channel, handwritten note, Hempstone told Moi that he meant no disrespect with his speech. "Indeed, if Kenya was to enter a new era of multiparty politics and clean government, I and the U.S. government would prefer that he lead (which was true). Change, I insisted, was inevitable. The choice was between becoming the beneficiary of change, or its victim. . . . Even if we disagreed politically, good economic relations were in the interest of both nations." Moi showed up to open the U.S. trade fair.

In fact, throughout Smith Hempstone's tour as ambassador, even as disputes grew and became still more public, even as Moi tried to have him removed, Hempstone remained able to get a wide variety of important things done with Moi personally. For example, Washington thought it would be very difficult to get Moi's support on giving safe haven to hundreds of anti-Qaddafi former Libyan soldiers and basing U.S. forces in Kenya for operations in Somalia. Hempstone was able to deliver these through his direct relationship with Moi. He understood that it was largely useless on the most sensitive and important issues to deal with the foreign minister or other lower-level officials, all of whom were deathly afraid of Moi and unable to make even minor decisions. Hempstone understood that dictators need us more than we need them and they will respect and cooperate with someone who stands up to them in the right ways. Hempstone notes that Moi seemed both to like him personally and to fear him, and I strongly believe that this is the right mix. Dictators live in a world of fear. They try to make everyone else, including foreign ambassadors, fear them; and the dictators themselves fear everyone else. It is the currency of their lives; it is a currency we need to learn to use. Ultimately, Ambassador Hempstone's case is a classic lesson that it is possible, though not simple, to do business with a dictator even as we pressure him and help local forces achieve a democratic breakthrough.

Hempstone lacked one crucial tool: full support from home. "While Jane Perlez, East African correspondent for the *New York Times*, had described me a week earlier as 'the only American ambassador on the continent to have publicly raised the matter of the expansion of democracy,'" Hempstone recalls, "the huzzahs from the State Department had not been exactly deafening."

On 18 May, Assistant Secretary of State for African Affairs Hank Cohen, along with Ambassador Hempstone, met with Moi in Nairobi, and Cohen made it clear that he hoped relations between the two countries could be conducted on a business-as-usual basis. "He said that the U.S. Government had 'not yet' made movement toward a multiparty system a condition for American economic assistance, although he admitted that 'individuals in the U.S. Congress' favored such an approach. . . . Cohen indicated [to Hempstone] that he did not want to meet with or talk to any Kenyan dissidents. . . . From then on it was the Kenyan government's publicly stated position that relations between the United States and Kenya were fine. If there were a problem it was Hempstone, who, they insisted, was a maverick acting on his own. And that situation could be easily remedied by having Hempstone recalled, or by being so unpleasant to him that he resigned or requested a transfer."

Cohen's undermining of Hempstone's authority and ability to help the democrats only grew worse. During a visit to Nairobi in August, Cohen even agreed to meet with Moi without Hempstone present. For nondiplomat readers such an act may not seem as extraordinary and appalling as it is. An American ambassador is the personal envoy of the president of the United States to another government, not an assistant secretary of state. The ambassador represents all elements of the U.S. government. Her own direct relationship with the leader of the other government is central to our ability to function as a nation overseas. You simply cannot undermine her and leave her in place. The choice really is up or down: either support her or replace her. Unfortunately, Cohen was not alone in agreeing to play the dictator's game. Kissinger made a fine art out of precisely this same approach with regard to U.S. ambassadors in communist countries, so much so that he once went to Moscow to meet with the leaders of the Soviet Union and the American ambassador did not even know he was in the country. In the case of Pinochet and others, the belief that higher authority in Washington did not support the U.S. ambassadors' democratizing efforts prolonged the dictators' time in power and risked large-scale violence. Sometimes sufficient support ultimately arrived from Washington and elsewhere—but it arrived too late for Kenyans and Hempstone.

The ambassador plowed ahead nonetheless. At his Fourth of July reception for six hundred government officials, principal dissident leaders, Kenyan and American business leaders, churchmen, ambassadors, ranchers, lawyers, wildlife experts, military officers, and physicians, Hempstone read out two key sentences from the Declaration of Independence:

> We hold these truths to be self-evident, that all men are created equal, that they are endowed by their Creator with certain unalienable Rights, that among these are Life, Liberty and the pursuit of Happiness. That to secure these rights, Governments are instituted among Men, deriving their powers from the consent of the governed.

Hempstone added, "America sought dominion over no nation, but . . . when we see a government that has been elected by the people in free elections, and that then honestly serves the people it represents, we rejoice and support that government."

This quotation from the Declaration of Independence ought to be read aloud by every American ambassador at every Fourth of July reception every year in every one of the remaining dictatorships until there are no more dictators. Ambassadors from other democracies certainly can find similar national or international texts to make the same points at their national days. This is a splendid example of the creative use of existing opportunities to promote freedom. It just requires the will to get started!

Ambassador Hempstone recognized early on that he needed to work with, and provide leadership for, a number of constituencies. En route to Nairobi, he stopped in London, Paris, Rome, and the Vatican in recognition of the critical role others can play. None of these governments or their ambassadors in Kenya was a good ally for democrats in Kenya and Hempstone's efforts in the beginning, but the Catholic Church and other faiths definitely were. The Danes, Swedes, and Norwegians were solid. In fact, Moi even broke diplomatic relations with Norway and expelled its ambassador over Norway's effort to provided legal counsel to some Kenyan democrats who had lived in Norway and whom Moi had arrested. "Two powerful ambassadors—because they gave so much money to Kenya—whom I desperately wanted to get on board were Naohiro Kumagai of Japan and Franz Freiherr von Metzingen of Germany. In neither case was I successful, although von Metzingen's successor, Bernd Mutzelburg, was to become my close friend, political heir apparent, and a courageous fighter for freedom. Kaumagai's successor, one of Japan's very few female ambassadors, helped a bit at the end. While I had good friends among them, it is an article of faith that no African ambassador will criticize an African head of state or his government. Large groups of ambassadors—the South Asians, the Latin Americans, the Arabs and the East Europeans—were either uninterested in the issue, too concerned about their personal careers, or too unsure of their status to take a stance."

Hempstone worked away at his colleagues, while Moi's own continuing barbarism helped focus the minds of other governments. By the summer of 1991 there had been a considerable evolution. With the arrival of the new German ambassador, Hempstone was able to constitute a formidable Gang of Five—the German, Danish, Swedish, Canadian, and American ambassadors. While the local British ambassador was still not on board, British Foreign Secretary Douglas Hurd and other politicians in London were increasingly embarrassed by their close relationship with the corrupt Moi.

Whatever a visiting State Department official might say to Moi, it helped Hempstone immensely that Democratic senators Pat Leahy, Dennis DeConcini, Paul Simon, Chuck Robb, and Barbara Mikulski came to Nairobi that summer "showing that they too cared about human rights and democracy, that I was not just a rogue ambassador pursuing his own maverick policies."

Hempstone also notes, "My personal view of the Kenyan government had evolved a great deal by the summer of 1991. When I arrived in Nairobi in 1989, I had a positive view of Moi. . . . I was prepared to give Moi a break, to believe that he was a good man surrounded by corrupt and brutal advisors. But as I moved deeper into this heart of darkness . . . the brutal suppression . . . made it clear that one man set the tone of the Kenyan government and that man was Moi."

This is an all-too-frequent way of thinking. Somehow it is not the president who is committing the atrocities and corruption, it is someone lower down whom he cannot quite control, or some pressure group, some extremists not allowing him to be more democratic—this in dictatorships where anyone close to the situation knows precisely who is responsible for the repression.

Taking Sides

At the end of July, Ambassador Hempstone was presented with "one of those rare moments in which the opportunity is given to alter the course of history. . . . The Anglican Church of the Province of Kenya, the National Council of Churches of Kenya, and the Law Society of Kenya were to hold a joint service of Thanksgiving and prayer at Nairobi's All Saints Cathedral on Sunday July 28. Would I read the lesson—Ephesians 6:10–20. . . . The lesson was an appropriate one. It was also, given the political climate of Kenya, dynamite. (Kenya's leading democrats had been threatened with arrest by security agents if they attended the service.)" The passage reads:

> Finally, my brethren, be strong in the Lord, and in the power of His might. Put on the whole armor of God, that ye may be able to stand against the wiles of the devil. For we wrestle not against flesh and blood, but against principalities, against powers, against rulers of the darkness of this world, against spiritual wickedness in high places. Wherefore take unto you the whole armor of God, that ye may be able to withstand in the evil day, and having done all, to stand. Stand therefore, having your loins girt about with the truth, and having on the breastplate of righteousness; and your feet shod with the preparation of the gospel of peace; above all, taking the shield of faith, wherewith ye shall be able to quench all the fiery darts of the wicked. And take the helmet of salvation, and the sword of the Spirit, which is the word of God; praying always with

all prayer and supplication in the Spirit, and watching thereunto with all perseverance and supplication for all saints: and for me, that utterance may be given unto me, that I may open my mouth boldly, to make known the mystery of the gospel, for which I am an ambassador in bonds; that therein I may speak boldly, as I ought to speak.

"I cabled Cohen telling him that . . . we had reached 'an historic moment, a watershed in the history of Kenya,'" recalls Hempstone, and that "the United States government 'might wish to line itself up finally and irrevocably on the side of the angels.' I admitted that such a move would further chill our relations with Kenya, but that 'great benefits in a post-Moi Kenya might accrue.' 'What say you?' I concluded. 'Shall I speak or remain silent?' I suppose I suspected what the answer would be. I was instructed that I should not read the lesson nor even attend the service."

In deciding whether to seek Washington's permission to attend the service and to speak, Hempstone faced an issue that deserves larger attention in the struggle for democracy and the role of embassies as freedom houses. Facing an earlier effort to undermine him, Hempstone had written Deputy Secretary of State Lawrence Eagleburger (then number two in the department) offering to resign. Eagleburger wrote back: "Do your job and stop worrying about the flakes, the nay-sayers and the old women who populate this place. I'll take care of them and you. The *only* danger you now face is that you will begin to second-guess yourself and your actions because of your worries about support back here. Don't fall victim to that disease! Everyone else here does. From you I expect your normal, nasty, sweet, self-effacing, modest, tough self!"

Before we leave Ephesians 6:10–20, let me recommend it to all ambassadors serving in dictatorships. It can and must be read in public to good effect in the future. Let ambassadors find occasions to free themselves from their "bonds" and speak "against rulers of the darkness of this world, against spiritual wickedness in high places . . . boldly"!

Despite the State Department's timidity in July, Kenyan democrats and some democratic ambassadors and their governments brought mounting pressure on Moi into the fall and winter. The opposition planned and requested permission for rallies but its members were preemptively arrested. When they managed to hold a rally on 16 November in Kamukunji, they were beaten and more arrests took place. Prime Minister John Major, Queen Elizabeth II, and Foreign Secretary Hurd had frank discussions with Moi in September and October. Major told Moi that human rights must be improved, that internal dialogue must be conducted with the opposition, and that new and clean elections had to be held. However, as Hempstone notes, the British, who had a low opinion of the dissidents, felt that change could only come from Moi.

This low opinion of democrats is widespread and it is a fundamental impediment to democratic governments' willingness to oust dictators. Governments rarely see a clear and desirable alternative leadership ready to replace the dictator. There are endless discussions in embassies and foreign ministries about the weakness of almost any movement and its leaders functioning as a future government. But of course this search for certainty is precisely the wrong approach. The strength of democracy is that it throws up new and unpredicted leaders all the time and provides a relatively quick and peaceful mechanism for removing those who fail to measure up. And the dissidents themselves very often are not the ones chosen by the populace to be their prime ministers and presidents, even though they are honored for bringing freedom. In fact they often do not have the right qualities to run a government. The point is that democracy will provide better governance than any dictator now present in any country.

Hempstone's own attitude toward, and relations with, the democrats seems to have been about right. From his earliest days as ambassador he recognized that not everything important happens inside the government or inside the capital. He established relations with all sectors of Kenyan society including personal relations with all the opposition leaders. He traveled extensively outside Nairobi, meeting with opposition leaders all across Kenya. He even went to England to meet with a key opposition leader living in exile. He worked closely with the dissidents, counseling, cautioning, and encouraging them, asking what he could do to be helpful, and repeatedly and fiercely intervening with Moi and his cronies to defend their rights. But through it all he maintained a healthy skepticism about the dissidents, both as individuals and as groups.

As pressures mounted, Moi became even more nervous and abusive. On 18 November, he had his foreign minister, Wilson Ndolo Ayah, call in and rake over the coals the ambassadors of Germany, Denmark, Sweden, Canada, Finland, and the United States. Ayah accused Hempstone of trying to overthrow the government, encouraging dissidents to disobey the law, and "managing the opposition." He called Hempstone a racist and regretted that President Bush had appointed a person of his caliber to be ambassador to Kenya. Next day the rubber-stamp parliament formally called upon the U.S. government to recall Hempstone, and one member of parliament suggested he should be "clubbed." Hempstone responded that the opposition would be considerably better organized than it was if in fact he were its manager, defended his right under the Vienna Convention to maintain contact with dissidents, and stated that he would always speak out against the denial of basic human rights and freedoms.

"Suddenly it occurred to Moi that Kenya's aid donors were due to meet in Paris within a week and that they were unlikely to be pleased with either the suppression of the Kamukunji demonstration or the campaign of invective against the American ambassador," writes Hempstone. "If Moi had any doubts about what the American attitude in Paris might be, they should have been clarified by a November 22 letter to Bush signed by twenty-one members of Congress from both sides of the aisle. . . . When its economic failures were combined with its heavy-handed suppression of democratic values, there was not much left to defend. Only the French and the Italians could be relied upon to stay out of the debate. Britain, once Moi's staunchest defender, was one no more." The donors announced that they would freeze all new aid for six months.

Solidarity Pays: Kenyan Democrats Hang Separately

The opposition in Kenya was encouraged by this decision, and FORD leader Shikulu declared publicly that "without Hempstone we certainly wouldn't have come as far as we have as quickly as we have." On 26 November, Hempstone had predicted in a cable to Washington that Moi would take some dramatic steps. Sure enough, "somewhat surprisingly, given the fact that, a few days before, government officials had been calling me 'a criminal, a drug pusher, and an enemy of the state,' Moi agreed to meet with Hempstone and visiting Deputy Assistant Secretary of State Bob Houdek on 2 December. Moi urged the United States to "detach itself from the dissidents and follow diplomatic conventions." Houdek said that he had been instructed to urge Moi to announce publicly and without delay that Kenya would hold fresh elections in which non-KANU candidates could participate. On 3 December, "to the astonishment of almost everyone," Moi announced publicly that he wanted to legalize multiparty politics once again, although he complained that he had been forced into the decision by foreigners and warned of the dangers of tribal warfare. In an article from Nairobi dated 6 December, the *Washington Post* reported:

> About 500 supporters of Odinga's FORD then marched down Moi Avenue to the U.S. Embassy, in what appeared to be a spontaneous and emotional show of gratitude for the prominent role played by U.S. Ambassador Smith Hempstone, whose pronouncements in favor of more pluralism have irked the Kenyan government but made him a hero to the opposition. The marchers, some waving tree branches, sat down in front of the embassy, chanting "Up with Hempstone!" and refused to leave until the ambassador emerged to speak briefly from behind a security grill.

Unfortunately, as Hempstone notes, "Multiparty politics had scarcely been legalized when the opposition began to fragment. . . . One did not need to be a mathematical genius to understand that a unified opposition could win the presidential race but a divided one could not." Hempstone, the German ambassador, and a number of leading Kenyan democrats failed to convince the Big Three leaders of the opposition to agree on a single candidate for president. The elections took place on 29 December 1992. "Given the disparity between the government and the fragmented opposition in national organization, money and coercive power, the fledgling opposition did very well indeed," writes Hempstone. "But the fact remains that they beat themselves through their own disunity. And, because under the Kenyan constitution ninety percent of the power resides in the presidency rather than the parliament, they lost all when they lost the presidency . . . no matter how many parliamentary seats they won."

Hempstone continues: "The sour mood that had engulfed Kenya since the elections prevailed during the visit to Kenya in February 1993 of Baroness Chalker, the minister for overseas development and the leading Africanist in Prime Minister John Major's government. When she came, despite opposition from Kenyan democrats who believed Britain still had not broken sufficiently with Moi, demonstrators pelted the British High Commission with rotten eggs, tomatoes, and garbage before moving on to the U.S. Embassy, where they shouted pro-American slogans." Hempstone left Kenya later that month, and the intervening years tragically and unnecessarily saw Moi continue in power for another decade of suffering and decline for Kenyans and repeated acts of terrorism against Americans and others.

At the end of his memoir, Ambassador Hempstone offers a few parting thoughts:

> Every American ambassador, it seems to me, should both comfort the afflicted and afflict the comfortable. Governments, after all, were instituted to serve men, not to prey upon them.
>
> It is profoundly racist to suggest that democracy is impossible in Africa. It will be difficult and messy. The process is likely to be a protracted one. But we owe it to ourselves as much as to the Africans to support the pro-democracy forces in their struggle. The support of human rights and the expansion of democracy will always be a component of U.S. diplomacy, but we need to decide how large a component it will be.
>
> I do not think that the more than $1 billion we have poured into Kenya since 1963 has done much to improve the life of the average Kenyan. More could be spent to support the creation and growth of democratic institutions, professional societies, women's groups, publications and the like.
>
> There's no shortage of villains [for Africa's poverty and backwardness]. Drought, locust pestilences, deforestation, declining world commodity prices, and the legacy of colonialism (which inflicted socialism on Africa) all have had

a deleterious effect on the continent. But the principal blame must lie with the criminally inept, corrupt, and venal leadership that has held sway over the continent for three decades of its independence. Until Africa's Daniel arap Mois are swept onto the rubbish heap of history, there cannot be much hope for Kenya or the continent. That process will be neither quick nor easy. But that does not excuse us from trying to help Africa, nor Africans from trying to help themselves. Tomorrow will bring another generation, and a new day.

Kenya also demonstrates the critical importance of *consulates and consuls* as well as embassies and ambassadors. In the BBC's *Focus on Africa* journal January–March 2002, Professor Mohamed Hyder, a leading member of Mombasa's Muslim community writes: "If we go back to 1991 we find that the United States was the darling of the Muslim population in Kenya in general and of Mombasa in particular. At that time US diplomats protected the interests of Mombasa Muslims. One of the most significant figures in all this was the American consul in Mombasa, Don Stader. . . . He forged a special relationship between the Mombasa Muslims and the United States government. . . . Through him they frequently met the US ambassador to Kenya, as well as leading US senators. But just as important, members of the Mombasa Muslim community [the Muslim capital of Kenya] could meet each other at a time when a gathering of more than ten people who were not members of the ruling party could be interpreted as an act of treachery. And when push came to shove, Stader provided actual physical security to Kenyan Muslims hounded by the police. But since then the US Consulate in Mombasa has closed and as a result the US relationship with Muslims here has deteriorated. On top of this came the increased police scrutiny that Muslims came under following the bombing of the American Embassy in Nairobi in 1998. Once the helpful intervention of Stader and other US diplomats had gone, Muslim anger with the Kenyan government and the radicalization of Kenya's Muslims increased. I tried to bring home to the Kenyan government that the answer to the political despair felt by Muslims was not to swing yet more police batons. Unfortunately, President Daniel arap Moi was not in a mood to listen. Since September 11th the government has done little to placate Muslim sentiment. . . . President Bush and Prime Minister Blair have made repeated assurances that the war they are waging is not against Islam but against terrorism. . . . What will count are positive actions to help Muslims raise their political and material fortunes in Kenya where they are being discriminated against wherever and whenever the government can get away with it."

In his memoirs, Smith Hempstone points out that the U.S. consulate in Mombasa was a one-man post and that Stader had no American help, not even a secretary. The cost for keeping the consulate open was minimal, and Smith Hempstone fought hard against its closing when Washington so decided, even offering to reduce his budget in Nairobi by a comparable amount. But there is a general failure to understand that maintaining—indeed, expanding—the number of democratic consulates inside dictatorships is one of the most cost-effective weapons we have for reducing the security threat to us and helping people gain control over their own destinies. Much of the process that starts, sustains, and eventually wins a nonviolent struggle to unseat a dictator and defeat terrorism unfolds outside the capital city.

Starting in 1975, I argued that the United States should have a diplomatic presence in Kosovo to develop Albanian language capability within the Foreign Service and to understand and influence developments within the Kosovar and larger Albanian world (for decades we had no embassy in Albania). No one can know now, but history might have been radically different had we been there earlier in this way; tens of thousands of lives might have been spared, and democracy in Kosovo, Albania, and even Serbia might have come much earlier. We now need to take full advantage of the network of consulates we and other democracies have in dictatorships like China. We should review all forty-five dictatorships to determine where a new presence outside the capital could make a critical difference. In places where we do not even have an embassy, like North Korea and Iran, we should move vigorously to open one. This does not legitimize a dictator unless we allow that perception to predominate; the main purpose in opening an embassy should be, and be seen to be, to help the forces for democracy.

Of course, the ultimate determinant of whether a country will return to or develop democracy is the quality of indigenous civic leadership. Without brave leaders in unions, political parties, and the Catholic lay community who were willing to take the calculated risk of confronting the regime nonviolently, Chile might have bucked the democratic wave in Latin America even longer. Had the Kenyans pulled together and applied the techniques of strategic nonviolence, they would have brought down Moi much earlier. This obvious fact does not absolve the democratic world from its duty to help fellow democrats living under dictatorship—indeed, it reinforces that responsibility to the democrats in the streets who do the difficult work.

Ambassador in Budapest

Ambassadors Barnes and Hempstone show how to deal with dictators in a Latin American and African context. Arriving in Budapest in 1986 as a freshly minted, forty-five-year-old ambassador, I learned on the job that many of the same techniques were effective in dealing with a European dictator. At various points in this book, I have cited examples from my four years' tenure. I allow the rest of the story of the American embassy's efforts during those years to be told by journalists who covered it. From helping Mickey Mouse and Ronald McDonald to break through the Iron Curtain, to founding the first business school in the communist world, to bearing witness at Imre Nagy's reburial, to marching in the streets, I hope the pictures and articles shown in figures 6.1–6.10 will give some flavor of how much fun, how exhilarating, and of course occasionally how tough it can be to help others gain their freedom. Staid, conventional ambassadors in despotisms are missing the best moment in their lives.

INTERNATIONAL HERALD TRIBUNE, THURSDAY, MARCH 16, 1989

Hungary's Opposition Marches Unhindered To Mark 1848 Uprising

By Henry Kamm
New York Times Service

BUDAPEST — Tens of thousands of opponents of the Communist government demonstrated freely in the streets of Budapest on Wednesday to commemorate the 1848 uprising against Austrian rule, which was put down with bloodshed and the help of the Soviet Army.

Among the crowd, which Western diplomats estimated at 75,000, was the U.S. ambassador, Mark Palmer. For more than three hours, Mr. Palmer walked inconspicuously amid the demonstrators and listened to speeches by opposition leaders at the bases of monuments and the steps of the national television headquarters.

He was accompanied by Miklos Haraszti, an author and editor of an opposition journal, who came to Hungary for the occasion from Bard College in Annandale-on-Hudson, where he is teaching for the current academic year.

Mr. Palmer said he had "no doubt where George Bush would have wanted me to be today."

He kept in good official standing by attending two wreath-laying ceremonies and the government's own celebration of the anniversary before joining the opposition marchers.

For the first time, the annual highlight of the opposition calendar received explicit parade permission from the authorities. The leadership of Prime Minister Karoly Grosz legitimized the march when it restoring March 15 to its former status as a national holiday. Businesses and schools were closed.

As recently as three years ago, the marchers were still met by the police, who blocked their way, tear-gassed and beat them and confiscated their identity cards.

In one speech, Gaspar Miklos Tamas, a philosopher, said: "If next year this country is a state ruled by laws, we hope we will celebrate together."

The liberalization in political comment and organization of the last months has caused considerable debate about the state of political freedom. The tens of thousands who marched Wednesday and cheered the speakers clearly believed that the Communist Party continues to hold virtually exclusive power, although it hesitates to exercise it to the full.

"Hungary has joined to a certain extent the free democratic nations, but not because of what the Communist Party does," Mr. Tamas said. "We have joined the ranks of democratic parties, but the Communist Party hasn't joined us."

In a particularly bold address, Viktor Orban, a 26-year-old representative of the major independent youth organization, won roaring cheers when he demanded that the Communist party withdraw from the army, the police and places of work.

Most Hungarians in opposition say that, no matter how liberal the present oratory of some party leaders, the party exercises undiminished power over the people through its absolute control over the security organs.

Demands for the official restoration to honor Imre Nagy, the executed leader of the 1956 uprising, recurred in speeches and on banners.

■ 'Freedom Billboards'

Warsaw authorities set up "freedom billboards" in the streets on Wednesday, Reuters reported. They recalled the "Democracy Wall" established in Beijing during political liberalization in 1978-79.

Figure 6.1.   "Hungary's Opposition Marches Unhindered," by Henry Kamm, *International Herald Tribune*, 16 March 1989. Reproduced in part courtesy of the *International Herald Tribune*, 2002.

Figure 6.2. Aerial view of the 1989 march, Budapest, Hungary.

DAILY

of the Hungarian News Agency MTI/Budapest.

U.S. AMBASSADOR MEETS OPPOSITION ROUNDTABLE

Mark Palmer, US Ambassador to Hungary, held talks on economic political questions with parties and organizations belonging to the Opposition Roundtable in Hungarian Parliament on Tuesday.

During the course of the meeting, representatives of the Bajcsy-Zsilinszky Friendship Society, the Federation of Young Democrats (Fidesz), the Independent Smallholders' Party, the Christian Democratic People's Party, the Hungarian Democratic Forum, the Hungarian People's Party, the Social Democratic Party of Hungary and the Federation of Free Democrats set out their views on Hungary's future investment policy, the cut in state subsidies and the implementation of an anti-inflationary policy. They also touched upon the subject of how guarantees to protect foreign investments could be established in Hungary, and how the West could assist the Hungarian economy in finding its footing.

Figure 6.3. "US Ambassador Meets Opposition Roundtable," *Daily News*, 29 July 1989. Reprinted courtesy of the Hungary News Agency, MTI, Budapest.

Figure 6.4.   Ambassador Mark Palmer in front of the U.S. Embassy in Budapest with Mickey Mouse and Donald Duck.

Un ambassadeur américain omniprésent

Un personnage inattendu est en train de prendre une place de plus en plus active à la vie politique hongroise : l'ambassadeur des Etats-Unis à Budapest, Mark Palmer, omniprésent ces temps-ci dans les médias officiels hongrois, tout particulièrement dans les moments de crise.

C'est ainsi que les téléspectateurs hongrois ont eu la surprise de voir au journal télévisé, la veille des grandes manifestations du 15 mars, un reportage sur une visite de M. Palmer au chef de la milice ouvrière, corps de forces de l'ordre très impopulaire. « De cordiale, commentait le journaliste, cette rencontre est devenue amicale lorsque les deux hommes se sont aperçus qu'ils parlaient tous deux le russe »... De quoi faire

pâlir l'ambassadeur soviétique, qui, lui, ne se risquerait pas à se montrer dans de telles circonstances sous peine de soulever l'indignation générale.

Les allures de Kennedy et les invariables nœuds papillon de M. Palmer n'expliquent pas à eux seuls l'engouement des médias hongrois. Ardent défenseur d'une politique de resserrement des liens entre les pays réformistes de l'Europe socialiste et l'Occident, il est perçu par les dirigeants hongrois à la fois comme une caution à l'égard de leur opinion publique, et comme une planche de salut économique potentielle. En échange M. Palmer, ne se contente pas, dit-on à Budapest, de jouer au tennis avec le premier

ministre Miklos Nemeth : il se permet de prôner prudence et stabilité dans la transition au gouvernement à la veille d'un plenum crucial du comité central, ou d'expliquer au contraire que les réformes ne progressent pas assez. C'était il y a trois jours à la télévision. M. Palmer a eu droit à un gros plan sur les petits écrans lors de la cérémonie officielle de la fête nationale de mercredi... Quelques heures plus tard, il se mêlait à la foule des manifestants de l'opposition... et les caméras étaient encore là. Il ne faut pas plus pour faire dire à certains que M. Palmer se comporte déjà en proconsul.

S. K.

Figure 6.5.   "Un ambassadeur américain omniprésent," by Sylvie Kaufmann, *Le Monde*, 17 March 1989. Reprinted courtesy of *Le Monde*, Paris.

SATURDAY, JULY 8, 1989 **13**

The Man Who's Was Always There

By WILLIAM ECHIKSON
The Christian Science Monitor

BUDAPEST — To his admirers, Mark Palmer is the prototype U.S. ambassador, ever active and imaginative, formulating original new ways of piercing the Iron Curtain. To his detractors, Palmer is too visible and too vocal.

One thing is sure: Ambassador Palmer is visible. Hungarian television showed him milling about the crowd both during the March 15 opposition demonstration and the June 16 reburial of executed Premier Imre Nagy. His ties with Hungarian Communist Party leaders also are excellent. His regular tennis partner is Harvard-educated Prime Minister Miklos Nemeth.

Perhaps more than any other single individual, Ambassador Palmer is responsible for articulating a Western policy toward a region where economic failure is forcing change, and where room for maneuver has expanded thanks to Mikhail Gorbachev's policies. In Palmer's opinion, the West should traverse the East-West divide with all kinds of links between governments, businesses, churches, environmentalists, students, journalists.

The United States, for example, could send 1,000 English teachers to Eastern Europe, Palmer says. That would be a bargain way of propagating Western ideas. More students from Eastern Europe also could come live and study with Western families.

In economics, the Palmer approach calls for explicit market-oriented lending. World Bank and IMF credits would become conditional on specific reforms: reducing bureaucracy, promoting private enterprise and liberalizing rules for foreign investment. Debt relief should be granted, but only "in the context of far-reaching reform." Large-scale credits to the governments would be wasted in inefficient state industries. Instead, Palmer says, loans should be smaller and targeted to specific projects. Direct foreign investment should promote private enterprise.

Palmer has helped sponsor the communist world's first Western-style business school. It opened its doors in Budapest this spring. He has increased the amount of fellowships for study in the United States, ensuring that many go to leaders of Hungary's budding democratic opposition.

President Bush reportedly will announce a set of "Palmerite" proposals during his trip to Budapest. One is the launching of a 100-million-dollar mutual fund to invest in Budapest's stock market. Another is private funding for the democratic opposition.

These measures, ironically, draw applause from Hungary's reform-minded Communists.

"Palmer is a good friend of Hungary," says Janos Barabas, the Communist Party's new ideology chief. "He's active, strong."

But many other Hungarians find him too active or too strong. They criticize him for permitting a painting of himself to be hung in the new business school, and for reportedly trying to ensure that opposition members do not adopt a too radically anti-Soviet stance.

"He acts like a proconsul," complains Janos Betlen, a journalist at Hungarian national radio. "The Russian ambassador here could never afford such an appearance. If he were American ambassador to a Latin American (nation), he would be expelled in 24 hours."

"I'm no proconsul," Palmer responds. "I'm just . . . keeping lines of communication open to everyone. We don't have any special powers here, we just have our values."

Figure 6.6.   "The Man Who Was Always There," by William Echikson, *Christian Science Monitor*, 8 July 1989. Reprinted with permission.

Figure 6.7. "Martyr's Funeral," *Daily News*, 12 June 1989. Reprinted courtesy of the Hungary News Agency, MTI, Budapest.

'EW YORK TIMES **INTERNATIONAL** WEDNESDAY, OCTOBER 4, 1989

Godollo Journal

How to Disarm Hungary (Hamburgers? Tennis?

By HENRY KAMM
Special to The New York Times

GODOLLO, Hungary, Sept. 29 — A large American flag covered a window by the entrance to the House of Culture in this college town 20 miles northeast of Budapest. Pinned to it was a photograph of a boyish-looking man with a bow tie, whose smile has become familiar throughout Hungary.

A notice under the portrait announced a meeting of the Godollo Opposition Club, which the man in the bow tie would address this evening. A Louis Armstrong tape resounded over the public-address system to make him feel at home.

Not all the people milling about before the meeting were members of the opposition. "Heaven forbid!" Istvan Safrany said. "We're Reds."

"Speak for yourself," rebuked a man standing next to him. "I'm no Communist. I prefer Mr. Palmer."

Both Sides of the Street

But Ambassador Mark Palmer is popular not only with the opposition.

Mr. Safrany, too, said he preferred the American envoy. "We expect more from that side," he said with nonideological pragmatism. "Those over there fooled us." There was no doubt about which country he meant by the vague allusion.

It is difficult these days not to find Mr. Palmer somewhere in the public eye.

He has been observed marching with the opposition, taking to lunch at the local McDonald's the general secretary of the Communist Party, Karoly Grosz, and on another occasion his friend, the Soviet Ambassador, an event the Hungarian press christened "the hamburger summit."

"There may be different views about what is diplomacy," the 48-year-old Mr. Palmer said in a conversation in his office. "Whether it's sitting behind the desk and going to cocktail parties or whether it's important to be visible, it's important to be the United States in another country, to speak out about our values and about the fate of the nation that you're sent to."

Friends in the Party

Mr. Palmer, former speechwriter to Secretaries of State, Deputy Assistant Secretary for European Affairs and one of the department's specialists on Soviet-American relations, has left Hungarians in no doubt which school he adheres to. He had hoped to be named Assistant Secretary of State in the Bush Administration, but when he did not get that post, he returned here as enthusiastic as ever for his job.

And at a time of transition, when Hungary seeks to show in many ways that it wants no longer to be seen as a satellite in the Soviet orbit, when a whole nation appears to "expect

more from that side," the Ambassador's style is attuned to its policy.

"I think probably it's fair to say that next to the Soviet Ambassador I have the best contacts with the party leadership of anybody in this city," the Ambassador said. "I'm very close to Pozsgay, I'm close to Nemeth, with Nyers I play tennis."

Together with Mr. Grosz, the three men constitute the party's Presidium. Imre Pozsgay is likely to be elected President of the republic before the year is out, Miklos Nemeth is Prime Minister, and Rezso Nyers presides over the Presidium.

The No. 2 Ambassador

"I've worked hard with him also," Mr. Palmer said of his Soviet colleague, Boris I. Stukalin. "When I called on him initially I said to him: 'You know you're the most important ambassador in this city, but I'm the second-most important ambassador. We can either fight or work together.' So we have a good, strong relationship. He does occasionally joke with me about how active I am."

The Ambassador emphasized the view that the United States had no interest in creating problems between Hungary and the Soviet Union or "to push them out of the Warsaw Pact."

Mr. Palmer is aware that he works close to the line that separates active diplomacy from interference. Asked

about it in a lively question session after his speech here, he replied, to roars of laughter followed by applause from the standing-room-only audience, "Other ambassadors had much more involvement with Hungarian politics before."

In his office, Mr. Palmer noted that he had associated openly with the opposition since he arrived in 1986. Dissidents in those days lived on the margin of society.

An Opening Gesture

"The very first thing I did was to invite Janos Kis and Laszlo Rajk, two very visible figures of the democratic movement, for dinner in the Gellert Hotel dining room," Mr. Palmer recalled. "I wanted to announce that this was my greeting card, my way of arriving in Hungary."

The Ambassador said that he avoided endorsing any single group and met with all. But, he said, "I have tried to show in a variety of ways that Americans side with the democratic forces in this country."

"I'm open about supporting the opposition parties, including getting money for them from the National Endowment for Democracy," he continued. "I think we should be proud of it."

He said that marching in the opposition demonstration on March 15, the

anniversary of the 1848 uprising, pressed by Austria and Russia, his high point.

A Nutritionist at His Side

While preaching democracy in tics, Mr. Palmer has been equ outspoken in praising free enterp and urging the privatization of gary's economy. He said he co ered his active role in creatin; American-style management t ing institute his second most im tant achievement.

The Ambassador is joined achievement by his wife, Dr. Sus Palmer. She spent a sabbatical here from her directorship of the and nutrition board of the Nat Academy of Sciences instru postgraduate physicians in Bud: in her specialty, the relationshi tween nutrition and cancer, hea ness and chronic diseases. She just returned here and is workin several projects.

Among those in the opposition office in the House of Culture, e siasm was high over Mr. Palr coming. They said they had no pl invite other ambassadors. So wh Palmer?

"Oh, everybody knows him," a replied. "On March 15 he par with the opposition. A very thing."

Mark Palmer, the United States Ambassador to Hungary, at the House of Culture in Godollo, a college to near Budapest, where he attended a meeting of the Godollo Opposition Club.

The New York T

Figure 6.8. "How to Disarm Hungary (Hamburgers? Tennis?)," by Henry Kamm, *New York Times International*, 4 October 1989. Copyright © 1989 New York Times Co. Reprinted by permission.

Americans Help Establish Hungary Managers' School

By HENRY KAMM

Special to The New York Times

BUDAPEST, Nov. 1 — With Abel G. Aganbegyan, economic adviser to the Soviet leader Mikhail S. Gorbachev, beaming approval, Hungarian, American and Italian partners today signed into being an American-style management training institute here, the only one of its kind in Communist Europe.

An American, Prof. Daniel S. Fogel, on leave as associate dean for executive and international programs at Tulane University in New Orleans, was appointed dean and academic director of the new International Management Center.

The university-level center is a tri-national joint venture of an American foundation created by George Soros, the Hungarian-born Wall Street financier; the Milan Chamber of Commerce; the San Paolo Bank of Italy; the Hungarian Credit Bank, the Hungarian Chamber of Commerce, and Szenzor, a management consulting concern.

The main interest at the signing ceremony focused on the surprising presence of Mr. Aganbegyan, chairman of the economics section of the Soviet Academy of Sciences. He sat on the dais together with the founding partners and Mark Palmer, the United States Ambassador to Hungary. Speakers credited Mr. Palmer with being the founding father of the institute.

In an interview, Mr. Aganbegyan suggested that he, too, had had a share in the creation of the institute and had run into resistance from some Kremlin officials who opposed more active Soviet participation.

In a brief speech of greeting, the Soviet academician said all members of his branch of the academy hailed the new management center. He said it marked the "friendship and active relations between East and West in the new conditions of perestroika," the Russian term for Mr. Gorbachev's program of restructuring.

Elaborating on this in the inter-

Continued on Page D7

view, Mr. Aganbegyan said: "We have new policies, perestroika, and surely we need new kinds of managers of all ranks. Management is not only a matter of feeling but also scientific work, and this must be studied not only through books and lectures but by really taking part in this process of education in real life."

After saying that "some chiefs, members of high rank" in Moscow had blocked Soviet participation in the project, he added, "They think we don't need this, that we can do it our own way." But he said he would work to send Soviet students to the institute and expected no obstacles.

Classes Begin in February

Dsudsanna Ranki, the institute's 34-year-old managing director, and Professor Fogel announced that short courses would begin in February and full-scale operations in September. The dean said two American professors, two Canadians and one Briton, along with five Hungarians, would constitute the faculty.

The center plans to enroll 200 to 300 full-time students for its first year of operation and hopes to have 500 to 600 eventually. They are expected to be young managers, sent by their employers. Education is usually free in a Communist country, but Professor Fogel said the tuition would be 500,000 to 600,000 forints, or $10,000 to $12,000.

The school will be housed in a renovated castle in a park on the outskirts of Budapest.

Figure 6.9. "Americans Help Establish Hungary Manager's School," *New York Times International*, 2 November 1988. Copyright © 1988 New York Times Co. Reprinted by permission.

Figure 6.10. Ambassador Mark Palmer and his wife, Dr. Sushma Palmer, with Hungary Manager's School Director Zsuzsana Ranki.

The Use of Nonviolent Force

Never doubt that a small group of thoughtful, committed citizens can change the world. Indeed, it's the only thing that ever has.

—Margaret Mead

There is ultimately no difference between the underlying functional basis of power in a democracy and in a dictatorship. No ruler can retain power indefinitely without the consent or acquiescence of the people. The majority of people cannot be compelled by force of arms to comply with the edicts of government if they are willing and able to resist. Stalinist Russia is always cited as the case that proves the rule that totalitarian control, if indeed it is total, can be stable. But had the German invasion in World War II not furnished Stalin with a cause that could rally popular support, it is likely that murdering potential and imagined opponents—his style of keeping control in the 1930s—would have eventually inspired a coup or an uprising against his unpredictable brutality. If you threaten everyone, all loyalty flees.

From time to time circumstances compel the international community or interested nations to put pressure on dictators to alleviate repression or change the way they rule. Trying to force dictators to modify the worst aspects of their behavior may certainly help to lessen the human suffering they cause. But softening repression does not eliminate its cause; eliminating the dictator is the only way to do that. History provides no account of a dictator being converted into a democrat while still in power or of relinquishing power of his own volition. The only way for democracy to emerge is for the dictator to go.

How the dictator is challenged determines whether and how quickly he can be ousted, and it also has a crucial effect on whether sustainable democracy ensues. Armed rebellions usually fail, often even before they can begin. Even if they succeed, what comes after is typically no better, and frequently worse, than what they displace. Leaders of guerrilla movements are adept at the use of violence and take those skills with them when they take over presidential mansions; that is why violent revolutions typically produce repressive regimes. The people inherit only a new set of jailers.

But there is another set of strategies for dissolving dictatorial power and establishing democracy, and it has a remarkable record of success. In their seminal book, A Force More Powerful, Peter Ackerman and Jack Du Vall document a dozen cases in which nonviolent popular movements prevailed against seemingly overwhelming odds and took power away from arbitrary rulers. My own experiences in the U.S. civil rights movement and in diplomatic service in communist countries confirm their view that political systems that deny people their rights can best be taken apart from the inside—by the people themselves.

No dictator can hold power without sowing the seeds of popular discontent. Payoffs to cronies and constables who crack down on opponents eventually exude the smell of corruption, which is always deeply unpopular. The mothers and fathers of young dissidents who are "disappeared" do not forget who is responsible for sundering their families. And few dictators are known for their brilliance in economic management: the economic crises that frequently follow can pile up more dry tinder of public resentment.

From the moment when the match of organized nonviolent opposition is first struck to the day that the dictator steps down, years can elapse—or only weeks. Almost a decade passed between the first stirrings of organized dissidence against the Polish communist regime in the early 1970s and the appearance of Solidarity in the midst of the Gdansk shipyard strike. But forty years earlier, a general strike by the citizens of El Salvador had toppled a military tyrant in a matter of days. The difference is not in how much violence the state is prepared to use—the Salvadoran general was one of his country's bloodiest rulers. What makes for success is developing and communicating clear objectives for the struggle, organizing and mobilizing people on a wide scale, applying maximum pressure to the pillars of a regime's support, and protecting the movement from inevitable repression.

In his landmark tract, From Dictatorship to Democracy (Boston: Albert Einstein Institution, 2002), which has been translated into a dozen languages and used as a bible by dissidents from Burma to Serbia, Gene Sharp—the master theoretician of nonviolent conflict—identifies 198 separate methods of nonviolent action. These are given in the appendix to chapter 7 and are classified into three broad categories: nonviolent protest and persuasion, noncooperation (social, economic, and political), and nonviolent intervention. A description and historical examples of each can be found in volume 2 of Sharp's *Politics of Nonviolent Action*.[1] From social and economic boycotts to industrial and rent strikes, and from outright civil disobedience to physical interventions such as sit-ins and occupations, the panoply of nonviolent weapons is far more diverse and inventive than the broadcast media's preoccupation with street marches would lead idle viewers to imagine.

That nonviolent resistance can be at once robust and precise, widespread and carefully timed, is typically unexpected by outsiders but not by the dictators who are its targets. They do not share the common misconceptions that nonviolent action is passive and reactive and that its leaders are amateurs or pacifists. As Ackerman and Du Vall observe, nonviolent movements that develop a systematic strategy to undermine their opponents and seize power are deliberately engaging in conflict, albeit with different resources and weapons. By choosing a method of struggle different from what their violent oppressors know best, they often put dictators at a disadvantage from the outset. Most nonviolent leaders work patiently for years to formulate the ideas and test the methods that will propel their movements forward; they may be ordinary citizens when they start, but they are seasoned veterans of fateful conflicts when they finish.

Even though these strategies do not use guns or explosives, they are not forms of conflict for the fainthearted. Nonviolent fighters often have to make protracted physical and economic sacrifices before they liberate their peoples. Many have to endure arrest, imprisonment, and torture. Many have been murdered. Yet tens of thousands of them, in conflict after conflict on five continents, have willingly faced these risks, in the interest of achieving freedom and justice.

Shrewd leadership can help them minimize risks and maximize the political damage their movement inflicts on the dictator. In movements that need people at the working level of society to join open or clandestine opposition, leaders can enlarge the ranks only by showing people that the goals of the struggle are worthy, the strategy sound. So unlike organizations that employ violence, nonviolent movements cannot be operated like an army, strictly from the top down. Their leaders have to rely on the same skills that are needed in running a democracy: persuading people to go along and encouraging initiative at the grass roots. A nonviolent campaign is effective when it overstretches the capacity of a dictator to maintain business as usual, but it can do that only when it empowers people everywhere to challenge his control.

Nonviolent power is therefore always rooted in the mind and action of the individual, and sometimes that action seems innocuous when the struggle is young. As Jan Bubenik, the Czech student leader noted to me, most of the movements against communist rulers in central and eastern Europe first took the form of samizdat, or self-published books, pamphlets, and other literature. The civic action to curb the military dictatorship in Argentina in the late 1970s began with a handful of unsophisticated mothers of the disappeared marching in the capital's central square. Nonviolent combatants understand something that dictators do not: to be sustainable, social or political action has to be built on the choice of individuals to engage in it, not on state edicts that prod unwilling subjects into compliance.

Although nonviolent resistance begins with the individual citizen, it has far more potential than violent insurrection to enlist all parts of the oppressed society in the cause. While violent skirmishing with police or soldiers may appeal to young firebrands, it frightens off older people and those without a taste for physical confrontation—in other words, the most stable elements of civil society, whose support is essential for lasting social or political change. By giving people from all walks of life (even children) ways of participating in a movement, nonviolent strategies enlarge the inventory of resources and tools available to undermine a regime.

This eclectic, inclusive approach to mobilizing support can even extend to people within the regime. Dissatisfaction with a dictator is not limited to those who are politically motivated to oppose him. From lower-level apparatchiks all the way up to the praetorian guard, there is often fear and ambivalence in the ranks of the dictator's chosen servants and defenders. The greater the repression that the dictator has employed, the greater the opportunity to subvert the loyalty of those defenders—but not if the movement vilifies them. When Ferdinand Marcos fell in the Philippines in 1986, and when Slobodan Milosevic fell in Serbia in 2000, their own military officers and police refused final orders to crack down on the opposition. That could not have happened had nonviolent organizers demonized or picked fights with security and military services.

Whether it is manifested in crowded public rallies or the emptiness of boycotted stores, in the boisterous occupation of key factories or the public stillness of a general strike, the vitality of a nonviolent movement necessarily raises popular expectations that it can work where other methods may have failed. Unless people are encouraged by the chance of victory to take action, they will never believe that change is possible. Nothing aids a dictator like the assumption that he cannot be vigorously challenged, and when he is challenged, the confidence of those whose support he requires to remain in power begins to erode. Then, when a movement's momentum builds from one engagement to the next, the whole nation will realize that the dictator's survival is in question.

No dictator is exempt from having to face this question once a nonviolent movement opens up space for opposition. If we think that the dictators in Beijing and Pyongyang are too ruthless to be bothered by nonviolent challengers, we should revisit the story of Charlotte Israel, the German woman who organized a sit-in demonstration in the heart of Berlin in World War II and forced the Nazis to release her husband and thousands of other Jewish spouses who had been taken to the death camps.

That a few famous totalitarian regimes were not dislodged in the past century does not prove a rule that dictators cannot be undone without violence. The roll call of dictatorships and colonial regimes that have fallen to nonviolent popular forces is too long to overlook, and it proves that the potential of new or revived democracy exists right in the very place that dictatorship appears to persist. A few examples[2] follow.

- French invasion of the Ruhr stymied by nonviolent resistance, 1923
- British viceroy in India forced to negotiate with Mohandas Gandhi, 1931
- Gen. Maximiliano Hernandez Martinez, El Salvador, forced to resign, 1944
- Legal segregation in the American South forced down by nonviolent action, 1960s
- Communist regime in Poland forced to legalize Solidarity, 1980
- Ferdinand Marcos forced to resign in the Philippines, 1986
- Gen. Augusto Pinochet in Chile forced to stand down by nonviolent organizing, 1987
- Communist regimes in eastern Europe and Mongolia forced out by nonviolent movements, 1989
- The regime in South Africa forced to negotiate an end to apartheid, 1990
- Slobodan Milosevic forced out of office by a nonviolent uprising, 2000

At the zenith of each of these regimes' power, they were thought to be invincible to everything but violent revolution. Indeed, while dictatorships may look invulnerable, they are actually extraordinarily fragile. They depend entirely on the cooperation of the population, on the combination of fear and isolation that compels people to go along with a system the dictator believes is right. Getting individuals and groups to stand up and declare openly that "the emperor has no clothes" is the essence of the task.

In almost every successful case, however, there was one further element in the eventual victory: the judicious support of external allies, who gave money and training to the movements or denied commercial privileges and political approval to the regimes. Without international support for poll watching and campaigning, popular fronts against Pinochet and Milosevic might not have succeeded. Without the crucial role of the Catholic Church in Poland and the financial sanctions against the white government in Pretoria, communism and apartheid would likely have taken longer to disintegrate. And sometimes belatedly, but nonetheless critically, democratic governments made clear that they no longer supported the dictator.

Nevertheless, in comparison to the West's frequent underwriting of violent movements against authoritarian regimes over the past fifty years, assistance to nonviolent movements has been comparatively meager. Although they have seen the willingness of indigenous people to apply nonviolent power against dictators, and their ingenuity in doing so, international agencies and Western foreign ministries have provided little physical and financial assistance. Evidently they fail to understand how versatile and universal are the uses of strategic nonviolent action in dissolving dictatorships. When conflicts arise, their impulse is to intervene militarily rather than to shift the means of revolution from violent to nonviolent strategies.

For the sake of the global democratic enterprise and the future peace of the world, this neglect of nonviolent conflict has to end. Nations must be governed "by the people." Nonviolent action by the people must make it so.

Two-Stage Campaign to Oust Dictators

Let us look at what the rest of the world can do to help those inside who want to conduct a nonviolent, two-stage campaign to oust a dictator. Democratic activists from sixteen countries, from successful campaigns and those still under way, created the following framework at a workshop sponsored by Freedom House and the International Center on Nonviolent Conflict in January 2002.

Stage 1: Communicating and Organizing

At the outset of this stage, civil liberties are nonexistent or very limited. Police are active in suppressing any sign of independent activity. Universities, media, parliament, and unions are either disbanded or under strict government control. At this point the objective of a nonviolent movement may simply be to come into existence. Initially the movement may consist simply of conversations among individuals and the beginnings of "writing for the drawer" or for very limited, clandestine distribution. Even brave citizens are reluctant to become involved in antigovernment activities, so education and spreading the word are key activities. Early campaign issues and organizations can be ostensibly nonpolitical and nonthreatening to the regime—health and the environment, for example.

As a campaign gains support, the goal can become to create groups and organizations that, acting together, can work as a shadow or parallel "counter-state." Underground press, think tanks, and political parties all work to weaken the authority and scope of the dictator and to create a working civil society. An experienced nonviolent operator noted that a movement can "create a situation where you have two parallel worlds. One is a ceremonial world, with pretty streets, dinner parties, and pleasant manners. And then there is the underground world." In *The Little Conspirator,* a master operator in this underground world reveals some of the tricks of the trade. Written and published by Czelaw Bielecki, Urszula Sikorska, and Jan K. Kelus in 1982, *The Little Conspirator* was the most popular pamphlet in the Polish underground that year and was the manual that guided the forces that ultimately brought down the communist regime. The excerpt that follows is from chapter 1, written by Czelaw Bielecki:

Conspiracy is based on the premise that the authorities and their activities are illegal. They not only violate treaties of human rights, which they have ratified, the Constitution, which they imposed on us, but even their own executive regulations for the police, including for example, the ban against using truncheons in closed spaces.

When you begin to build your underground organization it is important, first, to look for co-conspirators among your close friends. People you can be sure of, whom you have known for years, and whose background you have personally checked. Later, once your basic organizational structure is in place, and the enterprise is rolling, then, and only then, should you begin to make contacts with other underground groups. Don't play the role of grand conspirator without a real organization.

The rule of underground organization is that a small group can conduct big business. The more autonomous a group is, the less chance there is of it being wiped-out, and the fewer the organizational problems it will experience. A company should be organized to minimize contacts, both internally and with other groups. Each specialized cell, like any well-run business, transfers finished goods to other companies with the absolute minimum of contacts.

Establishing an underground press is an end in itself. Newspapers can serve as a means of communication between cells which otherwise would be isolated for security reasons. What is more, they are a forum which enables leaders to identify themselves with specific intellectual and political positions.

Newspapers do not only spread ideas; for the underground, they are the best source of information, money and materials. An underground press serves as a training ground, it schools novices in techniques of conspiracy. It teaches them how to cope with, and overcome fear. One measure of the novices' progress, in dealing with these problems, is how many bundles of newspaper are transported

The process of producing and distributing an underground newspaper teaches all the elementary techniques of conspiracy. It demonstrates the need for each section's isolation from other sections (like between the printers and distributors). It demands the use of dead-letter boxes, as, for example, between the editorial section and the printers. The rule of segregation between those engaged in the wholesale transportation and distribution, and those retailing the newspaper is observed.

In the beginning everyone experiences problems. Everyone is afraid when they first transport underground newspapers, and deliver them to an unknown man at a strange place. That man is frightened too, but when both overcome their fear, it is like the opening of a door between two prison cells. Later, together, they force open the next door, and the next. Then they will smile at each other, they realize that freedom is not something to believe in, but something to practice.[3]

International parties can help people overcome their initial fear and reluctance to participate, pressure the dictator, and support attempts to organize. Possible actions include:

- *Naming.* Nongovernmental organizations, media groups, individual countries, and international organizations can play a crucial role in highlighting dictators' human rights abuses and lack of democratic practices. They can collect information and reveal specific cases, bringing them to public attention. Amnesty International, Human Rights Watch, and other human rights groups play a particularly courageous and critical role here.
- *Shaming.* In today's global culture, there is a growing desire on the part of dictators to achieve at least a semblance of legitimacy. Public discrediting of despots by major international players can expose conjuring acts.
- *Strategic advice.* Workshop participants mentioned that it would have been helpful had they been aware earlier in their movements of strategic thought on nonviolent resistance. While all methods may not be applicable to all cases, a working knowledge of available options can open new avenues of action to a movement. Participants suggested multiple methods of information distribution, including distribution of a standardized textbook on strategic nonviolent conflict and radio programs geared toward civil resistance. Training is critical.
- *Material assistance for specific projects.* At this early stage seed money is needed—for example, for press equipment or information distribution. Financial and other support to get civil society groups started and functioning is important.

Perhaps the most important contribution outsiders can make at this early stage is to help raise expectations by showing an entire nation that others in similar circumstances have ousted dictators and that they too can succeed. It is striking how low expectations are, even among dissidents inside and among democracy advocates outside. The central task is to change assumptions, to get people excited by the vision of a free society, to jumpstart people power by showing that nonviolent means will work quickly and decisively once undertaken on a massive scale.

The central argument against raising expectations has been that it is "irresponsible," that encouraging people to organize and go into the streets will only lead to further repression, and that foreigners who do so must be willing to intervene with military force. But repression and suffering are an everyday reality in dictatorships, even without people organizing and going peacefully into the streets. While there are undoubtedly risks and sacrifices, and while the first efforts may not succeed, in most cases there is really no alternative. No one would condemn the North Koreans or Burmese or Iranians to suffer for decades more under oppression, corruption, and backwardness. Nor should the rest of the world have to endure these dictators' threats to peace and support for terrorism, drug smuggling, and other depredations.

The U.S. government and others have been slow to encourage struggles for freedom ever since 1956, when Radio Free Europe supposedly promised the people of Hungary that American troops would intervene if they rose against the occupying Soviet army. In fact, as Arch Puddington's excellent book *Broadcasting Freedom: The Cold War Triumph of Radio Free Europe and Radio Liberty* documents, Radio Free Europe never broadcast any such promise.[4]

Ultimately, the decision to confront a dictator is one only the individuals themselves can make. They know the dangers. What many of them do not know is that they can succeed and that today's democracies and democrats are ready to offer peaceful political assistance and resources (although there will be times when military intervention is sensible and required to supplement the efforts of local democrats). There is nothing irresponsible in helping oppressed people achieve democracy.

Stage 2: Facing and Ousting

At this phase, the opposition has gained enough power to face the state. As one movement leader put it, the government may be "the owners of the buildings, and ceremonial state. But we are the owners of civilian society." The conflict is now in the open, fought with strikes, protests, civil disobedience, or boycotts on one side and the threat of arrests, beatings, or exile on the other. While the opposition may not yet have the power to accomplish its large-scale goals, it has become large enough to ensure its continued existence even if major leaders are taken out. Initial fear has been overcome and organizational strength is growing.

The movement's goals at this point are to:

- *Create a sense of ubiquity.* For example, the Otpor movement in Serbia plastered the streets with 1.5 million stickers and pamphlets.
- *Cultivate external support.*
- *Apply pressure on the dictator* through a variety of nonviolent tactics, including but not restricted to strikes, speeches, underground press or radio, processions, public assemblies, boycotts, and social, economic, political, and legal noncooperation.
- *Search for legal means through which the government can be challenged* via elections, laws, or international regulations and treaties. In Chile, Pinochet's call for a national plebiscite provided the opposition movement with an ideal opportunity.
- *Attempt to co-opt the regime's pillars of support,* especially the repressive apparatus, including the army, police, and civil service. In Serbia, a deliberate plan to identify with police forces in the latter part of the nonviolent campaign helped protect protesters against brutality and bring down the dictator.

External actors can play a key role in the success of a campaign during this stage. As the process of resistance is underway, international parties can facilitate the process through:

- *Providing material assistance.* By this point, the movement should have formulated a coherent strategy and specific tactics, but it may lack the financial means to undertake them fully. Foreign aid, in response to need expressed on the ground, can be a critical factor in the success of the movement.
- *Training leaders in nonviolent tactics.* In Serbia, trainers provided by the International Republican Institute, Freedom House, and others proved extremely successful in preparing groups like Otpor for their nonviolent campaign.
- *Applying external pressure on dictatorship.* As the opposition gains power, international actors can help to pressure the dictator into more specific concessions (e.g., fair elections) through targeted sanctions and public denunciation. Participants mentioned forming a "world conspiracy" against the dictator.
- *Establishing rules of the game.* International actors can establish a set of rules to make a peaceful settlement possible and hold the dictator accountable through international treaties, laws, and tribunals.
- *Providing support for democratic actions.* External parties can also help by providing poll watchers, sponsoring public education on voting, or donating financial support to "get out the vote" campaigns.

- *Undermining the pillars of support*. The democracies either have or can establish contacts with the dictator's military, police, intelligence, and other security services. They should use their influence to persuade these services to refuse the dictator's orders to open fire on the democrats. Getting to that point is the key to the entire nonviolent process.

Finding a nexus of issues and events is key. Nonviolent action can be sparked by a variety of causes. The generalized discontent present in all dictatorships, the universal "we-they" attitude toward the dictators and their allies, can turn to action in response to a specific event or concern. The soft spot could be the jailing or murder of a popular figure, and an international inquiry could help unearth the facts and generate reaction. Sometimes the issue is economic, and outside help could be offered contingent on the dictator's taking certain actions. Or a perceived weakness can be created, leading to a loss of standing in the rest of the world. These windows of opportunity can be used to raise the level of crisis within the dictatorship and widen political space for the opposition.

Another way to support the forces of resistance is to organize events outside the country. For example, as a State Department officer working with the White House and with Afghan groups around the world, I helped organize "Afghanistan Day" on 21 March 1982 to protest the Soviet occupation. President Reagan issued a proclamation, we held a ceremony in the White House East Room, there was a rally around the Washington Monument, demonstrations were held around the world at Soviet embassies, and we issued a special publication documenting the horrors of occupation. (Of course, within Afghanistan the struggle against the Soviets was carried on by violent means; to this day the Afghans are trying to find ways to disarm resistance fighters and militias and find peaceful means to run their own society.)

Such opportunities abound today. Iran's teachers and students are in the streets demanding their rights. This calls out for support from democrats abroad to show their solidarity through declaring and organizing a worldwide "Iran Democracy Day." It should be followed with days for "A Democratic China," "Equality for Women in Saudi Arabia," and "A Dictator-Free Africa," among others.

People Power: Two Battlegrounds

The nonviolent strategies of people inside a dictatorship, searching for portals to democracy, and the mind-sets of foreign governments and democratic institutions that help or hinder them are closely intertwined. Nowhere are these complicated links better exemplified than in the cases of the Philippines of the 1980s and Serbia in 2000.

In the Philippines, an indigenous democratic movement fashioned the effective nonviolent strategy that has entered the language as "People Power" and used it to break the back of the dictatorship. This was accomplished without the full support of the world's most powerful democracy. America's long, special relationship with this former colony and the Philippines' steady assistance during the Vietnam conflict shaped a policy of acceptance that could not quite give up on Marcos. No matter that the regime had devolved from a popular, democratically elected one to a corrupt, brutal dictatorship—one did not let down one's friends. In a sense, people power worked here in spite of American policy, except toward the very end—when it was decisive.

By contrast, American involvement in the ouster of Serbia's president Slobodan Milosevic was sharp, and violent, with NATO bombers striking targets in Serbia and Kosovo, where a Serbian-led "cleansing" of ethnic Albanians had murdered and displaced thousands of citizens of what remained of Yugoslavia. NATO and Russia also sent thousands of peacekeepers into Kosovo to help the battered region back to its feet. This might have been avoided if we had backed Serbia's democratic opposition earlier. In any case, once democratic opposition bloomed again following the bombing and aggressively applied the tactics of strategic nonviolence to overthrow Milosevic, it was aided with money and training from the West. Here people power worked because America and other democracies pitched in on the side of nonviolent transition.

The Philippines

The story of Ferdinand Marcos in the Philippines perfectly illustrates how democracies tend to stand by old "friends," no matter their crimes. But it also shows how the United States and other established democracies can play a key, if belated, role in ensuring that the democrat-turned-dictator exits the scene. I have relied heavily on Peter Ackerman and Jack Du Vall's book, *A Force More Powerful*, and George Shultz's memoirs, for different aspects of the story.[5] In addition, I had the opportunity to discuss the situation with a number of the senior American officials involved, whose contributions are appreciated. And I used relevant oral history interviews with still others involved.[6]

Following its victory in the Spanish-American War of 1898, the United States became colonial overlord of the Philippine archipelago, a collection of about seven thousand islands in the South China Sea. The Philippines were not without ardent advocates of independence, and the new colonial power brutally suppressed this option, as a number of American anticolonialists, most notably Mark Twain, documented very well at the turn of the century in the *Atlantic Monthly* and other publications. However, by the 1930s, the United States was on a trajectory to give the Philippines their independence; the process was derailed by the Japanese invasion. The Philippines received their independence in 1947, retaining a special relationship with the United States.

Ferdinand Marcos was born into a political family and became a political figure in his own right with a reputation for violence in the newly independent Philippines in the 1950s. He was elected to the presidency in 1965 on a platform of fighting corruption and promoting land reform to narrow the vast gulf between rich and poor. However, he concentrated on public works, with massive attendant borrowing. Marcos was a staunch supporter of the growing American war effort in Vietnam, and the major military installations in the archipelago, the naval base at Subic Bay and the air force base at Clark Field, played an important role in that conflict. Marcos was reelected in 1969, but that election was widely criticized domestically for bribery and political violence. The *Philippines Free Press* commented, "No election since 1949 has touched off louder cries of fraud and terrorism than this one."

Integral to the feudal system that developed under Ferdinand Marcos was his wife, Imelda, a former beauty queen. Many observers deemed their relationship, especially at later stages, as a political marriage of convenience. She certainly exhibited remarkable ambition and apparently later saw herself in the role of successor to her older husband. One American diplomat said of her, "I don't think that I have ever known any other person whom I would truly describe as amoral. . . . Simply without the instincts that most of us have that there is a right and a wrong. . . . She required constant adulation and attention." Another described her as "shameless in her pursuit of money and power." As with other dictatorial power couples (Slobodan Milosevic and Mira Markovic spring to mind), views vary as to which of the two was dominant.

As his second term moved toward its end, the Marcoses grew increasingly worried about maintaining their control. Students protested the war in Vietnam, and there was general discontent about the Marcoses' heavy-handed and increasingly flamboyant exercise of power and patronage. The criticism from established political opponents was also on the rise. A communist insurgent group, the New People's Army (NPA), was becoming a serious problem. The Marcoses saw the plurality election of socialist Salvador Allende in 1971 in Chile as a frightening portent, but they also regarded it as an opportunity to blunt any potential criticism from the United States for their increasingly autocratic collective rule. According to American diplomat Richard Finn, who served in the American embassy in Manila in 1971, Imelda Marcos related to both the U.S. ambassador and the director of the Central Intelligence Agency

(CIA), Richard Helms, the fear that the Marcoses "faced a very similar threat in the form of a communist threat to the government, a political threat at first but backed by violence to attempt to take over the government." Finn's own view was that Marcos was "blowing up what was admittedly a nasty problem . . . but never an unmanageable one or one threatening to take over the whole system in the Philippines." Even were Marcos constitutionally eligible to run for a third term in 1973, it was doubtful whether he could win. The political officer at the embassy felt that Marcos's motivation in pushing the Chile analogy was as self-serving as it was realistic. However, given Marcos's general support for the United States, the embassy "went along" with "our friend and supporter [who] would do almost anything we asked him to do."

This pliant American posture apparently emboldened the Marcoses to push further. In September 1972, President Marcos imposed martial law and made radical changes to the country's political and legal system, beginning with removing the two-term limit, nullifying the constitution, banning public assembly, suspending habeas corpus, and arresting political opponents on charges of plotting the overthrow of the government. Marcos also launched a frontal assault on freedom of the press by closing newspapers and taking over broadcasters. At the time, the United States was winding down its involvement in Vietnam, and many Asian allies feared the United States would withdraw from the region altogether. The Marcoses benefited from America's preoccupations elsewhere. In fact, their regime actually received *increased* American backing following the declaration of martial law, with military aid doubling in the Nixon-Ford era.

With the strictures of rule of law and democracy now completely swept aside, the Marcoses pursued a level of corruption and graft hitherto unseen even in the freewheeling Philippines. Skimming from all major economic activity in the country and building a staggering web of patronage, the couple became enormously wealthy and spared no expense in promoting themselves. Foreign capital in the form of loans continued to be readily available to the Philippines after martial law was declared, nearly quadrupling the country's debt from $2.7 billion in 1972 to $10.7 billion by 1977. The downward trend in the Philippines' economic fortunes, especially relative to other Asian countries, accelerated greatly. As Robert G. Rich, who later served as deputy chief of mission in Manila, said: "For almost 20 years 10 percent of the GNP had been siphoned off into nonproductive activities, much of it abroad. Now that 10 percent probably made the difference between the Philippines being as economically successful as Taiwan, Hong Kong, or South Korea and just rocking and stumbling along as they did. They started out with more advantages than the others. They had the English language, good business ties with the United States . . . reasonably good infrastructure, a literate population and hard working people."

In addition to profligacy, political repression was a hallmark of the new Marcos dictatorship. There were sixty thousand political arrests between the declaration of martial law in 1972 and the 1977 inauguration of American president Jimmy Carter, who had made human rights a focal point of his campaign. This focus did scare a number of dictators in the noncommunist world and won freedom for some three thousand prisoners in the Philippines and many others worldwide. But here, as elsewhere, the Carter administration's focus on human rights was never subsumed in a broader focus on dictatorial governance as the cause of the problem.

The communist New People's Army meanwhile made significant advances during the martial-law period and held sway in large swaths of the rural provinces. U.S. congressman Steve Solarz, who served as chair of the House Foreign Affairs Subcommittee on Asia, thought that Marcos was the best "recruiting sergeant" for the NPA, and events on the ground seemed to prove the accuracy of that view. A second insurgency, this one of Muslims in the southern islands, particularly Mindanao, took off during Marcos's rule. In self-destructive counterpoint, the Philippine armed forces became steadily less professional, as cronyism festered in this once respected institution.

To keep up democratic appearances, elections took place. On 6 April 1978, Marcos held a parliamentary election. Benigno "Ninoy" Aquino, former Liberal Party leader in the Philippine senate and political prisoner since the advent of martial law, formed the Laban ("fight") Party from jail and stood for a seat in the national assembly. Originating a tactic later repeated with local variations from Santiago to Prague to Belgrade, Laban called for Manila residents to launch a noise barrage—using car horns, pots and pans, or their own voices—the night before the "election." The election results were shocking in their fraudulent audacity: seven of the Philippines' thirteen provinces showed 100 percent of the vote for Marcos's KBL party. In the Manila district, the official tally gave the opposition 31 percent of the vote.

Following the elections, some members of the opposition, in a group calling itself Project Public Justice, decided that arson attacks on regime targets, broadly defined to include beneficiaries of the dominant patronage system, might expose cracks and help bring the government down. The effort came to naught, and the perpetrators were arrested without converting their sparks into embers of popular opposition: the regime-controlled press utterly ignored the fires.

In 1979, Aquino was convicted of the murder for which he had been arrested seven years before and was sentenced to death. However, the U.S. State Department finally intervened in the case in 1980, pressuring Marcos to have the sentence suspended so Aquino could be treated for a heart condition in the United States. Following surgery, Benigno Aquino and his wife, Corazon, relocated to

Massachusetts, where he had fellowships at Harvard and MIT. While in the United States, Aquino publicly associated himself with the April 6 Liberation Movement, named for the day of the Manila noise protest but committed to the use of political violence against the Marcos regime, which was defined to include "corrupt presidential cronies and cabinet members," according to Aquino. The group detonated a number of bombs in Manila in 1980, including one at a conference of American travel agents where Marcos personally welcomed attendees to allay their fears of a threatened attack. A number of people were injured in that and other bombings. Filipinos failed to rally after the attacks. Imelda Marcos met with Aquino in New York in late 1980, pledging on her husband's behalf free elections. Martial law was formally lifted in January 1981, but the extraordinary powers remained in Marcos's hands. Elections were announced for June 1981, but the minimum age for candidates was set at fifty, disqualifying the forty-eight-year-old Aquino. The opposition boycotted the poll, and the situation remained static. Sometime after this, when Sir Richard Attenborough's film *Gandhi* was released, Aquino was apparently quite affected and renounced violence.

Assassination Triggers Reaction

In 1983, despite warnings from a great many friends and officials that his safety was in jeopardy, Benigno Aquino decided to return to Manila. Some American diplomats thought his desire to return was sparked by reports that Ferdinand Marcos, long ill, might be near death, with the potential for a power struggle looming. The fact that some in the Philippines had derisively called him a "steak commando" for being comfortable in the United States probably played a role. Political allies on the ground told him he was needed, as resolve for democratic nonviolence was flagging, and people were more likely to turn to the communists. In the words of former Philippines senator Francisco Rodrigo, "Marcos wanted to radicalize us so he could tell the Americans, 'You don't like me? What's your alternative? Communism. I may be a bastard, but I'm your only bastard.' And the Communists also wanted that. They knew that people were angry with Marcos. They wanted to make it seem as if only the NPA could succeed in driving Marcos out. We were trying to give them a viable alternative." Ninoy Aquino was seen as a necessary galvanizing force.

At his farewell party, Aquino said, "According to Gandhi, the willing sacrifice of the innocent is the most powerful answer to insolent tyranny." Upon his arrival in Manila in August 1983, Aquino was shot as he was leaving the plane, escorted by police. His alleged killer, Ronaldo Galman, was also found shot dead on the tarmac. While the official media in the Philippines kept the story quiet, Catholic Radio Veritas got the word out and prompted a great public outpouring of grief from a cross section of Filipino society. There was also suspicion, both among the Filipino population at large and the diplomatic community in Manila, that such an assassination could not possibly have taken place without high-level backing. One American diplomat saw the killing as a final, intolerable straw for a population that had learned to live under the corrupt, violent weight of the Marcos regime. "Although there were a lot of dirty tricks . . . prior to the assassination, there was a very clear sense . . . to the Filipino people that this had gone too far," he said.

The U.S. ambassador in Manila, Mike Armacost, requested an immediate audience with President Marcos as soon as he heard of the killing. Armacost and visiting Congressman Steve Solarz, a vocal critic of the Marcos regime, had met with Marcos a few days before the Aquino murder, and though Marcos was obviously seriously ill, the three had a solid and substantive discussion. When he arrived for the meeting, Armacost suspected Marcos had to be assisted into the room before the ambassador was allowed to enter. However, the president was "lucid" and kept up his end of the hour-and-a-half discussion, though the ambassador found his explanation of the killing "fishy." As the official investigation into the killings began, it became Armacost's conviction that the murder of Benigno Aquino could only have occurred with Ferdinand Marcos's consent.

Armacost made himself very visible at Aquino's funeral, which was a massive event in Manila. Cardinal Jaime Sin, who was to become a key figure in helping Filipinos reestablish democracy, gave the funeral eulogy, saying Aquino had given his life for democracy. The funeral procession drew nearly two million mourners, who chanted in Tagalog, "Ninoy, you are not alone!" and other slogans. Tellingly, the state-controlled media utterly ignored the events, with only Radio Veritas covering the funeral. To Armacost, the killing of Ninoy Aquino was "a wake-up call in two respects: (1) it was a reminder of the lengths to which the regime would go to snuff out any serious opposition; and (2) it revealed the extent of growing middle class disaffection with Marcos."

The human rights preoccupation of the Carter administration had pressured the Marcos regime into releasing some political prisoners, including Aquino, but had done little to promote a return to fully democratic government in the Philippines. In sharp contrast, the Reagan administration saw the Philippines through the lens of the recent shocks in Iran: twisting a dictator's arm on human rights could undercut his rule, creating a vacuum that would fill with religious extremists or, worse, communists. Marcos would not be sacrificed in the name of human rights. Besides, the Reagans and the Marcoses were friends, a fact that ultimately made it that much more difficult for the

American president to turn the page on Marcos and throw in with the clearly articulated will of the Filipino people.

With Aquino's assassination, a search began at a number of levels in the U.S. foreign policy establishment to find an alternative to Marcos. In the U.S. Congress, the reaction of some members was to push to cut aid completely to the Philippines, though most, including vocal Marcos critic Solarz, saw the strategic imperative to maintaining the bases at Clark Field and Subic Bay as too strong. However, it was clear to many that "the status quo was unacceptable."

From the assassination forward, Ambassador Armacost was "preoccupied" with putting "real distance between [the United States] and the regime in the eyes of the public." Armacost attempted to "persuade Marcos to set up a neutral and honest 'Warren Commission' to investigate the assassination" and met frequently with Cardinal Sin. He also made contact with officials who had been sent safely abroad by Marcos after they had "disassociated themselves from him" and with "business and political figures known to harbor growing distaste for the regime." Armacost returned to the United States in April 1984 to become undersecretary of state for political affairs (the number three position in the State Department), a position from which he would continue to play a key role in the Philippines. He was succeeded in Manila by Ambassador Steve Bosworth.

According to Frederick Brown, a former Foreign Service officer who later worked under Senator Richard Lugar at the Senate Foreign Relations Committee, by 1984 "it was clear that the Marcos regime was going to crumble. Either in a neat pile or a messy pile. The name of the game at that point was to protect U.S. interests in the Philippines, to make sure that the transition would not cause chaos and be harmful to our political interests, not to mention the interests of the Filipino people."

Still, there was no obvious ferment in the United States to make fundamental policy changes. There was "a lot of unhappiness. . . . It was a matter of great concern," according to Morton Abramowitz, the former ambassador to Thailand who soon after headed the State Department's Bureau of Intelligence and Research. He recalls a visit to much of Asia, including the Philippines, in 1984. After doing some touring and making observations on the general situation, Abramowitz was certain that Marcos was "driving the country into the ground." He shared his opinion with Ambassador Bosworth, who, Abramowitz recalls, was "not persuaded." Upon his return to Washington, he told Mike Armacost, Paul Wolfowitz (now assistant secretary of state for East Asia), and Richard Armitage (assistant secretary of defense for Asia) that he believed that Marcos was a lost cause. Still, with no clear alternative, there was little impetus for a major shift in American policy toward Manila.

To Ambassador Bosworth, the case against military chief Gen. Fabian Ver was the "litmus test" for the Marcos regime. Should it choose to whitewash the Aquino murder, there would be no hope of the government reforming itself. In late 1984, investigative panel chair (and former Supreme Court justice) Corazon Juliano Agrava determined that Aquino's purported lone killer was a member of an antiterrorist squad and that his killing was part of a cover-up. Agrava reported to Marcos that six men under the former head of the Air Security Command plotted the assassination. The report of the majority of the panel went much further up the command chain, all the way to General Ver. Relieved earlier of his position as army chief of staff under American pressure for the lack of progress against the New People's Army, Ver was put on trial for the Aquino killng with twenty-four other officers and one civilian.

Meanwhile, the opposition tried to agglomerate into a more coherent force. Many local businessmen, hitherto willing to accept the Marcoses' system, decided with the Aquino murder that a change had to occur, with free elections and a free press. President Marcos relented by allowing the National Movement of Citizens for a Free Election (NAMFREL) to register and appointing some new board members to the Commission on Elections. The Congress of the Filipino People, an umbrella organization representing a broad cross section of Filipino society, met to determine the strategy for the upcoming 1984 National Assembly elections. The communists pushed through a resolution calling for a boycott of the elections unless the Marcos regime met a list of demands, including the release of all political prisoners. Some political parties were unwilling to boycott the election, despite the supposition that they would be rigged. Salvador Laurel's United Democratic Action Organization (UNIDO) and Benigno Aquino's Laban Party both decided to contest the elections; Laban was now led by Aquino's widow, Corazon, or "Cory." NAMFREL was critical to the conduct of the elections, as it monitored their conduct and could report on fraud. In addition, NAMFREL was to conduct its own vote count, so that it could be cross-referenced with the official version. The elections drew 90 percent turnout and showed some real gains for the opposition, especially where there was independent monitoring through NAMFREL. Though it did not greatly shift the balance of power, this election gave valuable experience in election monitoring to some two hundred thousand NAMFREL volunteers—a crucial resource.

Washington still hoped that Marcos could clean up his act and still saw only a communist alternative to his regime. In the 1984 U.S. presidential debates, President Reagan responded to a question about the Philippines becoming another Nicaragua, "I know there are things there in the Philippines that do not look good to us from the standpoint of democratic rights. But what is the alternative? It is a large Communist movement to take over the Philippines. I think we're better off trying to retain our friendship and help them right the wrongs we see rather than throwing them to the wolves and then facing a Communist power in the Pacific." Ambassador Bosworth recalls that Reagan confidant Senator Paul Laxalt of Nevada and CIA director William Casey both visited the Philippines in 1985 to impress upon Marcos the need to open the country up politically and economically, to allow more space for political opposition. However, as Bosworth notes "Marcos was no dummy. . . . On the big issues, no one could move Marcos." He saw that fundamental reform would call into question the legitimacy of his rule and be the end of him. So on these matters he was "unshakable." According to former secretary of state George Shultz, after a mid-1985 visit, Armacost assessed the opposition to Marcos as "unimpressive" and still divided.

Senator Laxalt was a direct conduit to Marcos and, as a close friend of President Reagan, was a natural for the role, according to Armacost, who noted that there was a "constant search for people whom Marcos would treat as credible representatives of U.S. policy." According to former National Security Council (NSC) Asia specialist Gaston Sigur, a visit by Laxalt in late autumn 1985 prompted Marcos to announce on the 3 November 1985 episode of ABC's Sunday news analysis program *This Week with David Brinkley* a snap presidential election for 17 January 1986, nearly two years ahead of schedule. In his announcement, Marcos dismissed opposition claims of past fraudulent elections as "silly" and "sour grapes." "If all these childish claims to popularity on both sides have to be settled, I think we'd better settle it by calling an election right now, or say give everybody 60 days to campaign and bring the issues to the people, I'm ready. I'm ready." The date was later adjusted to 7 February, after Corazon Aquino demanded that Marcos sign a bill from the National Assembly calling for the vote. Marcos must have been confident he could keep the divided opposition at bay and win the election handily (with a little insurance), thereby reducing Washington's pressure.

Once the election was called, the approach among the activist Americans was to do whatever was possible to ensure a free and fair contest, one covered in local and international media. In his memoirs, Secretary of State Shultz said he saw the call for elections as a cynical attempt to disadvantage the opposition, which many felt was not ready for prime time. Ambassador Bosworth made a statement that "we would do business with any government that won the elections, so long as [the election was] fair and open." The final caveat, tellingly, was taken as an insult by the Marcoses. The Filipino parliament moved to have Bosworth declared persona non grata for calling for a democratic election. Marcos communicated this feeling to Washington, and Bosworth was instructed forcefully to drop the line, as it favored the opposition.

On 2 December, Gen. Fabian Ver and the other defendants were acquitted of the murder of Benigno Aquino, with the three-judge panel asserting that the killing was the act of a single (and conveniently deceased) gunman. Marcos even reinstated Ver as army chief of staff. The findings, completely at odds with the Agrava panel's findings, were met with skepticism in the United States. Charles Redman, deputy spokesman for the State Department, noted, "It's very difficult to reconcile the exemplary, thorough work of the Agrava Board, and the conclusions it reached after a year of hard work, with the outcome of this trial." Congressman Steve Solarz was more biting in his assessment, labeling the trial a "mockery of justice" and calling for military aid to the Philippines to stop altogether until General Ver was again removed.

The reaction to the verdict in the Philippines was strong and immediate. Manila saw major public demonstrations, and general strikes began in rural provinces. Meanwhile, with the filing date, 11 December 1985, rapidly approaching, the opposition had still not settled on a single ticket. Salvador Laurel and Corazon Benigno were set to run independent campaigns, guaranteeing a Marcos victory. Cardinal Jaime Sin worked to get Laurel to accept the running-mate slot, with Cory Aquino topping the ballot, as he thought she stood a much stronger chance of winning. The opposition ticket was announced on 5 January.

The campaign moved forward, with the opposition snowballing in popularity in the brief preelection period. Mort Abramowitz, on his way back from a trip to Pakistan about a month before the election, stopped in the Philippines and came away "very impressed" by the opposition campaign, comparing the atmosphere in Manila to a "religious revival" in terms of popular fervor. Secretary Shultz in his memoirs recalls being "worried about our activism" and the perception that the State Department might be favoring an opposition victory. He held the view that the United States would not "serve our interests by the appearance we are trying to oust Marcos."

Shultz appears to have been more concerned with impartiality. Others believed that Marcos would lose a democratic election, but there was a general wariness of Aquino. Donald Regan, President Reagan's chief of staff, was strongly in favor of continuing to support Marcos. More important, Reagan himself was not disposed to turn his back on Marcos. "However bad the Philippine situation might be, Ronald Reagan felt that Marcos had been a friend and ally of the United States, and Reagan stood up for people when the going got tough," Shultz writes. Reagan and Regan were the last to grasp the threat to America's long-term relationship with the Philippines, and thereby American interests, that a continuation of Marcos's rule posed

As the campaign wound up, its momentum continued to build. Corazon Aquino crisscrossed the archipelago in a private plane lent by a supportive businessman, drawing hundreds of thousands of spectators. The campaign ended with a massive rally at Manila's Luneta Park attended by a million supporters. Marcos's campaign was weak by comparison, and the man himself seemed uninspired.

Election Fraud Backfires

The U.S. Congress decided to send a delegation to observe the Filipino election. The delegation was headed by Senator Richard Lugar of Indiana, chairman of the Senate Foreign Relations Committee, and Congressman Jack Murtha of Pennsylvania. While Congressman Solarz, like some others, worried that the delegation might pronounce its report too soon and grant a fraudulent election an American blessing, he thought the risk worth taking. He felt that he should not participate, as it would be difficult for him to be seen as objective after his vocal criticism of Marcos in Congress. Though the delegation's members could not come close to observing all of the nearly eighty-six thousand precincts, their presence could serve as "a deterrent to fraud," in Shultz's eyes. Ambassador Bosworth, who recalls their efforts as critical, maintained "virtually constant contact" with the delegation throughout the trip.

The election process was characterized by serious irregularities from the beginning of polling; some voters were removed from the voter register, and many names were added. NAMFREL's chair for the metropolitan Manila area, a major opposition center, estimated that 15 percent of voters were unable to exercise their right to vote. Violence was observed throughout the country, as was vote buying and intimidation of opposition campaigners and voters. The vote tabulation was necessarily complicated, given the Philippines' geography. But it appeared that provincial votes were being held back until it was clear how many votes Marcos would need. Lugar and the rest of the delegation had the distinct feeling they were seeing a sanitized portion of the election, but they wanted to wait to see the results and more of the process before making any statement.

Thirty-one vote-tabulation technicians walked out from the election commission headquarters in Manila on 9 February after noticing that the figures being reported publicly did not match those they had in computer printouts. The workers sought safety in a church and then issued a statement that they were nonpartisan and had quit "when we realized something wrong was going on."

The constant coverage of the election and its aftermath by CNN, the Cable News Network, was being rebroadcast on local media. The overwhelming impression was that fraud was rampant but that Corazon Aquino had won and was going to be denied her victory by Marcos. The considerable allegations of fraud created pressure for some sort of American policy response.

Already, it appeared to senior sdministration officials that Marcos was trying to steal the election. The Bureau of Intelligence and Research at the State Department was writing regular reports on goings-on in the Philippines that provided further evidence for the conclusion that Marcos was a lost cause. On 9 February, Secretary of State Shultz convened a meeting of senior foreign policy officials at his home. Those attending included Paul Wolfowitz, Mike Armacost, Gaston Sigur from the NSC, and Admiral William Crowe, commander in chief, Pacific Forces. Considering the reports from the scene, it appeared clear to Shultz that "a great deal of fraud" had taken place and that there was "an outpouring of people who want democracy." He and the others concluded that "the Marcos era [was] over" and that the United States should do what it could to "accelerate the succession," by sending an envoy to Manila to pressure Marcos to step down. It was apparent that Marcos was contemplating moving against NAMFREL, as he had asked the CIA whether the United States would object! And it appeared that more repression was in store.

On 10 February, the nineteen-nation international observation mission issued the following statement: "The electoral anomalies which we have observed are serious and could well have an impact on the final result. Occurrences of vote-buying, intimidation and lack of respect for electoral procedures were present." No violations by Aquino supporters were noted. Despite this information, White House spokesman Larry Speakes said in a press briefing on 10 February that Marcos had won the election, and he called upon the opposition to join with Marcos in national reconciliation, much to the chagrin of Shultz. Later, the White House issued a semiretraction, stating that the result remained unclear and the president would soon meet with Senator Lugar.

A cable from Ambassador Bosworth, recounted by Shultz in his memoirs, was damning in its conclusions about the election:

> The bottom line conclusion is inescapable: Mrs. Aquino would have won if there had been an even minimally fair count. The opposition, therefore will not accept the National Assembly proclamation [of Marcos's victory]. Our urging that they join together in national reconciliation on reform would not change their position. Such a U.S. position would however subject the U.S. to charges of "whitewash" after our principled emphasis throughout the campaign on free and fair elections. This election has effectively cost Ferdinand Marcos most of his remaining political legitimacy and credibility, both in the Philippines and the U.S. . . . Our overriding policy objective is to manage our way into the post-Marcos era.

Shultz's own thoughts moved in the same direction. "The Filipino people had taken the democratic process seriously. . . . So the U.S. faced a big moment: we represented democracy to these people."

In his meeting with President Reagan, Secretary of State Shultz, and Secretary of Defense Caspar Weinberger, Senator Lugar gave a "sober, measured, detailed and devastating" account of "massive election fraud" on behalf of a unanimous delegation, according to Shultz. It was agreed that Philip Habib would be sent to the Philippines to meet with Marcos, Aquino, and other opposition leaders. Despite this report, President Reagan gave a press conference later in the day at which he announced that there was "the possibility of fraud, although it could have been that all of that was occurring on both sides." Lugar, when asked about the statement, said he had no evidence of fraud by Aquino supporters and was uncertain how Reagan had determined any had occurred. The true motivation for the presidential statement appears to have been a desire not to betray a friend. "Shultz is trying to push the president further than he wants to go," Larry Speakes told Bernard Kalb, then at State. Despite all the evidence that Marcos had blatantly flouted the popular will, Reagan still thought of him as a friend.

Senator Lugar estimated two days later that had the vote been free and fair, Aquino would have pulled between 60 and 70 percent of the vote. Senator Sam Nunn, ranking Democrat on the Armed Services Committee, wrote President Reagan a letter accusing Marcos of "making an all-out effort to steal the election by massive fraud, intimidation, and murder." Senate Majority Leader Bob Dole went as far as to say that the United States should consider moving its bases from the Philippines, because "unrest" would result from the Marcos election grab.

Events on the ground were moving forward, however, despite policy paralysis at the very top in Washington. Corazon Aquino reacted sharply to Reagan's statement, saying, "I would wonder at the motives of a friend of democracy who chose to conspire with Mr. Marcos to cheat the Filipino people of their liberation." The Catholic Bishops Conference of the Philippines soon convened to issue a strong statement, characterizing the elections as "unparalleled in the fraudulence of their conduct." The bishops condemned the incitement of "naked fear" and the "criminal use of power to thwart the sovereign will of the people." They urged the citizenry to organize active nonviolent resistance: "The wrong was systematically organized. So must the correction be . . . in a peaceful, nonviolent way." In a strongly Catholic country, already agitated by the theft of the democratic process but uncertain how to proceed, such a strong statement had enormous impact. Ambassador Bosworth believes the bishops' statement was one of the absolutely critical events that led to the ouster of Marcos.

Undeterred, Marcos's deputies in the National Assembly completed the official vote count on 15 February, leading to an opposition walkout and the proclamation of Marcos as the official winner of another six-year presidential term. The only country to recognize the Marcos "victory" was the Soviet Union. NAMFREL, in its own vote tally, which covered 70 percent of the precincts, found Aquino to have beaten Marcos by nearly eight hundred thousand votes out of nearly fifteen million cast in those polling stations. A White House statement issued the same day noted that the "elections were marred by widespread fraud and violence perpetrated largely by the ruling party. It was so extreme that the election's credibility has been called into question both within the Philippines and the United States." However, despite this apparent shift, Shultz was convinced that Reagan "had no intention of abandoning Marcos, nor could he conceive of Marcos's departure from office."

Shultz, however, was not reluctant to conceive of such a future. In testimony to the Senate Budget Committee on 19 February, he was sharply critical of "fraud and violence carried out on a widespread scale" by Marcos and his backers. He continued: "We have a big stake there. We have a stake in freedom. We have a stake in democracy. Let's put that first, over and above the bases." In his memoirs, he adds, "I was making the point that we should not be willing to accept a fraudulent election simply to keep the bases; in fact, the way for the United States to lose the bases would be to accept a fraudulent election under these circumstances!" Both houses of the U.S. Congress voted to find the Filipino elections fatally flawed.

Ousting Marcos in Washington and Manila

In response to Marcos's declaration of victory, supporters of Aquino converged in Manila the following day, 1.5 million strong, for a "Triumph of the People Rally." At the rally, Aquino told her supporters that if Marcos did not yield, "we shall escalate. I'm not asking for violent revolution. . . . Now is the way of nonviolent struggle for justice. This means active resistance of evil by peaceful means." This was the launch of the People Power movement, seen worldwide on CNN. An integral part of the plan was economic boycotts against Marcos-connected companies, and the campaign had an immediate impact on these firms and the economy overall. However, each side appeared convinced that it could wait the other out. In any event, Marcos showed no sign of budging.

Some officers in the military had long chafed under Marcos resenting the political commanders foisted upon them, diluting a proud professionalism many brought from training at West Point and other American staff schools. Some had organized a secret group known as RAM, for "Reform the Armed Forces of the Philippines Movement." The group, connected to Defense Minister Juan Ponce Enrile, had been contemplating a coup before the election. One of these officers, Lt. Gen. Fidel Ramos, had been named chief of staff after General Ver was sacked once again under American pressure. Following the National Assembly's declaration of Marcos as the winner, it became clear that purges directed by Marcos and Ver were coming soon, with potential assassination of RAM members and arrest of opposition leaders. At Malacanang Palace, the presidential residence, security had been bolstered by provincial units. In addition, four RAM officers had been arrested and had revealed the coup plan. Defense Minister Enrile and General Ramos moved their forces, both army and national police, into two adjoining bases, Camps Aguinaldo and Crame, drawing more defecting troops, police, and the international press corps, which began live broadcasting. Soon, Enrile and Ramos held a press conference at Camp Aguinaldo. Enrile said that he could not "in conscience recognize the president as commander in chief of the armed forces. . . . I believe the mandate of the people does not belong to the present regime." He went on to ask for the support of "all decent elements in the cabinet . . . government, decent Filipinos, and . . . decent soldiers and officers." General Ramos echoed that call and said, "We are committed to support Corazon Aquino. . . . I think deep in my heart, that she is the real president of the Philippines." They had thrown in their lot with the people and thrown down the gauntlet to Marcos.

Cardinal Sin received calls for help from both Ramos and Enrile and called on people to go to the two camps and try to forestall any attempt to clear them out. Benigno Aquino's brother, Butz, went on Catholic Radio Veritas to call for people to join him and march to the two camps. In scenes that recalled the Paris taxicabs driving troops to the front, Manila's taxis, buses, and private cars ferried people through the night to the camps and back. The next morning, the crowd was estimated to number fifty thousand. Marcos called on the rebels to end the "stupidity" and to "surrender." Enrile later led his forces across the road to Camp Crame to concentrate the forces in one location for better defense.

Soon, the expected confrontation came, and Marcos's loyalist marine tanks advanced on the rebel positions. Civilian demonstrators, including nuns, students, and others, were told to meet the force and prevent government troops from advancing on the outgunned rebels. They bravely did so, risking life and limb. "I saw no one yield to fear," said a Jesuit priest who was among the human wall separating the forces of Marcos and the rebels. Despite attempts to advance through the crowd, marines in their armored vehicles were unable to intimidate the pro-democracy civilians. Ambassador Bosworth warned Marcos that the United States would not tolerate firing on unarmed demonstrators, to which Marcos objected that he had the right as commander in chief to maintain law and order. But the forces did not shoot at the demonstrators. Undersecretary Armacost later said that he thought this was the definitive last gasp for Marcos, as his "last line of defense was the military. Once it became clear that it was at best deeply divided, and even the loyalists were unwilling to do what needed to happen, his rule was measured in days." In a cable to Shultz, Armacost said he didn't believe that statements would deter Marcos—this was one of his "unshakable" moments. Cory Aquino was on the island of Cebu, where the rebels had told her she would be safer until the rebellion was over.

During the people-power demonstrations, Congressman Solarz, chairing the Subcommittee on Asia for the House International Relations Committee, moved to suspend all aid, military and economic, "to show we were on the side of the people." He recalls Assistant Secretaries Paul Wolfowitz and Richard Armitage, from State and Defense, respectively, coming to him to make the case that such a cutoff would force Marcos out and help the NPA. However, Solarz continued to believe, even more than before, that Marcos and the communists were in a symbiotic relationship and that only recognition of the popular will be expressed in the election could stop the downward spiral. The subcommittee voted unanimously to cut off aid.

American policymakers feared the Philippines were on the verge of potentially massive bloodletting, and they undertook efforts to calm emotions in the Philippines. Illustrating further evolution, White House spokesman Larry Speakes gave a statement supportive of Ramos and Enrile's actions, noting that their rebellion and the popular support for it "strongly reinforce our concerns that the recent presidential elections were marred by fraud, perpetuated overwhelmingly by the ruling party. . . . Many authoritative voices in the Philippines have been raised in support of nonviolence. We support these voices and expect them to be respected. We also support resolution of the issues involved by all the people of the Philippines as quickly as possible." Such statements notwithstanding, in a 22 February cable, Ambassador Bosworth told the secretary of state that nothing less than a call by President Reagan for Marcos to step down would have an effect.

Immediately upon Philip Habib's return on 23 February, a senior-level staff meeting on the crisis was held. Habib, who had met with Marcos, said he looked "horrible" and was unable to accept that there was a broad-based movement to get him out of power. Shultz intended to get a unified position to make the case to Reagan that dumping Marcos immediately was the only viable option and that Reagan himself would have to act. He managed to get agreement among the disparate group that Marcos was at a dead end and that the United States would have to engineer a way to convince him there was no choice but to leave. Shultz noted that the United States had missed a number of "tidal shifts" in the past, including the fall of the shah of Iran: "We have paid a heavy price for our handling of these matters. We have gotten the worst of both worlds: we have gotten on the wrong side, and we have appeared disloyal to our friends."

A later meeting was called in the White House Situation Room with the president and many of the same players who had met at Shultz's home earlier that day. Reports came in of the armored troops advancing on the camp being halted by unarmed civilians. It appeared that Marcos was mustering forces for a major assault on Camp Crame for the following dawn. The rebels were calling the U.S. embassy to see if they could count on American support.

Habib gave his report of events in the Philippines, ending it by stating, "The Marcos era has ended." Shultz argued that Marcos could no longer govern and that Aquino represented the democratic alternative to the NPA. "The United States must find a way to support the democratic forces for change and to treat Marcos with respect and courtesy. We should be ready to bring him to the United States." Reagan's chief of staff, Don Regan, opposed pushing Marcos out, convinced a power vacuum favoring the communists would result. Shultz then reminded Reagan of the unanimity of his advisers on the issue: "Mr. President, there's not a person here, other than Don, who believes Marcos can stay in power. He's had it."

Reagan then called for a private message to be sent to Marcos calling on him to refrain from using violence against the rebels and warning that military aid would be severed should any such attack go forward A second message called for Marcos to step down. A public White House statement the next morning called on loyalist forces not to use force against rebels or demonstrators: "Attempts to prolong the life of the present regime by violence are futile. A solution to this crisis can only be achieved through a peaceful transition to a new government," the statement read, in part. However, Ambassador Bosworth reported back to Washington that Marcos had rejected the personal message calling on him to step down when it was presented to him in person. "Marcos said it was a ridiculous conclusion we have drawn: he is in full control. He has no intention of doing what we suggested. He rejects our conclusions."

The likelihood of massive bloodletting increased with Marcos's digging in his heels. The rebels' firepower was augmented on 23 February by the defection of an attack helicopter squadron, which had been ordered to attack the camp, making the defense of the camps militarily viable. The next day, the helicopter squadron went on the offensive for the opposition, destroying three presidential helicopters and helping capture the government-controlled television station. Another station fell to rebels as well. In the meantime, loyalist troop movements were cut off by civilians blocking their way; they then offered food to the troops. Corazon Aquino insisted on coming back from Cebu at this time to be with her supporters, marveling at their willingness to put "life . . . on the line." CNN, reporting from Malacanang Palace, saw shooting in both directions; the population was called to reinforce the stations to prevent a government reconquest of them. Aquino urged her supporters to maintain their stance to protect the gains made. On local television, Marcos called on his supporters to come from outside the city with weapons. Manila was on the brink of civil war. Ambassador Bosworth called the people-power revolt "the first CNN event"; it made for compelling—and influential—television. "People power and the media" had a "galvanizing effect" on the American public, according to Bosworth. What was seen on-screen had a direct impact on the policy options available to American and Filipino officials.

Marcos began to wilt. On 24 February, he called the Senate to speak to Paul Laxalt, saying he was "willing to bargain." En route to the White House with Laxalt to inform the president, Shultz received a call from Armacost that the Marcos family had been in touch indirectly to discuss conditions. When Laxalt made the call, he was firm, telling Marcos that the United States would work on assuring his security if he were willing to leave. Marcos was not pleased with the news: "There were long silences. . . . He was very emotional. Marcos said he would go through with his inaugural ceremony in a low key and then telephone me [the next day] I was very direct on 'no power sharing' and that he should go out with dignity. There was a long pause." He told Marcos to "cut and cut clean." The following day, the Philippines had two inaugurations: a popular ceremony to welcome the people's choice, Corazon Aquino, to the presidency, and a somber wake of a ceremony for the defeated dictator. Even the television transmission of the ceremony was abbreviated. Marcos soon left on a U.S. Air Force plane on his way to Hawaii. The Marcos era was definitively over.

As George Shultz recounts in his memoirs, the United States still had some hiccups on the way to recognition of the Aquino government. Reagan and Regan were still reluctant to fully embrace the product of democracy. When Shultz came to the White House with a draft statement of recognition, Regan exploded, and the president objected to the strength of the language about Aquino and the democratic process: "Those words would make us look as if we wanted to dump Marcos," Shultz summarizes their position. He successfully argued: "If we equivocate about Aquino's position at this moment, it can turn a triumph of democracy into a catastrophe. The Filipino people are sending a message. It's loud. It's dramatic. It's clear." Shultz then delivered the statement, promising cooperation with the Aquino government, praising her for her commitment to nonviolence, but still assessing Marcos as having been in the totality of his rule "a constructive force."

Following the elections, Senator Lugar, Senator Alan Cranston, Congressman Jack Kemp, and Congressman Solarz sponsored the Multilateral Aid Initiative for the Philippines. The fund, to which a number of countries contributed, was to total roughly $1 billion to support the Philippines' transition to democracy.

The transition in the Philippines required a number of tough decisions on the part of Aquino and her new team. As former NSC Asia specialist Gaston Sigur recalls, when he arrived in March 1986, she was preparing to take "some very important political steps: to dissolve the legislature, throw them all out, and to, in effect, assume dictatorial powers until plans for elections could be put into effect and she could move toward democracy. None of us had any doubts she was going to establish a democratic system, we never doubted that for a minute, but she was going to assume dictatorial powers temporarily," against the advice of Vice President Laurel and Defense Minister Enrile. Their feeling was that this was too broad a sweep of the old regime and that some talented administrators, particularly governors, would be removed. Aquino, before she announced the decisions on television, asked Sigur what he thought. Sigur told her, "'Look, the United States government fully, completely supports you. We've made that very clear. You are the president of the Philippines. We believe that you are going to take the steps that you have to take to move the country forward toward democracy, and economically, to strengthen the military and so forth. . . . And therefore what you feel is essential to do, we will support.' I was rather impressed with her at the time. . . . She stuck by her guns there, to do what she felt was necessary to really change the situation in the Philippines. Maybe it wasn't all correct, but nonetheless she took tough decisions and she did it," Sigur remembers. "I've always felt that she's got a bit of iron in her."

The Marcoses landed in Hawaii on a plane with forty-five people and a second plane full of cargo. Their fate was not yet clear, and legal questions regarding the wealth they took with them, as well as assets already in the United States, were burgeoning. Congressman Solarz had had Marcos's landholdings in the United States investigated some years before and found that the couple had sunk roughly $350 million into real estate purchases in Manhattan. This was just the tip of the iceberg. One unlucky Foreign Service officer, Robert Rich Jr., had to deal with the complications. Among the items on the second plane were items of jewelry that "would have made any museum or the Hapsburgs envious," and Rich thought the plane should not have been part of the deal at all. In addition, for fear of having assets attached in lawsuits, the Marcoses could not open a bank account, so they could not pay for their expenses. Imelda Marcos played the poor act to the hilt, trying to portray herself as a victim. The U.S. government attempted to shuffle the Marcoses to Panama, but the deal fell through after Aquino pressured Panamanian leader Manuel Noriega not to accept the couple, as efforts to retrieve stolen assets would be easier through the American legal system. When confronted with the infamous shoe collection, Imelda Marcos quipped, "I have a lot more shoes down in Tacloban," a palace in the southern Philippines. Rich notes that "the way she reacted was so typical: What is wrong with all this? There was a total opaqueness in her moral understanding of why anybody should get excited over such things. Why was it an issue?" Most of the entourage families were later able to work in the United States, but none of these factors was considered before flying the Marcoses out. The Marcoses eventually moved to a house on the water that was "spoken of in the press as a much more palatial place than it was. There too the charade of not owning anything continued."

President Reagan remained unconvinced by Aquino, according to Shultz. Some time after Aquino was inaugurated, in discussing an upcoming visit to Washington, President Reagan remarked that he had "a wait-and-see attitude toward Aquino." Shultz told the president, "The Filipinos are waiting to hear you say you support her government." Reagan replied, "I'll support a legitimate government—when she gets elected." "She thinks she *did* get elected," Shultz told Reagan. On a subsequent trip through Asia, Reagan bypassed Manila, though Shultz went there to meet Aquino. Though wary of her reception in Washington because of the Reagan administration's mixed signals, Aquino accepted the invitation after being assured that she would be enthusiastically welcomed by Congress and cordially received by the White House.

In September 1986, President Corazon Aquino of the Philippines addressed a special joint session of the U.S. Congress, and her speech was greeted with thunderous applause. Congressman Solarz decided to capitalize on the moment and sponsor a unanimous-consent decision to grant the Philippines $200 million in economic aid. Senate Majority Leader Bob Dole, who was among those escorting President Aquino through the chamber, called it "the largest honorarium in U.S. history."

While her term as president saw a number of serious difficulties—attempted coups, flagging support among other Filipino leaders for whom she had gone to bat, administrative difficulties, and natural disasters—President Aquino's tenure markedly improved the prospects of the Philippines. Furthermore, by insisting on clearing out the old guard after coming to power, she helped reestablish democracy. "She aspired to turn over a functioning democratic system to an elected successor. This great goal she achieved," says former Secretary Shultz in his memoirs. Former ambassador Armacost sees Aquino as having been "an important symbol" of the popular will to return to democracy and says that she did a "good job cleaning house" after the ousting of Marcos. Fidel Ramos, for whom she campaigned, was elected the next Filipino president, and Armacost assessed him as the best post-Marcos administrator.

What are the lessons and questions for the future that emerge from the Philippine experience? The Filipino people-power example was significant in several respects. First, it showed that a number of American policymakers, albeit not at the commanding heights to start, were able to see the nexus between security, American interests, and respect for the will of the people in a foreign country. In the words of Gaston Sigur: "If you are really going to have a strong security system in a country, you have to in fact have a democratic society. . . . In order to enhance the American security relationship with the Philippines, it was necessary to restore a democratic form of government to their country." The idea that the bases at Subic Bay and Clark Field were the sum total of our interests, though widely held, was false. "I think the preservation of a democratic Philippines should be an important element in American policy," Sigur says, "regardless of the bases . . . because of our long relationship with the Philippines and also . . . because . . . I feel very strongly that security and the people's participation in their own affairs go hand in hand, and that you can't separate the two."

Those bases have since closed. Had the United States maintained its support for the Marcos regime for the sake of these bases, we would have lost at least one—Clark Field—anyway, owing to the eruption of Mount Pinatubo. Furthermore, the Filipino people might well be under a government with an understandable chip on its shoulder toward the United States because of Washington's support of Marcos. It is even conceivable that the cause of democracy could have been long delayed by a shift of popular support to an active insurgency as the only viable avenue of resistance to the dictator. The Philippines remain a democratic ally, even to the point of accepting American military assistance in rooting out the Abu Sayyaf terrorists in Mindanao.

Toward the end of the Marcos regime, there were machinations behind the scenes to open channels with the Soviet Union—evidence of the desperation and unreliability of dictators in crisis. Their fundamental yardstick is what keeps them in power, and ideological consistency rarely gets in the way. In the event, the Soviet option was never really a serious one, as the Marcos regime was crumbling and the Soviet Union was already overextended. But the fact that dictators cannot be counted on is a recurring lesson policymakers in the United States and the rest of the democratic world appear to need to relearn with stunning frequency.

The Philippines example also shows how executive branch and congressional leaders, both in Washington and in the field, can collaborate and work to outmaneuver a failed or static policy. A number of factors in the policy process were crucial to the eventual, though late, consensus that Marcos had to go. The leadership of certain members of Congress at various points was indispensable. Their unanimous position on the extent of Marcos's malfeasance, once presented to the president, made it possible for advisers to step into the breach and make their case. Election campaigns are enormous social mobilizers and often backfire on dictators who believe they can channel public discontent. Even where the cards seem stacked against the opposition, going through with the campaign is usually worthwhile if only to expose the unpopularity of the regime. Having trained foreign monitors on hand helps deter or at least expose fraud, while inevitably revealing the ugly underbelly of repressive, dictatorial systems.

On the executive side of the equation, it is clear that those closest to the situation in a dictatorship are often able to see how rotten it is. Of course, it is equally true that the desire of diplomats to keep bilateral relations smooth leads to "clientitis" and an inability to see things as they really are. In the case of the Philippines, a number of individuals at the State and Defense Departments and in the U.S. embassy became convinced over time that Marcos was a lost cause and that efforts needed to be made to remove him from the scene. More became convinced over time, and not all for the same reasons. For example, many senior officials noted that Admiral Crowe was a key player, as he felt both that the two strategic U.S. bases in the Philippines were at risk and that the communist insurgency was gaining ground. Marcos was becoming an albatross for the United States.

Others felt that the American relationship with the Philippines was long term and that continued support for such a dictatorial regime would poison the well there for years to come. In any event, the fact that there was a cadre of officials already convinced that Marcos was a lost cause helped build the strategy around the elections and build the case against Marcos for those, including President Reagan, who remained unconvinced.

What did the United States actively do to get rid of Marcos? According to Mort Abramowitz, who headed the State Department's Bureau of Intelligence and Research at the time, "not much." From his standpoint, the real question was whether the United States would stop helping a leader who had repeatedly quashed the democratic will of the people. The reporting of what was happening on the ground, through official channels or in the media, made much of the case for this.

But there were important things that helped the opposition and spotlighted the ugly underside of the Marcos regime. Ambassador Armacost's attendance at the funeral of Ninoy Aquino no doubt sent a strong message—one that the senior level of the U.S. government did not find to its liking. Ambassador

Bosworth's contact with NAMFREL and the opposition, including consulting with Cory Aquino on security matters, was also of great import. And country director John Maisto was lauded by Abramowitz and Senator Lugar's foreign relations staffer Frederick Brown as ahead of the curve on seeing the Marcos regime for what it was: a dictatorship that was bad for our long-term interests in the Philippines and East Asia and bad for the Filipinos.

Many of the tools now commonly employed to monitor elections and assist opposition parties were largely untried at this stage. The National Endowment for Democracy and its associated core institutes were brand-new. The international election-monitoring operation in the Philippines was critical in showing to the most recalcitrant of American policymakers, up to the president himself, that Marcos was bankrupt as a leader and "friend" of the United States. Since this election, election monitoring has become a de facto institution. Countries in transition want the seal of approval it provides, and a series of reasonably well-conducted and clean elections usually "graduates" countries to the ranks of "mature" democracies. This is the case with Poland and Hungary, who returned to the democratic world in 1989. Election monitoring has become so ubiquitous that dictators sometimes select their own "observers" to assure that they get the desired seal of approval, as Aleksandr Lukashenko and Slobodan Milosevic have done.

One of the most important lessons is also one of the most difficult: the United States and other democracies often find their policies behind the power curve. The inability of policymakers to imagine a future without dictator or monarch X in charge of country Y is a constant repeated to this day. This lack of imagination leaves policymakers completely reactive, leading them to misunderstand the processes at work. It also cripples their ability to promote friendly and *democratic* alternatives to violent revolt. The importance of cultivating leaders and allies at the civic level is shown in the Filipino example. Unforeseeable opportunities do arise, and there must be good people on the ground to step into the breach.

Bringing Down Milosevic

The twenty-first century's first nonviolent overthrow of a dictator happened in October 2000, when an army of civilian resisters from all over Serbia defended the results of an election that the country's president, Slobodan Milosevic, had lost but tried to ignore. This dramatic collapse of a regime that many Western policymakers had thought would yield only to violent force confirmed the power of civilian resistance as a means of replacing dictators with democratic rule. Many may think of the mutiny in terms of a few newsvideo images in which smoke rose from windows of the parliament building in Belgrade after it was taken by demonstrators. But the images told the wrong story. The building and the country were taken without violence.

While there had been significant resistance to Milosevic in the mid-1990s and NATO bombing clearly weakened his credibility, the game of bringing down Milosevic became really serious after the bombing stopped. Resistance to him within Serbia was suspended during the bombing. When the dust settled, a student organization called Otpor ("Resistance" in Serbian) picked itself up and brushed itself off—and proceeded to jump-start the dormant coalition of forces that yearned for real democracy. The group was the perfect political duelist for Milosevic, a man who had long papered the walls of Serbia with his chubby image and political slogans and had no sense of irony.

Otpor ridiculed the dictator's birthday celebrations with mock parties on public sidewalks, cutting up a cake in the shape of Yugoslavia to represent the way his wars had lopped off parts of the country. They staged boisterous rock concerts, lacing the revelry with raplike sarcasm aimed at the president. When the regime declared Otpor illegal, its members surprised local police stations by showing up in droves and pretending to turn themselves in, flummoxing the authorities. Refusing to regard the police as the enemy, they treated them as potential coconspirators in a kind of public theater intended to expose the dictator's pretensions to grandeur.

While their energy and ingenuity were entirely homegrown, their funding was not. Accepting support from any source, foreign or domestic, willing to provide it, Otpor and other oppositionists—including independent media, unions, and other pro-democracy groups—took up to $20 million from Western sources. The latter included such organizations as the Open Society Institute, Freedom House, the American Center for Labor Solidarity, the Center for International Private Enterprise, the Institute for Democracy in Eastern Europe, the German Marshall Fund, the International Research and Exchanges Board, the International Foundation for Election Systems, Star-Delphi Women's Network, Network of East-West Women, the American Bar Association's Central and East European Law Initiative, World Learning, the U.S. Institute of Peace, the National Endowment for Democracy, the International Republican Institute, and the National Democratic Institute. Numerous European funders and organizations also reached serious levels of participation, including the British Foreign Office; the German foreign ministry; all the German party foundations; the Netherlands foreign ministry; the governments of Switzerland, Sweden, Norway, Greece, Hungary, Canada, Denmark, Luxembourg, and the Czech Republic; Press Now (Netherlands); the Swedish Helsinki Committee; Norwegian People's AID; the Westminster Foundation; and others. I list all of these players to indicate how many within the democratic community can be brought together in a single coalition of the willing to unseat a dictator when the will is generated.

While the U.S. State Department had been "clumsy" and tried to "micromanage" Serbian groups in exchange for support, according to Otpor leader Srdja Popovic, this constellation of independent organizations developed a sophisticated understanding of local conditions and never tried to impose their views. This was crucial: Milosevic's opponents could honestly maintain that their decisions and actions were their own. But the strategic ideas they employed in their nonviolent conflict with the regime had been strongly influenced by key Western experts.

In particular, Popovic and his Otpor colleagues translated the nonviolence scholar Gene Sharp's book *From Dictatorship to Democracy* into Serbian, and student dissidents circulated it among themselves. A hardheaded, concise framework for undermining a dictator's base of support, it was "an amazing experience" to hold the book in their hands and read it, according to Popovic. It complemented a training seminar in Budapest that retired U.S. Army colonel Robert Helvey conducted for Otpor leaders. Helvey, whom Popovic recalls as "a quite impressive character," told the young Serbs that nonviolent conflict "is a form of warfare . . . so the principles of war that apply to a military struggle have tremendous overlap into strategic nonviolent struggle." Helvey told them to analyze Milosevic's pillars of support and design messages and methods to exploit his vulnerabilities.

What the Otpor kids and many other democrats in Serbia were learning was a kind of do-it-yourself liberation. By organizing at the grass roots, shattering Serbs' acquiescence in Milosevic's rule, and propagating acts of resistance beyond the logistical or psychological readiness of the police to suppress them, the movement was transferring political power from the dictator to the people even before he was actually removed. They democratized the spirit of Serbia before political democracy formally arrived.

In addition to Western strategic advice and funding for nonviolent opposition groups in Serbia, another invaluable outside contribution to the Serbian people's campaign against Milosevic was training and support for campaigning, getting out the vote, and monitoring polling places and voting returns. Noticing the erosion of his popular support, Milosevic moved up the date for a presidential election that he still thought he could win—or steal—handily. But the opposition was ready for him. When the election returns came in and it was obvious that he had lost, he tried to distort the results and call for a run-off. That was the moment for the movement's supporters to head for the streets, and they did. From all over Serbia they streamed into Belgrade, in such a massive show of civilian power that the army and the police (with whom resistance leaders had initiated a dialogue) stood aside, and Milosevic was forced to step down.

Zoran Djindjic, an opposition leader and later prime minister of Serbia, said that "It was Gandhi's idea, just to show that we don't accept this government" that was the final strategic move in collapsing its hold on power. In the words of Gene Sharp: "All governments can rule only as long as they receive replenishment of the needed sources of their power from the cooperation, submission and obedience of the population and the institutions of the society." When this replenishment stops, they have to stop. Slobodan Milosevic had been indicted at The Hague and bombed by NATO, and belatedly the West made clear it no longer supported him. And finally when his people refused to obey him, he fell.

Wayne Merry, a former Foreign Service officer who served in East Germany in the 1970s and on the German desk in the 1980s, recalls being asked repeatedly by East German friends, mostly Lutheran pastors, how the Filipinos managed to oust Marcos. They had watched it on West German and Danish television. According to Merry: "The lesson for them was that, at least in principle, a nonviolent opposition to an authoritarian regime could succeed if the opposition thought through its strategy and exercised both self-discipline and a willingness to communicate with the authorities. These lessons proved very important in the crisis of the GDR [German Democratic Republic] and certainly owed much to the experience of 'people power' on the far side of the world."[7] This principle is even more pronounced today. When one considers the fact that anti-Mugabe demonstrators compared him to recently ousted Serbian ruler (and indicted war criminal) Slobodan Milosevic, and that others in Africa have also used the example of the 5 October popular uprising in Serbia, it is impossible to conclude that democracy is not a universal human goal.

The real lesson of the interplay between the nonviolent strategies of people power and the policies of democratic governments and institutions is that everything is connected. The victories in the Philippines and Serbia, the elections won in Nairobi and Santiago—all of these compose a kind of collective experience. Optor students drew from the Filipino nonviolent arsenal and sharpened its weapons for the fight in Serbia. What happens on one side of the world spreads like a starburst, illuminating the way to democracy half a planet away. Nothing occurs in isolation.

Appendix: The Methods of Nonviolent Action

The Methods of Nonviolent Protest and Persuasion

Formal Statements
1. Public speeches
2. Letters of opposition or support
3. Declarations by organizations and institutions
4. Signed public statements
5. Declarations of indictment and intention
6. Group or mass petitions

Communications with a Wider Audience
7. Slogans, caricatures, and symbols
8. Banners, posters, and displayed communications
9. Leaflets, pamphlets, and books
10. Newspapers and journals
11. Records, radio, and television
12. Skywriting and earthwriting

Group Representations
13. Deputations
14. Mock awards
15. Group lobbying
16. Picketing
17. Mock elections

Symbolic Public Acts
18. Displays of flags and symbolic colors
19. Wearing of symbols
20. Prayer and worship
21. Delivering symbolic objects

22. Protest disrobings
23. Destruction of own property
24. Symbolic lights
25. Displays of portraits
26. Paint as protest
27. New signs and names
28. Symbolic sounds
29. Symbolic reclamations
30. Rude gestures

Pressures on Individuals
31. "Haunting" officials
32. Taunting officials
33. Fraternization
34. Vigils

Drama and Music
35. Humorous skits and pranks
36. Performances of plays and music
37. Singing

Processions
38. Marches
39. Parades
40. Religious processions
41. Pilgrimages
42. Motorcades

Honoring the Dead
43. Political mourning
44. Mock funerals
45. Demonstrative funerals
46. Homage at burial places

Public Assemblies
47. Assemblies of protest or support
48. Protest meetings
49. Camouflaged meetings of protest
50. Teach-ins

Withdrawal and Renunciation
51. Walk-outs
52. Silence
53. Renouncing honors
54. Turning one's back

The Methods of Social Noncooperation

Ostracism of Persons
55. Social boycott
56. Selective social boycott
57. Lysistratic nonaction
58. Excommunication
59. Interdict

Noncooperation with Social Events,
Customs, and Institutions
60. Suspension of social and sports activities
61. Boycott of social affairs

62. Student strike
63. Social disobedience
64. Withdrawal from social institutions

Withdrawal from the Social System
65. Stay-at-home
66. Total personal noncooperation
67. "Flight" of workers
68. Sanctuary
69. Collective disappearance
70. Protest emigration (hijrat)

Economic Boycotts

Actions by Consumers
71. Consumers' boycott
72. Nonconsumption of boycotted goods
73. Policy of austerity
74. Rent withholding
75. Refusal to rent
76. National consumers' boycott
77. International consumers' boycott

Action by Workers and Producers
78. Workmen's boycott
79. Producers' boycott

Action by Middlemen
80. Suppliers' and handlers' boycott

Action by Owners and Management
81. Traders' boycott
82. Refusal to let or sell property
83. Lockout
84. Refusal of industrial assistance
85. Merchants' "general strike"

Action by Holders of Financial Resources
86. Withdrawal of bank deposits
87. Refusal to pay fees, dues, and assessments
88. Refusal to pay debts or interest
89. Severance of funds and credit
90. Revenue refusal
91. Refusal of a government's money

Action by Governments
92. Domestic embargo
93. Blacklisting of traders

94. International sellers' embargo
95. International buyers' embargo
96. International trade embargo

The Strike

Symbolic Strikes
97. Protest strike
98. Quickie walkout (lightning strike)

Agricultural Strikes
99. Peasant strike
100. Farm Workers' strike

Strikes by Special Groups
101. Refusal of impressed labor
102. Prisoners' strike
103. Craft strike
104. Professional strike

Ordinary Industrial Strikes
105. Establishment strike
106. Industry strike
107. Sympathetic strike

Restricted Strikes
108. Detailed strike
109. Bumper strike
110. Slowdown strike
111. Working-to-rule strike
112. Reporting "sick" (sick-in)
113. Strike by resignation
114. Limited strike
115. Selective strike

Multi-Industry Strikes
116. Generalized strike
117. General strike

Combination of Strikes and Economic Closures
118. Hartal
119. Economic shutdown

The Methods of Political Noncooperation

Rejection of Authority
120. Withholding or withdrawal of allegiance
121. Refusal of public support
122. Literature and speeches advocating resistance

Citizens' Noncooperation with Government
123. Boycott of legislative bodies
124. Boycott of elections
125. Boycott of government employment and positions

126. Boycott of government depts., agencies, and other bodies
127. Withdrawal from government educational institutions
128. Boycott of government-supported organizations
129. Refusal of assistance to enforcement agents
130. Removal of own signs and place marks
131. Refusal to accept appointed officials
132. Refusal to dissolve existing institutions

Citizens' Alternatives to Obedience
133. Reluctant and slow compliance
134. Nonobedience in absence of direct supervision
135. Popular nonobedience
136. Disguised disobedience
137. Refusal of an assemblage or meeting to disperse
138. Sitdown
139. Noncooperation with conscription and deportation
140. Hiding, escape, and false identities
141. Civil disobedience of "illegitimate" laws

Action by Government Personnel
142. Selective refusal of assistance by government aides
143. Blocking of lines of command and information
144. Stalling and obstruction
145. General administrative noncooperation
146. Judicial noncooperation
147. Deliberate inefficiency and selective noncooperation by enforcement agents
148. Mutiny

Domestic Governmental Action
149. Quasi-legal evasions and delays
150. Noncooperation by constituent governmental units

International Governmental Action
151. Changes in diplomatic and other representations
152. Delay and cancellation of diplomatic events
153. Withholding of diplomatic recognition
154. Severance of diplomatic relations
155. Withdrawal from international organizations
156. Refusal of membership in international bodies
157. Expulsion from international organizations

The Methods of Nonviolent Intervention

Psychological Intervention
158. Self-exposure to the elements
159. The fast
    a) Fast of moral pressure
    b) Hunger strike
    c) Satyagrahic fast
160. Reverse trial
161. Nonviolent harassment

Physical Intervention
162. Sit-in
163. Stand-in
164. Ride-in
165. Wade-in
166. Mill-in
167. Pray-in
168. Nonviolent raids
169. Nonviolent air raids
170. Nonviolent invasion
171. Nonviolent interjection
172. Nonviolent obstruction
173. Nonviolent occupation

Social Intervention
174. Establishing new social patterns
175. Overloading of facilities
176. Stall-in
177. Speak-in
178. Guerrilla theater
179. Alternative social institutions

180. Alternative communication system

Economic Intervention
181. Reverse strike
182. Stay-in strike
183. Nonviolent land seizure
184. Defiance of blockades
185. Politically motivated counterfeiting
186. Preclusive purchasing
187. Seizure of assets
188. Dumping
189. Selective patronage
190. Alternative markets
191. Alternative transportation systems
192. Alternative economic institutions

Political Intervention
193. Overloading of administrative systems
194. Disclosing identities of secret agents
195. Seeking imprisonment
196. Civil disobedience of "neutral" laws
197. Work-on without collaboration
198. Dual sovereignty and parallel government

The Forty-Five Least Wanted

Power tends to corrupt, and absolute power corrupts absolutely.

—Lord Acton

A few exemplary cases aside, we have thus far looked at dictators primarily as a plague-bearing species that should be extinguished by the year 2025. To achieve that goal, however, we must now look further down the taxonomic chain, to understand the intraspecies divisions and, finally, the forty-five individual dictators themselves (see figure 8.1).

As far as I know, this chapter is the first attempt to profile each of the world's dictators. It should not be the last. Just as the FBI systematically publishes its Ten Most Wanted list, we need to create an annual Most Wanted—or perhaps Least Wanted—Dictators publication and poster. It should be updated each year with the dictators' latest crimes, accumulating evidence for an indictment and trial, and it should focus as well on their vulnerabilities. Remaining a member of this particular club will help erode legitimacy because it becomes more exclusive as, one after another, the rogues lose power. Once we get to know them, we can think about ways to bring them down. Too often, the dictators are allowed to hide behind supposed regimes, systems, cultures, or traditions. Reports are written about countries when in fact the problem is a few individual criminals.

We first divide dictators into six categories as follows:

- *Personalistic dictators.* Saddam Hussein, arguably one of the most murderous dictators of the twentieth century, ranking after Stalin, Hitler, and Mao, included as a fresh, familiar example of the category of personalistic dictators—tyrants whose primary claim to power is their own "greatness."

Figure 8.1.   A cross-section, a dirty dozen, of the world's tyrants.

- *Monarch dictators.* The paradigm is Saudi Arabia's Crown Prince Abdullah ibn Abdul Aziz Al Saud, seventy-eight, who has effectively governed since 1995, when his brother King Fahd suffered a stroke. Such
  fraternal succession raises the possibility that a series of aging, sickly
  rulers will fail to confront this strategically important country's mounting problems, including domestic and exported Islamic extremism.
- *Military dictators.* Military dictators are exemplified by Gen. Omar Al-
  Bashir of Sudan, who has divided and waged war upon his own people
  while profiting from a lucrative slave trade in women and children.
- *Communist dictators.* A vanishing but still virulent species now found in
  Cuba, China, North Korea, and a handful of other Asian states.
- *Dominant-party dictator.* A dominant-party dictator bases his "legiti-
  macy" on a ruling party he runs, such as Hosni Mubarak's deeply corrupt
  National Democratic Party, which controls over 80 percent of the seats

in parliament. Though Egypt has fourteen political parties, all receive state financing and can be shut down at any time.

- *Theocratic dictator.* With the removal of Mullah Omar in Afghanistan, the last theocratic dictator is Iran's Ayatollah Ali Khamenei. His backwardness, brutality, and refusal to respect those elected to office has led to massive disaffection and renewed student antiregime activism. His days are numbered.

In all, there are twenty personalistic, seven monarchic, five military, five communist, seven dominant-party, and one theocratic dictators. What they have in common is a keen awareness of how thin the legitimacy of their rule actually is. In their countries, criticism of the dictator himself is banned. Their number one priority is internal security and—especially—personal safety. They fear their own people more than any external enemy. Their nearly universal corruption and flagrantly extravagant lifestyles, in the face of widespread poverty and need, have alienated their subjects. Eternal preservation of their personal power is a common goal. Nationalism and other ideologies are used in extreme forms, mainly as smokescreens. Equity flows from the state, and therefore from the leader. And they are not getting any younger. Many are old enough that they will not see 2025. A minimum objective must be to ensure that their successors are not dictators—to guarantee a succession to democracy in the manner of Spain and Portugal. In every case, the sooner these men give way to democracy the better it will be for their people, for regional and global security, for prosperity, and for freedom.

Personalistic Dictatorships

For all their idiosyncratic differences, many of the world's dictators head regimes that, beneath the surface, look remarkably similar. Lacking any real ideology and unconstrained by democratic checks and balances, they use both patronage and fear to accrue and maintain power and usually wealth. Many siphon off natural resources and tax revenues to line their pockets and reward compliant military leaders, businesspeople, advisers, and local officials. They also dole out jobs and other perks to supporters. In these societies, economic success depends on maintaining a mutually beneficial relationship with the ruler.

Depending on the political challenges they face, personalistic dictators often resort to terror and coercion to stifle opposition. Some use the security forces to harass, torture, and sometimes kill dissidents. Displaying a lighter touch, other strongmen tolerate independent newspapers, civic organizations, and even opposition parties. But they also rig elections, intimidate the judiciary, and do whatever else is necessary to make sure these groups do not become too powerful. Given that personalistic rulers can intervene in economic, social, and political affairs on a whim, life in these societies is not only brutal at times but also highly unpredictable.

Saddam Hussein, Iraq

Although Saddam Hussein was ousted by a military force led by the United States in spring 2003, we decided to leave him in the book. He may still be alive and a threat to his people, neighbors, and the world. He became a threat again after being soundly defeated in the Gulf War of 1991, after which many assumed he would be driven from power by the Iraqi people; indeed, there were uprisings, but he put them down with great brutality. We also left him in because he is such a fresh and familiar reminder of the havoc that dictators wreak around the world.

After Saddam Hussein officially came to power in 1979, he started two wars, murdered countless political opponents, attempted to exterminate Iraq's Kurdish population, and committed atrocities against Shiite Muslims in southern Iraq. In recent years, he built grandiose monuments and palaces while Iraqis suffer a humanitarian crisis of epic proportions under United Nations sanctions. All told, Saddam's casualties numbered well into the millions. In addition, he continued to threaten neighboring countries, sought to develop weapons of mass destruction, and encouraged his sons to carry on his reign of terror. He rewarded the families of Palestine's suicide bombers and sponsored international terrorist groups.

Those who have studied him closely say he is neither mad nor irrational. According to Dr. Jerrold M. Post, director of the political psychology program at George Washington University, he is indeed very dangerous, but not unpredictable. He is ambitious in the extreme, deeply paranoid, devoid of conscience, exceptionally violent, and loyal only to himself. But he is also a shrewd tactician who makes decisions based on careful consideration. His highest priority, says Dr. Post, was to survive in power with his dignity intact.

Massive bloodshed was a defining characteristic of Saddam's rule. His campaigns against ethnic Kurds have been classified as genocide by Human Rights Watch and other watchdog organizations. By itself, the Anfal operation, a systematic extermination of Kurds between February and September 1988, by conservative estimates killed sixty thousand people. The total number of Kurds killed by Iraqi armed forces between 1983 and 1993 is "well into six figures," according to Human Rights Watch. A constant menace to his neighbors, Saddam attacked Iran in 1980, sparking an eight-year war of attrition, which according to some estimates killed up to a million people, wounded many more, and created millions of refugees. The Persian Gulf War, the result of Saddam's 1990 invasion of neighboring Kuwait, claimed as many as twenty-five thousand Iraqi lives. The regime also tortured and murdered many religious leaders, particularly Shiites. In southern Iraq, the army tried to flush out small numbers of Shiite guerrillas by targeting their villages, razing homes, and draining the Amara and Hammar marshes, all but obliterating the six-thousand-year-old culture of the indigenous Marsh Arabs.

In *Republic of Fear: The Politics of Modern Iraq*, writer Kanan Makiya describes Saddam's complex network of overlapping and often competing security organizations. The interior ministry had grown so vast that the police and militia far outnumbered the armed forces. Saddam's staying power had much to do with his ability to recruit vast numbers of ordinary citizens into the security apparatus, thus turning as many people as possible into collaborators. Any perceived threat to the regime was eliminated swiftly and decisively. Citizens were routinely kidnapped, imprisoned, tortured, and murdered for allegedly insulting the president. Officials took relatives as hostages when suspects could not be found. Threats against, and assaults on, family members were used to extract confessions of wrongdoing.

Saddam, who has no military background (he failed the entrance exam for the military academy), had a tenuous relationship with the armed forces. To keep the military from threatening his power, Saddam rotated and at times executed military officers.

The Iraq that produced Saddam has long endured political and social violence. The country has seen ongoing ethnic, tribal, religious, and class conflict; local rivalries; interference by foreign states; and bloody coups and attempted coups.

Born in 1937 to a family of peasants, Saddam was raised and educated early on by his uncle and political mentor, Kairallah, who had fought the British in a 1941 uprising, spent five years in prison for nationalist agitation, and later became mayor of Baghdad. Kairallah evidently planted the first seeds of Arab nationalism, xenophobia, hatred of Jews, and contempt for Western imperialism in young Saddam. Indeed, an article written by Kairallah and later republished under Saddam's government was entitled "Three Whom God Should Not Have Created: Persians, Jews, and Flies."

Gamal Abdel Nasser's revolution in Egypt also profoundly influenced Saddam, and he joined the Ba'ath (Renaissance) Party as a secondary school student. Ba'athism advanced a vision of a modern, unified Arab nation, freed from colonialism and Western imperialism, developing economically through socialism. It also portrayed the Arab world as oppressed by the creation in 1948 of Israel. Ba'athism provided Saddam with the opportunity to prove his loyalty to the Arab cause and to demonstrate his capacity for violence. He advanced quickly in the party and took part in its unsuccessful assassination attempt against Iraqi president Abdel Karim Qassem in 1959.

During a brief period of Ba'athist rule in the early 1960s, Saddam reputedly worked as a torturer and interrogator at a detention facility. When an ideological split erupted within the party, Saddam aligned with Ba'ath founder Michel Aflaq and leader Ahmad Hassan al-Bakr, and reportedly offered to assassinate leftists within the party. In 1968, the Ba'ath took power again, with Bakr as president. However, Saddam from early on was seen as the strongman behind the regime. He built up the internal security apparatus and the regime's propaganda machine. He also began eliminating his political rivals. The beginning of Ba'ath rule in 1968 was marked by widespread public denunciations, show trials, and executions of "spies."

Following a dispute with Bakr over Iraqi-Syrian federation, Saddam convinced Bakr to step down in 1979. The inauguration of Saddam's rule was described as a "baptism of blood" by Judith Miller and Laurie Mylroie in their book, *Saddam Hussein and the Crisis in the Gulf.* The new leader called a meeting of some one thousand top-level party members. First, a Shiite party secretary read a fabricated confession of treason. Saddam then read a list of condemned "traitors," including heads of labor unions and members of the Revolutionary Command Council. Senior party members were forced to execute as many as five hundred supposed political opponents, beginning a campaign of government-sponsored killings and disappearances.

Saddam's close relatives were not immune from his reign of terror. Two of his sons-in-law, who were brothers, defected to Jordan in 1995, prompting allegations involving millions of dollars in stolen money and a possible attempt to overthrow Saddam. The brothers returned to Iraq in 1996 after Saddam promised amnesty and safe passage in exchange for information about the stolen money. Their uncle, a high-ranking member of Saddam's regime who led the chemical attack on the Kurds years earlier, along with Saddam's sons Uday and Qusay Hussein, raided the brothers' house, killing them and several other members of their immediate family.

Uday and Qusay built their own reputations for violence and excess. Stories abound about Uday's exploits, which include clubbing to death a servant of Saddam, shooting women who refused his advances, and gunning down an uncle during a quarrel. After a 1996 assassination attempt that left him partially disabled, Uday ran the media and overseas trade, which mostly involved his father's lucrative smuggling of goods, food, and medicine on the black market. He was also the head of the national soccer team and reportedly had players tortured for losing games. Qusay, the younger brother, was responsible for the military, intelligence, and security services and overseas annual purges of many prison inmates. He was seen as his father's likely successor.

Initially, Saddam's rule was not based exclusively on terror. Beginning in the early 1970s, he pursued social policies that boosted his popularity among Iraqis. He nationalized Iraqi oil companies in 1972 and used the money to implement a huge economic development program. The country saw improved standards of living, education, literacy, and health care. The government permitted the functioning of trade unions loyal to the Ba'ath Party and launched social security and land reform programs. In addition, Saddam championed a personal-status law that was relatively progressive for the Middle East, affording Iraqi women greater protections than those enjoyed by their counterparts in neighboring Iran or in Saudi Arabia. His understanding of the concerns of ordinary Iraqis helped cement his monopoly on power.

The leader who once used oil revenues to bring to his country a degree of modernity ended up using the oil-for-food exception to UN sanctions to enrich himself while his people starved. At least 1.25 million Iraqis reportedly died, including more than 500,000 children under age five, as indicated by a sharp escalation of the mortality rate between 1991 and 1999, according to UNICEF. The UN Human Development Index, which ranks 174 countries on quality of life as measured by social indicators such as education, health care, and material wealth, rated Iraq 55th in 1990. By 2000, Iraq had dropped to 126th, despite marked improvement in living standards under the oil-for-food program in Kurdish-administered northern Iraq.

Meanwhile, observers estimated Saddam's personal fortune at around $6 billion in unfrozen foreign assets. He spent untold sums of money on monuments to himself in the form of palaces, sculptures, amusement parks, and mosques. Baghdad boasted two victory arches, a complex in the shape of Iraq with a presidential residence in the center, and dozens of smaller memorials and fountains. An attempt to reconstruct the ancient city of Babylon used bricks inscribed with tributes to Saddam. But perhaps the most astonishing project is the brand new "Mother of all Battles" mosque. Named for the first Gulf War, the mosque featured towering minarets in the shape of scud missiles, a massive water-and-stone relief map of the Arab world, and a 605-page Koran allegedly written in Saddam's blood. Mosque-building was largely seen as a cynical attempt by Saddam to claim religious legitimacy. An even bigger mosque, intended to be the world's largest, neared completion, as did another presidential palace—the latest of dozens—which included "four huge busts of Saddam's scowling visage staring out over the city's squalor," according to London's *Daily Telegraph*.

Saddam blamed the international community, and particularly the United States and Britain, for his country's humanitarian crisis. His defiance of the

West, combined with an international weariness with sanctions, particularly within countries that wanted to invest in Iraq's oil industry, had enhanced his status among fellow Arab states. In addition, the embargo on Iraq was gradually eroding as Arab, European, and African countries defied it with increasing frequency. But in the end, his defiance of the international community and his brutality to his own people led to his removal from power by military force.

Isaias Afwerki, Eritrea

For a fleeting moment in the 1990s, it seemed that the Great Lakes region of eastern Africa and the Horn of Africa, a swath of the continent sorely in need of benevolent leaders, had finally found a few good men. In a handful of countries, youthful rulers who had proven their mettle as guerrilla leaders were emphasizing clean government over cronyism and pragmatism over ideology. During his 1998 trip to Africa, U.S. president Bill Clinton hailed what he called a "new generation of African leaders" who seemed poised to reverse the fortunes of their troubled lands. These hopes have largely been dashed, as the onetime saviors are looking increasingly like garden-variety autocrats. Even when Clinton spoke, none of the new-generation leaders were true democrats. But Clinton saw Isaias Afwerki of Eritrea, Meles Zenawi of Ethiopia, Yoweri Museveni of Uganda, Paul Kagame of Rwanda, and, potentially, Laurent Kabila of Congo as benign rulers who would focus on economic development, good governance, and free markets.

President Afwerki of Eritrea arguably is the most repressive among this new group of leaders. His government has refused to hold elections, stunted the growth of independent civil society groups, and sharply curbed press freedom.

Afwerki has tried to justify restrictions on political rights by citing the difficulties faced by his young, impoverished country. "Constitutionality, political pluralism and free and fair elections are naturally the best institutional tools" for achieving stability and economic development, Afwerki said at an April 2000 speech at Princeton University. But, he added, these processes must "be allowed to develop with appropriate rhythm and pace that takes into account the prevailing cultural and political realities in the specific country in question."

Having come to power as the popular head of the guerrilla movement that won Eritrea's independence from Ethiopia, Afwerki has given no hint about when he will hold presidential elections. Parliamentary elections once scheduled for the end of 2001 have been put off indefinitely.

In refusing to put their fate in the hands of voters, Afwerki and the other new-generation leaders seem to be squandering a chance to build democratic institutions and other safeguards against a future relapse into even more dictatorial rule. Lacking a popular mandate at the polls, Afwerki and the other new leaders have instead based their legitimacy largely on their success in either toppling brutal dictators or ending mass killing. Before they came to power, their countries had experienced some of the worst horrors visited on postcolonial Africa: genocide in Rwanda, Idi Amin's maniacal rule in Uganda, famine in the Horn of Africa, and terror and state collapse in Mobutu Sese Seko's Zaire, now Congo.

With their talk of good governance, the new generation offered the prospect of enlightened leadership for impoverished countries that had been battered by civil conflict and run into the ground economically by indifferent despots. Some were former Marxists, but they had long ago shed their ideological baggage. Rejecting the arguments of many Third World leaders and intellectuals, Afwerki argued that the greatest obstacle to economic development was not capitalism or past colonialism but corruption.

Criticized widely for failing to intervene in the 1994 massacres in Rwanda, which killed at least five hundred thousand civilians, Washington apparently viewed solid ties with these leaders as the foundation for greater regional engagement. The Clinton administration no doubt also saw these generally pro-Western rulers as bulwarks against the Islamic fundamentalist regime in Sudan.

But Clinton's hopes began fading almost as soon as his visit ended. Within months, Eritrea and Ethiopia began a war that would kill one hundred thousand people and displace one million others, while Museveni and Kagame sent arms and troops to aid rebels in neighboring Congo. There, Kabila's government had already banned political parties and demonstrations and was routinely harassing journalists, while doing little to end the conflict engulfing that sprawling land. Called by some Africa's first world war, the fighting drew in forces from at least eight countries. Kabila was assassinated in January 2001 to be succeeded by his relatively inexperienced son, Joseph.

Nearly every stage of Afwerki's adult life has been intricately linked to the Eritreans' decades-long struggle to create a viable, independent country. Born in 1945, he joined the nationalist, Marxist Eritrean People's Liberation Front (EPLF) in 1966 in its fight against the Ethiopian government, then headed by the self-styled emperor Haile Selassie. Afwerki received military training in China the same year and later became an EPLF deputy divisional commander. He was named the guerrilla movement's secretary general in 1987 and became president of independent Eritrea in 1993.

Initially, Afwerki's calls for national self-reliance resonated in a battle-hardened country where men and women fought side-by-side in the trenches during the long independence struggle. The new country rejected most foreign aid, and the government required youths to perform national service. But in the aftermath of the border war with Ethiopia, many Eritreans are questioning whether they should continue sacrificing for their country or instead focus on their own survival, says George B. N. Ayittey, a professor of economics at American University and the president of the Washington-based Free Africa Foundation. "What did they get out of this war? Nothing. They fought over a barren strip of land." He notes that Afwerki's calls after the war for Eritreans to make further sacrifices in order to restore the country's self-reliance rang hollow given the conflict's devastating effect on the economy. By the time the fighting ended in 2000, Eritrea had become partially dependent on food aid and was saddled with huge debts for arms purchases. Ayittey believes that Afwerki faces little immediate threat from the decimated political opposition but could be overthrown by disgruntled soldiers or even the military brass. "I don't think he can hold out much longer."

By most accounts, the war began in May 1998, when Eritrean forces invaded the border town of Badme, claimed by both sides but in Ethiopian hands. Evoking the carnage of World War I, the two countries fought more than two years of trench warfare that saw waves of Ethiopian soldiers advancing and then being cut down, the 620-mile desert border barely budging throughout the conflict.

Adding to the senselessness of the war, Afwerki and Meles Zenawi, his Ethiopian counterpart, are distant cousins who worked together for years to overthrow Ethiopian dictator Mengistu Haile Mariam in 1991. Two years later, Ethiopia ceded control over Eritrea after its would-be citizens voted overwhelmingly for independence in a referendum.

Facing growing opposition at home in the war's aftermath, Afwerki's regime began cracking down on freedom of expression in September 2001. That month, authorities shut down the country's eight independent newspapers for allegedly failing to abide by the press law and detained ten leading journalists and eleven dissident politicians. The human rights group Amnesty International said in September 2002 that it had learned of dozens of other detentions of business people, civil servants, journalists, former liberation fighters, and elders who had tried to mediate between the government and its critics. All were being held without charges or trials.

Even if trials were held in these cases, prospects that they would be fair are bleak. Eritrea's judiciary is "weak and subject to executive interference," according to the U.S. State Department's global human rights report for 2001.

So far, the promise of Afwerki and his new-generation counterparts has not been realized. Most of them seem focused primarily on maintaining power. Ayittey even thinks that President Clinton's praise of Afwerki may have emboldened the Eritrean leader to put his small country at risk by challenging Ethiopia. "All that went to his head," Ayittey says. "His ego outstripped him and he started throwing his weight around in the region. Then everything started to unravel." But the people of these countries still want to achieve the promise—to emerge finally and fully from decades of civil conflict, economic mismanagement, and repressive rule.

Teodoro Obiang Nguema Mbasogo, Equatorial Guinea

Teodoro Obiang Nguema Mbasogo, Equatorial Guinea's autocratic president, is actually fairly tolerant compared with his uncle, Francisco Macias Nguema, whose vicious reign in the 1970s drove one-third of this tiny central African country's population into exile. But Obiang, who has wielded near absolute power since helping to overthrow Nguema in 1979, has not shied away from using brute force to fend off challenges to his rule.

Thanks to offshore oil, Equatorial Guinea, consisting of a patch of land on mainland central Africa and an island in the Atlantic, has one of the highest per capita incomes in sub-Saharan Africa. Relatively little wealth, however, has trickled down to the average person in this former Spanish colony, where most people are illiterate subsistence farmers.

Obiang's unchecked grip on power raises the concern that oil revenues will simply prop up the regime, which is dominated by members of the president's Fang ethnic group. Observers say the government wields power not through formal institutions but in part by doling out patronage to compliant business leaders, bureaucrats, and other powerful interest groups.

"The worst of the old dictatorship's violence is gone, but what you are left with is a patrimonial state with a complete absence of the rule of law," a foreign diplomat told the New York Times in 1998. "The President's clan controls everything and there is total confusion between state resources and personal wealth." Though his health is reportedly failing, Obiang could try to keep power and wealth in the family by installing one of his sons as president. Many expect his two eldest sons, Teodorin Nguema Obiang and Gabriel Nguema Lima, to compete to succeed him, the London-based Africa Confidential newsletter reported in 1999.

Obiang has long been sensitive to outside criticism of Equatorial Guinea's bleak human rights record. Authorities in 1993 expelled the American ambassador, John Bennett, on charges of witchcraft after he complained openly about the regime's human rights abuses. Nevertheless, the president admitted publicly for the first time in 1997 that some civilians, as well as security and military officers, were "systematically violating human rights." Obiang claimed that his government would take steps to end these abuses. But authorities have punished few human rights violators, and Obiang's security forces continue to commit abuses. During a private visit to the United States in March 2001, Obiang returned to old form and denied that any violations were taking place. "There is no abuse with respect to human rights," Obiang pointedly told reporters.

Since the early 1990s, however, Amnesty International has recorded hundreds of cases of torture and ill treatment in Equatorial Guinea, often of members of the opposition. A court in June 2002 handed down prison terms of between six and twenty years to nearly 70 people on the sole basis of statements extracted through torture under incommunicado detention, Amnesty International reported. They were among more than 150 people arrested in March on charges of undermining state security.

In one of the few signs of positive change, soldiers appear to be harassing ordinary citizens somewhat less than in the past. "People can walk freely," Isabel Tonka, twenty-five, a member of the Bubi ethnic group, told the *New York Times* in July 2000. "It is not like before. I can go to my village and come back to Malabo without hassle." Tonka's Bubi ethnic group had suffered during a chilling orgy of violence following a January 1998 guerrilla attack on a military barracks on the island of Bioko, where Malabo, the capital, is located. Following the attack, which killed three soldiers and several civilians, the government arrested about five hundred people, most of them solely because they were ethnic Bubis, according to Amnesty International. The Bubis are the indigenous people of Bioko. Six died after being tortured by security forces, while soldiers watched as mobs beat and raped ethnic Bubis, the report added.

Obiang blamed the barracks attack on an outlawed separatist group, the Movimento de Autodeterminación de la Isla de Bioko, and sentenced fifteen of its members to death and seventy other people to prison terms of between six and twenty-six years for their alleged involvement. All of the convictions were based on confessions made under torture, a 1999 Amnesty International report said. Obiang later commuted the death sentences to life imprisonment.

Obiang has been a dominant figure in Equatorial Guinea for much of its turbulent history since the country gained independence in 1968. Born in 1942, he received military training in Spain and seized power in 1979 after leading a military coup that overthrew and later executed his uncle, Francisco Macias Nguema. During a brutal eleven-year reign, Nguema had jailed and executed opponents, closed schools and churches, and even forbade local fishermen to use their canoes. Some experts suggest that Obiang himself played a major role in fomenting the terror. "As head of the army, Obiang was Macias's main enforcer," a foreign diplomat told London's *Daily Telegraph* in 1992.

The president won a new seven-year term in 1996 with more than 97 percent of the vote in an election that both opposition and outside observers said was marred by fraud and intimidation. Obiang has in recent years somewhat loosened his grip on the media but still severely restricts freedom of expression. A few small independent newspapers publish occasionally and two of them, *Tiempo* and *La Opinión*, are often critical of the regime. At the same time, courts handed down prison terms, in one case for three years, to five people arrested in 1999 for possessing a two-year-old Amnesty International appeal document, photocopying a Spanish newspaper article, or possessing an opposition paper.

Prison conditions continue to be dismal, even though the government has granted the International Committee of the Red Cross access to Equatorial Guinea's prisons. "There have been reports that prison authorities tortured, beat, and otherwise abused prisoners, and that such abuse, combined with a lack of medical care, resulted in the deaths of prisoners," according to the U.S. State Department's report on Equatorial Guinea's human rights record in 2001.

Whoever controls this country in the coming years will have the opportunity to use the oil boom to improve the dreary lives of ordinary citizens. Recent evidence suggests, however, that the government is already playing fast and loose with oil revenues. In its typically oblique language, the International Monetary Fund noted in an October 1999 report that the government's "management of oil production-sharing contracts continues to lack transparency, with no fiscal control over the payments made by the oil companies."

Led by the American giant ExxonMobil, those companies pump up to 120,000 barrels a day. That's paltry compared with nearby Nigeria, but a significant amount in a country of 465,000 people. Already, Equatorial Guinea is the fourth largest destination for American investment in sub-Saharan Africa. This investment gives Washington and the companies enormous potential leverage over the government's human rights actions and its accounting of the oil revenues.

Per capita gross domestic product (GDP) increased to $1,170 in 1999 from $370 in 1995, the year before the country's first major oil field began production, according to World Bank figures. It is hard, however, to determine from these aggregate national numbers just how much wealth is actually trickling down to ordinary citizens.

The government says it has used oil revenues to build new paved roads and an electricity plant that provides power to most of Malabo. Infant mortality declined to 104 per 1,000 births in 1999 from 112 per 1,000 in 1995, according to the World Bank.

But other signs hint that at least some of the oil revenues are simply enhancing the lifestyles of the rich and powerful. The international airport boasts a sparkling new presidential wing, new villas are sprouting up in the rich Malabo neighborhood of Little Spain, and the government built a convention hall and seventeen villas for visiting dignitaries before hosting a 1999 conference of central African countries.

For now, most ordinary citizens are simply waiting for the good life to arrive. With around 44 percent of the population under the age of fifteen, relatively few Equatorial Guineans can remember the terror of the Nguema regime in the 1970s. But Obiang's legacy so far—rampant human rights abuses, continued abject poverty, and decrepit state institutions—has given them ample reason to demand more enlightened leadership.

Idriss Déby, Chad

Idriss Déby has ruled Chad since 1990, when he led an insurgency that toppled the dictatorship of Hissène Habré. Both army soldiers and rebels from the Movement for Democracy and Justice in Chad, headed by former defense minister Youssouf Togoïmi, are accused of killings and torture. In a country that has been wracked by almost constant civil conflict since gaining independence from France in 1960, Déby has kept control of the army and most key government posts in the hands of members of the Zaghawa and Bideyat ethnic groups. They are found mainly in the president's home region in the northeast. International and domestic observers cited serious flaws in the May 2001 presidential elections that gave the military-backed Déby a second five-year term. Born in 1952, Déby, a career army officer, had helped Habré come to power in 1982. After being accused of plotting a coup, he fled in 1989 to Sudan, where his forces regrouped before ousting Habré.

Gnassingbé Eyadéma, Togo

Africa's longest-standing leader, Gnassingbé Eyadéma, sixty-five, led an army coup in 1967 to seize power from a democratically elected government, then suspended the constitution and extended his rule through fraudulent elections. Political parties were legalized in 1991 and a democratic constitution was adopted in 1992, but soldiers and secret police suppressed opposition through the harassment, intimidation, and murder of opposition supporters. The country's main opposition leader, Gilchrist Olympio, lives in exile. Eyadéma won fraudulent presidential elections in 1993 and 1998. The opposition boycotted October 2002 legislative elections, and Eyadéma's Rally of the Togolese People won seventy-two of eighty-one seats. In December, parliament changed the constitution, which restricted presidents to two terms, to allow Eyadéma to run for reelection in 2003. Parliament amended the media law in September 2002 to impose heavy sentences for "defaming or insulting" the president. "Insulting the head of state" now carries a penalty of up to five years' imprisonment. Human rights groups continue to denounce killings, arbitrary arrest, political detention, and torture. Amnesty International has accused Eyadéma's administration of widespread human rights abuses, including summary executions in the run-up to the 1998 presidential election.

Paul Biya, Cameroon

Paul Biya, sixty-nine, is one of Africa's most enduring dictators, having ruled Cameroon since 1982 following the resignation of another strongman, President Ahmadou Ahidjou. Biya's security forces routinely commit extrajudicial killings, torture, and politically motivated disappearances, while slavery reportedly persists in some northern areas. Having legalized opposition parties in the early 1990s, Biya resorted to intimidation, manipulation, and fraud to ensure his victory in presidential elections in 1992 and 1997. Opposition leaders claimed massive vote rigging in June 2002 parliamentary elections, which resulted in the ruling party increasing its already overwhelming majority in the legislature. The next presidential vote is due in 2004.

Observers of both Chad and Cameroon are concerned that ordinary citizens will see few benefits from a controversial oil pipeline project backed by the World Bank. Scheduled for completion in 2004, the 680-mile, $3.7 billion pipeline will take oil from Chad to Cameroon's Atlantic port of Kribi. The bank says that adequate safeguards are in place to deter corruption once the oil revenues begin flowing, but many observers remain wary given the pervasive graft in both countries. Transparency International has ranked Cameroon at or near the bottom of its annual corruption surveys. The Berlin-based organization has not rated Chad, but anecdotal evidence suggests that corruption and fraud are also rife in that country.

Charles Taylor, Liberia

A onetime warlord and escapee from an American prison, President Charles Taylor has been a dominant force in Liberia since 1990, when his National Patriotic Front of Liberia (NPFL) took control of much of the countryside after invading from neighboring Cote d'Ivoire on Christmas Day in 1989. His government is increasingly isolated from the international community amid reports of continued human rights abuses and concerns that Taylor is seeking to dominate the Manu River region, which also includes Guinea and Sierra Leone. The United Nations imposed sanctions in 2001 to punish the regime for supporting Revolutionary United Front rebels in Sierra Leone. Taylor denied the charges. The sanctions prevent Taylor and his associates from traveling abroad, buying weapons and selling diamonds.

Meanwhile, Liberia and Guinea have accused each other of harboring dissidents seeking to overthrow their governments. Taylor has reportedly sponsored cross-border attacks in Guinea that began in earnest in 2000 by fighters based in Liberia and Sierra Leone. At home, the regime has faced an insurgency since 1999 by a rebel group calling itself Liberians United for Reconciliation and Democracy. The government declared a state of emergency in February 2002 in response to a rebel attack near the capital, Monrovia. As 2003 unfolded, fighting intensified and international concerns increased. Taylor's security forces, meanwhile, continue to commit abuses with impunity, including illegal detention, torture, and extrajudicial killings.

Taylor was elected president in 1997 after leading his rebel forces for seven years against rival guerrilla groups and a Nigerian-led intervention force that mostly protected the capital. The conflict was notorious in part for the widespread use of child soldiers, often drugged and intoxicated to steel them for battle. The 1997 presidential election, in which Taylor won around three-quarters of the vote, were held in an atmosphere of intimidation. Some observers said Taylor's victory reflected a vote for peace more than any real support for the man himself, since many Liberians believed that Taylor would go back to war if he lost.

Born in Liberia in 1948 to a Liberian mother and American father, Taylor graduated from Bentley College in Massachusetts in 1977 and later joined the Liberian government of Samuel Doe. Charged with embezzling $900,000 as the director of the government's General Services Agency, he fled to the United States, where he was arrested. He escaped from prison in Massachusetts and made his way back to Africa, where he joined and later became the leader of the exile-based NPFL.

Lansana Conté, Guinea

In neighboring Guinea, President Lansana Conté took power in 1984 following the death of Ahmed Sékou Touré, the Marxist dictator who had ruled this West African country since its independence from France in 1958. Born in 1944, Conté served in the French army and later became the Guinean army's chief of staff, putting him in position to succeed Touré.

Though Conté is quick to resort to repression, his maintenance of power depends in large part on being able to dole out ample jobs, business concessions, and other patronage to civilian and military supporters. He was nearly toppled in 1996 by an army mutiny. In another threat to his power, parts of southern Guinea have been destabilized since the late 1990s by the attacks of Liberia-based rebels and the presence of tens of thousands of refugees fleeing violence and repression in Liberia and Sierra Leone. Backed by state patronage and government-controlled media, Conté won reelection to a second five-year term in 1998. He then had hundreds of political figures arrested. They included Alpha Condé, the official third-place finisher, who later received a five-year prison term for sedition.

Robert Mugabe, Zimbabwe

Once revered by many of his countrymen for his leading role in overthrowing white minority rule in Zimbabwe, President Robert Mugabe now faces widespread discontent over a stolen election and food shortages and other economic hardships. In his struggle to retain power, in March 2002 he staged presidential elections deemed unfree and unfair by independent observers. Tens of thousands of urban opposition supporters were denied the right to vote because of last-minute polling-station closures and changes. In the long campaign of intimidation prior to the poll, Mugabe detained, harassed, and had his supporters assault leaders of the opposition Movement for Democratic Change (MDC), student activists, and labor organizers. A number of deaths were associated with the campaign, almost all traceable to the ruling Zimbabwe African National Union–Popular Front (ZANU–PF) and its supporters. State authorities, including the army and the police, have been employed in an overtly political role. Despite government intimidation of its candidates and supporters, the opposition Movement for Democratic Change, led by Morgan Tsvangirai, won 57 out of 150 seats in the 2000 parliamentary elections. Opposition candidates had won only 3 seats in the 1995 vote. For roughly a year prior to the election, Mugabe instigated the violent takeover of white-owned farms by "war veterans" in the name of land redistribution—for which a legal procedure was to be devised.

The aging Mugabe, who was born in 1924, is one of the last of a generation of African anticolonial leaders. He became a leader in the 1960s of a violent guerrilla movement against the white minority regime in what was then Southern Rhodesia. That government unilaterally declared independence from Britain in 1965. Mugabe helped found the ruling Zimbabwe African National Union in 1963 and, along with Joshua Nkomo of the rival Zimbabwe African People's Union, later negotiated the end of white rule. Mugabe became prime minister of the new state of Zimbabwe in 1980 and took office as president in 1987. Since achieving power, Mugabe has not shrunk from employing violence to achieve political ends. The worst such instance was in 1984, when he sent the North Korean–trained Fifth Brigade to Matabeleland, in the west of the country, home of the Ndbele people. In a campaign to establish dominance over the local population, his Fifth Brigade is reputed to have killed more than ten thousand people. His opponents continue to be killed. Economic mismanagement, meanwhile, has contributed to a famine that affects nearly two-thirds of Zimbabwe's twelve million people. Some 70 percent of working-age Zimbabweans lack jobs.

Muammar al-Qaddafi, Libya

Strongman Muammar al-Qaddafi is trying to end Libya's international isolation as economic mismanagement, corruption, and high unemployment continue to plague ordinary Libyans. They reap relatively few benefits from Libya's roughly $10 billion in annual oil revenues. Qaddafi's diplomatic offensive began in 1999 with the surrender of two Libyan nationals suspected in the 1988 bombing of Pan Am Flight 103 over Lockerbie, Scotland. The United Nations later suspended sanctions imposed in the wake of the bombing, which killed all 270 people aboard the aircraft. Qaddafi has also agreed to pay compensation to the families of 170 people killed in the 1989 bombing of a French airliner over Niger, accepted responsibility for the 1984 killing of a British police officer by shots fired from the Libyan embassy in London, and expelled from Libya the Abu Nidal terrorist organization. The United States, however, has maintained unilateral sanctions, imposed in 1981, because Libya is still on Washington's list of countries that sponsor terrorism.

As commander in chief of the armed forces and chairman of the ruling Revolutionary Command Council, Qaddafi rules by decree with the aid of a small group of close associates. Amnesty International estimates that Libyan jails hold at least one thousand political prisoners. Independent political parties, civic groups, and media are illegal.

Born in 1942 near the desert town of Sirte, Qaddafi attended the University of Libya before joining the army. He has ruled Libya since leading a 1969 coup as a twenty-seven-year-old that overthrew the monarchy of King Idris. The Libyan leader calls his political system, which draws on Arab nationalism, Third World socialism, and Islamic beliefs, a *jamahiriya*, loosely translated as a "state of the masses." But so-called people's committees, which in theory translate grassroots demands into state policy, have no real power. Qaddafi's Green Book purports to chart an economic alternative to both communism and capitalism. In practice, this has meant state control over oil and other key industries.

Joseph Kabila, Democratic Republic of the Congo

Both the Democratic Republic of the Congo and Somalia have only nominal central governments with little real power. In Congo, President Joseph Kabila has shown willingness to cooperate with the United Nations in implementing a 1999 peace accord aimed at ending the fractious central African country's civil war. With the withdrawal of the last Rwandan troops in October 2002, the country was mostly free of foreign forces, although local militias continued to hold sway in parts of the country. But observers question whether Kabila, who took power in January 2001 as a thirty-one-year-old following the murder of his father, Laurent Kabila, has the clout to stand up to the many powerful interests that have profited from the mineral-rich country's war economy. Kabila had relied for support on Zimbabwe, Angola, and

Namibia while facing rebel groups backed by Rwandan, Ugandan, and Burundian troops.

Musa Sude Yalahow, Somalia

With much of its territory carved up among clan-based warlords, Somalia continues to be a failed state. A transitional government, elected in 2000 by a conference of businesspeople, academics, and former officials, controls only half of the capital of Mogadishu and a short sliver of coastline. Meanwhile, Musa Sude Yalahow, a former driver, controls the rest of Mogadishu, local strongmen control fiefs in southern and central Somalia, and northern Somalia has two de facto ministates, Somaliland and Puntland.

Islam Karimov, Uzbekistan

The Soviet Union may molder in the dustbin of history, but Islam Karimov, the president of Uzbekistan, is running his corner of the former empire much as he did in the days when he was Moscow's placeman in the republic. An engineer by training and a onetime Soviet factory boss, Karimov heads a secular dictatorship that bans true opposition parties and prevents Muslims from worshiping freely in Central Asia's most populous country. Authorities allow Muslims, who make up 90 percent of the population, to pray only at government-sanctioned mosques and have arrested thousands for alleged links to Islamic fundamentalists.

Uzbekistan—at least until recently—faced a small but deadly Islamic insurgency, but human rights groups and other observers say that Karimov uses this threat as a pretext to crack down on political opponents, both real and imagined. In a society where followers tend to practice a tolerant version of Islam, authorities have arrested many men simply for wearing the long beards favored by devout Muslims.

As a strongman who heads a strategically situated country, Karimov has been both courted and occasionally criticized by Western leaders. For the most part, they view Uzbekistan, which borders Afghanistan and sits astride potential oil pipeline routes, as a critical buffer against the spread of Islamic fundamentalism in resource-rich Central Asia. Washington has been promoting the development of a trans-Caspian pipeline that would transport oil from Uzbekistan and other regional countries to the West as an alternative to the existing Russian energy grid.

Uzbekistan's importance to the United States in particular rose during the American-led campaign against terrorism in the wake of the September 2001 terrorist attacks in the United States. Karimov allowed American troops and warplanes to use an Uzbek airbase to launch attacks on targets in neighboring Afghanistan.

At home, Karimov has maintained power in part by allowing traditional clan and family heads to control local fiefdoms in return for their support, according to Roger Kangas, a professor of Central Asian studies at the George C. Marshall Center in Garmisch-Partenkirchen, Germany. Karimov also keeps top government officials off balance by shuffling portfolios and assignments and rewards loyalty—and perhaps keeps potential rivals outside of Uzbekistan—by doling out plum diplomatic postings. By basing access to power and privilege on fealty to himself, Kangas notes, Karimov makes it clear to his backers that "if someone else can muster more support, your days are numbered."

In relying on patronage networks, Karimov is using a system that he inherited from his days as the head of the republic's Communist Party during the waning years of Soviet rule. During the seven decades that Uzbekistan was part of the Soviet Union, Moscow split up many tribes and fostered regional, rather than tribal, identities among the population. Today, regional bosses continue to oversee the production of cotton, which accounts for some 85 percent of Uzbekistan's GDP.

Karimov's political fate in the coming years will depend in part on his ability to control these regional leaders and reap the benefits of cotton production and trade, according to Pauline Jones-Luong, a professor of political science at Yale University. "The system can unravel if they produce less or sell on their own," she argues, referring to the tendency of local leaders to adjust their loyalty to Karimov according to their perceptions of his strength.

These regional leaders became more brazen in defying Karimov after a series of car-bomb attacks rocked Tashkent, the capital, in early 1999, killing sixteen people. "Perceptions of weakness in the regime gave regional leaders more leeway to take advantage" by keeping more of the cotton proceeds for themselves, Jones-Luong says. The United States will reverse this trend and strengthen Karimov's grip on power, she believes, if it rewards Uzbekistan in the years ahead with significant aid and diplomatic support for its role in the war on terrorism.

Without offering any real evidence, Karimov blamed the 1999 bombings, which he called an attempt on his life, on the Islamic Movement of Uzbekistan (IMU), a shadowy fundamentalist guerrilla outfit. In the aftermath, authorities arrested suspected supporters of outlawed Islamic opposition groups as well as members of the banned Erk and Birlik secular opposition parties and independent human rights workers. The crackdown on suspected Islamists intensified after IMU rebels in August 1999 entered neighboring Kyrgyzstan from Tajikistan on their way to Uzbekistan. Authorities handed down lengthy prison sentences to thousands of devout Muslims following hugely flawed trials, according to Amnesty International.

Karimov also used fighting words to condemn what he called religious extremism. He reportedly said in 1999 that he would order authorities to arrest the father of any suspected militant if the son could not be found. "If my child chose such a path, I myself would rip off his head," he was quoted by the local press as saying.

Kangas believes that while many Muslims in Uzbekistan are rediscovering Islam, the actual threat to the regime in the coming years from religious extremism is limited. He notes that the IMU lost every engagement it fought against government troops in 1999 and 2000 and suffered a drop in financial support after the United States launched its antiterrorism campaign. But, Kangas cautions, "if the economy doesn't do well, people may start falling into the extremist camp."

Though it still provides a convenient pretext for government repression, the IMU now appears to pose even less of a threat to the regime after having lost secure bases in Afghanistan during the U.S.-led campaign to oust the Taliban in that country. The group, which says it seeks to turn Uzbekistan into an Islamic state, has been bankrolled by Afghanistan's drug trade and by Osama bin Laden, the Hong Kong–based *Far Eastern Economic Review* reported in 2000. Previous attacks resulted in considerable suffering among ordinary villagers. After Uzbek forces clashed with IMU guerrillas in August 2000, authorities forcibly rounded up and resettled thousands of mostly ethnic Tajiks from the southern Surkhandaryan region on the border with Tajikistan, reportedly because rebels had infiltrated these villages, Amnesty International said.

Before Uzbekistan achieved independence in 1991, Karimov's career path seemed to be that of a typical Soviet functionary. Born in 1938 in the central Uzbek town of Samarkand, he received graduate degrees in mechanical engineering and economics and worked in the state industrial sector before entering government in 1966. Beginning with a posting in the State Planning Committee, Karimov rose to become the first secretary of the republic's Communist Party before becoming president of Uzbekistan in 1990. Karimov was reelected for a second five-year term in 2000 (parliament extended his first term for five years in 1995). The Vienna-based Organization for Security and Cooperation in Europe (OSCE) considered the electoral process to be so flawed that it declined to send observers. International human rights groups strongly criticized a referendum in January 2002 that extended the presidential term from five to seven years.

Though he owes his rise to his agility in the old Soviet system, Karimov has claimed that Uzbekistan's communist legacy is an obstacle to democratic rule. "We will build democratic institutions—but keeping in mind our own special circumstances," he told *Time* magazine in July 1994. "Do you think it was possible to create other political parties in a state long dominated by the Communist Party?" Twelve former communist countries in Europe have, however, managed to replace one-party regimes with multiparty systems.

Measuring the true popularity of a leader in a closed society that lacks opinion polling is difficult, but Kangas believes that many Uzbeks support Karimov. He says that ordinary citizens realize that their country avoided the civil conflicts that destabilized neighboring Afghanistan and Tajikistan. Moreover, the economy did not contract as much as in Russia and many other post-Soviet states.

At the same time, Uzbekistan has many teachers, engineers, and other professionals who seek a more accountable and effective government. Karimov has used intimidation and harassment to try to marginalize secular opposition groups such as Birlik and Erk, driving some of their members into exile. But independent nongovernmental groups such as the Human Rights Society of Uzbekistan continue to defy official pressure and publicize government wrongdoing.

Perhaps equally important, many ordinary Uzbeks feel frustrated that independence has not led to increased prosperity. The average income of $620 in 2000 placed Uzbekistan in the ranks of the world's low-income countries, albeit above the group average of $420, according to the World Bank. "There was lots of hype and expectations about post-Soviet economic development," Kangas says. "People know they don't have a lot compared with people in other countries."

Saparmurad Niyazov, Turkmenistan

As in Uzbekistan, personalistic dictators hold sway in the other four Central Asian states. Altogether four of the five Central Asian dictators are communist-era party bosses. This lack of change in the people in power goes a long way to explain the region's backwardness vis-à-vis the European former communist states. Under strongman Saparmurad Niyazov, Turkmenistan shows little sign of easing the blanket repression that has made him the worst human rights violator in the region. Niyazov had parliament declare him president for life in 1999, making Turkmenistan the only former Soviet republic to dispense with even the pretense of presidential elections. The government also controls all print and broadcast media, dominates the judiciary, restricts religious freedom, and maintains a ban on opposition parties, including the main opposition Agzybirlik group. Early in 2003 Niyazov conducted show trials of political opponents for allegedly trying to assassinate him, which the Western press compared to the worst of Stalin's show trials. The landlocked country has the world's fourth largest natural gas reserves, but limited export routes have largely prevented it from selling gas to lucrative Western markets.

The former Soviet-era communist boss has created an elaborate cult of personality as the self-styled Turkmenbashi, or leader of the Turkmen. As the *Washington Post* pointed out on 8 July 2002, the money—every denomination—bears the portrait of Turkmenbashi the Great. So do local brands of vodka and tea. The national television network constantly superimposes a small, golden profile of the Dear Father, neatly placed in the upper-right-hand corner of the screen. He lives in a gold-domed palace. A gilded statue of Turkmenbashi the Great, atop a two-hundred-foot-high arch, towers over downtown Ashkhabad, turning with the desert sun, so it always lights his face. Turkmen gas brings substantial revenues—not to the national treasury but to Niyazov's "presidential fund," currently said by Western specialists to hold about $2.5 billion. Only the Great Leader can disburse these funds, which are held offshore. Meanwhile, the national treasury is strapped; foreign currency reserves reportedly have fallen to $25 million or less.

Niyazov underwent major heart surgery in 1997, and his current health status is not known.

Nursultan Nazarbayev, Kazakhstan

Like Niyazov, President Nursultan Nazarbayev appears intent on running Kazakhstan well into the future. Already holding sweeping executive powers, Nazarbayev in 2000 got parliament to grant him executive authority for life. Lawmakers gave Nazarbayev permanent membership on key advisory bodies and effective control over future presidents and governments. His regime has in recent years used this concentration of political power to gain control over most strategic resources and economic distribution networks. Nazarbayev now seems well positioned to channel expected revenues from recent oil discoveries into his own pockets and those of his supporters. In April 2002, his prime minister acknowledged to parliament that the president had put a $1 billion payment from Chevron Corporation into a secret Swiss bank account. The president claims that oil deposits in the East Kashagan field off the Caspian shelf will prove to be among the world's largest, although Western oil companies and industry experts remain more cautious in their assessments. Nazarbayev won reelection to a seven-year term in 1999 in a vote that the OSCE said fell "far short" of international norms. During the course of 2002 he jailed leaders of opposition movement Democratic Choice and independent journalists. In a sign that middle-class Kazakhs are increasingly willing to defy the regime, however, tens of thousands signed the registration papers of an opposition group called White Path in 2002. This allowed White Path to overcome a seemingly impossible new membership requirement and apply to reregister as a party.

Born in 1940, Nazarbayev was elected president in December 1991 on the eve of his country's declaration of independence from Moscow. He is an engineer by training and a Soviet-era Communist Party boss.

Imomali Rakhmonov, Tajikistan

President Imomali Rakhmonov's grip on Tajikistan is tenuous, as regional warlords, paramilitary forces, and criminal gangs hold sway in much of the mountainous countryside. His country, the poorest in Central Asia, is still recovering from a destabilizing five-year civil war that ended in 1997. That conflict pitted the Soviet-era communist elite against Islamic and anticommunist forces, thousands of whom have been demobilized and integrated into the Tajik army. A former Communist Party heavyweight, Rakhmonov took over from another party official during the height of the war in 1994 and has since strengthened presidential powers. He won reelection in November 1999 with 97 percent of the vote after most opposition candidates failed to muster the 145,000 signatures needed to obtain a spot on the ballot. Citing serious flaws during the preelection period, the Vienna-based OSCE declined to send observers.

Askar Akayev, Kyrgyzstan

In Kyrgyzstan, President Askar Akayev has steadily tightened his grip on power by sidelining political opponents, but his failure to carry out deeper economic reforms has left his poor, landlocked country heavily dependent on Russia and neighboring states for trade and energy. Analysts say that Akayev fears that privatization of large state enterprises and the energy sector and other market-based reforms would weaken the regime's control over key sectors of the economy. Human rights groups and Western governments have criticized Akayev for holding flawed elections, pressuring the judiciary, and harassing the media through tax audits and criminal libel cases. For the first time since independence, security forces in March 2002 killed several people by firing into a crowd of antigovernment protesters, some of whom were throwing stones. Before Akayev had three rivals disqualified from contesting the 1995 presidential elections, his Kyrgyz Republic had gained a reputation as an outpost of democracy in a region dominated by despots. Again barring key opposition leaders from running, Akayev won a third five-year term in 2000. Born in 1945, Akayev, a physicist by training, headed the Soviet-era Academy of Sciences before becoming president in 1990.

Aleksandr Lukashenko, Belarus

In Belarus, another troubled former Soviet republic, Aleksandr Lukashenko took power after winning a relatively free 1994 presidential election. Lukashenko, forty-eight, then used a 1996 referendum to change the constitution to extend his term and increase his powers. He also stacked parliament with handpicked supporters and fired opponents from government posts, while his security forces ruthlessly suppressed dissent. Western governments, most of which have refused to recognize Lukashenko as head of state since his original term expired in 1999, take seriously allegations that the government employed death squads to eliminate some dissidents. Lukashenko claimed a landslide victory with 76 percent of the vote in the September 2001 presidential election, which the OSCE denounced as fraudulent. The runner-up, Vladimir Goncharik, a trade unionist, received officially 15 percent. Opposition politicians, activists, students, and journalists faced intense harassment and intimidation throughout 2002 and into 2003.

Hun Sen, Cambodia

Cambodian prime minister Hun Sen faces few overt challenges to his power as he presides over a country wracked by lawlessness, poverty, and corruption. While international donors have conditioned aid on progress in carrying out legal and judicial reforms and curbing graft and illegal logging, respected opposition leader Sam Rainsy has urged donors to consider suspending aid entirely. He says Hun Sen's dictatorial government has made minimal progress in tackling poverty and corruption and in strengthening land rights.

Born in 1952, Hun Sen joined the Khmer Rouge in 1970 and then fled to Vietnam in 1977. After Vietnam invaded Cambodia and pushed the Khmer Rouge into the jungles, it installed a communist government, which Hun Sen took over in 1985. Following his Cambodian People's Party's (CPP) defeat in this Southeast Asian country's first free elections in 1993, Hun Sen muscled his way into a coalition government with Prince Norodom Ranariddh of the royalist FUNCINPEC party. He regained full power in a violent 1997 coup that overthrew Ranariddh and then tried to gain legitimacy for his regime in 1998 by holding elections. That vote was marred by political killings, harassment of opposition parties and candidates, and changes to the electoral formula, while ballots were being counted, that ensured the CPP a parliamentary majority.

Following lengthy negotiations, the United Nations in 2002 withdrew from a proposed UN-Cambodian tribunal for former leaders of the Khmer Rouge, saying that it could not reach agreement with Phnom Penh on mechanisms to ensure independent and impartial trials. Cambodia pledged to set up the tribunal and try cases on its own, although many observers question whether the country's corrupt and rudimentary judiciary has the capacity to conduct fair and open trials. Some say that the trials of former Khmer Rouge could expose embarrassing details about Hun Sen's own past with the shadowy movement, whose rule between 1975 and 1978 killed more than one million Cambodians through execution, disease, overwork, or starvation.

Maumoon Abdul Gayoom, Maldives

Unlike most other dictators, President Maumoon Abdul Gayoom of the Maldives has relied more on subtle pressure and coercion than outright repression to stave off challenges to his rule in this Indian Ocean country. In office since 1978, Gayoom won a fifth five-year term in a 1998 presidential referendum. Under the constitution, Gayoom has been the sole candidate in these tightly controlled, yes-or-no referendums that give voters no real choice. His regime does not allow political parties and occasionally detains opposition figures and other dissidents.

Born in 1937, Gayoom received degrees in Islamic and civil law from Cairo's prestigious Al Azhar University and also studied at that city's American University.

Monarch Dictators

Like personalistic rulers, ruling monarchs use jailings and other repressive means to keep dissidents at bay while ladling out patronage to reward loyal supporters. But they also claim legitimacy based on dynastic lines of power and expect their children or other relatives to inherit the throne. Notably, even a significant number of nonmonarchic dictators, like the late Kim Il Sung in North Korea and Hafez al-Assad in Syria, have emulated this practice of dynastic succession by handing power to their sons, and many of the forty-five dictators are positioning their sons to take over, creating hereditary dictatorships.

Today, most of the world's kings, sultans, and other potentates, including many in Asia and Europe, serve as constitutional monarchs. Others may be edging in this direction.

Abdullah ibn Abdul Aziz Al Saud, Saudi Arabia

In Saudi Arabia, Crown Prince Abdullah ibn Abdul Aziz Al Saud, seventy-eight, has effectively governed since 1995, when his brother, King Fahd, suffered a stroke. Amid declining living standards, a soaring population, and ballooning debt, the royal family still spends lavishly on palaces (more than three hundred in Jeddah alone), cars, vacations, and other luxuries. It also devotes some 30 percent of the GDP to the military. Many Saudis have become increasingly open in denouncing official corruption and mismanagement, while the puritanical clerics who underpin the regime's legitimacy grow more critical of its ties to the West. Critics inside and outside the royal family have called for political reform, including some form of popular participation in the political process and an end to pervasive gender discrimination. Under a constitution based on the government's interpretation of Islamic law, political parties are outlawed and the monarch rules by decree.

The five other Gulf monarchies are somewhat less repressive. Bahrain moved up in 2002 from the ranks of Not Free to Partly Free, and Kuwait is already rated Partly Free.

Qabus bin Said al-Said, Oman

During his thirty-two years on the throne, Sultan Qabus bin Said al-Said has transformed Oman from an impoverished desert land into a country with a fairly modern physical infrastructure as well as improved social services, public utilities, health care, and schools. At the same time, Oman faces the prospect of a difficult succession since Qabus, alone among Gulf leaders, has no offspring and has not groomed an heir. The sultan has granted citizens few political rights, having implemented hardly any of the provisions of Oman's de facto first constitution, which he promulgated in 1996. He has appointed a woman as a minister in the government.

Hamad bin Khalifa al-Thani, Qatar

In Qatar, Sheikh Hamad bin Khalifa al-Thani, fifty, took power in 1995 by deposing his father, Sheikh Khalifa. Since then, he has gradually introduced modest political reforms. Qatar in 1999 became the first Persian Gulf state to hold a direct election under universal suffrage. In voting for an advisory municipal council, several women contested seats, but none was successful. A directly elected parliament is currently in the planning stages. While not attacking its own government, al-Jazeera satellite television station presents lively coverage of human rights and other controversial issues, much to the chagrin of neighboring regimes. With its decidedly anti-American and anti-Western bent, al-Jazeera has also staked out a distinct Arab nationalist identity.

Zayed ibn Sultan an-Nahayan, United Arab Emirates

Sheikh Zayed ibn Sultan an-Nahayan, some eighty-five years old, has been the president of the United Arab Emirates (UAE) since the country's establishment in 1971. Having headed Abu Dhabi, the largest emirate, since 1966, he was nominated to head the new country by a council of the seven emirate rulers. The emirs, their extended families, and their allies all wield tight political control in their respective emirates. The only real chance that ordinary citizens have to influence policy is a traditional consultation process that allows them to petition their leaders at open gatherings. Like neighboring Qatar and Oman, the UAE's citizens enjoy a high standard of living based on oil and gas exports.

Hassanal Bolkiah Mu'izzaddin Waddaulah, Brunei

Asia has two of the world's most tightly controlled monarchies, Brunei and Bhutan. Sultan Haji Hassanal Bolkiah Mu'izzaddin Waddaulah of Brunei ascended the throne of this Southeast Asian ministate in 1967 following the abdication of his father. The sultan, fifty-five, has ruled under emergency law since his reign began. He serves as prime minister, minister of defense, minister of finance, chancellor of the national university, superintendent general of the Royal Brunei Police Force, and leader of the Islamic faith. Oil and gas accounts for more than half of Brunei's GDP, although known reserves are being depleted rapidly. Corruption and abuse of power have increasingly become targets of public scrutiny and dissatisfaction, highlighted by the discovery that the sultan's brother, Prince Jefri, drained billions in government foreign currency reserves to support his lavish lifestyle. Not wanting to appear indifferent to this public display of corruption, the sultan, who himself lives in a 1,788-room palace, had the government sue Jefri for financial misconduct. The suit was settled out of court.

Jigme Singye Wangchuk, Bhutan

Bhutan's King Jigme Singye Wangchuk continues to maintain tight control of this tiny Himalayan land, detaining pro-democracy dissidents and preventing Bhutanese from forming political parties, civil society groups, or trade unions. A Dzongkha-speaker from northern Bhutan, King Wangchuk probably directed, and in any case has never held any soldiers accountable for, gross human rights abuses against Nepali-speakers in the early 1990s. Citing an alleged threat to the cultural survival of the Buddhist Dzongkha-speakers, security forces beat and raped many Nepali-speaking villagers, who formed the majority in several southern districts, and forced tens of thousands to flee the kingdom.

King Wangchuk came to the throne in 1972 at the age of seventeen, assuming the title of *Druk Gyalpo*, or Dragon King. Born in 1955, the king was partly educated in Britain and has four wives, who are sisters.

Mswati III, Swaziland

In southern Africa, Swaziland's King Mswati III faces pressure for democratic reforms from the country's trade unions, which are backed by their powerful South African counterparts. The king rules by decree and is supported by elites from his Dlamini clan. Continuing the reign of the Dlamini dynasty, King Mswati III was crowned in 1986 at the age of eighteen upon the death of his father, King Sobhuza II. He was born in April 1968, just five months before Swaziland won independence from Great Britain, where the future monarch received his education. King Mswati III has publicly urged citizens to overcome cultural biases inhibiting efforts to curb the HIV virus, which afflicts roughly one-fifth of Swaziland's population.

Military Dictators

In military dictatorships, power is derived from the armed forces as a whole. If the military dictator dies or is ousted by junior officers, the military may try to put another officer in his place. In contrast, when a personalistic dictator dies or is overthrown, the regime sometimes collapses—although another personalistic leader may take his place. Crucially, in a military dictatorship the armed forces generally are the most cohesive institution in the country. This presents a unique challenge for civil society groups in overthrowing these dictatorships and often assures the military a key role in managing any democratic transition. Some have retaken full power. But other military dictators have been definitively ousted, including Paraguay's Alfredo Stroessner, Bangladesh's H. M. Ershad, and South Korea's Chun Doo Hwan.

Omar Al-Bashir, Sudan

General Omar Al-Bashir has presided over the worst deterioration of human rights and civil liberties in the history of war-torn Sudan. Since the 1989 coup that installed him as president of a radical Islamic regime, he has divided and waged war against his own people, banned political parties and public gatherings, imposed *sharia* (Islamic law) on Christian and traditional believers in the south, and indiscriminately bombed civilian population centers. Famine and disease have contributed to some two million war-related deaths. Soldiers and government agents have abducted tens of thousands of children, forcibly converting many to Islam and recruiting them to fight alongside government forces in Sudan's protracted civil war. Soldiers also profit from a lucrative slave trade in women and children. Famine is widespread as the government spends massive amounts of money on its war effort while often intercepting international aid.

Long considered a figurehead for Hassan Al-Turabi, the Islamic ideologue and head of the fundamentalist ruling party, the National Islamic Front (NIF), Al-Bashir has since sidelined his rival, although he continues to carry out Al-Turabi's extremist policies. Authorities have crushed most political opposition through harassment, intimidation, arbitrary arrest, detention, and torture, which officials commit with impunity. Under sharia, punishments include flogging, amputation, and crucifixion. Women are summarily tried and frequently flogged for violating the government's standards of modesty in their dress.

Sudan's civil war, which began in 1983, broadly pits the country's Arab Muslim north against the black African animist and Christian south. Bolstered by revenues from oil reserves in southern Sudan shipped by a pipeline that opened in 1999, Al-Bashir's government spends an estimated $1 million per day on the war while it diverts or bans humanitarian aid. Al-Bashir has denied the existence of famine in Sudan and accused Western media of trying to harm Sudan's image. He has also responded to international concerns over displaced people (there are some five million internally displaced Sudanese) by calling the issue an internal matter with which foreigners should not be involved.

Government forces under Al-Bashir commit atrocities against the southern population, including bombing, raiding, and looting of villages; forced conscription of children; the selling of women and children into slavery; rape and forced pregnancy; and forcible conversion to Islam. Officials have used the word "jihad" to describe the war and the government's policy of "depopulating" the Nuba mountains, a 30,000-square-mile area in the heart of Sudan. While continuing this policy, aimed at extinguishing the nearly one million black Sudanese in the Nuba region, Al-Bashir encourages Arab Sudanese to "aid development" by increasing the population. "We should achieve this by having many wives," he said in August 2001. In 2002, the government signed a series of agreements with rebels, including a cease-fire in the Nuba mountains, the establishment of peaceful zones in which health programs would be implemented, an investigation into slavery, and an end to attacks on civilians. But war-related crimes and human rights abuses continued largely unabated.

Though its abominable human rights record has drawn international condemnation, the regime's export of terrorism also has made it an international pariah. Under Al-Bashir, Sudan has given refuge to militant Islamic terrorist groups, including Egypt's Islamic Group and Islamic Jihad, the Palestinian Hamas, and Osama bin Laden's Qaeda network. For his part, Al-Bashir has publicly called the United States "the number one terrorist state" and accused it of plotting to invade Sudan. Regarding U.S. sanctions against Sudan, former ambassador Donald Petterson writes that Al-Bashir "described the United States as a thief plundering and robbing Sudan's wealth and said Sudan would reply with further holy war."

Since the 11 September 2001 terrorist attacks, Al-Bashir supposedly is cooperating with the United States in fighting terrorism and also in trying to find a settlement to Sudan's internal warfare. It is not clear that he is sincere on either front.

Al-Bashir emerged as the regime's strongman in 1999 following a dispute with Al-Turabi. Backed by the military, he dissolved parliament, declared a state of emergency, and began consolidating his power. Al-Turabi was arrested in 2001, along with a number of his supporters. With Al-Turabi effectively neutralized, Al-Bashir began calling for improved ties with the United States and the West, offered a general amnesty to political opponents and opposition exiles who returned from abroad, toned down his hard-line Islamist stance, and mended relations with some Arab neighbors.

Despite these positive moves, war-related crimes and human rights abuses continue. The presidential and parliamentary elections held in late 2000 were hugely flawed. They reaffirmed the supremacy of Al-Bashir's ruling National Congress Party. The European Union declined an invitation to monitor the polls to avoid bestowing legitimacy on the outcome. Indeed, Al-Bashir has made clear that he has little use for democracy. "Partisan practices perpetrated during and after the [1986] elections made us believe that the democracy practiced in Sudan is not at all good for Sudan," he said. The 1986 vote brought to power a government led by Sadiq Al-Mahdi of the moderate Islamist Ummah party.

Al-Bashir faces a splintered but significant opposition, most notably from John Garang's Sudan People's Liberation Army (SPLA), the southern-based rebel group that controls large patches of territory. The SPLA is the largest group in the National Democratic Alliance (NDA), a coalition of more than a dozen opposition groups, mostly based in the northeast. The NDA also includes the Beja Congress, a northeastern-based, armed Muslim opposition group. Moreover, many soldiers loyal to Al-Turabi have turned against the government. Rebels have attributed their success in repelling recent government offensives to dissension in the army, according to author Dan Connell, who has covered Sudan for more than twenty-five years. Connell says that the opposition may be gaining military strength and increasing its political coherence by default, as the regime is weakened by the rift between Al-Bashir and Al-Turabi.

Forces outside Sudan pull in different directions. The present Bush administration has provided financial assistance to the NDA as a whole. Many endorse this policy, presumably with the aim of encouraging a broad-based solution to the war, and perhaps eventually a broad-based leadership for postwar Sudan. Egypt, however, would rather see the political status quo prevail. A breakup of Sudan could endanger Egyptian control of the Nile headwaters. International religious, human rights, and other groups promote sanctions against the Al-Bashir regime, while those hoping to invest in the country's oil industry favor dialogue and improved relations with Khartoum. These outside forces will likely be factors in both a future settlement of the civil war and democratic development in Sudan, two processes that may well be inextricably linked.

Pervez Musharraf, Pakistan

In Pakistan, the army has toppled several elected governments since the south Asian country won independence in 1947 with the partition of British India. General Pervez Musharraf continues to wield decisive power in Pakistan despite having turned over the reins of government in 2002 to an elected prime minister. Musharraf, who declared himself president in 2001, has the authority to sack both the government and parliament and still heads Pakistan's powerful armed forces.

Musharraf's decision to back the United States in its war on terrorism following the September 2001 terrorist attacks in the United States prompted Washington to reschedule debt and waive nuclear-related sanctions. But the south Asian country remains hugely indebted, impoverished, and crippled by a crumbling public education system that has left Islamic fundamentalist religious schools to educate—and, many say, indoctrinate—a generation of young Pakistanis.

Musharraf took power in 1999 in a bloodless coup after he and the army balked at Prime Minister Nawaz Sharif's orders to pull back from the disputed Himalayan territory of Kashmir. Musharraf has taken some steps to root out graft but has undermined the judiciary, cracked down on party activists, and backtracked on some social reforms in the face of pressure from Islamic fundamentalists.

Born in Delhi in 1943, Musharraf emigrated with his family to Pakistan after the partition and joined the army in 1964.

Than Shwe, Burma (Myanmar)

In Burma, Gen. Than Shwe heads a regime that has been condemned internationally for widespread, gross human rights abuses including extrajudicial killings, torture, and forced labor. He is reportedly ailing, and observers say his two most likely successors are Lt. Gen. Khin Nyunt, the intelligence chief, and his rival, the more hard-line Gen. Maung Aye, the army commander. Reaping sizable profits from its real estate and other business interests, some of which are built up using forced labor, the army has shown few signs that it plans to cede power to an opposition headed by Nobel laureate Aung San Suu Kyi. Known formally by its Orwellian name, the State Peace and Development Council, in 2002 the junta allowed political parties to reopen offices and released hundreds of political prisoners. In May 2002, the regime freed Suu Kyi after keeping her under house arrest for nineteen months. Burmese jails, however, reportedly continued to hold 1,500 political prisoners, and in 2003 Suu Kyi and her supporters were attacked and detained again. Suu Kyi's National League for Democracy won Burma's first free elections in three decades in 1990, but the army has refused to recognize the results. Soldiers have ruled this Southeast Asian land since 1962, when the army toppled an elected government struggling to contain an economic crisis and several ethnic-based insurgencies.

Born in 1933, Than Shwe took power in 1992 and is a specialist in psychological warfare.

Pierre Buyoya, Burundi

Pierre Buyoya seized power in Burundi in a 1996 coup on the pretext of staving off further upheaval in this strife-torn land, where since 1993 ethnic-based fighting has killed an estimated two hundred thousand people. Buyoya deposed Sylvestre Ntibantunganya, a Hutu who had served as president under a 1994 power-sharing arrangement between the central African country's main political parties. A more recent power-sharing agreement between Buyoya's Tutsi-dominated government and several Hutu opposition parties created a transitional government that remains in place, but the government and the main Hutu rebel group have been unable to agree to a cease-fire.

Members of Buyoya's ethnic Tutsi minority have ruled almost continuously since independence. Buyoya first took power in 1987, when he overthrew Jean-Baptise Bagaza, an unelected Tutsi president. He gave up office in 1993 after being beaten in Burundi's first presidential election by Melchior Ndadaye. The assassination of Ndadaye later that year plunged the tiny country into widespread violence.

Born in 1949 to a family of stockbreeders, Buyoya attended military academies and studied in Belgium, France, and Germany. Under the power-sharing agreement, Buyoya is due to hand over power to his deputy, a Hutu, in 2003.

Abdelaziz Bouteflika, Algeria

In Algeria, President Abdelaziz Bouteflika's efforts to end the violent conflict between radical Islamists and government forces, which has killed more than one hundred thousand people, have yielded few tangible results. The Islamist insurgency began in 1992, after the army seized power and canceled a second round of legislative elections, which the Islamic Salvation Front was poised to win. The government has also faced pressure from members of Algeria's Berber minority, who mounted nationwide protests in 2001 and 2002 following the death in custody of a Berber youth. Dozens of Berbers were killed in clashes with security forces. Authorities blocked Berber marches and rallies demanding political and language rights during 2002, and some Berber activists resorted to violence and intimidation in trying to effect a boycott of parliamentary elections in May 2002.

Bouteflika came to power in a 1999 presidential election in which the generals who seized power in 1992 openly favored him over six other military-approved candidates. His opponents withdrew from the race on the eve of elections, charging electoral fraud. Algeria has been ruled by dictators since winning independence from France in 1964 following a bloody liberation struggle.

Communist Dictators

Beginning with the Bolshevik Revolution in 1917, communist regimes in Moscow, Beijing, and their satellite states created the world's first totalitarian societies. Under the guise of utopian ideologies, they set up single-party states, ran command economies, exhorted citizens to meet dubious production goals, and prohibited any independent religious, civic, and social groups. The communist regimes still around today—China, Vietnam, Laos, North Korea, and Cuba—have a range of economic policies, from North Korea's classic total state control to China's partial economic reforms. But in these remaining communist countries, the party still controls nearly all organized political, social, and cultural affairs. Authorities deter opposition by jailing dissidents, curbing religious freedom, and tightly controlling the press.

Jiang Zemin, China

When China's aging shadow rulers needed a hard-liner to head a fractious ruling Communist Party, refurbish Beijing's international reputation, and regain control and punish dissidents in the wake of the 1989 Tiananmen Square massacre, they turned to Jiang Zemin, a colorless but experienced apparatchik who lacked the legitimacy of having fought in the 1949 communist revolution. Jiang has since ruthlessly suppressed political dissent while adroitly maneuvering to ensure his own survival as China's peak leader. Having turned seventy-six in August 2002, Jiang formally gave up power at a 2002 party congress as part of a long-planned transition to a younger generation of Chinese leaders. Designated years earlier by Deng Xiaoping to be Jiang's successor, Hu Jintao, the sixty-year-old state vice president and an engineer by training, took the reins of the Communist Party. Jiang, however, held on to a key military post, leading to speculation that he intends to wield power behind the scenes just as Deng Xiaoping did from this same post.

The leadership jockeying came as the Communist Party faces critical decisions on how far and fast to pursue market reforms, which have in recent years fostered unprecedented economic growth while also threatening to undermine the party's rigid political control.

Jiang has tried to balance the party's desire to foster economic growth as a long-term strategy for deferring political reform against the reality that shutting large factories and other painful reforms could lead to even more widespread discontent. While the student activism of the late 1980s has largely receded, factory workers and farmers have in recent years held thousands of street demonstrations and strikes over local political corruption, hardships associated with the government's privatization of small- and medium-size state factories and efforts to roll back China's cradle-to-grave welfare system. Privatization has already cost millions of workers their jobs. These hardships are expected to increase as the government slashes tariffs and takes other measures to open China's economy to trade and foreign investment as part of Beijing's World Trade Organization commitments.

Jiang also fears that further liberalization will weaken the party's control over the economy. The economic reforms that began in the late 1970s have created a new generation of entrepreneurs and other private-sector workers who increasingly can choose where to live and work. Jiang knows that organized pressure groups from an emerging middle class helped overthrow dictators in South Korea, the Philippines, and other Asian countries. In an apparent effort to marshal the support of students and other interest groups, Jiang has tried to position the Communist Party at the vanguard of a nascent Chinese nationalism.

Jiang has not wavered from the party's absolute ban on political dissent and has not improved China's dismal human rights record. Zealous local officials and security forces actually carry out most of these human rights abuses, but it is clear that policy is set by Jiang himself. Beijing has introduced judicial reforms in recent years aimed at increasing the fairness of ordinary criminal and civil trials. However, Jiang has clearly instructed soldiers, police, and bureaucrats to violate human rights. Jiang personally ordered the repression of the Falun Gong and is directly responsible for the thousands of deaths and tens of thousands sent to labor camps and prisons. He regularly orders nationwide

"Strike Hard" campaigns against crime, which have led to thousands of summary executions and have given security forces and local authorities wide latitude in punishing dissent and maintaining order. Moreover, he himself sets out overarching policies sharply restricting the press, civil society, religious freedom, and political life.

In pursuing cautious economic reforms while cracking down on dissent, Jiang is following a path set by his mentor, the late Deng Xiaoping. Deng emerged as China's paramount leader following Mao Tse-tung's death in 1976 and began efforts to free up China's centrally planned economy in late 1978. Like Deng, Jiang hopes to hold onto power long after giving up some of his official titles.

For now, Jiang seems intent on holding on to one of those titles—chairman of the Central Military Commission—for the foreseeable future. This powerful post effectively keeps him in charge of China's 2.5-million-man armed forces. Analysts say, moreover, that five or six of the cadres on the powerful, nine-member Politburo Standing Committee, which Hu heads, are Jiang protégés.

Jiang has surprised many observers simply by holding on to power for this long. Deng Xiaoping tapped Jiang, then the mayor of Shanghai, to become party general secretary in June 1989, largely because he was personally untainted by the Tiananmen massacre. Jiang had defused pro-democracy demonstrations in Shanghai by talking to students and then banning protests without having to call in the army.

At the same time, Jiang had proven his hard-line credentials by firing a top liberal newspaper editor, Qin Benli of the *World Economic Herald*, shortly after the demonstrations began in the spring of 1989. Jiang later joined Deng and some other party elite in calling for the punishment of cadres like his ousted predecessor, Zhao Zhiyang, who had tolerated the student pro-democracy protests. "Toward these cruel enemies there must not be even one percent of forgiveness," he told the *People's Daily*, the party's mouthpiece, just weeks after the massacre. Jiang became state president in March 1993 but wasn't recognized as China's true paramount leader until Deng's death in 1997.

Jiang's formative years contain a smattering of Western influence but largely reflect a typical career path of a rising Communist Party functionary. He was born on 17 August 1926 to "an intellectual family" in Yangzhou, in eastern Jiangsu province, according to his official English-language biography, posted on the website of the *People's Daily*. He attended an American missionary school where he learned English before receiving an engineering degree in 1947 from Shanghai's Jiaotong University. Jiang studied economics in the Soviet Union in the early 1950s during a stint at the Stalin Automotive Plant. He then worked as an engineer and factory boss, surviving

Mao's chaotic Cultural Revolution by keeping a low profile and then heading to Romania to represent the Ministry of Machine Building. Beginning in 1980, Jiang held a series of central government posts before becoming mayor of Shanghai in 1985. His *People's Daily* biography says that Jiang speaks good English, Russian, and Romanian and knows some Japanese and French.

Jiang may ultimately be remembered as a partial economic reformer, but he also will leave a legacy as a merciless dictator. By most accounts, Chinese prisons, labor camps, and detention centers hold thousands of political prisoners, although the exact number is not known. Since December 1998, courts have sentenced more than thirty members of a fledgling dissident group, the China Democracy Party, to prison terms of up to thirteen years on subversion and other charges.

Ordinary citizens routinely suffer abuses. Chinese "reeducation through labor" camps held some 310,000 people in early 2001, Amnesty International said in 2002. Meanwhile, officials use a system called "custody and repatriation" to detain one million Chinese each year, many of them homeless people and other "undesirable" city residents, Amnesty said. Both reeducation through labor and custody and repatriation are administrative procedures that allow authorities to imprison people without trial.

China executes thousands of people each year, more than all other countries combined. Many of those put to death are convicted of nonviolent offenses including hooliganism, theft of farm animals or rice, embezzlement, or corruption. Torture of criminal suspects, political dissidents, and others is "widespread and systemic, committed in the full range of state institutions, from police stations to 'reeducation through labor' camps, as well as in people's homes, workplaces and in public," Amnesty International reported in February 2000.

Beijing requires all religious groups to submit to the tight control of state-sponsored associations and cracks down on religious leaders and ordinary worshipers who reject these bodies. Local officials harass and at times fine, detain, beat, and torture church leaders or ordinary worshipers and raid, close, or demolish underground churches, mosques, temples, and seminaries, according to the U.S. State Department's global human rights report and other sources.

Press accounts suggest that courts have since 1999 imprisoned tens of thousands of followers of the Falun Gong spiritual movement without trial. Thousands have been beaten or tortured to death. Authorities have also ruthlessly targeted devout Buddhists in Tibet and Muslims in northwestern Xinjiang province as part of Beijing's efforts to weaken independence movements in both regions.

In sifting through Jiang's overall record in office, some analysts detect an overarching goal of completing China's transformation from a communist state to a system where ordinary Chinese have wide latitude to go about their daily lives as long as they steer clear of politics. These observers believe Jiang is influenced by a group of so-called neo-authoritarian intellectuals who emphasize nationalism and a strong, benevolent state but with very limited democracy, the Hong Kong–based *Far Eastern Economic Review* reported in May 2001. To this end, Jiang has failed to make good on a 1997 pledge to expand China's village elections to a higher level.

At the same time, Jiang's reluctance to introduce political reforms may simply be more evidence of the cold pragmatism and ability to shift tack with the prevailing political winds that have kept him in power. Not for nothing is he nicknamed "the Weathervane." At the very least, he has unabashedly put his own survival in power ahead of concerns about the means used to achieve these ends. When television's Barbara Walters asked Jiang about the events of 1989, when the army killed hundreds of student protesters after more than a million people had demonstrated for democracy in some 150 cities across China, he responded, "It's like much ado about nothing."

Kim Jong Il, North Korea

Kim Jong Il is a reckless lunatic whose country's nuclear and ballistic missile programs threaten South Korea, Japan, and even the United States. Or the North Korean dictator is shrewd and calculating, using these weapons programs simply as bargaining chips to gain aid and other concessions from Washington, Seoul, and Tokyo. He is a recluse who is out of touch with the world, traveling little outside North Korea and rarely emerging in public. Or he is well informed about global events, surfs the Internet regularly, and enjoys Hollywood movies. He is eccentric, paranoid, and deeply insecure. Or he is arrogant and basks in the glow of a Stalinist cult of personality that portrays him as a genius and glorifies his every move.

These are the rival images of a dictator the outside world knows little about, one painting Kim as a secretive psychotic, the other as a cunning pragmatist. And to some extent, both are accurate. The former view has its roots in the cold war, when South Korean intelligence officials portrayed Kim as an unstable playboy. Since succeeding his father as North Korea's supreme leader in 1994, Kim has provided ample material for this image with his almost comical obsession with his personal security. In 1998, a North Korean ballistic missile flew over Japan. Such antics have convinced many that Kim is a regional menace. He has given his East Asian neighbors a bad case of the jitters. More ominously, the regime's admission in 2002 that it was producing weapons-grade plutonium in violation of a 1994 agreement created a fresh international crisis.

Kim's brutality toward his own people makes him a mass murderer. North Korea denies its citizens even the most basic rights, regularly executes dissidents and repatriated defectors, and holds tens of thousands of political prisoners in horrendous conditions. The government's political and economic policies have led to massive malnutrition and even widespread starvation; overall since 1995 close to two million North Koreans are estimated to have starved to death. Kim himself has been implicated in the 1980s bombing of a South Korean airliner and other terrorist acts.

At the same time, South Korean and American officials have emerged from meetings with Kim describing him as an engaging, perhaps even rational, person with whom they can do business. Former South Korean president Kim Dae Jung called Kim Jong Il "a pragmatic leader with good judgment" following the first ever summit in June 2000 between leaders of the two Koreas.

These soft words may be diplomatic niceties aimed at fostering a dialogue. But they apparently also reflect an awareness that Kim is more lucid and informed than many previously believed. An American official who accompanied Secretary of State Madeleine K. Albright to Pyongyang for an October 2000 meeting with Kim said that the North Korean leader could discuss "market economics, the Internet, coming technologies, [and] economic trends," according to the *Washington Post*. Some veteran Kim watchers say they never bought into the conventional wisdom about him. "I've never fallen into the mindset that Kim Jong Il is a mysterious, hermetic semi-loon," Jon Wolfsthal, a Korea expert with the Carnegie Endowment for International Peace in Washington, told the *New York Times* in August 2001. "Here's a guy who does have some contact with reality, whether it's surfing the Web or movies or whatever."

The North Korean dictator may indeed be in touch with global affairs, but he is unlikely to be mistaken anytime soon for a statesman. Kim, who fears flying, arrived in Moscow for an August 2001 state visit after a bizarre, six-thousand-mile rail journey across Russia. Along the way, he spurned scheduled meetings with local officials and conducted his few brief forays off the train, including one to a pig farm, in almost complete secrecy. Feeding longstanding suspicions about his alleged paranoia, Kim's twenty-one-car train was armor plated, carried ten bomb-sniffing dogs and two food tasters, and was preceded by two minesweeping locomotives. The Russian general on board accompanying Kim wrote an exposé revealing that he has extravagant tastes in food, having live lobsters and expensive French wines flown in by special aircraft while they were en route.

A movie fanatic, Kim once had North Korean agents kidnap a South Korean movie actress and her husband in Hong Kong and spirit them to

Pyongyang. But many other tales about Kim's lifestyle were wrong or simply fiction. There is apparently little truth to rumors that Kim receives blood transfusions from young virgins to slow the aging process and has orgies with Swedish blondes, U.S. officials told the *Los Angeles Times* in October 2000. Some of these stories were based on South Korean intelligence before that country's democratic transition, the *Times* added.

Like his lifestyle, Kim's background is shrouded in confusion, sowed in this case by North Korea's Stalinist propaganda machine. According to official hagiography, Kim was born in 1942 in a hut used by communist guerrillas and perched on the slopes of Mount Paekdu, a sacred Korean mountain. More objective sources say that Kim was born that year in a Red Army hospital in the Soviet city of Khabarovsk. His father was stationed there as an army officer fighting the Japanese during World War II.

The future dictator was educated in Pyongyang, where he studied Marxist-Leninist thought in college. As the son of President Kim Il Sung, who dominated North Korea for forty-six years, Kim Jong Il rose quickly through the ranks of the ruling Korean Workers' Party. He was put in charge of agitprop and then the all-important party personnel department, where careers were made and shattered based on loyalty to Kim Il Sung.

Kim Jong Il's assumption of power upon his father's death in 1994 was the world's first hereditary transfer of power in a communist state. Since then, Kim has tinkered little with the totalitarian regime created by Kim Il Sung. Defectors say the regime holds some 150,000 political prisoners, while the South Korean government puts the figure at 200,000. The UN Human Rights Committee commended North Korea in July 2001 for cutting the number of offenses carrying the death penalty to five from thirty-three but noted that four of the remaining offenses are largely political. There are no accurate figures on the number of North Koreans executed each year for political crimes.

Kim has also shown stunning indifference to the extreme suffering of his impoverished people. While regime-induced chronic food shortages have caused widespread death and forced many ordinary North Koreans to forage for grass to survive, the regime continues to build monuments depicting heroic workers and soldiers or honoring Kim and his father. Kim himself reportedly muses about building a North Korean space program and a city with a skyline to match that of Shanghai, the dynamic Chinese coastal city.

North Korea's economy, never a powerhouse, and agriculture have faltered catastrophically since the collapse of the Soviet Union and East Bloc led to an abrupt cutoff of critical subsidies and preferential trade. Famine killed "an estimated several hundreds of thousands to two million persons" in the 1990s, according to the U.S. State Department's global human rights report for 2001. Some three hundred thousand North Koreans have fled to China since 1995.

Notwithstanding the impact of drought and floods that struck the country in the mid- and late 1990s, North Korea's economic mismanagement and virtual ban on private property and free enterprise are the major cause of its plight. No democratic government has ever allowed famine. Moreover, though the two Koreas were economic equals in the early 1970s, regional economists say that capitalist South Korea's GDP is about one hundred times greater than North Korea's, the *Los Angeles Times* reported in October 2000.

Kim's meetings with South Korean president Kim and Secretary Albright in 2000 and a January 2001 tour of stock exchanges and factories in Shanghai raised speculation that he was looking for ways to ease North Korea's isolation and boost its economy. To this end, the regime has in recent years allowed families to cultivate small private gardens and farmers to sell produce at small markets. In another implicit admission that past policies have failed, the government in 2002 also began raising wages; easing price controls on food, housing, and other necessities; and paying farmers more for their produce. By early 2003, however, it appeared that these changes had caused still more hardship for the people. South Korean and Japanese firms have recently been refurbishing North Korean factories and using local workers to produce goods.

Kim's Shanghai tour also suggested that he might be seeking to mimic China by reforming North Korea's economy while maintaining tight political control. In August 2002, Kim made a similar trip to cities in Russia's far east. North Korea's ability to attract significant foreign investment to rejuvenate its decaying factories is limited, however, by a severe energy shortage and its crippled railways and ports. And unlike Deng Xiaoping in China, who reformed agriculture beginning in the late 1970s, Kim has yet to tranform agrarian policies that have caused systemic mass malnutrition and starvation. In any case, Kim would undermine his own regime's guiding philosophy of national self-reliance by really opening North Korea to foreign investment. "What he saw in Shanghai was the product of 23 or 24 years of real hard work, full of dangers [for the Chinese leadership]," Kim Byung Kook, a professor at Korea University in Seoul, told the *Washington Post* in January 2001. "The odds against him succeeding are exceedingly high."

For now, there is no sign of the type of underground dissident movements that helped topple communist rulers in central and eastern Europe. Most North Koreans struggle each day simply to feed themselves. Nevertheless, many are clearly aware that life is better in neighboring countries. From what other country do people flee to communist China (or for that matter to any other dictatorship)? But huge numbers have tried to flee despite the difficulty and danger of trying to get out and the consequences of being returned. One North Korean who recently managed to escape estimated that 60 percent of North Korea's twenty-two million people would leave if given guarantees of their safety once out. He noted that this would be the simplest way to destabilize North Korea. "It would take only six months for there to be a flood. The cities would be empty" (*New York Times*, 21 August 2002). Such an exodus was central to bringing down the communist regime in East Germany.

Ultimately, Kim's extreme emphasis on personal security, refusal to carry out virtually any reforms, and attempts to secure foreign aid without opening up his country to outside influences seem more informed and calculated than paranoid or irrational. In keeping his people poor, hungry, and isolated, Kim is no doubt pulling out all the stops to avoid the fate of hard-liners across the border in South Korea, where in the late 1980s an emerging and increasingly organized middle class brought down a repressive regime.

Nong Duc Manh, Vietnam

Nong Duc Manh, who took over as general secretary of Vietnam's Communist Party in April 2001, faces tough economic choices that go to the heart of the ruling party's efforts to maintain absolute power. The government faces long-term problems if it fails to modernize the economy and create enough new jobs for the 1.4 million Vietnamese who join the workforce each year. But accelerated reforms of the ailing state industrial sector would potentially throw millions out of work, possibly leading to a backlash against the regime. Moreover, the reforms to date have already allowed millions of farmers to work for themselves and many other Vietnamese to enter the private sector, where they cannot be monitored as easily and no longer depend on the state for their livelihood. Manh, who previously chaired the national assembly, has a reputation as someone who could build a consensus between the party's conservative old guard and younger cadres who favor deeper economic reform. Born in 1940 to an ethnic Tay farming family, Manh studied in the Soviet Union for five years and is the party's first leader who lacks the legitimacy of having fought in Vietnam's anticolonial struggle against the French.

Khamtai Siphandon, Laos

Khamtai Siphandon, the head of Laos's ruling People's Revolutionary Party, leads an old-guard faction of the regime that also faces pressure from moderates within the party for more extensive economic reforms. The government ended collectivized agriculture and introduced other market-based reforms in the 1980s, but Khamtai and other hard-liners apparently fear that further efforts to boost the private sector, such as selling off large state enterprises, could undermine the party's tight grip on power by reducing its control over the economy. Khamtai has held the post of general secretary of the party, the most powerful position in the country, since 1992. Born in 1924, he joined the Laotian communist forces in the late 1940s during the struggle for independence from France.

Fidel Castro, Cuba

In power since 1959, Cuba's Fidel Castro has repressed his people longer than any other of the forty-five remaining dictators. His economic policies are such a failure that Cubans face tight rationing of energy, food, and consumer goods. Castro controls every key lever of power in Cuba, including the judiciary, and is responsible for every important appointment. He punishes dissidents through jailings, beatings while in custody, and intimidation by uniformed or plainclothes police. Cubans have little opportunity to work or take part in group cultural and social activities away from the government's prying eyes. Elections are a total sham, a point underscored by the fact that the Cuban Communist Party is the sole legal political party. It controls government bodies from the national to the municipal level. Castro seized power after leading the overthrow of the U.S.-backed dictatorship of Fulgencio Batista. Born in 1926, Castro received his early education at Jesuit schools before going to Havana University, where he received a law degree.

Dominant-Party Dictators

Dominant-party dictators tend to be less totalitarian than the communists. That is, they and their ruling parties control the political process but do not seek to impose a guiding philosophy or use the party to mobilize and monitor the population, at least not to the same extent. With China and some of the rest of the world's last communist countries moving toward partial market economies and giving their citizens somewhat greater social freedom, the practical distinction between the two dictator types is narrowing.

Dominant-party states also differ from personalistic regimes in that the former have ruling parties, as well as one individual controlling the levers of power. But here, too, the difference in practice is more one of degree. Powerful leaders like Ali Abdullah Saleh of Yemen, who heads the ruling General People's Congress, run their countries much like personalistic strongmen.

Hosni Mubarak, Egypt

Egypt has become increasingly a one-man show since Hosni Mubarak succeeded assassinated president Anwar as-Sadat in 1981. Mubarak has increased government control over political, social, and cultural affairs and alone appoints government ministers, senior military officers, media heads, judges, bankers, corporate bosses, university presidents, and even heads of religious institutions (this approaches the power of the cadre/personnel departments of the Communist Parties of Stalin and Mao and is quite typical of the Last Forty-five). Though Egypt officially has fourteen political parties, they receive state financing and can be shut down at any time. The deeply corrupt ruling National Democratic Party controls at least 80 percent of the seats in parliament. Mubarak easily wins elections with 90 percent or more of the vote, though the opposition, which faces numerous restrictions on its participation, points out that turnout may be close to 10 percent.

Mubarak's larger-than-life image is reinforced by excessive, fawning media coverage and by the fact that he has never appointed a successor, or even a vice president. He is believed to be grooming his son Gamal to succeed him. A *Middle East Times* article in May 2001 entitled "Exaggerated Birthday Coverage for Mubarak Makes Many Cringe" called the flattering state media reporting of the occasion "more suited to a dictatorship." It noted that many Egyptians consider the coverage "embarrassing" or "a farce." The article, which was censored from the print edition of the paper but appeared online, quoted one woman who believes that high administration officials maintain their positions through such worship. "Minister of Information Safwat Al Sharif has been in office for such a long time because he doesn't let a chance go by without describing Mubarak in the most cheesy way," she said. Like most leaders lacking legitimacy, Mubarak is extraordinarily sensitive about his image. The government has amended press laws to punish those who criticize his family and high government officials.

In the absence of criticism, transparency, and accountability, corruption has flourished. In her book *God Has Ninety-Nine Names: Reporting from a Militant Middle East* (New York: Simon & Schuster, 1996), Judith Miller describes the "gang of sons"—the children of high-ranking officials—who have used their fathers' positions to enrich themselves. According to Miller, Alaa Mubarak, son of the president, was a partner in a number of joint Libyan-Egyptian ventures. Alaa's brother Gihad, an investment banker, had earned tens of thousands of dollars in bonuses for, among other things, helping Egypt finance a multimillion-dollar trade deal with China.

Meanwhile, unemployment in Egypt is estimated at nearly 20 percent, and close to 50 percent of Egyptians are underemployed. Per capita annual income is around $1,800, although the income distribution is skewed toward the wealthy and most Egyptians earn far less. Roughly 45 percent of Egyptians are illiterate, with the figure rising to 76 percent for rural women. Only 14 percent of pregnant women receive prenatal medical care. Of the roughly $57 billion in aid provided to Egypt by the United States in the last twenty years, about $41 billion has gone for arms.

Mubarak has waged an aggressive military campaign, combined with political repression, to tackle two major Islamic terrorist organizations operating in Egypt, the Islamic Group and Islamic Jihad. Both claim to seek to overthrow the government and form an Islamic state. Thousands of suspected members of banned Islamic groups have been imprisoned, some for more than a decade. Torture and mistreatment in detention are common, and at least twenty-two people were executed in 2000, according to Amnesty International. Although the militants have been effectively quashed, emergency laws restricting civil liberties remain in force. Human Rights Watch noted that the government used national security and antiterrorism concerns to justify an intensified crackdown on political opponents during 2002.

Mubarak has kept relatively moderate Islamists, including the Muslim Brotherhood, at arm's length. Muslim Brothers can stand in elections as independents, but the party itself is banned and authorities routinely arrest its members by the hundreds during electoral campaigns in an attempt to reduce their influence.

At the same time, Mubarak has increasingly made concessions to political Islam in the hopes of neutralizing opposition and shoring up his own Muslim credentials. As Islamists consider Israel and the United States the root of the evils plaguing Egypt, ranking right after Mubarak's own regime, Mubarak is only too happy to urge Egyptians to blame their discontent on others. He has distanced himself from, and even apologized for, Sadat's peace with Israel and has effectively maintained a "cold peace." He has allowed Muslim scholars to ban books that are deemed heretical or insulting to Islam and has not only allowed but also encouraged anti-Israel campaigns in educational curricula and the media. Egyptian newspapers, including government papers, brim with anti-Jewish sentiment, and, in cartoons described by Miller, portray Jews as "knife-wielding sadists with giant hook noses, pockets bulging with American dollars, and tongues dripping with blood." Mubarak has also sanctioned severe repression against Copts, or Egyptian Christians, who are occasionally massacred by Islamists while security forces look the other way.

While allowing rabid anti-Jewish and anti-Western sentiment to flourish, Mubarak's regime stifles democratic opposition. Laws restrict the ability of nongovernmental organizations, many of which have called for greater political openness and democracy, to operate or obtain funding. Saad Eddin Ibrahim, a prominent sociologist and political analyst, was sentenced to seven years' hard labor in 2001 after an unfair trial for "defaming Egypt" and accepting foreign funding. The sentence was upheld upon appeal in 2002, but quashed by the Court of Cassation in December under heavy pressure from abroad. Ibrahim, a onetime friend and adviser to Mubarak, has criticized the government's failure to establish democracy, investigated and denounced discrimination against Egyptian Christians, advocated normalization with Israel, and monitored elections. He was arrested in the summer of 2000 in a raid on his home, and his center, the Ibn Khaldun Center for Development Studies, was ransacked by police. Courts sentenced twenty-seven of his colleagues along with Ibrahim, though most of these sentences were suspended. In response to the international outcry from human rights groups over Ibrahim's arrest and sentencing, Mubarak has asked, "Why is everyone so concerned about this stupid man?"

Mubarak's policy of stifling democratic debate while placating Islamists denies Egyptians the possibility of a viable democratic alternative. Mubarak was sitting next to Sadat and was injured when the latter was shot to death in 1981 by Islamic fundamentalists. But instead of encouraging democratic reform, which could have undermined Sadat's assassins, he made surviving in power his priority. He thus increased the Islamists' appeal by keeping Egypt backward and poor. Still, the existence of Ibrahim and like-minded Egyptians means that extremist political Islam is not the only choice for a post-Mubarak Egypt.

Bashar al-Assad, Syria

In Syria, Bashar al-Assad, thirty-six, took power following the death of his father, the longtime dictator Hafez al-Assad, in June 2000. An initial slight relaxation of restrictions on free expression was quickly reversed in 2001, signaling that Bashar, a British-educated ophthalmologist, either is constrained by the entrenched interests of his father's cronies or is himself content to continue in his dictator father's shoes. Syria remains on the U.S. State Department's list of sponsors of terrorism and continues to support radical terrorist groups, including the Lebanon-based Hizbollah. With some thirty-five thousand to forty thousand troops occupying Lebanon, Syria dominates that country politically and militarily. Syrian-picked leaders in Lebanon follow the Syrian line on internal and regional affairs, although Lebanon does enjoy a greater degree of civil liberties, including some press freedom, than its occupier.

Zine al-Abidine Ben Ali, Tunisia

Under strongman Zine al-Abidine Ben Ali, sixty-six, dissatisfaction is growing in Tunisia over declining living standards, corruption, and unemployment. Western governments and rights monitors have criticized repeated government crackdowns on dissent. An attack by al-Qaeda on North Africa's oldest synagogue in April 2002 killed twenty-one people. The government responded with an intensified crackdown on political opposition in the name of national security. In a May 2002 referendum widely criticized as a "masquerade," Ben Ali won the right to amend the constitution, thus allowing him to run for a fourth term in 2003. Ben Ali's secular Constitutional Democratic Rally (RCD) has governed Tunisia since 1987, when he had his predecessor, Habib Bourguiba, deemed medically unfit to govern.

José Eduardo dos Santos, Angola

In Angola, José Eduardo dos Santos has faced little opposition to his rule since making peace in 2002 with the rebel UNITA movement to end a civil war that had plagued Angola since before independence from Portugal in 1975. The end to the conflict followed the death of UNITA leader Jonas Savimbi, who during the cold war was backed by Washington but more recently used the civil war to pocket revenues from the illicit diamond trade. In office since 1980, dos Santos has long justified clamping down on basic freedoms and concentrating power in his own hands by citing the war against UNITA, an excuse that now rings hollow. He is president, prime minister, and head of the ruling MPLA party and has reportedly used his posts to enrich himself. Hundreds of millions of dollars are "missing" because of high-level official corruption and what diplomats have called "a complete privatization of the war." Diplomats and aid workers warn that the war could resume if the government fails to carry through on its promises to give demobilized UNITA fighters vocational training and other help in returning to civilian life. Dos Santos has also pledged to hold elections in 2004.

Ali Abdullah Saleh, Yemen

Since becoming president of a unified Yemen in 1990, General People's Congress (GPC) leader Ali Abdullah Saleh, sixty, has gradually marginalized opposition groups, particularly the southern-based Yemeni Socialist Party (YSP). A February 2001 referendum approved constitutional amendments that extended Saleh's term in office and increased his powers. The changes essentially lock the YSP out of politics at least until 2003. It is widely believed that Saleh is grooming his son as his successor. Yemen is plagued by official corruption, poverty, and intertribal violence. Its notorious lawlessness also has made it a source and transit point for terrorists, weapons, and funding for Osama bin Laden's Qaeda organization. Yemen has recently undertaken joint efforts with U.S. military forces to curb terrorism and increase security within its borders.

Jean-Bertrand Aristide, Haiti

Popularly elected in 1990, overthrown in a military coup in 1991, and rein-stalled under threat of a U.S. invasion in 1994, Jean-Bertrand Aristide, forty-nine, was again elected president of Haiti in November 2000. This time, however, the election was boycotted by the opposition and marred by civil unrest and voter intimidation. While his supporters call him a champion of the powerless, Aristide's opponents accuse him of seeking to establish a one-party state. Economic disarray has made Haiti a breeding ground for corruption, money laundering, and drug trafficking; members of Aristide's Lavalas Family Party, which controls the senate, have been connected to Colombian drug cartels. Having made it safe for him to return to office, the United States has in recent years distanced itself from Aristide's increasingly dictatorial regime. Among other signs of Washington's shift, the U.S. Justice Department in 2000 ended a long-running, scandal-ridden police and prosecutorial training effort in Haiti, though it gave no official reason for its decision. In September 2002, the Organization of American States proposed a set of re-forms aimed at restoring stability and democracy. However, the opposition ac-cused the government of stalling on the reforms.

Paul Kagame, Rwanda

Long viewed as the leader of Rwanda, Maj. Gen. Paul Kagame, forty-five, of-ficially became president in 2000 after the resignation of President Pasteur Bizimungu. Kagame was military commander of the Rwandan Patriotic Front (RPF), which invaded Rwanda from neighboring Uganda to end the 1994 genocide of Tutsis by the Hutu majority. The RPF later invaded eastern areas of neighboring Congo, which harbored Hutu refugees as they rearmed along the Rwandan border. The government has extended its mandate until at least 2003, citing continued threats to domestic security. It also closely controls the news media, which were used by Hutus to broadcast incitements to slaughter. Often described as ascetic and disciplined, Kagame himself is careful to down-play the issue of ethnicity; he publicly identifies himself as a Rwandan rather than as a Tutsi.

Theocratic Dictator: *Ayatollah Ali Khamenei, Iran*

With the collapse of the Taliban in Afghanistan, Iran became the world's only theocratic country. Theocratic rulers claim legitimacy based on their status as clerics, in this case Islamic. In contrast, the rulers of other Muslim-majority countries that also base some or all of their legal systems on Islamic law claim legitimacy according to hereditary authority, as in Saudi Arabia, or on the basis of some type of elections, as in the Maldives.

Since 1989, Ayatollah Ali Khamenei has presided over an Iranian regime known for its sponsorship of international terrorism and its systematic, brutal human rights violations. As successor to the late Ayatollah Ruhollah Khomeini, architect of the revolution that made Iran an Islamic theocracy, he enjoys none of the popularity that Khomeini did when he joined in ending the brutal and corrupt regime of Shah Reza Pahlavi in 1979. Khamenei inherited a society devastated by war and, at least at first glance, cowed into submission by an interpretation of Islam that dictates everything from citizens' political views to their dress and behavior. But discontent has flourished, particularly among those too young to identify with the revolution. And it has found expression in a reform movement led by renascent vestiges of civil society, student protesters, and an elected president and parliament that, while holding little real power, present Khamenei with formidable demands for modernization and reform.

Mass execution and torture persist under Khamenei, as does the denial of the rights of women and a vigorous campaign to assassinate Iranian dissidents abroad. Hundreds of thousands of people are arrested every year for "moral corruption," which can include wearing jeans, possessing videotapes, or, in the case of women, exposing too much hair under a scarf. Lashing and amputation are common punishments, and women are frequently stoned to death for "moral" offenses such as prostitution.

Amnesty International believes that tens of thousands of Iranians have been executed since the revolution, and the true number may be much higher. Iranians who denounce such harsh punishments do so at their own risk. In response to a newspaper reporter who recently advocated scrapping capital punishment and vengeance laws, Khamenei said, "Any newspaper or writer wanting to renounce the fundamental principles of Islam or questioning the vengeance law is an apostate and subject to the death penalty."

As a two-term president under Ayatollah Khomenei, Khamenei served as an adviser to the supreme leader and participated actively in government decisions to commit acts of terrorism abroad. These included street bombings in France in 1986 that killed about a dozen people. But when Khamenei was named supreme leader following Khomeini's death in June 1989, Western observers predicted a moderation of the regime's behavior. Khamenei not only lacked his predecessor's charisma and ability to unite diverse political and ideological factions, they noted, but his religious credentials were also deficient. His junior rank in the clerical hierarchy did not meet the constitutional requirements for a supreme leader. In fact, Khamenei was selected only because Khomeini had pushed aside his designated successor, Ayatollah Hossein Ali

Montazeri, after a dispute. In order to enjoy any legitimacy, analysts said, Khamenei would have to adopt a more moderate approach.

Instead, he did exactly the opposite, looking to right-wing religious hardliners for allies and institutionalizing his dictatorship. The Iranian constitution was promptly changed to increase the powers of the supreme leader, making Iran legally far less democratic than it had been even under Khomeini. Provisions requiring that the supreme leader have a popular mandate and be a preeminent jurist with an established following were deleted. Presidential powers were diminished, and the supreme leader was given control over the military, foreign affairs, and the judiciary; the power to appoint and remove the president and legislature; and the final word on virtually every aspect of internal and external government policy. The regime launched a propaganda campaign with the aim of securing Khamenei's position among Iran's foreign proxies, including the Lebanon-based Hizbollah terrorist group.

Vigilantes working with the tacit consent of the Iranian government and spurred on by "divine duty" target perceived infidels and opponents of the regime at home and abroad. Supporters of the current reformist president, Mohammad Khatami, with whom Khamenei has a difficult relationship, have been particular targets in recent years. A number of writers and intellectuals were gunned down in late 1998 by "rogue elements" in the intelligence services, according to officials. Many of the suspects in the killings were released, while the prime suspect allegedly committed suicide in prison.

Khamenei's position has become tenuous since Khatami's 1997 election. Soaring unemployment and inflation, a marked decrease in living standards because of declining oil revenues, economic corruption and mismanagement, and restrictions on personal freedom led 70 percent of the electorate to vote for Khatami. He promised political and economic reform and signaled his commitment to the rule of law. Faced with an opponent who enjoys the popular mandate that he himself does not, Khamenei has assailed publicly Khatami's policy positions and denounced his supporters as morally bankrupt liberals. Khamenei's denunciations have brought the wrath of hard-line politicians and vigilantes upon Khatami supporters. They have been tried for corruption, lost government jobs, had their newspapers closed, been arrested and physically assaulted and, in some cases, assassinated.

Even before Khatami's election, the regime had sought to silence moderate or liberal voices. Dozens of Iranian and foreign nationals, including Turkish journalists, Iranian professors, and Kurdish leaders, have been murdered by Iranian vigilantes in recent years. Perhaps the most notable target is Indian-born author Salman Rushdie, whom Khomeini accused of apostasy for his book *The Satanic Verses*. Referring to Khomeini's declaration of a death sentence against Rushdie, Khamenei said in 1993: "The imam fired an arrow toward this brazen apostate. The arrow has left the bow and is moving toward its target and will sooner or later strike it. This sentence must definitely be carried out and it will be carried out." Rushdie has been in hiding in Europe and the United States.

The U.S. Department of State has for years considered Iran a chief state sponsor of terrorism. Iran provides material and financial support to Hizbollah, which it helped establish in Lebanon in 1983. Since then, Hizbollah has been involved in numerous anti-U.S. and anti-Israel terrorist attacks, including the June 2001 bombing of a Tel Aviv nightclub that killed twenty people.

Failed economic policies and rampant corruption have crippled the Iranian economy and impoverished a once-thriving middle class. Following the end of a devastating war with Iraq in 1988, Iran's leaders chose to forgo reconstruction in favor of a massive, rapid military procurement program, including efforts to acquire nuclear weapons. The United Nations Development Programme's 2002 report ranks Iran ninety-eighth out of 173 countries in terms of human development, an aggregate indicator that includes data on life expectancy, educational attainment, GDP per capita, and other measures of socioeconomic well-being. Twenty-five percent of adults are illiterate, 27 percent have no access to health services, and 36 percent have no access to sanitation. Meanwhile, clerics have enriched themselves through huge Islamic charitable institutions, called *bonyads*, which were established with the assets and possessions abandoned by the shah, his entourage, and other Iranians who fled the revolution. Bonyads are unregulated by the government and overwhelmingly corrupt. Furthermore, it is telling that this largely agricultural country imports 30 to 50 percent of its food.

In response, public outcry has intensified. In July 2002, a well-respected cleric publicly issued a letter resigning his post as a Friday prayer leader and denouncing the corruption of the clerical establishment. Students took to the streets by the tens of thousands in 1999, shouting unprecedented anti-Khamenei slogans. Police brutally beat them back, and Khatami later called on them to be patient. Patient they have been, and in 2001 they again helped give Khatami another landslide election victory. But the genie is out of the bottle; in 2002, students nationwide protested the death sentence for blasphemy against Hashem Aghajari, leader of a reformist political group. In 2003 they were again in the streets. The reawakening of Iran's tradition of student activism, a predominant force in the 1979 revolution, cannot be lost on Khamenei. In the end he will have to step aside for this growing wave of opposition, or be swept away as it clears the way for a post-theocratic Iran.

So here they are: forty-five bosses, kings, generals, communists, and an ayatollah. They import fear and export terror and war. They hold onto personal power at all costs—paid for by their enslaved people and long-suffering neighbors. Of course these dictators live very well themselves.

They are the major barrier to a civilized world.

9

Out by 2025

Democratization has been a global tide . . . and those who join it will prosper while those who resist will perish.

—Li Rui
Mao Zedong's former Secretary

Having now studied the world's last forty-five, we can begin to think how they might be brought down, applying the principles laid down thus far. Our stated priority is to have them all gone by the year 2025 and, to the degree possible, gone through nonviolent means. It remains to develop plans specific to each remaining dictatorship and to set priorities.

There are three basic regions within this arc of tyranny, which spreads from China and North Korea in the north to Zimbabwe and Angola in the south:

- *Asia,* with eight dictatorships: China, North Korea, Vietnam, Cambodia, and Laos are communists; Brunei and Bhutan are royalist dictatorships; and Burma is a military dictatorship. While the dictatorships in this region are far outnumbered by the Free and Partly Free nations, China makes up roughly half of all the people in the world still suffering under a dictator.
- *The "Stans," the Middle East, and North Africa,* with half of all the world's dictatorships—twenty-three. This is the only uniformly undemocratic region in the world.
- *Sub-Saharan Africa,* with eleven dictatorships: Angola, Burundi, Cameroon, Congo-Kinshasa, Equatorial Guinea, Guinea, Liberia, Rwanda, Swaziland, Togo, and Zimbabwe. There are twice as many Free and Partly Free countries in this region as there are Not Free countries.

There are also the three outlying dictatorships—*the last dictatorships in Europe and the Americas*: Belarus, Cuba, and Haiti. These two continents have been almost entirely swept clean of despots in the past quarter century. The three holdouts are anomalies in seas of freedom.

Asia

All of Asia's dictatorships deserve attention. For the prime movers, those living inside, say, Laos or North Korea, ousting the local dictator is more important than what happens anywhere else in the region. It is almost impossible to predict which of the eight is most likely to oust its dictator first.

North Korea certainly is the most isolated of the eight and, according to conventional wisdom, the least likely to move soon. But it is also the most brittle precisely because it is so oppressed and such a transparent failure in meeting even the most minimal of its people's needs—for food and heat. The South Korean comparison is powerful, as is the peaceful reunification of East and West Germany. A sudden, unpredictable change is entirely possible.

It would be particularly powerful to help one of the Asian communist dictatorships to cross the divide to democracy. We should learn from eastern/central Europe where Poland led the way and created a massive tidal wave that lifted and carried other European communist countries in its wake.

Burma also deserves special attention in part because it almost rid itself of its dictator in 1990 with free elections.

China

The country that clearly demands the most attention is China, also in part because it came so close to democracy in 1989. And because success in China will bring democracy to 1.3 billion people—one out of every five people on Earth, and one out of every two still living under a dictator today.

Let us apply the action agenda of this book.

What will China and the world look like if China continues under dictators, and what will it look like if China becomes a democracy? Many serious military analysts believe that China is the single greatest threat to American and global security. In the eyes of its communist leaders, the United States and the West are the enemy. As China specialist Professor Ross Terrill points out, "We are needed as an adversary to shore up the legitimacy of the Communist-party state."[1] Communist China already has strategic missiles capable of reaching the western United States. Today China is "the only nation targeting the United States with nuclear weapons," as Shanghai-based attorney Gordon G. Chang writes in his perceptive book *The Coming Collapse of China,*[2] although North Korea also has some limited capability to strike the United States. China is a serious and growing threat to all neighboring states. A democratic China would have a profoundly different orientation. Some form of unification with a democratic Taiwan could be accomplished peacefully. China would see the United States and the rest of the democratic world as allies, not enemies. The political balance of forces in Asia would be transformed as it was in Europe when that communist house of cards collapsed.

Is it feasible for China to become a democracy by 2025? The country has seen three campaigns for democracy over the past three decades: the Democracy Wall movement in the late 1970s, the nationwide movement of 1989 culminating in the demonstrations in Tiananmen Square, and the struggle started by the Falun Gong and other groups at the end of the last decade.

Thus far they have failed. But we know from the experience of India, Poland, Hungary, Yugoslavia, and many other countries that sometimes repeated campaigns of nonviolent conflict are necessary before dictators can be ousted permanently. Every failed campaign demonstrates *the* most important ingredient—that the will to struggle and sacrifice for democracy is alive and strong in the society.

Few recognize that Chinese democrats nearly succeeded in ousting the dictator, Deng Xiaoping, in 1989, the same year that success was achieved in central and eastern Europe. As documented in the *Tiananmen Papers,* on 15 May 1989, according to China's Ministry of State Security, 1.2 million people demonstrated in Beijing alone.[3] There were demonstrations that day in 132 Chinese cities—in every part of the country. Students from virtually every university participated in the protests. According to a State Security Ministry report, demonstrators in Beijing came not only from schools, even grade schools, but also from a wide range of factories, party offices, government ministries, broadcast and print media, museums, intellectual salons, hotels, food markets, department stores, and other places. Some military commanders refused to follow orders. And, as always in dictatorships, there was the fear that when the crunch came, soldiers would not fire on their own civilians.

A majority of the Standing Committee of the Politburo led by Zhao Ziyang opposed declaration of martial law and the use of force against the students. In this they were strikingly similar to Gorbachev and other Communist Party dictators in most central and eastern Europe countries who also refused to use force and, as a result, were forced to allow democracy. Unfortunately, in China, the ultimate dictator, Deng Xiaoping, supported by other "Elders," recognized that this was a "life-and-death turning point for the future of our Party and State." Deng Xiaoping and his Elders realized, "We could all have been put under house arrest." Deng Xiaoping also stated that while they did some useful things on economic reform, "the last two general secretaries (Hu Yaobang and Zhao Ziyang) both stumbled on . . . opposition to bourgeois liberation." So Deng Xiaoping did authorize the use of force. But it is at least as significant that Deng also allowed the student demonstrations to continue for many weeks, to embarrass the regime in front of a visiting Mikhail Gorbachev, even to "paralyze" the heart of Beijing. He was clearly concerned whether the police and army would stay with him, as his use of force might have ignited his overthrow. It is also possible that Deng's long exile after the Cultural Revolution inclined him to be less repressive, at least initially.

What lessons are to be learned from 1989? Most important, it almost worked. Had Deng Xiaoping not been alive, or had Zhao Ziyang publicly opposed martial law, the troops and police would not have stopped the democrats. Deng Xiaoping, the Elders, and Li Peng, their proxy within the Politburo, won their power struggle with Zhao Ziyang and other reformers in part because the democratic world—and specifically the U.S. government—was seen within Zhongnanhai (the leadership compound) to be urging caution. Secretary of State James Baker had said it was not in the interest of the United States to see major instability in either China or the Soviet Union. When asked why the United States did not support the Chinese students, Baker replied that "the United States supports democracy and the freedoms of speech and assembly, but that it was also very important, in the present situation, that the United States not be seen as in any way inciting political unrest."[4]

Some of the student leaders of 1989 from Shanghai and Beijing have confirmed to me that this lack of support, or even opposition, from the United States and other leading democratic governments was a factor in their own decision making. And they are certain it had an impact on the decisions and actions of Deng Xiaoping and Zhao Ziyang, as well as the police and military. One lesson to be learned: do not desert and undermine your natural allies. Think how different a democratic China would be today, and how different would be its relations with the United States, Taiwan, and other democracies.

It is striking and encouraging that despite the brutality of the repression in 1989, with thousands shot and tens of thousands jailed, and continuing repression since, a decade after Tiananmen Square, nonviolent conflict once again spread across the face of China. According to government officials, 307 "sieges" occurred between 25 April and August 1999 throughout the country. Labor strikes occur virtually daily, some involving tens of thousands of workers. Perhaps most dramatic, without warning, ten thousand practitioners of the Falun Gong appeared before the Chinese leadership compound and peacefully but powerfully insisted on their right to practice their faith—by doing their spiritual exercises in full view of the dictator. Once again the

Chinese communist leadership was confronted with the choice between dialogue and repression. After Premier Zhu Rongji's initial meeting on 25 April
1999 in Zhongnanhai with several participants and reported commitment to
them not to repress the Falun Gong, and Jiang Zemin's surreptitious drive
to watch through the tinted windows of his car as the Falun Gong did their
exercises, Jiang decided on repression. According to *Time* magazine, he was
reportedly impressed by the discipline of the vigil and the Falun Gong's
capacity to mobilize so many people so quickly. He has, according to *Time*,
"become obsessed with the Falun Gong and its ability to organize in cyber-
space."[5]

As Danny Schechter states in his detailed book on the Falun Gong, this is
a movement "Gandhian in its breadth and historic in its proportions."[6] Estimates of the number of practitioners range from 30 million to 100 million
people—a very large number even for China. Rooted in Buddhist and Taoist
traditions and practices thousands of years old, Falun Gong has proved a powerful attraction to every segment of the population, including many in the
Communist Party, the military, and police and security services. Practitioners
have demonstrated immense courage and determination by nearly weekly
public demonstrations of their faith in Tiananmen Square and throughout
China. Hong Kong's *South China Morning Post* reported in February 1999 that
"President Jiang Zemin has warned that the Falun Gong sect poses as much of
a threat to the Communist Party as the Solidarity movement did to the Communists in Poland in the 1980s." Or as Gordon Chang writes, "The Communist Party looks at Li Hongzhi and his Falun Gong spiritual movement and
sees the image of Mao's peasant army of the late 1940s sweeping across the
plains. No wonder China's leading political organization acts as if it were
fighting for its survival."[7]

Once again the democratic world's response has been "tepid," to use
Schechter's term, and once again the dictator has interpreted this as a green
light to proceed with suppression. As the repression deepened in November
1999, President Bill Clinton and President Jiang Zemin were pictured smiling
with one another during a bilateral meeting in New Zealand. Jiang presented
Clinton with a government propaganda tract against Falun Gong. When local practitioners presented President Clinton with a book by Falun Gong's
leader, Li Hongzhi, he said nothing. As Schechter writes, at one point during
the summit, Jiang delayed attending the official dinner for heads of state for
three hours until Falun Gong posters outside the hall were taken down. Similarly in England and France, security officials blocked protests and shielded
the traveling Chinese dictator from their view. Not a single head of a democratic government, including now two presidents of the United States has met
Li Hongzhi, who lives in forced exile in New York City. This man of peace

and spirituality is not welcomed at the White House, partly because of communist propaganda about this "cult" and partly from fear of the dictator Jiang Zemin's reaction. Thus, the leader of the most popular movement in China, and what may be the best hope for a peaceful democratic China, is still not considered our partner. The U.S. government is not alone in this timidity. When I asked the German foreign ministry in Berlin to allow me to introduce a major figure in the Falun Gong, which has no contact with Germany, I was told it would not be possible because "it might be misconstrued by officials in Beijing." How profoundly shortsighted, superficial, and wrongheaded is our understanding of national interest and international security.[8]

The democratic world needs to realize that democracy in China is feasible, that its achievement would transform the globe's security, and that we should make the achievement of democracy in China our number one priority in international affairs. We need to pursue a dialogue with all elements of Chinese society premised on an unambiguous and public assertion that full democracy will come within a single generation, at the absolute latest by 2025. We need to make clear that we support the Chinese people's struggle to become a democratic and prosperous nation worthy of the world's trust and respect.

Sanctions must be tailored against the dictators of China, not the Chinese people, and a new consensus must be developed among democrats. The classic debate between those who want to "engage" versus those who want to "contain or isolate" China is wrongheaded. The objective must be to engage the people and contain, influence, and ultimately oust the dictators. The most powerful sanction is for outside democrats to work with all elements of Chinese society to bring about a peaceful democratic revolution.

We need to participate in bringing together the key groups inside China behind a single strategy. We need to participate actively in the democracy campaign.

Part of the strategy should be to set a deadline for the achievement of full-scale democracy. Waiting until 2025 seems much too long, but setting a deadline of five years for a country as large and early stage seems unrealistic. Perhaps 2015 is a realistic target, which could be met by achieving each of the three stages set forth below in approximately four-year increments. Stage 1 should be completed by the 2008 Olympics. (The alternative is that the following sentiment expressed by a BBC correspondent will spread: "As China becomes a bigger power in the world its government is becoming ever more fascist. In the run up to the Beijing Olympic games one can't help thinking of Berlin in the 1930s.")[9]

Bringing in the multinational business community is critical for China to achieve democracy. Our proposed Business Community for Democracy, including the world's largest and most successful corporations and therefore the largest investors in China, should develop a special program for China including the following elements:

- It must be agreed that the rule of law and democracy are required for the protection and success of business in China as elsewhere.
- China's membership in the World Trade Organization (WTO) affords new possibilities to promote public accountability and the rule of law; violations of WTO standards need to be vigorously pursued through the organization's procedures; functioning contract, property, and commercial law is conducive to public expectations of other rights and obligations on the part of state authorities.
- Programs to promote the rule of law and democracy within China will be funded from the Business Community for Democracy's Global Democracy Fund.
- As was done in South Africa, a corporate code of conduct will be established: treating workers in a manner consistent with International Labor Organization standards; allowing independent labor unions to organize in foreign-owned plants; conducting outreach to the community, including environmental and other civil society groups; posting free press on their premises; allowing Falun Gong and other spiritual groups to practice their faith on the premises; hiring those active in the democracy campaign.
- Businesses must agree not to engage in corrupt practices, and specifically not to offer financial support for the dictator, his support mechanisms, family, or friends.

Some will argue that the business community cannot possibly attempt these things without being chased out of China. This ignores the fact that China's rapid growth has been, and continues to be, overwhelmingly fueled by foreign investment from these very firms and by exports they produce in China. Without foreign investment, technology, and markets, China will cease to grow altogether and the communists will be overthrown, quite possibly in a less than peaceful manner. They know the outside world economy has huge leverage; the problem is that the business community itself is not organized to take advantage of this leverage and does not have the right conceptual framework. This will have to change. An informal China Working Group, which includes companies and organizations such as Amnesty International, the International Labor Rights Fund, and Global Exchange, already exists. The group shares best-practices information and members' experience working or operating in China and educates members about Chinese government policies and human and labor rights abuses.

We must galvanize and organize the communities of democracies and democrats to work together and to help the democrats inside China. The difficulty of rallying governments behind this task is demonstrated by the truly deplorable unwillingness of most democratic governments to support resolutions in the UN Commission on Human Rights calling upon China's Communist leadership to respect its human rights commitments. In 2003 even the United States did not offer such a resolution. This is precisely the reason that the Community of Democracies is so important as a new initiative. If Community of Democracy groups to focus on each region of the world are created, it will become more difficult to ignore the largest democracy holdout in the world. It may be that a coalition of the willing from within the Community of Democracies would allow democratic governments with the courage and commitment to do so to work together on China. Initial common projects would probably have to be fairly tame—for example, promoting education in democracy ("civics" classes) within China and some of the other "opening" programs we recommend.

Galvanizing and organizing nongovernmental democrats to help the Chinese is somewhat easier. There already are non-Chinese willing to go to China and get arrested to show their support for the Chinese people's rights. Tens of thousands of Chinese are studying abroad, many at American universities. They offer an enormous resource. While many are reluctant to discuss politics, these students need to be engaged by Chinese Americans and our democracy/human rights community. Some may consider working to change the system upon their return. Training even a handful in nonviolent resistance techniques would increase knowledge of these methods among Chinese youth—potentially the most powerful agent for change in the country.

China has an enormous and politically significant diaspora in Asia, and it should be viewed as a resource to promote democracy in China. Taiwan's transition to full democracy in the past decade gives the lie to Singaporean Lee Kwan Yew's "Asian values" argument that democratic openness is alien and cannot take root in Chinese societies. Ethnic Chinese investors and others who have regular access to China could use their "in" to great effect by helping encourage nonviolent resistance and public demands for basic civil and human rights.

Freedom House rates Hong Kong and Macao, both now under Chinese control, as Partly Free, because of their residual civil structures. The democracies need to help the citizens of these enclaves maintain these freedoms and continue to test the limits. Every encroachment by the communists and their local stooges on agreements made needs to be vociferously protested by the democracies, in direct protests to Beijing. These two enclaves should be piedmonts of a free China, and political party foundations need to be active there. Other specialized nongovernmental organizations (NGOs), such as Article 17 and others concerned with press freedom and the AFL-CIO's Solidarity Center with its focus on labor rights, should have more room to maneuver and should be supported in strong programming.

Individual citizens of democracies can do their part to help the Chinese yearning to break free. Tourism is a major opportunity for foreigners, allowing for low-risk democracy action. The Falun Gong practitioners from abroad who exercised together with Chinese in Tiananmen Square in late 2001 and 2002 had precisely the right idea. "Volunteers for democracy" organizations should be created to stage planned actions in China; this is the purpose of the proposed Students for Democracy. For example, a demonstration at the Three Gorges Dam site by Greenpeace and the developing Chinese environmental movement would get important press and could spark similar stands in other areas of China. The very first large demonstration in Hungary in the critical late 1980s was staged by environmentalists to protest a dam. This is the sort of public demonstration that willing embassies could attend, protect, and support.

Another step to unite and galvanize nongovernmental elements and governments alike could be the proclamation of an annual China Democracy Day around the world. This could provide a focus for statements by prime ministers, presidents, parliamentarians, and other democratic leaders, demonstrations and pressure for more programs and concrete support. Most important, it would help undermine the legitimacy of the communist dictatorship.

A truly massive opening program is warranted for China and will achieve massively valuable results. But programs cost money. Of the already meager resources available for democracy promotion, no more than 5 percent is directed toward China—a country that represents 50 percent of all those still suffering under dictatorship, and which poses the largest single security threat to the United States and its neighbors. The U.S. Congress should pass a special China Democracy Act, as it did with great effect for Serbia. We and other democracies need dedicated resources for this challenge and opportunity.

Substantially increased China programs for the National Endowment for Democracy, the AFL-CIO's American Council for International Labor Solidarity, Freedom House, and the other democracy-promotion organizations could make a difference. The International Republican Institute has had for a decade a village-level-elections program in China. We should press Ziang Zemin and Hu Jintao to allow elections at the provincial level and offer the institute's assistance in setting them up.

Within the new Dictatorship-to-Democracy Center, there should be a special, large-scale program for China, to help with strategy for the national movement, training in techniques, and funding. Chinese dissidents and activists urgently need resources with which to operate. In China, the dollar goes far. Those willing to take the risks in opposing the system need the wherewithal to do so. Their families need support when they are in jail or underground. Innovative methods of getting these funds to them, with a minimum of bureaucracy, are imperative.

The more traditional opening programs also deserve high priority for China. Exchanges and visits of all types and at all levels are important.

China is increasingly promising in terms of media, considering the growing affluence of the population and proliferation of televisions. Radios are nearly universal. Access to the Internet, though filtered, is growing. The importance of getting messages into China is primarily to show the Chinese that the world at large is on their side and concerned with their languishing under a geriatric, repressive regime. Notable inroads have been made by Radio Free Asia, which has significant listenership, despite the regular use of jamming by the Chinese authorities.[10] Radio Free Asia has listeners calling in to discuss issues of the day, including strikes, and police crackdowns and to help Chinese see that their compatriots share their troubles. The rottenness of the system is on regular display to Radio Free Asia's audience. Prohibited works are serialized and read on the air. A new program suggestion: a reading of Peter Ackerman and Jack Du Vall's *A Force More Powerful* or Gene Sharp's works on strategic nonviolence would help disseminate this wisdom and hope throughout the population. The party's denunciations of Radio Free Asia have *increased* the profile of the station, exposing it to a wider audience. Thirteen years after Tiananmen Square, in which information technology played an important role, the communists remain behind the power curve of technology and effective public relations.

Another potential topic for discussion on Radio Free Asia and other international broadcasts to China in native languages (Mandarin, Cantonese, Tibetan, Uighur) is the Chinese constitution itself. Like the Soviet constitution, it enumerates rights that have never been respected by the communist authorities. China has signed a multitude of international agreements that guarantee respect for human and civil rights that are severely curtailed. A program on Charter 77 in Czechoslovakia, which used the communist regime's signing of the Helsinki protocols in 1975 as a lever, could be useful.

But our media efforts should enter the age of television as well. The satellite channel from Los Angeles to Iran in Farsi demonstrates the power of this medium in getting directly to a mass audience, and particularly young people, with a message of democracy and resistance and the ability to create new leadership figures within a society.[11] While the dictator Jiang Zemin has his own satellite channels covering Chinese and Chinese Americans in the United States, the democrats have nothing comparable to reach Chinese viewers in China. For an initial investment of $50 million and with annual support in the range of $10 million, a first-class news and entertainment channel could be beamed to China and around the world in Mandarin and

Cantonese. But it should not be run by the U.S. government. Television is different from radio. The experience with the U.S. Information Agency's Worldnet and other government television failures demonstrates that they are, almost without exception, incredibly boring and achieve little audience loyalty and impact. A new corporation should be set up with government backing but an independent management and board with professional television experience. We earlier proposed a $1 billion international fund for independent television; in its absence the U.S. government should fund this Chinese channel.

Just as Solidarity in Poland broke into official state television broadcasts to show programming of its own, so the Falun Gong has managed in the northeastern Chinese city of Changchun to tap into the cable and take over local cable stations with its own programming. Even more dramatically, the official New China News Agency reported on 24 September 2002 that the Falun Gong has used Taiwan as a base to hijack satellite transmissions and repeatedly beamed its messages all over mainland China and for up to twelve hours at a stretch.

China is an ideal candidate for a multiyear democracy development plan and program. Like other communist countries, it has long experience with five-, ten-, and even fifteen-year economic development plans; it is currently pursuing its tenth five-year plan. From Mao onward, all of China's communist dictators also have talked about long-term political development plans and objectives. China's own constitution guarantees numerous rights, including freedom of speech, of the press, of assembly, of association, and of religion. China is one of the original signatories of the Universal Declaration of Human Rights and more recently of the International Covenant on Civil and Political Rights and the International Covenant on Social and Cultural Rights. These three documents contain specific commitments to each of the building blocks of democracy and our proposed democracy plan/program; China is committed to freedom of association, independent trade unions, multiparty elections, a free press, freedom of religion, an independent judiciary, and so forth.

In terms of the three stages of democratic growth that provide the basis for a multiyear democracy plan and program (see chapter 5, pp. 84–86), China is at an early part of stage 1.

To raise and pursue such a three-stage democracy program with the Chinese, we recommend the establishment of a Dictatorship-to-Democracy Center by the Community of Democracies with a United Nations affiliation. The purpose of the center is precisely to guide nations to implement such democracy programs. If the center has not been established in the near term, a coalition of willing governments and NGOs could approach the Chinese government.

While the initial reaction may not be positive, beginning the process of setting benchmarks is useful in itself. The dialogue, public and private, can then shift from individual human rights cases and violations to the more fundamental issues of changing the political system—without which there will be human rights violations without end. Over time and with the strategy recommended here, even China's dictators can be brought to the table. Most important of all, these three stages provide a vehicle to raise the expectations of Chinese students, intellectuals, workers, and others and to focus their nonviolent movement for change. Perhaps the 2008 date for the Olympics could be used as a lever and reference point for this multiyear democracy development program; The program should be announced and launched well before the Olympics. Stage 1 should possibly be completed by then, and a process and target dates extending beyond the Olympics should be formulated.

We cannot know in advance when the communist leadership will be prepared to engage. There is clearly a debate within the party about political reform. One example is an article by Mao Zedong's former secretary, Li Rui, eighty-five, in *China Chronicle*, a magazine widely read by party officials. He warns that China must embrace democratic politics and free speech to avoid stagnation and possible collapse. He proposes wide-ranging measures to limit the Communist Party's powers, to begin introducing the popular election of government officials, and to protect freedom of speech and independent rule of law.[12] We cannot know what new party general secretary Hu Jintao and the other members of the new Politburo may be willing to try—especially if we do not talk with them about it.

A Chinese pollster noted about a recent public opinion poll: "Ten years ago, the frequent concern was getting access to decent food, like meat and vegetables, but after a decade of stability and economic development people have aspirations that go way beyond. . . . There is general hope that after the Party Congress there will be slow, steady progress in the legal system and improving our political institutions." He notes that people specifically mentioned a desire to expand local elections to higher levels of government. Two-thirds hoped that new methods would be quite different and allow expressions of public opinion.[13]

We must realize the full potential of democratic embassies and consulates as active freedom houses within China. They must be visible, active parts of the Chinese cultural and political landscape, not just in the major cities but also in the hinterland and in Tibet and Xinjiang, the western territories that are essentially Chinese colonies. A visit to a factory where workers are being fleeced by corrupt managers, with the complicity of state officials, would send a message to the Chinese people that their fight against arbitrary power is recognized. Diplomats should elbow their way into political trials of Falun Gong members and should exercise with them publicly in Tiananmen Square and other public spaces. Going to sites of tension or unrest, including the Korean border to show solidarity with and encourage North Korean refugees, is necessary. Our diplomatic missions are supposed to represent not only our governments but also our societies and the values we hold dear as democratic, self-governing peoples. Embassies and consulates must not devolve into being mere trade-promotion offices. Democracies can—and must—perform their traditional diplomatic roles and promote democracy at the same time.

To realize this, the right personnel need to be selected for the job. These individuals, both professionals and appointees, need to be prepared to raise the thorny, "rude" questions to the Chinese authorities about their systematic trampling of civil and human rights and need to get on with building democratic institutions. Keen participant-observers like former Freedom House chair Bette Bao Lord note that the United States and other democracies rarely exact reciprocity from Chinese authorities on the composition of delegations and other nuts-and-bolts issues. Regularly, the communists nitpick at incoming delegations for critics and potential critics, while the United States rarely does this. When such obstructionism occurs, democracies should exercise similar stalling, methodical scrutiny. The obstructions would soon decrease.

Within democratic embassies, ambassadors need to hold regular democracy coordination meetings with their section heads, including intelligence and military. Soon after these regular meetings, the democratic ambassadors need to hold similar meetings among themselves. These meetings should also take place outside the capital, in cities that have large diplomatic communities.

On the social circuit, embassies need to ensure they do not hew to the party line in drafting their guest lists. Beyond the usual official and diplomatic set, nonstate actors, including independent labor figures, strike leaders, and private businesspeople; Falun Gong, Catholic, Protestant, and other persecuted religious figures; released Laogai prisoners; students; and others should also be present.

The democratic embassies need to be freedom houses by providing unfettered information and, when necessary, sanctuary. Cybercafés should be created at embassies, consulates, and other official offices. By opening these centers in China's major cities, democracies can facilitate coordination of civic action throughout the country. In addition to helping them communicate with one another, this interaction will also permit democracies to identify potential leaders and avenues to assist them.

We should also initiate a regular process of fireside chats about democracy. Every week at least one ambassador should give a talk on a new China Democracy Hour broadcast via Radio Free Asia, the BBC, Voice of America, and anyone else who will carry it. This should be supplemented by addresses given

by presidents, prime ministers, and others, either on visits to China or as fireside chats from their capitals. President George W. Bush's speech at Tsinghua
University in Beijing on 22 February 2002 was a solid beginning; it was broadcast via Chinese government channels throughout the country. He argued
that the strength of America is our democratic political values and system.
"Life in America shows that liberty, paired with law, is not to be feared. . . . In
a free society, diversity is not disorder. Debate is not strife. Dissent is not revolution. A free society trusts its citizens to seek greatness in themselves and in
their country."[14]

Subsequent speeches should talk more explicitly about China itself. For example, President Bush missed an opportunity at Tsinghua to mention that
over three hundred of its students and faculty have been put in prison or sent
to reeducation camps because of their peaceful practice of Falun Gong. He
missed an opportunity to state explicitly that China must and will become a
full-scale democracy within a generation because that is what its people
want—and as they have demonstrated every decade. There is ample time for
him and other democratic leaders to fully voice the aspirations of a people
who cannot yet do so freely by themselves.

A point of paramount import is the need to professionalize the People's
Liberation Army. In 1989, Deng was loath to test the army's willingness to fire
on unarmed demonstrators and had to maneuver to find units he thought
were a safe bet before playing his last deadly card.[15] The United States needs
to lead the way in using its contacts with the Chinese army to promote a professional, civil ethos. Armies are to protect the people from foreign enemies,
not to protect the government from the people. Junior- and middle-ranking
officers should be a particular focus. Not only are they more likely to be open
to new patterns of thinking, but also they are the company- and platoon-level
commanders who may well be forced to decide whether to follow or refuse an
order to shoot fellow citizens.

We must deal directly with China's dictators. If history is any guide, Jiang
Zemin will try to continue to be number one until he dies. But Hu Jintao, his
ostensible successor, will be restless with this situation. We have repeatedly
witnessed in China the presumed successor and other senior leaders try to accommodate to pressures for democratic change only to be reined in or ousted
by the aged number one. It is clear from a new book, *Zhu Rongji in 1999*, that
Jiang feared China's premier because of his popularity and systematically
worked to undermine his reformist and personal influence.[16] This argues for
the American ambassador in Beijing and the ambassadors of other leading
democracies to develop direct relations with Jiang, Hu, and other key leaders.
Fissures can develop and be used. Time together is required and the more private, the better. It is critical to find ways to meet not only in offices but also

elsewhere, over meals, at sports, whatever is possible. Hosting Hu Jintao on another trip to and around the United States would provide one way to deepen a relationship, especially with the U.S. president. Visitors to China provide another reason to meet. There should be three components to the dialogue:

- First, the ambassador and the president should talk with Jiang, Hu, and the others about the nature of twenty-first-century societies, about the relationship between the free market and a political infrastructure of independent trade unions, an independent judiciary, a free press, and competing political parties. China is facing an enormous set of problems: massive and growing unemployment, numerous and sometimes violent strikes, slowing rates of growth, and banks and state enterprises that are basically bankrupt. Modern, open, democratic societies can absorb and manage these problems peacefully; repressive regimes will stifle the initiative required in a world increasingly driven by intellectual product as opposed to pure manpower.

- Second should be a discussion about the personal situation of Hu and the others. Hu should be helped to understand that students, Falun Gong, and others are reasonable people (here the ambassador's known direct relationship with students and the Falun Gong is critical to his or her credibility) and willing to work with Hu if he too is reasonable. The growing number of cases where former communist leaders are able to play a significant role in postcommunist societies is a central point. Hu and the others need to be brought to understand that they can become positive, historic figures in the Chinese pantheon if they are willing to accommodate to democratic change.

- Third, Hu needs also to understand the negative consequences for himself if he resists. The ambassador should indicate that more democratic "risings" are inevitable; Hu will again face the choice of slaughtering his fellow citizens or entering a dialogue leading to full democracy. With the students occupying Tiananmen Square, Deng believed "We will be under house arrest" or worse if he did not use force. But the world has evolved. Another Tiananmen Square could lead to charges being brought in The Hague before a special tribunal for crimes against humanity such as Slobodan Milosevic and the Rwandan leaders have faced. And next time, the students and workers may be joined by young soldiers who turn their guns against the oppressors rather than the oppressed.

According to the International Criminal Court classifications, Jiang has committed over ten varieties of crimes against humanity just in his persecution of the Falun Gong. Furthermore, he has violated nearly every article in the Universal Declaration of Human Rights and the International Covenant on Civil and Political Rights. Jiang is directly responsible for the wrongful imprisonment, torture, and death of tens of thousands of Chinese.

We must depart from former secretary of state James Baker's stated view that "the United States [must] not be seen as in any way inciting political unrest." Quite the opposite, we must state that political stability in China can be achieved only through democracy and that the path there lies through open and active support for Chinese democratic and nonviolent movements. We already have mentioned the Falun Gong and the various pro-democracy groups in China. We know from the experience of 1989 that there is a huge desire for freedom and willingness to go into the streets across China among students and intellectuals and the growing middle class. In 1989 some workers also joined at late stages. Strikes among workers have been growing in number and scale in recent years; strikes are now massive and nationwide, most protesting plant closures or the corruption of plant managers and the collusion of local party and government officials. "Corruption is routinely the top complaint of people queried in internal government polls, surpassing unemployment. . . . Sources close to the Chinese security apparatus note that unrest, killings and demonstrations linked to corruption cases are on the rise," reported the *Washington Post* on 6 March 2002. But these strikes remain diffuse, not yet connected by independent national trade unions or a movement like Solidarity in Poland. A way must be found to weave together workers, spiritual practitioners, and democracy activists into a national movement. What issues resonate throughout the working population? The pervasiveness of corruption? Unemployment? The environment? Chinese themselves will define the strategy and tactics they want to use. But outsiders familiar with other successful nonviolent campaigns can play a critical role.

We must narrow our focus to the issue of a single dictator versus an entire nation's right to elect and reject its own leaders. Until further notice, China's dictator is Jiang Zemin. He personally decided to ban, jail, and murder members of China's largest spiritual movement. Hu Jintao, emerging as his possible eventual successor, was personally responsible for the terrible repression in Tibet during his tenure there. They should not be allowed to hide behind "regimes" or "cultures." We need to make clear that they are personally responsible for their acts; they are, after all, all-powerful. We should issue an annual report on their personal crimes against humanity, their personal vulnerabilities, their lack of legitimacy. At the same time, we should be on the lookout for agents of change within the leadership—for latent Mikhail Gorbachevs and Boris Yeltsins. Zhao Ziyang was becoming one when he was removed by Deng Xiaoping just prior to the bloody 1989 crackdown. Zhu

Rongji leaned in this direction before being reined in by Jiang Zemin. Inherent in the transition relationship now under way between Jiang and Hu Jintao are tensions that might be exploited to encourage a more tolerant policy, the real retirement of Jiang Zemin, and the eventual holding of free elections by the Chinese people.

North Korea

Dubbed "the hermit kingdom" by many observers, North Korea has long been the most isolated of countries, under the most totalitarian system in the world today. It is also among the world's most impoverished countries, with a slow-motion famine that is devastating its population. In the 1990s, humanitarian aid to North Korea became necessary for the regime to maintain itself, and while humanitarian workers have not been given much latitude to travel freely and ask questions, a clear picture emerges. By all accounts, the results of the regime's rule have been demographically catastrophic; children are far below their weight targets and mentally disabled owing to systemic malnutrition. The economic mismanagement inherent in communism has resulted in an agricultural society that cannot feed itself. Even more than Cuba or Vietnam, North Korea preserves the cold war era perfectly in amber; it stands as a nightmarish twentieth-century anachronism in the new era of globalization of information and freedom.

In an effort to break through that isolation, South Korea's former dissident and president Kim Dae Jung embarked on his own version of Ostpolitik, an engagement with Pyongyang known as the "Sunshine Policy." Initially, this looked as if it was making inroads into North Korea and gaining new insights for a population that had been separated from its northern brethren for over fifty years. South Korean companies were encouraged to invest in North Korea. Development of the Tyumen River Basin on the Manchurian border with China and Russia was studied. A few families were reunited, if only briefly, after decades of being separated by the world's most fortified frontier. North Korea, hungry for foreign exchange from rich South Koreans, encouraged very strictly controlled tourism to a few sites. The Kims even met in 2000 in Pyongyang.[17] But by 2001, the Sunshine Policy appeared to have hit the wall.[18] South Korean investors lost a great deal of money in their investments in the North. Efforts to build on the advances of 2000 and 2001 stalled. There was no liberalization to speak of in North Korea. The little the South Koreans (and other Pacific powers, including the United States and Japan) were able to learn about North Korea in this brief thaw did nothing to allay their fears of a paranoid, insular regime determined never to open to the rest of the world.

With the advent of the second Bush administration, a new skepticism entered U.S. policy toward Pyongyang. Departing for his February 2002 Asian tour, President Bush underscored his concern with North Korea's posture on the demilitarized zone, noting the reason the United States maintains a strong presence in South Korea. He added, "On one side of the military zone are people who are starving to death, are people who are imprisoned, are people who can't speak their mind freely. . . . On the other side are a free people with a fantastic economy and great opportunity. And I'm going to remind people of the fundamental question: Why? And it's because of freedom."[19] In his press conference with South Korean president Kim Dae Jung, Bush noted that he supported Kim's Sunshine Policy and questioned North Korea's unwillingness to act in its spirit and avail itself of the new opportunities the policy provides. He then vigorously defended his placement of the Pyongyang regime in the "axis of evil," saying that he was "troubled by a regime that tolerates starvation" and develops weapons of mass destruction, and that dictator Kim Jong Il had to prove to the world that he cared for his people. Bush then outlined his vision for Korea: "My vision is clear—I see a peninsula that is one day united in commerce and cooperation, instead of divided by barbed wire and fear. Korean grandparents should be able to spend their final years with those they love. Korean children should never starve while a massive army is fed. No nation should be a prison for its own people. No Korean should be treated as a cog in the machinery of the state."[20]

The issue now is how to bring this change about.

In December 2002, Kim Jong Il created a new crisis by admitting that he had been conducting a secret program to develop nuclear weapons, in violation of the 1994 agreement with the United States. He threatened war if the United States did not agree to negotiate a nonaggression pact and restart economic assistance in return for his again promising not to develop nuclear weapons. This was an extraordinary opportunity for the United States and South Korea to move "From Helsinki to Pyongyang"—the title of a statement of principles that Michael Horowitz of the Hudson Institute and I conceived and drafted and for which we secured leading Americans as cosigners. The *Wall Street Journal* published the statement on 17 January 2003. We argue that just as President Richard Nixon in 1972 agreed to negotiations on Leonid Brezhnev's demands for nonaggression and improved economic cooperation but insisted on broadening the agenda to include human rights, so President Bush should propose to open negotiations on such a Helsinki-like three-basket agenda with North Korea. The animating insight of Helsinki was that, by publicly raising human rights issues to high-priority levels, the United States would set in motion forces that would undermine the legitimacy of the Soviet communist empire, and so it turned out to be. By formally acknowledging in Helsinki the legitimacy of such rights as the free exchange of people, open borders, and family reunification, the communists opened the floodgates of dissent and brought about their eventual ouster.

Would Kim Jong Il agree to enter into such a negotiation and agreement? In 2002 and early 2003 he is showing signs of desperation and searching for new solutions to mounting problems. In 2002, he introduced a modest reform in the setting of wages and prices, quite likely in part the result of his study trips to China and Russia. In his belligerent way, he is literally begging for relations with, and help from, the United States. While he is no Gorbachev 1984–1985, there are some similarities, which we should exploit.

Of all the Not Free countries, North Korea is the only one that has yet even to take a cautious step into stage 1 of the three stages of democracy development. It has no proto–civil society, no legalistic culture to influence, no free media. It is far more isolated than the pre-Helsinki Soviet Bloc. Material privation surpasses that in the 1960s and 1970s Soviet Bloc, which failed its citizens miserably but made at least some pretense of having a consumer base.

In fact, thanks to the resilience of the human spirit and imagination, countries are rarely as locked down as they seem from without. The people of North Korea can be persuaded that there *is* light at the end of the tunnel and that they *will* eventually—within a generation—rejoin with their relations in the South in a united, democratic, and open Korea. The democracies, especially those with a strong presence in the region like the United States and Japan, in partnership with the Republic of Korea, a charter member of the Community of Democracies, need to make communicating with the people of North Korea their first priority. Once the brutalized people of North Korea begin to believe that they can work to change their destiny and that they will have all the help the democracies can possibly provide, the rotten edifice will begin to crumble. But there is no time to lose.

An invaluable avenue is media penetration, which is not impossible even in North Korea. People have radios even in the countryside. Radio Free Asia has a Korean-language service, and South Korean stations can be received.[21] Building up the Radio Free Asia Korean Service from its current four hours a day to a full-time service would take a modest spike in funding, and considering the potential dividends, the resources need to be found. A concerted effort to get through to the North Korean public in this manner is essential, even with the attendant jamming and monitoring.

Members of the elite in North Korea have greater access to information from outside, through satellite television, the Internet, and other media. They must get a consistent message that there is a future for those who are willing to switch their allegiance to the side of the people—and that the regime is doomed in any case owing to its own failings. They must also understand that should the leadership lash out in its self-imposed death throes, the response will be withering and total. The military, security, and foreign affairs elites' access to international media is essential to the regime. By using these conduits, the democracies can work to reduce the chance for a conflagration when the regime crumbles. High-level officials have defected before, some in recent years. There is no doubt they are taking the risk of defection for a reason. Certainly they know how low North Korea's dictators have laid the country, and how backward it is today. Now they must be shown a way out. The intelligence services of the democracies need to recruit agents of influence in this rarefied stratum. If the North Korean army and security forces can be persuaded not to turn on dissidents at home or against "enemies" abroad, and if the North Korean people can be empowered to take the necessary risks, the shift to democracy could follow very quickly.

The democratic world must work within Japan's sizable Korean community to find ways to get inside and funnel information out.[22] While this community contains a great many North Korean agents and still more sympathizers, even this can be turned into an asset. Interrogating and turning North Korean agents, with all the attendant risks, will at the very least give a clearer picture of North Korea's support network. If these resources are squeezed, or redirected toward the struggle for democracy, the regime will feel real pressure.

Such exchanges with the outside world as still exist must be exploited. Russia, at least nominally a democracy, continues to court cold-war-era allies. But North Korea cannot be seen as an ally that produces any financial or strategic gain for Moscow. Following the terrorist attacks on the United States, Russia's president, Vladimir Putin, has tried to draw closer to the United States. An opportunity to change tack is now at hand. President Bush should communicate to Putin that he sees a peaceful transition to democracy in North Korea as being in the interests of both the United States and Russia and that Moscow has an important role to play in assuring a "soft landing." Broadcast facilities in the Russian far east could help increase the radio footprint—and the frequencies used—for reaching the North Korean general population. Russia's border with North Korea, though relatively short, allows for some defections, refugee flows, and interaction with North Korean authorities. Furthermore, a declared policy of offering political asylum to those who escape should be adopted. A sufficient flow of refugees could, as in former East Germany, lead to the collapse of the regime without any bloodshed or war. If Russia wants to be considered a democracy and a partner in the war on terrorism, its actions with regard to North Korea, as well as the post-Soviet "near abroad," rogue states, and its own dirty war in Chechnya, need to be the proof of such a commitment to a common goal.

China, which shares a much longer border with North Korea, has a deeper, more significant relationship with Pyongyang—a relationship among dictatorial regimes that feel besieged by the democratic world's pull. While China is somewhat more open, it is integral to maintaining the regime it saved from annihilation in the Korean War. There is far greater interchange between China and North Korea. Defections and refugees from North Korea are common—some three hundred thousand in the past few years. Consistent with the rest of Chinese human rights practice, some are forcibly returned to North Korea. Others, as is the case with illegal aliens the world over, are kept in essentially chattel-slavery conditions in China. The communist Chinese regime's quest for international respectability, though doomed by its own essential nature, could be used to advantage in this most dire circumstance. It is against international law to return refugees to countries where they will likely be tortured or killed. Chinese commitments—indeed exhortations—that international law must be the basis for relations among nations should be invoked. In addition, this is the most permeable border into North Korea, and better intelligence on the state of the regime and the people of North Korea is best gathered here. Democracies should fund the resettlement in South Korea of Koreans who manage to escape the North Korean border guards. A volunteer cadre of these escapees, with other defectors, should be trained in nonviolent organization and conflict techniques. Getting South Korean veterans of the Kwangju street battles of 1980 to undertake this training first, and to become the trainers, is an approach worthy of consideration.

The bottom line is that Beijing needs to be forced to accept that North Korea will eventually reunify with South Korea in a democratic Korean state and that the democracies wish to manage this, starting the process sooner rather than later. Of course, if China is democratized by 2015, as described earlier, this problem evaporates.

In addition to all this external activity, the democracies need to work to get *inside* the country directly. The United States has already offered to initiate talks with Pyongyang "anytime, anyplace." Why not up the ante by announcing that the United States and other democracies wish to open embassies in Pyongyang? With the right talent in even a handful of democratic embassies, the influence of democracies in North Korea—and over developments there—would increase exponentially. Like all embassies, these should be freedom houses, with Internet access and facilities where people can safely meet. The ambassadors and all their diplomatic staff need to make themselves visible on the scene in Pyongyang, testing their limits, traveling to the hinterland, reporting and networking and influencing, even passing out free radios able to receive foreign broadcasts, as our diplomats have been doing in Cuba.

Under the leadership of the South Koreans, the democracies and NGOs need to vastly expand educational, cultural, scientific, people-to-people, and other exchanges with North Koreans. This tried-and-true method had a huge impact on opening up the USSR and eastern Europe and can work in North Korea as well. Kim Jong Il has been willing to explore exchanges, although very tentatively and with repeated backsliding. Even if the initial areas the dictator is interested in should be restricted to such subjects as management training, learning how the World Bank and other international development institutions function and how commercial law works, the democracies should see this as the beginning of a process. While nervous and paranoid, Kim Jong Il, like most dictators, may begin to think he is smart enough to avoid the fate of others before him who thought they could control everything. We need to believe that he will fail once enough opening occurs.

Managing the shift to reunification should start now. Because regimes rarely crumble according to a timetable, having a plan in place for the disintegration of the North Korean regime is imperative. The neighborhood needs to buy into the overall plan, or, as with China, be willing to stay out of the way. The whole democratic world must reassure the region, and Seoul most of all, that it will have resolute backup—including resources—when the process gains its own momentum. Fear of being overwhelmed is palpable, and understandable given the massive disparity that has grown between North and South Korea. This fear is perhaps the largest barrier to active South Korean support for regime change in the North. They need reassurance that the process can be managed. The time to begin planning for what can be done in all conceivable scenarios is now.

A major reason to begin postcommunist planning now is to do it publicly, broadcast it to North Korea and therefore help raise expectations there, create momentum, make the prospect of radical change seem real and near-term. Remember that no dictatorship can long survive once the people withdraw their cooperation.

Already, South Koreans and others are studying how Germany went about its unification in 1990 and what is to be avoided. While the analogy is imperfect, there are still lessons to learn. One obvious "don't" is not to convert the North Korean currency on a basis too favorable to it. This killed East Germany's one competitive advantage—low labor costs. Labor mobility will also have to wait for some time, until the North's economy has made some advances, so as not to swamp the South with cheaper labor and, again, not to deny northern Korea its natural advantage in attracting investment. Squaring this need with the inevitable drive for family reunification and freedom of movement will be a difficult equation, and one that requires serious thinking now. Perhaps Korea should be reunited in principle after the dictator's ouster but with some degree of separation and autonomy for a transition period. A positive lesson from Germany's unification: building up infrastructure pays big dividends in enabling economic growth, attracting domestic and foreign investment, and stemming the exodus to more affluent areas. North Korea was once the country's industrial base, and industry requires serviceable roads, ports, railways, and communications systems.

Cadres of South Korean police, administrators, and other managers will need to move north to help make the transition as smooth as possible. Northerners need to be brought into the process at all stages. Most important will be the early introduction of democratic political institutions and getting to the point where North Koreans can manage local matters in the same way South Koreans already do.

One of the most positive models for a liberated North Korea is the example of South Korea. In a single lifetime, South Korea has risen from being considered a hopeless backwater under dictators to joining the Organization for Economic Cooperation and Development—the club of the world's richest democracies. The ingenuity and know-how are already on hand, as is the will. A campaign to help bring the world's most repressive regime down, with the North Koreans themselves leading the way for their own liberation, can make an entirely free and united Korea a reality.

Burma

Burma, or Myanmar, stands out as one of only three noncommunist dictatorships left in Asia (monarch-oppressed Bhutan and Brunei are the other two). A military dictatorship, it scores a "perfect" 7/7 on Freedom House's ratings for political rights and civil liberties—the worst possible rating, shared by only eight other countries. In August and September 1988, the army opened fire on massive, peaceful, student-led pro-democracy demonstrations, killing an estimated three thousand people. The same regime remains in power. Viewed from this perspective alone, it would seem a formidable task to help the Burmese people achieve their freedom. But military dictatorships have historically been somewhat easier to oust than communist or monarchical tyrannies.

The Burmese people have repeatedly organized and demonstrated for democracy, and they have real leaders. Nobel laureate Aung San Suu Kyi, the country's preeminent pro-democracy campaigner, has strong national and international legitimacy. Her party, the National League for Democracy, won 392 of the 485 parliamentary seats in 1990 in Burma's first free elections in three decades. While under house arrest in Rangoon, she still managed periodic meetings with other Burmese democratic leaders and some communications with the outside world. Released in May 2002, but detained again in May 2003, she has pursued a long-proposed dialogue about democracy with the military leaders. For the dialogue to succeed, she will need outside support and engagement. Burma could be the first project for a caucus of Asian-Pacific democracies.

Bringing together the Asian-Pacific members of the Community of Democracies into a regular caucus could be profoundly helpful. The participants would be Australia, New Zealand, Indonesia, the Philippines, South Korea, East Timor, Fiji, Japan, Kiribati, the Marshall Islands, Micronesia, Mongolia, Nauru, Nepal, Bangladesh, India, Sri Lanka, Palau, Russia, the Solomon Islands, Tonga, Tuvalu, Vanuatu, the United States, and Canada. Invited observers could include Taiwan, Malaysia, and Singapore. These twenty-five participants and three observers constitute a powerful set of democracies, even if some are still in transitional phases, and are a huge majority of the countries in the region.

They might initiate an Asian variant of the Helsinki process that has been so vital to the introduction and consolidation of democracy in Europe. The Helsinki process gave birth to both a founding document and an operating entity, the Organization for Security and Cooperation in Europe (OSCE).

The Asian variant could begin with a founding document drafted and approved by the democracies. This would set the goal of having all Asians share the full range of democratic institutions and also show how this relates to peace and economic growth in the region. The Community of Democracies' Warsaw document already approved by these Asian nations could be a precursor. A specific element of the document could be to set up an organization to work with each nondemocracy on a democracy development plan. The Asian Democracy Organization, like its OSCE counterpart, could carry out a number of practical functions, such as election observation and enforcement, democracy training, and so forth.

Burma could be the first country for the Asia-Pacific Democracy Caucus and the Asian Democracy Organization to tackle. It is less sensitive than China and is a more manageable first task. The Asian-Pacific democracies could try to bring the Burmese dictators to the table with the following offer:

- Asian-Pacific democracies would agree to lift all investment and trade sanctions and offer an aggressive program of economic assistance.
- The military dictatorship would agree to participate in the democracy development process, establishing a national roundtable and setting a date for free and fair elections.
- As part of the process, a private dialogue would be entered into with the dictators. They must be offered a way out, but it also must be made clear that if they choose to reject this route, other means will be employed,

including the prospect of trial, ouster, and removal from Burma to incarceration.

In parallel, the full range of assistance and encouragement must be offered
to Burmese democrats. Of particular importance will be assistance in the pursuit of strategic nonviolent conflict. The Burmese generals will not go without considerable internal as well as external pressures.

The "Stans," the Middle East, and North Africa: The Heart of Democratic Darkness

At the heart of the geographic arc of dictatorship is an area of democratic
darkness containing twenty-three tyrannies. It runs west from the "stans,"
from Pakistan and Kazakhstan, through Iran and the Gulf states, and on
through Egypt to Algeria, then south to Chad, Sudan, and Somalia. Some
have begun to call this region "the Greater Middle East." Next to China, it
represents the largest number of oppressed peoples on Earth. There has been
less progress toward democracy in this region than in any other in the world.
It is a nearly unbroken mass of dictators, with just a single Free country, Israel,
and a sprinkling of Partly Free countries—Kuwait, Bahrain, Jordan, Turkey,
Morocco, Ethiopia, Djibouti—in its midst.

Paradoxically, while this wide region represents the largest concentration
of dictators, it has received the least attention from the democratic world—
though after September 11 that has begun to change. Among so-called experts, there is a long-held skepticism about the capacity of people in these
states with Islamic majorities to oust their dictators, even to successfully rule
themselves. In fact, conventional wisdom has argued that it would be a mistake to promote aggressively democracy in these nations, as that would usher
in still worse regimes. And of course, there is the conventional wisdom among
the practitioners of so-called realpolitik and national security that protecting
oil supplies and Israel requires that we support King Fahd and President Hosni
Mubarak. So Mubarak gets the second-largest amount of aid from the United
States of any leader, and King Fahd is our "close ally and friend." Worse, we
have corrupted our own terminology, calling these dictators "moderates."
Anyone who has had anything to do with the Saud family regime knows it is
anything but moderate. These dictators do more to damage the interests of
the United States, Europe, and Japan than to be helpful. All dictatorships by
definition—including all of those in the oil-producing lands—are unstable
and will be overthrown sooner or later. The central question is who, and
what, comes next.

Klaus-Dieter Frankenberger of the *Frankfurter Allgemeine Zeitung* was dead right when he wrote: "Whatever the U.S. trains its sights on next, it will have to consider the future of the Middle East. From now on, Washington will have to pay far more attention to whether or not it should continue to found its political, strategic and energy interests on ruling cliques whose repressive, anti-liberal character is masked by the qualifier 'moderate.' If there is to be one big project for the coming years . . . it must have something to do with this region's coming to terms with the modern world, with pluralism, and with something resembling democracy. The removal of the regime in Baghdad would be one part of this. . . . The United States should not be left alone to this task, but neither should it claim exclusive rights."[23]

The democratic world needs to recognize that our only true and durable allies are the people of each of these countries. Only by helping them achieve democratic governments will the security and other problems of the region be resolved. We also need to recognize that the successors to the current dictators will only be Islamic fundamentalist extremists if the democrats inside and outside these countries fail to join hands to produce moderate, democratic alternatives. The palaces must give way to democracy—or to the mosque.

But the problem is individual dictators, not Islam. Over half of the world's Muslims live in democracies today. Indonesia is the world's largest Islamic country, and it recently broke through from a long ordeal under dictators Sukarno and Suharto. A Muslim cleric, Abdurrahman Wahib, was the first democratically elected president of the nation and the longtime head of Indonesia's largest Muslim social group and an equally long-term committed fighter for democracy. India has the world's second-largest Muslim population—about 150 million—and, except in Kashmir (and even here the elections of 2002 were better), Muslims are full participants in India's vibrant democracy. The only solution to Kashmir is to introduce democracy in Pakistan. The citizens of that country, which has the third-largest Muslim population, have repeatedly shown that they want democracy. Bangladesh, the world's fourth-largest Islamic populace with 125 million Muslims, has feisty, turbulent politics but is no dictatorship. Turkey is in a virtual tie with Iran and Egypt as the next-largest Islamic nation, and Turkey too, despite its serious problems, is no dictatorship. In Iran the 1997 and 2001 election and reelection of democracy advocate (and Muslim cleric) Mohammad Khatami as president demonstrates that the vast majority of Iranian Muslims want democracy. Nigeria has a comparable Muslim population (half of its people) and is an emerging, struggling democracy.

Thus, seven of the eight largest Muslim populations in the world do not exhibit an intrinsic tension between Islam and dictatorship (and does anyone seriously believe that Egyptians prefer dictators?). Yet many so-called experts justify and accept the continuation of dictatorship in this heart of democratic darkness as the fault of Islam—and engraved in stone.

The dictators, with whom our government and nongovernment leaders and experts spend most of their time, argue that this is the case. Of course, they argue it from contradictory viewpoints. The Mubaraks argue that their dictatorship is justified to keep Islamists from taking over; King Fahd argues that his dictatorship is justified because it is needed to protect and promote "pure" Islam. The common thread is that all dictators everywhere claim some basis for their legitimacy. Their claims are as specious as those of medieval kings, who justified their rule as necessary to the defense and spread of Christianity.

Another reason for this acceptance of Islam's supposed bias toward dictatorship is simply intellectual laziness. It is an all-too-common phenomenon that experts "predict" more of the same; few have the intellectual energy, creativity, or professional courage to go out on a limb and predict fundamental change when it is not imminent or overwhelmingly obvious.

The impact of these broadly held views is devastating for the people of these countries and for international security. This is a region striking in its economic stagnation, a factor that is intrinsically related to dictators. It is also a region of massive social backwardness. Although more women have led Islamic countries than have led non-Islamic democracies, many women in these countries endure the cruel bondage of rampant male chauvinism. There is no greater mass crime in the world today than the oppression of women in this region. If we cannot press for democracy here on humanitarian grounds, perhaps we can apply the leverage of geopolitical necessity. The region's oil and gas reserves are among the largest on the planet.

As a practical matter, then, the democracies need to change their present policies and bring these nations into the democratic camp. First, the democracies and the democrats must show Islam the respect we show any other great religion and recognize that its adherents make up a quarter of humanity. Next, we must find ways to bring together the world's democratic Muslim leaders and movements with their non-Muslim, natural democratic allies. A Helsinki-like process is clearly needed. We need new means to talk with each other, to develop strategies and programs for ousting the dictators oppressing Muslim peoples. We need action programs for each country, and we need vastly increased "democracy" resources for the entire region.

The Bush administration is well ahead of previous American administrations and the European and other democracies. Speeches over the course of 2002 and into 2003 by the president, Secretary of State Colin Powell, and State Department policy planning director Richard Haass state the goal of democracy for all countries in the region. Their Middle East Partnership Initiative, announced 12

December 2002, launched a few specific programs. But the *Washington Post*'s editorial assessment is correct that this initiative "follows the same timid logic as existing U.S. programs in the region: It seeks to promote liberalization in Arab states without challenging many of the autocratic rulers now in charge. . . . If it is possible in Iraq and the Palestinian Authority, free elections and free speech ought to be possible soon in Jordan and Egypt, too. The Administration . . . should be preparing not only to depose its enemies, but also to demand hard decisions by its friends."[24]

As former CIA Middle East expert and American Enterprise fellow Reuel Gerecht has written: "Practical support for liberal ideals in the Arab world has been virtually nil. . . . Corrupt stability (in Egypt and elsewhere) does us no honor and ultimately harms our interests. Bin Ladenism's appeal is unlikely to end in a Muslim world dominated by such unchanging despotism."[25]

Some of these countries deserve particular, early attention because they offer particularly interesting opportunities and because a breakthrough there could have ripple effects across the region. As geostrategists, we need to look at the map and determine how best to break up this continuous monolith of oppressors by attacking its weakest links. My own list would be Pakistan, Uzbekistan, Iran, Iraq, the Gulf states and other monarchies, Palestine, Lebanon, Egypt, and Algeria. (Fortunately, a case can be made for focusing early attention on any of these twenty-three countries, and at some increased level of effort we should.)

Pakistan

Many argue that the most dangerous confrontation in the world is between nuclear-armed India and Pakistan, who have fought three wars in just the last four decades. But no civilian elected government in Pakistan has ever gone to war with India. Gen. Pervez Musharraf, Pakistan's former army chief of staff, overthrew an elected government in October 1999. The proximate cause was that democratically elected prime minister Nawaz Sharif had ordered Islamic militants backed by Pakistani troops to withdraw from strategic heights they had seized on the Indian side of the Line of Control in Kashmir. This operation was General Musharraf's personal project. Sharif had been trying for months to assert civilian control over the military—Pakistan's endemic problem. He had sacked the previous army chief of staff on 7 October 1998 and then on 12 October 1999 sacked Musharraf, who wanted to continue fighting with India.[26] With a military dictator in power, there is no durable solution to the conflict over Kashmir and between India and Pakistan. Without Kashmir, the Pakistani military and its military dictator boss could not justify the high levels of military spending or the military's political power. So it has an organic, vital stake in perpetuating the issue. It is a facile illusion to believe dictators are better able than democrats to make and stick to hard decisions. History demonstrates the opposite. The same point can be made about dealing with al-Qaeda, the Taliban, and other terrorists who have made Pakistan their home base. As a Pakistani attorney, Afrasiab Khattak, remarked, "America is making things worse by supporting the General. After September 11, democracy is indispensable here. Only democracy can root out terrorism."

The second reason for giving early priority to the democratization of Pakistan is that there is a real basis on which to build an early return to democracy. For intervals covering over half of Pakistan's fifty-five years as a nation, Pakistanis have been able to elect their own leaders and operate with a certain amount of democratic freedom. After three periods of military rule, "Pakistanis have grown leery of generals who promise a return to democracy, then adopt endless stratagems to delay it," according to *New York Times* correspondent James Burns.[27]

Finally, because it affected 140 million people, the 1999 coup against democracy was the single largest act of backsliding in the era of extraordinary democratic revolutions. A return to democracy could have a huge effect not only on Pakistanis but also on the development of democracy throughout the heart of democratic darkness.

What needs to be done? A dialogue with the dictator himself is essential. Perhaps former Secretary Powell, a former general, could be a key participant in this dialogue. Musharraf must be persuaded to agree to a specific timetable for democratization and to his withdrawal from the post of president by 2007—a post and period of time he gave himself on 20 June 2001 in a transparent stratagem designed to allow himself to stay on as the real power even after the elections for prime minister and parliament in October 2002 (this date was set by Pakistan's Supreme Court as its deadline for restarting democracy). The elections resulted in a parliamentary coalition backing Musharraf's candidate for prime minister and, for the first time in Pakistan's history, a significant elected fundamentalist Islamic representation in parliament. Fundamentalists also won control of two of four provincial assemblies.

When General Musharraf lived in Turkey, where his father was an attaché, he witnessed Kemal Ataturk's secularist model, for which he has indicated some support. Members of Pakistan's military, however, have had a strikingly different relationship with Islamists than Turkey's military. The militant Islam that now faces Pakistan was unleashed, even encouraged, by another army general, Zia ul-Haq. As the *Washington Post* editorialized: "The Islamists clearly benefited [in the 2002 elections] from General Musharraf's concerted campaign against Pakistan's secular parties, which have been resisting his attempts to rewrite the constitution and extend his term as president. The Bush

Administration could have avoided this outcome by pressing General Musharraf to negotiate with the civilian parties; instead it has effectively supported his power play."[28]

The Musharraf dictatorship received a great deal of international recognition following the terrorist attacks on 11 September 2001 because of the need to get backing from Islamabad for an attack on al-Qaeda in Afghanistan. This is one of the great ironies of our young century. It is well to remember that General Musharraf, in both his pre- and postcoup incarnations, backed the Taliban to the hilt. Only the bluntest threats forced him to stop supporting the Taliban he helped create; he continues to support violent Islamists in Kashmir and overall has not moved unambiguously and strongly against them inside Pakistan itself.

Fortunately, there is a base on which to build democracy. Pakistan's print press is largely unfettered and has a number of very professional journalists. As a society, Pakistan remains relatively open, and by the deplorable standards of the Last Forty-five the Musharraf regime has not been particularly repressive. Public dissatisfaction is growing as the economy is in a shambles and has been on a downward slide for well over a decade, while democratic India has over the past decade achieved and sustained one of the world's highest rates of economic growth. The civil service and public officials in general are poorly paid, and corruption is rife. Pakistan consistently ranks among the most corrupt countries in the world, far ahead of all its neighbors and in the same rank as Nigeria. The military keeps a debilitatingly large proportion of a meager state budget.

The new centrality of the Washington-Islamabad relationship means that America must play a leading role. The Community of Democracies can best assist in the evolution of democratic and responsive politics in Pakistan by holding Musharraf to his own timetable. The five-year window should be used to expand the powers of the new prime minister, Zafarullah Khan Jamali, and his government; to strengthen the political parties and other democratic institutions; and to start the clock for presidential elections. There is clearly a role here for the party-building and, eventually, campaigning skills of the National Democratic Institute and the International Republican Institute, the German party foundations, and others.

The seating of the elected parliament launches a new phase for the democracies and their engagement with Islamabad. Again, taking Musharraf at his word, and holding him to it, is the first move in this political judo. The democracies need to engage the new government and parliament as the *sole seats of legitimate authority* in their areas of responsibility. Perceptions matter and can help build the Pakistani public's own expectations. Part of this effort will necessarily be devoted to encouraging these elected officials to take their roles seriously, exercise their constitutional authority, and gradually expand their power.

The five-year timetable also affords an interregnum during which Musharraf should be pressured to substantiate his oft repeated promise of reform and allow the new prime minister to act and independent political parties to function. A number of structural problems have long impeded the establishment of a broad democratic base. Pakistan remains a stratified society, with most of the wealth in the hands of landowning families. The tax base is essentially nonexistent; many of the wealthiest are exempt from supporting the society they have ruled oligarchically since independence. Musharraf himself, like the elected civilians Sharif and Bhutto, comes from the upper level of society. It is no accident that the richest man in India is an Indian Muslim software entrepreneur, while the richest Pakistanis are the fifty leading feudal landowning families. So long as real power remains concentrated at this level, it is difficult to envision a bright future for democracy in Pakistan. An already poor country has fallen even further behind because the ruling stratum is disinclined to pay its way.

The most obvious victim here is the public education system, which is unworthy of the name. At least a whole generation of Pakistani youth has been handicapped by this failed system, and radical Saudi-funded madrassas have filled the social vacuum. The results can be seen in Pakistan and Afghanistan and around the world. Saudi Arabia's Wahabist strain of ascetic, antimodern Islam has gained strong currency in what had been wholly alien territory. Musharraf's forced efforts to move Pakistan back toward secularism need to address this critical aspect. To ensure that this occurs, the affluent democracies should help fund the reconstruction of public education there, without, however, letting Musharraf or the Pakistani establishment evade the hard choices to maintain a decent education system. The essential corollary of this deal for Pakistan must be the dramatic overhaul of the country's revenue structure so that the government can support public education—including uniforms and meals for students—within Musharraf's term. While the developed world may well need to supplement Pakistani resources for a time after reforms are made, there is no excuse for Pakistan's inability to provide a decent education to its citizens. Similarly, reform of the legendarily corrupt civil service, law enforcement, and judicial systems is also sorely needed, and the competent authorities—both elected and self-appointed—need to be pressured to make these wrenching adjustments as well.

As with other impoverished and dysfunctional societies, one of Pakistan's potentially most valuable resources is its educated and relatively affluent diaspora. Economic opportunity abroad led many away, though their ties to Pakistan remain strong. The stagnation of Pakistan's economy owes less to intrinsic factors than to the maladies of its political system and social structure, and many Pakistanis abroad would return to invest their skills and wealth if the opportunities looked promising. To harness this valuable resource in the cause of democratization, Pakistan's electoral code needs to provide for simple, verifiable absentee voting. Democracies should consider funding public information campaigns where diasporas are concentrated, coupled to those ongoing in Pakistan itself.

While some in the diaspora support and fund extremism, most are moderate. My Indian Hindu nephew who now lives and works in the United States has numerous Pakistani Muslim friends who openly express their disinterest in the Kashmir "cause" and want democracy in Pakistan above all. We need to bring younger leadership elements from Pakistan to the United States to experience this moderation and to train them in democracy and good governance—giving them some stature when they return to Pakistan. The more-senior people are too set in their ways to train, and many are discredited.

The final stage in the five-year democracy plan for Pakistan is the presidential election in 2007. The stronger the civilian government, and the more prominence and prestige real political parties are given by democratic nations, the more likely a popular challenger will emerge to vie for the presidency with Musharraf. Best of all would be to dissuade Musharraf and any military figure from running. If that fails, the unity of the democratic forces will be key, as we have seen in so many dictator-to-democracy transitions. Kenya's Daniel arap Moi managed to manipulate elections only so long as the democrats were split; he fell as soon as they united around a single candidate. By holding Musharraf to his own statements, the democracies have a very real opportunity to help Pakistan construct a viable democracy. Clearly, this presents a major challenge. Civil-military relations will probably continue to be a touchy issue beyond the five-year window. But by embracing, monitoring, and participating in a process announced by General Musharraf himself, the democracies can make it exceedingly difficult for him to backtrack.

Uzbekistan

Uzbekistan is typical of the five Central Asian personalistic dictatorships. It is tightly in the grip of its Soviet-era apparatchik ruler, Islam Karimov. Karimov managed to defraud the Soviet system by dramatically inflating the figures of the cotton yield in the late Brezhnev period, and he deftly weathered the dissolution of the USSR. President Karimov, whose last election in 2000 was deemed so crooked that the OSCE would not monitor it, is king of his fiefdom, as are the dictators of the other four formerly Soviet Central Asian states.

Karimov was taking advantage of Uzbekistan's strategic location and relatively large population well before 11 September made it an important factor in the war on terrorism. Karimov has fiercely resisted Moscow's efforts to reassert its influence in Uzbekistan since independence, unlike such troubled neighbors as Tajikistan, which has seen civil war, and Kazakhstan, which has a large Slav population. Under Karimov, Uzbekistan moved close to the United States, avidly participating in NATO's Partnership for Peace program and aligning itself with NATO against Russian efforts to regain control of the "near abroad."

The repressive measures undertaken by the Karimov regime are well known among those willing to see, thanks to the work of groups like Human Rights Watch and others. Practice of the region's traditional Islam is viewed as a threat by Karimov, as is any potential alternative locus of power. State-controlled religion, on the Soviet model, is the order of the day. Civic groups are harassed with regularity, and torture is rife. In this environment, Karimov has managed actually to drive disgruntled citizens into the arms of groups like the Islamic Movement of Uzbekistan (IMU), which became active in the late 1990s as a guerrilla force with support from al-Qaeda and the Taliban. Before the 11 September attacks, it appeared that Karimov and the IMU could become locked in a downward death spiral of feeding each other's outrages and destroying domestic peace for Uzbekistan's repressed, but calm, populace.

Karimov has been a primary beneficiary of the American war against the Taliban and al-Qaeda. Uzbekistan's border with Afghanistan made the country a vital staging area for U.S. airpower and ground forces, as well as a transit point for humanitarian aid through Termez—a goal that was largely unrealized. The IMU was hit extremely hard in the U.S. air strikes on the Taliban and al-Qaeda in Afghanistan, where its members, along with other Islamic militants, provided muscle for the Taliban regime. It is unclear how much of the organizational structure survives, and the IMU's military commander, Juma Namangani, is presumed dead. What is clear is that the threat the IMU poses, real but inflated by Karimov and flogged as pretext for repression of any opposition, is greatly reduced.

The United States has a great deal of leverage with the Karimov regime. Now that the threat posed by the IMU has been beaten back, there is no reason for the United States not to push for liberalization and democratic progress in the immediate term. Unless this is undertaken soon, the United States risks being drawn into a client relationship that will poison its reputation—and interests—in Central Asia, much as the uncritical client relationship with Mubarak in Egypt has created a backlash in Egypt. Repression of civic and religious freedoms has already fed an Islamist insurgency that otherwise might not have built up any steam, and this threat will rise again unless discontent can be channeled constructively in the public domain.

The fact that neighboring Afghanistan, a real threat to Uzbekistan's population when under Taliban rule, is now trying, albeit with difficulty, to move in a democratic direction with a pronounced and expanding international commitment is of great significance for all the bordering states. As is the case with Iraq, all of Afghanistan's dictatorially run neighbors—Iran, Pakistan, Turkmenistan, Uzbekistan, Tajikistan, and even China—fear a democratic Afghanistan with strong ties to the United States. Iran's controlling religious and security establishment, along with Pakistan's, is nervous about the example a stabilized and increasingly democratic Afghanistan would show to its own young and frustrated population. There is so much at stake, and not only for Afghanistan, that the effort *must* succeed.

Uzbekistan's current situation falls somewhere between stages 1 and 2 in the democracy development continuum, with the possibility for rapid progress. There are already courageous elements of civil society, including opposition figures, who dare to speak out and a small coterie of lawyers who will defend those brought up by the regime on politically motivated charges. On the eve of a visit to the United States in March 2002, Karimov finally allowed a single human rights group to register—after ten years of trying. However, the media situation is bleak, and there is no democratic self-governance at any level.

The democratic world has sent positive signals, through the OSCE's refusal to supervise the January 2002 referendum to extend Karimov's rule. Washington criticized the referendum publicly, an important statement of principle. However, considering the increased attention to the country, especially in the security realm, following the war against the Taliban and al-Qaeda, a number of mixed signals have been sent, leading wily survivor Karimov to believe he can evade meaningful criticism that would otherwise have been directed at his repressive rule. Maintaining multifaceted pressure after the fraudulent referendum is imperative so that the democratic world's criticism is seen to have depth and meaning. Without persistence, such statements are worse than meaningless—they are devalued and lead those under repression to doubt the commitment of the democracies to their stated values.

In their dealings with Karimov, democracies should make clear that the new presence and focus on his country is in no way an endorsement of his governance, which we have (only by implication, unfortunately) found to be illegitimate. A reasonable stance should include pronounced work with civil society, including local democracy activists, and the official electoral bodies to prepare for upcoming elections. The democracies need to make a protracted effort to get the regime to declare its intention to hold new presidential and parliamentary elections in the next three years. They then should work to build a viable system for such elections to be free and fair, not a mere coronation, as the last referendum clearly was. This will be no mean feat, considering the level of oppression employed by Karimov. However, countries with similarly oppressive histories have made democratic transitions.

One of the first changes that can be made is to alter the international posture toward and within Uzbekistan. The OSCE mission in Tashkent is well positioned to do some very important work, but thus far it is viewed by observers on the ground to be underpowered and muted in its efforts to promote openness and accountability in Uzbekistan. The American and British embassies have frequently bypassed the OSCE and its statements to make (frequently stronger) statements on their own. However, their efforts could help push the OSCE in the right direction and strengthen its spine. A senior political figure, for example a former prime minister with strong backing and a willingness to take on a public role, should be chosen from an established democracy to head the OSCE mission in Tashkent. Working with democratic embassies in Tashkent, this individual could steer the OSCE away from a mere pro forma presence and toward a role befitting an organization that is mandated to promote democracy. A first and important project for a bolder OSCE in Uzbekistan, as well as in the four other Central Asian dictatorships and the still Not Free Belarus (all OSCE members), would be to develop and pursue multiyear democracy development plans and programs with specific target years.

Public diplomacy is a key to any pro-democracy campaign, and Community of Democracies members in Tashkent should hold meetings at least once a month to coordinate strategies and share information. The ambassadors of the democracies should be women and men who are familiar with efforts to open closed societies and who are willing to become fixtures in the public life of the country, beyond the diplomatic cookie-pushing circuit. Some new democracies have an abundance of former opposition civic action figures in their diplomatic corps, and all should have them. Men like Slovak ambassador to the United States Martin Butora, who was active in 1989 and later in efforts to oust postcommunist authoritarian premier Vladimir Meciar, would be appropriate for such a role. Meeting publicly with opposition figures, attending trials of those political targets, and holding receptions with civic figures along with the usual regime members are all active methods that could be employed in Uzbekistan to open more public space. As often as possible, independent newspapers and other media should be given "exclusives" in interviews with diplomats, visiting dignitaries, and military officials. Many professional diplomats will shrink from such behavior for fear of offending the government; those who are failing to take on this role should be replaced by men and women who are not looking at the next assignment but at their necessary role in the here and now. Democratic ambassadors also need to have dedicated funds to use at their discretion to assist indigenous democratic and civic actors. With such funds on hand, they can actively take advantage of opportunities as they present themselves, without having to wait for clearance from their national capitals. Democracies could pool resources to build a legal defense fund for journalists, NGO activists, and the like, to assure that they can defend themselves against political harassment. When necessary, the Tashkent embassies (and whatever consulates exist in Bukhara and Samarkand) should act as refuges for political targets of the regime. Under no circumstances should they be turned away or handed over to local authorities.

Democratic governments worldwide, but especially from within the OSCE membership, need to apply pressure on Karimov to adhere to the international treaties and covenants his government has signed since independence. As we saw in central Europe in the 1970s and 1980s, such commitments, often entered into pro forma, can become powerful tools in the hands of brave individuals and groups that highlight the yawning gap between word and deed. Many civic groups have not been allowed to register and are therefore technically illegal and subject to prosecution. International pressure, especially from the United States, could be useful in effecting their legalization. In addition, Tashkent should be prevailed upon to invite the specialized United Nations mechanisms, such as the special rapporteur for the prevention of torture. Similarly, the UN High Commissioner for Human Rights should be invited to send a regional representative to Tashkent—an invitation that Karimov has been unwilling to issue. The presence of such structures in Uzbekistan would send a message throughout the region that with the augmented Western attention since 11 September comes added scrutiny of the lack of democracy and protection of basic rights.

Secretary of State Colin Powell told the House International Relations Committee in February 2002 that "America will have a continuing interest and presence in Central Asia of a kind that we could not have dreamed of before." The new American military presence throughout Central Asia, consisting of thousands of troops, aircrews, and contractors, with hubs in Uzbekistan and Afghanistan, could be an enormous opportunity to raise the profile of democratic practice in countries whose dictators would prefer not to have such examples in their midst. The U.S. military presence in Uzbekistan, Kyrgyzstan, Tajikistan, and elsewhere in the region will be the most conspicuous representatives of the democratic world in Central Asia. The tone set by U.S. forces and diplomats will have enormous resonance throughout the region, and beyond. This is not a time to repeat previous mistakes of "one-stop shopping" with dictators or to delude ourselves that our security can be hermetically sealed from our democratic values, which are the only true guarantor of our security.

The basis of our involvement needs to be made clear. It is a matter of mutual interest that U.S. and other forces are active regionally; it is not a matter of selfless largesse on the part of the dictator Karimov. Language and terminology are of fundamental importance in defining the democratic world's public position. Therefore, despite common diplomatic practice, lauding "cooperation" with undemocratic leaders like Karimov to the point of declaring them "strategic partners" is dangerous beyond the immediate term. To the extent statements are made, they should be careful to assert that this is a partnership with the legitimate polity—that is, the Uzbek people. There should be no praise for Karimov at all. Otherwise, the United States will almost certainly be associated with the regime's repression. It is imperative that our policies and posture point in precisely the opposite direction.

Among the most important things the United States (and other Western military powers, such as the United Kingdom, France, and Australia) can do is assure that their efforts and contacts are coordinated among their own national contingents, including their embassies, militaries, and other relevant security branches. In the U.S. case, this would include not only the forces on the ground at bases like Khojand and Khanabad but also the ambassador, the CIA station chief, and the Justice Department representative. In addition, these representatives need to share information with their colleagues from other involved democracies. A common front needs to be shown not only to Uzbekistan's armed forces but also to the MVD (Interior Ministry forces) and secret services. These nonmilitary services are more often employed for repressive purposes, and inroads that could be used to influence them away from outrageous and illegal behavior could smooth the way to a democratic transition.

Promoting an international, interagency security dialogue is also imperative. The apparent demise of the IMU provides a perfect platform for such discussion. As the revival of the IMU constitutes a threat to U.S. forces, addressing the problem is in the American national interest. At the same time, the social forces that helped fill IMU ranks—government repression of religious and civic freedoms—also constitute a threat to our forces. Declaring publicly, especially through local media, that the democratic world believes that the IMU has been contained, would help remove from Karimov's arsenal a favorite bogeyman for repression. An active NGO such as Freedom House, in cooperation with the U.S. military, should sponsor an intensive program on civil-military relations, drawing in international and indigenous human rights groups and the Uzbek security spectrum. Such a program would not only allow these segments of Uzbekistan to interact under the eye of democracies but would also give American forces a chance to get a better feel for the measures their local counterparts employ to defend the regime from its own people. This could have an impact on their attitude and posture while stationed in Uzbekistan and elsewhere in the region.

The interaction of American forces and other personnel with the local population needs to be encouraged. The current understandable fixation on "force protection" hinders such contact, to the benefit of dictators like Karimov (or the Saudi regime, for that matter). The less these forces are seen as sequestered on base, and the more they are able to present themselves as partners of the local populations in their communities, the less enemies of such a presence will be able to vilify them as "occupiers." These basing arrangements are actually enormous opportunities to exhibit the strengths of professional, volunteer militaries and the democracies they represent. Their economic footprint is significant and should have benefits for the general population, not merely those representing (or handpicked by) the regime.

There is no independent broadcasting in Uzbekistan, so the only conduit to the population is from without. Radio Liberty broadcasts in Uzbek and other languages spoken in Uzbekistan and the region and should make its programming as connected to its audience as possible. Call-in programs, such as those on Radio Free Asia, are relatively inexpensive but have enormous impact.

Dictatorships are always at a distinct disadvantage in providing entertaining and informative television programming. The opening up of Afghanistan therefore provides an opportunity to develop a terrestrial TV broadcasting channel catering to the Uzbek-speaking population over the border, as well as the Uzbek speakers inside Afghanistan. While care needs to be exercised not to undermine the provisional government in Kabul, the ability of citizens of Uzbekistan to see entertainment and news programming produced by their compatriots would weaken Karimov's ability to control information in the country. Alternatively, pressure could be brought to bear on Karimov to license a television station within Uzbekistan to an independent Uzbek group, possibly with a foreign partner to help guarantee its independence.

Beyond the policies and posture of American and other democratic diplomats and forces in Uzbekistan, the democratic world needs to actively engage Uzbekistan's unofficial sector. Educational and professional exchanges provide enormous value for the money spent on them. The Fulbright program has proven an incalculable asset to democratization and has helped build American expertise on the world at large. Augmented attention to Uzbekistan and its Central Asian neighbors is clearly in order.

The activity of international NGOs, like Human Rights Watch, in Uzbekistan is exceedingly important. Their independent monitoring capacity will remain vital even as the democratic world increases its level of engagement in the cause of democracy. Groups like the American Bar Association's Central and East European Law Initiative, which works to promote the independent rule of law throughout the former Soviet bloc, also play a critical role. Beyond their engagement with the judicial and law enforcement bodies, programs such as the "street law" education program, as practiced in Belarus, help citizens understand their rights as guaranteed by the laws already on the books. The concept of having rights that can be employed when confronted by state authority is one that needs to be driven deep into the marrow of Uzbekistan's body politic. There are few more important concepts in the foundation of a democratic society.

On the more overtly political level, political party foundations, like the German liberal Naumann Stiftung and the American International Republican Institute, should publicly engage with beleaguered secular opposition Birlik and Erk groups to help them prepare for elections that the democracies will push the regime to hold.

In October 2002, Freedom House held a very public inauguration of a Human Rights and Resource Center in Tashkent. The ambassadors of the United States, Britain, and Germany spoke at the event, bringing significant international and Uzbek attention to the center and the appalling human rights situation in the country. Use of the center has far exceeded expectations; its presence and accompanying support have allowed Uzbek human rights activists to pursue a more strategic approach with aggressive tactics.

The environment is a promising public issue that would undoubtedly have political ramifications. The stranglehold of water-intensive cotton cultivation on Uzbek agriculture has had ravaging effects on the ecological stability of the country and the health of the population. In many repressive polities, environmental civic organizations have helped hold leaders accountable for malfeasance, corruption, and disregard for public welfare. Uzbekistan may well be ripe for such a crosscutting wedge issue. Clearly, the current reliance on cotton agriculture is unsustainable, and those who benefit most from the current structure are a minority of the population, which remains very poor. International environmental engagement, particularly at the local level, must be encouraged—indeed promoted—by the democracies. Lessons learned in the past three decades in the West about the need for openness on the environmental impact of military bases could be employed to great effect in Uzbekistan. Such visible concern for the local population would not only promote positive relations but would also put the regime on the defensive for not showing similar concern.

None of these efforts alone will assure democracy's eventual victory in Uzbekistan. But if employed robustly, consistent with a plan and program to introduce real democracy, they could have a major impact in a relatively short period of time.

Iran

Iran is the world's last real theocracy after the destruction of the Taliban regime in Afghanistan. The aftermath of the war that led to the Taliban's collapse vividly exposes the contradictions in neighboring Iran's government. While the elected government of President Mohammad Khatami has vocally supported the fragile provisional government of Hamid Karzai in Kabul, Iran's military and security services, along with Ayatollah Ali Khamenei's Guardian Council, have worked to subvert it. Their long-standing ties to regional figures in Herat—a traditional area of influence—are undercutting Karzai's effort to build some semblance of central control. Iranian conservatives are unnerved by the prospect of a democratic government in neighboring Afghanistan and by a monarch returning to his land. After all, the heir to the throne, Reza Pahlavi, who lives in exile in the United States but broadcasts to Iran, has become increasingly popular in the absence of other role models.[29] He appears to be far more committed to democracy than his father, Shah Mohammad Reza Pahlavi.

At the same time, Iranians are growing weary of elected representatives who cannot—or will not—deliver. The will to achieve democracy among the vast majority of the Iranian people is clear. The extraordinary story of the past few years speaks volumes about the country's determination to rid itself of dictatorship. Mohammad Khatami, a former culture minister who was forced to resign in 1992 for being too liberal, ran for president in the 1997 elections on a platform of economic reform, rule of law, civil society, and improved foreign relations. He won the support of intellectuals, women, youth, and business groups seeking greater social openness and an end to state interference in the economy. Ninety percent of the electorate turned out to vote, and 70 percent voted for Khatami. After four years of Khatami battling the unelected dictator Ayatollah Ali Khamenei and his equally unelected Council of Guardians, in the 2001 elections the Iranian people again spoke resoundingly in favor of democracy with another big turnout and another huge vote for Khatami as their only elected, and therefore only legitimate, leader. To date, President Khatami has urged moderation and caution in confronting the dictator, despite the arrests and persecution of Khatami's closest supporters, members of parliament, and the press.

Increasingly impatient with this caution, young Iranians regularly flood into the streets chanting antidictator slogans. After 11 September, thousands came out in the streets with pro-American signs and held vigils.[30] Protests by teachers and other workers over pay are growing. In one example reported by the *New York Times* on 9 July 2002, "In a powerful expression of popular frustration with repressive government, protesters clashed with police, marking the third anniversary of a violent crackdown on student protests at Tehran University—spurred by a long drive on opposition radio and satellite television." The Guardian Council has been reluctant to test the military's loyalty by calling on it to intervene. Observers believe a significant number of Islamic clergy (ulema) would consider supporting democratic forces if they appear to be on a trajectory for victory.

Iran's demographics work against the continued institutionalization of the 1979 Islamic revolution. With more than half of Iran's growing population born since the revolution, the primacy of the ulema was never a matter of choice for Iran's youth.

The inability of this potentially vibrant economy to provide satisfying job opportunities or prosperity to its population diminishes whatever popular legitimacy the regime might have. Furthermore, the people's faith in the power of their vote is thoroughly eroded. The once legitimate fear of Iraqi aggression was effectively destroyed by the 1991 Gulf War. Two presidential elections later, they believe that they have waited long enough for a chance to decide the country's direction.

Iran is far riper for fundamental change than many policymakers in the democracies (other than the United States) seem to believe. Even with the massive tectonic shift produced by the destruction of the Taliban in Afghanistan, they have yet to grasp what incredible benefits could accrue were Iran to enter the democratic fold. And to the extent it has dawned on even American policymakers, the idea has yet to be translated into a coherent strategy.

Despite continued repression and recurring arrest, incarceration, beating, and murder of opponents of the theocracy, significant international political, social, and economic engagement is possible in Iran. Every possible opening needs to be exploited; a major breakthrough could occur at any time.

First, the Community of Democracies needs to declare and demonstrate its support for the Iranian people's struggle. Backing President Khatami per se is insufficient, and probably counterproductive. Following his constituents' lead, the democracies need to call on Khatami to deliver. If he and other elected officials cannot effect change owing to the hard-liners' opposition, they need to tell this to the people and then join them in their struggle. If Khatami does not do this, then those who contend that he is an integral factor in the theocracy's machine will have been proven correct. It is decision time. The decision of the Community of Democracies also must be clear: we stand with the Iranian people.

President George W. Bush moved in this direction in his 2002 State of the Union speech. He noted that Iran was a member of an "axis of evil," with Iraq and North Korea, but that Iran's people were along for the ride only because of their "unelected leaders."[31] In July 2002, President Bush made a clear statement recognizing the fissure in Iran between the majority who have voted and demonstrated for democracy and those who oppose it. But he still did not use the occasion to introduce a new set of policies and programs actively to support those fighting for change in Iran.

President Bush should announce a comprehensive "Contract with the Iranian People." The president should express regret for America's backing in the early 1980s of the Iraqi aggression against Iran. It would have enormous impact, considering the devastation that war caused to Iran and the fact that Ayatollah Ruhollah Khomeini was able to use the invasion to consolidate control after the revolution. The contract should include specific commitments: to assist in economic restructuring once Iran reaches democracy, to help modernize the oil industry, to track Iranian assets stolen by the shah and the theocratic elite, and to unblock Iranian state assets once the country is democratically run. An Iran Democracy Act, similar to the 2001 Zimbabwe Democracy Act, would easily pass Congress and should be drafted forthwith. With congressional backing and attendant resources, such an act could give real substance to the commitments made in this contract.

Speaking to the American Iranian Council 13 March 2002, the chairman of the Senate Foreign Relations Committee, Senator Joseph Biden, set forth a five-point plan based on the following premise: We must recognize that the most entrenched elements in Iran seek to perpetuate Iran's isolation through confrontation with the outside world. Those who seek change want to increase Iran's international linkages. Biden's opening steps moved in the right direction. Unfortunately he did not go far enough, and he underestimated the capacity of the United States and other democracies to help. He stated that "the United States is not in a position to have a major impact on the ongoing power struggle underway in Iran. Nor should we intervene in any direct way. . . . [the experience of 1953] should counsel us to be extra-cautious."

I profoundly disagree with this view of the potential for the rest of the democratic world to help Iranians get rid of their dictator. We can have a decisive impact. The lesson of 1953 is that we have influence; in that case we used it against the forces of democracy. But we need to be able to "walk and chew gum" at the same time. Both Biden and Bush are wrong—we need simultaneously to openly call for the dictator to be removed, by general strike if necessary, and to actively engage in opening up the country.

American efforts should move forward in coordination with the rest of the Community of Democracies. As have other dictatorships, Iran's regime has been able to rely on divisions among the democracies to dissipate pressure on weapons proliferation and other topics of concern. With the United States making a decisive shift, it needs to work to bring the rest of the world's democracies into alignment behind this common front. One gesture consistent with the tone of the contract would be to convene an international donors' conference, inviting the major donor nations, international financial institutions, and some members of the Iranian opposition. This conference could create a set-aside fund for quick-start projects to help support a democratic transition. News of this commitment will have great resonance with a population hungry for freedom and real improvement in their lot.

One policy shift that could be effected in the immediate term, with direct and perhaps decisive impact, is to fund satellite television broadcasts by the Iranian diaspora to their compatriots. National Iranian Television, beamed by satellite from studios in Los Angeles to Iran, was watched by tens of thousands until the station was no longer able to pay for the strongest satellite transmission. While the finer points of strategy are being drafted and coordinated, just bankrolling this service for about $5 million per year would make communication with Iran substantially better. As we witnessed in revolutionary situations in the Philippines and Serbia, seeing compatriots in action has an emboldening multiplier effect that can help build momentum at pivotal (and unforeseeable) moments.

In addition to backing these television broadcasts, substantive cooperation among the democracies is necessary in designing and implementing a democratization strategy for Iran. Embassies in Tehran need to reopen, including the American embassy, and their staffs should make clear that they see themselves as accredited to the Iranian people. Comparative advantages among democracies should be identified and maximized, within a common strategy. All democratic embassies should be freedom houses, providing to Iranians cyber-cafés with access to the Internet and other communications equipment, as well as safe rooms for meetings. These embassies need to be prepared to protect demonstrators and persons threatened by the regime.

The U.S. trade ban on Iran should be lifted, and the American companies should agree to sign a publicized code of conduct. Integral to this should be a commitment to treat workers fairly, allow them to organize, and protect employees as best they can in the event of a crackdown.

Cultural, academic, and professional exchanges and programs must form an integral part of our efforts to assist Iranians in the democratization of their country. Visiting professors and scholars—even tourists—have freedom of movement and association that diplomats do not. Brave young activists from democratic countries could also enter Iran as tourists to meet with their Iranian counterparts; these visits could be coordinated with democratic embassies that could help look out for them. In the current environment, Iran's antidemocratic forces may not shrink from killing foreigners. But the opportunity to help will be seized by some, so long as the means are available. Conversely, it is vital to get young Iranian democratic activists abroad for short seminars with counterparts who have been successful in organizing civic campaigns in Serbia, the Philippines, Indonesia, and elsewhere. Public support for these efforts can help make them happen.

We should not shrink from helping to organize a general strike to topple the dictatorship, as we helped Serbs to do.

Iran's own sizable diaspora is also a critical factor, as shown by the theocracy's assassinations of notable émigré figures worldwide. There are divisions among Iranians abroad, most notably between those who backed the shah and those who opposed him or left later. However, a democratic Iran should be a unifying goal for all of them. The shah's son, Reza Pahlavi, has made great strides in helping bridge the differences through his vocal support for the Iranian people's democratic aspirations. He could emerge as an interesting and important figure. Under no circumstances, however, should a monarchy be imposed on Iran without the explicit consent of its people, and even then it should be only a constitutional monarchy on the model of Spain or the United Kingdom, not a return to the shah's dictatorship.

Events in Iran may move very quickly. The stakes are extremely high for the region and indeed the entire world. A democratic Iran would cease acting as a source of state terror through its backing of Hizbollah and Hamas. It would cease to be a weapons proliferator and potential nuclear threat.

Once again, a quiet dialogue with the dictator Khamenei is needed. Perhaps the British ambassador to Iran could conduct this dialogue.

Iraq

While the Bush administration correctly diagnosed the Saddam Hussein problem as one requiring not just continued quarantine but radical surgery, it did not fully consider the option of using nonviolent force to oust Saddam Hussein. This option would have taken longer than an invasion-only approach, and I did personally favor invasion over a failure to act at all to oust Saddam Hussein, over trying to just contain and live with him. But as we look at Iraq and beyond it is well to remember the view of super-hawk Richard Perle: "We're not going to make war on the world for democracy. . . . We should be using all the instruments of American influence to accomplish that purpose, and most of these instruments are not military."[32]

I must admit that over the year and more before the U.S.-led coalition's invasion, those of us who believe in the power of nonviolent methods to complement a larger strategy received a fairly cool reception from key Iraqi opposition figures. Some Iraqis agreed to participate in training sessions; but most argued with us that Saddam Hussein was different, too bloody-minded to be ousted in the way other dictators had been. Even someone sympathetic to our case, Iraqi oppositionist Laith Kubba of the National Endowment for Democracy, said to us in 2002, "Saddam has altered the mind-sets of the Iraqi people through sowing fear, mistrust and apathy."

Could America once again have helped raise the expectations of the Iraqi people and persuaded them that they could play the decisive role in their own liberation? Such hope was largely abandoned after the allies turned a blind eye to Saddam's post–Gulf War suppression of uprisings in the Kurdish north and Shiite south. By adopting such a strategy, Washington could have put all the other democracies and erstwhile critics on the spot. If they demurred in favor of continuing to engage Saddam for financial gain, their decision would have been remembered by the Iraqi people when the ouster came. The sad truth is, if we could not have stimulated a broad-based challenge to Saddam's rule from within, nothing short of a full-scale invasion would have brought it to an end. To begin to build hope among the Iraqi people, the two- to three-million-strong Iraqi diaspora needed to be a central part of the solution. As Kubba estimates, only one or two thousand of the Iraqis living outside the country were politically active, but many more would have participated had there been a serious and sustained Western effort aimed at ousting Saddam and help in building a coherent internal opposition.

Together we needed to launch a classic two-phase campaign, first organizing and then acting. The strategy needed to determine: What messages could resonate within Iraq? What fissures in the regime could be exploited? What sort of activist organization would work in Saddam's Iraq? The democracies needed to work with a broad spectrum of pro-democracy Iraqis, without fixating solely on the Iraqi National Congress or any other single group. This campaign would have required coordinated support in the form of grants and other aid, such as polling.

This effort would have involved northern Iraq, which was protected by the U.S./UK-patrolled no-fly zone. Some five million Iraqis lived there, in markedly superior conditions to those living under Saddam's control. Here, funds from the oil for food program actually reached the people. The Kurds of northern Iraq were politically divided, but they were united in their skepticism of bellicose American rhetoric. They had seen saber-rattling and plots evaporate before, and therefore were more open to trying political means. These leaders, including Massoud Barzani and Jalal Talibani, in 2002 had reaffirmed their desire to see a united democratic Iraq. As one of their representatives stated, "We are not interested in changing a dictator for another one.

We want a democratic and federal Iraq, in which Kurds can live as first class citizens and as full partners to other Iraqis in government."[33] If the U.S. led the democratic world in creating, recognizing, *and defending* a provisional democratic government for Iraq from this northern piedmont, it could have changed the entire dynamic. Far greater resources would have been needed. The possibilities were vast, and well worth the expenditure, especially when one considers the amount spent on deterring Saddam's aggression over the previous decade (which Saddam outlasted), the cost of the invasion itself, and the complexity of its aftermath. In the northern, protected zone, Iraqis would have been able to vote in elections for an all-Iraq assembly, administered by trained locals and monitored internationally. Once constituted, those elected to the assembly could have created a Transitional Council, including representatives for occupied Iraq. The Transitional Council would have been recognized by the democracies as the legitimate representative of the Iraqi people until the rest of the country had been liberated. Every stage of the process needed to be broadcast on Radio Free Iraq, the BBC World Arabic Service, among others.

The second phase would have been to launch an active resistance in the rest of Iraq to bring Saddam Hussein down. Prior to the invasion, a leading Iraqi oppositionist expressed exasperation that the Bush administration seemed to be considering every possible military strategy for regime change without realizing "that 22 million Iraqis detest Saddam Hussein" and that they represent an enormous potential resource in ungluing critical levels of control. Another Iraqi oppositionist had noted that Saddam's regime could not function without oil revenues and there was a limited number of oil workers who, if they were to abandon their jobs, could create a crisis by themselves, and there were other industrial points of vulnerability. If Saddam started shooting oil workers or workers at electrical utility installations, how would that have kept the oil fields running or the power running in his palaces or military garrisons? So, one tactic would have been to organize a boycott/strike by oil field and utility workers. Such actions by mine workers in Serbia, shipyard workers in Poland and many other countries have been at the heart of successful nonviolent campaigns to oust dictators.

Another tactic is to get people into the streets. At the moment when most resistance movements begin, most observers think that success is impossible because they can only see the costs of resisting and the brutality of the regime. But there are techniques for initial steps, which are difficult for the regime to target—for example large numbers *not* going into the streets, emptying city streets at certain times, or go slow movements. The success of even modest initial steps encourages bolder ones. When asked about the impact of getting five thousand people to march in Baghdad, an Iraqi oppositionist, a former general, just shrugged and said that Saddam would shoot them down. Asked the same question about 50,000 or 100,000 in the streets, the oppositionist said, "Of course, the next day Saddam would be gone."

So the goal could have been to organize and act—initially in the north and underground and eventually in the streets—as has happened in dozens of other countries. Should the United States and other democracies have been prepared to intervene militarily to stop Saddam from trying to crush such a movement—as we failed to do in the 1990s? At a minimum, under such circumstances we should have militarily protected the free zone and interim government in northern Iraq. But I would argue that in the face of a massive resistance effort throughout the country, we should have put Saddam's security forces on notice that we would attack them (and first of all him) if they opened fire on peaceful demonstrators.

The broad two-phase campaign outlined here would have had a direct impact on Saddam-controlled Iraq. Furthermore, regardless of how regime change was ultimately effected in Baghdad, the awakening and empowerment of such a critical mass of active, organized, resisting Iraqis both inside and outside of Iraq would have dramatically eased the transition to democracy there. That, in turn, would have eased the transition to democracy throughout the Arab world.

For these reasons, this phased plan to oust Saddam would have been opposed by many in the Middle East and Europe. But, while shifting gears so radically after a decade of consistent policy draws in untested variables and dangerous unknowns, this strategy for Iraq would have been more palatable to many than the invasion-only approach we decided upon. It would have been more difficult for other democracies to oppose a policy of working with democratic Iraqis—in the West, in northern Iraq, and underground in the rest of Iraq—and beginning to challenge the regime. An atmosphere of common purpose and cooperation might have replaced one of dissonance and recrimination. Assisting the Iraqi diaspora and the population of northern Iraq would have been a catalyst for producing new leaders and hope *throughout* Iraq that they could, with some help, liberate themselves. If we wanted regime change in Iraq, and wanted it to cease being a regional threat, making the Iraqi people our allies might have been a better path for us to choose. That said, there is no question in my own mind that the U.S. military action to depose Saddam was a net gain for democracy, in Iraq and throughout the Arab world.

The Gulf States and Beyond: Monarchs for Democracy

Below Iran and Iraq along the western shore of the Persian Gulf—a region of enormous strategic importance—are six states ruled by monarchs. Bringing

Iran into the democratic camp along the full length of the Gulf's eastern shore would create one anchor of freedom and stability and would build momentum for democratic breakthroughs in the region; a democratic breakthrough in Iraq would further enhance the strategic equation for the democratic camp. There are already stirrings in the six west-coast monarchical states.

Strategically placed Kuwait already is in the ranks of the Partly Free. By definition, this means Kuwait is not yet a full democracy. For example, in November 1999, the Kuwait parliament, with Islamists holding twenty out of fifty seats, narrowly voted to reject granting women full political rights. But it is well to remember that women received the right to vote in the United States only in 1920 and in France only in 1947—a full century and a half after our two democratic revolutions. What is exciting about Kuwait is that it demonstrates that by bringing "Islamists" into the democratic political process, long-deferred core human rights issues can be openly addressed, and extremism and feudalism can be tempered. It is clear that women will get the vote in Kuwait and it will be done with persuasion and consensus-building rather than force.

In 2002 Bahrain moved up to join Kuwait in the category of Partly Free nations. Sheikh Hamad bin Isa al-Khalifa, fifty-one, has launched reforms since taking power in March 1999 following the death of his father, whose iron rule lasted for four decades. Sheikh Hamad has relaxed censorship, repealed emergency rule, allowed exiles to return home, and granted citizenship to stateless people. In a February 2001 referendum, in which women voted, Bahrainis approved constitutional changes including the creation of a parliament that will have a directly elected chamber. And on 24 October 2002, for the first time women ran for office and voted in elections for parliament. The government has yet to define the powers of the new legislature, and the Shiite opposition boycotted the elections as nothing more than a show. In February 2002, Sheikh Hamad retitled himself king and declared the country a "constitutional monarchy."

In Qatar, Sheikh Hamad bin Khalifa al-Thani has gradually introduced modest political reforms and in 2002 proclaimed a commitment to transform the country into a democracy, to qualify for full participation in the Community of Democracies. Qatar in 1999 became the first Persian Gulf state to hold a direct election under universal suffrage. In voting for an advisory municipal council, several women contested seats but none was successful. A directly elected parliament is currently in the planning stages. With the regime no longer overtly censoring the press, al-Jazeera satellite television presents lively coverage of human rights and other controversial issues, much to the chagrin of neighboring governments, even as its virulently anti-American bias presents a substantial threat to the democracies' overall interests in the region.

Further down the western shore of the Gulf, the United Arab Emirates (UAE) is another Not Free country but one that already has experienced enormous economic and social change, laying the basis for political reform as well. While Sheikh Zaid ibn Sultan an-Nahyan of Abu Dhabi and the other six emirs who together rule the United Emirates have not permitted political parties and some other democratic institutions as has the Kuwaiti emir, the UAE has been transformed from an impoverished region of small desert principalities into a modern, wealthy state. The 2002 United Nations Development ment Programme report placed the UAE among the world's top performers in terms of quality of life as measured by real income, life expectancy, and educational standards. Human Rights Watch called the UAE "the most wired state in the Arab world" with some 143,000 Internet users. Women are treated more nearly equally here than in most other Arab states.

During his thirty-one years on the throne, Sultan Qabus ibn Said al-Said has transformed Oman from an impoverished desert land into a country with a modern physical infrastructure as well as social services, public utilities, health care, and schools that are on par with those in the West. At the same time, Oman faces the prospect of a difficult succession since Qabus, alone among Gulf leaders, has no offspring and has not groomed an heir. The sultan has granted citizens few political rights, having implemented few of the provisions of Oman's de facto first constitution, which he promulgated in 1996. He has allowed women to vote for the purely advisory Majlis al-Shura, which he consults on new laws and public policy. Women won seats on the council in the elections of 1997 and 2000.

Saudi Arabia may be the world's most repressive extant monarchy, its rulers linked by a system of fraternal succession that guarantees a series of aging, sickly royals attempting to steer the country around its problems of social repression and economic decay. As a theocratic anchor to windward, the House of Saud remains strongly identified with Wahabist Islam, whose tenets it spends lavishly to propagate. Despite this religious linkage, the greatest threat to the Saudi throne is the rise of homegrown Islamic extremists, who, among other things, provided most of the 11 September hijackers.

In the search for ways to bring democracy to Saudi Arabia, the qualities of monarchy are both the problem and a possible solution. Stability must somehow be distilled from the dangerously unstable brew of kingship, Islamic extremism, tradition, and modernity. There are signs that this is happening. Prince Wali bin Talal has reportedly discussed with other members of the royal family what might be done to reduce domestic discontent. An outspoken advocate for lifting restrictions on free expression, he has gone so far as to raise the possibility of moving the country toward limited democracy. Pressures for greater freedom for the Saudi people seem to be growing. Were the

West to give less fawning attention to the dictatorship, that evolutionary process might be greatly accelerated.

To the west, east, and south of the Gulf, there are five other ruling monarchs. New, young kings now rule Jordan and Morocco. Both countries are rated by Freedom House as Partly Free countries, that is, qualitatively freer than countries under the world's other ruling monarchs. King Abdullah took power upon his father's death in 1999 and has made Jordan's economy his priority; he inherited a kingdom beset by 20 to 30 percent unemployment, rampant poverty, and an inefficient bureaucracy perceived by most to be widely corrupt. He must attempt a precarious domestic balance, trying to maintain the support of Islamists and Arab nationalists, while striving to limit their influence. Overall, Jordan is a step ahead of the Gulf states in terms of tolerance; for example, Judaism and Christianity are recognized faiths, and there is continuing pressure for—and some movement toward—political and economic reform.

Morocco's King Mohammad VI also took power in 1999, confronting high levels of unemployment, poverty, and illiteracy, which the Islamist opposition exploits to make gains among the poor. His father's program of gradual and limited evolution of democratic institutions and a more market-oriented economy produced some results, but ultimate retention of central control and corruption have somewhat eroded the monarchy's legitimacy. Mohammad VI's own government has a mixed record to date on economic and political reform. The king promised in 2000 to turn his country into a constitutional monarchy, but he has yet to take an unambiguously reformist course.

Asia has two of the world's most tightly controlled monarchies, *Brunei* and *Bhutan*. Sultan Haji Hassanal Bolkiah Mu'izzaddin Waddaulah of Brunei faces few restrictions on his power and has ruled under emergency law since his reign began. Corruption and abuse of power have increasingly become targets of public scrutiny and dissatisfaction. Bhutan's King Jigme Singye Wangchuk continues to maintain tight control of this tiny Himalayan land, detaining pro-democracy dissidents and preventing Bhutanese from forming political parties, civil society groups, and trade unions. In southern Africa, *Swaziland*'s King Mswati III faces pressure for democratic reforms from the country's trade unions, which are backed by their powerful South African counterparts. The king rules by decree.

The goal with all of these ruling monarchies, including such relatively tolerant states as Jordan, must be to help their transition to a constitutional monarchy. One initiative worth exploring would be a summit and eventual association of monarchs—Monarchs for Democracy—in which the world's remaining ruling monarchs could share experiences and explore routes to constitutional monarchy. Under the auspices of the Community of Democracies, a dialogue could benefit from the extraordinarily rich dynamic of recent decades as numerous monarchs have made this transition. That dynamic is still unfolding in places such as Afghanistan, where former king Mohammad Zahir Shah is one of the new legitimizing figures and advocates for full-scale democracy. In Bulgaria, former king Simeon may be the first monarch ever elected to public office, having become prime minister in a completely free and fair election in June 2001. Thailand's king also has intervened a number of times in recent years to restore and protect Thai democracy. In 1992, when the Thai army was suppressing and shooting pro-democracy demonstrators, King Bhumibol summoned the army chief, along with the most prominent advocate of reform, for an evenhanded dressing down, paving the way for a peaceful restoration of democracy.[34] In the absence of their own king, Laotians under a communist regime are filling their hunger for royalty by avidly watching King Bhumibol via the three Thai television stations receivable in Laos. Having dethroned Laotians' own last king, the communists are now paying homage to an earlier Laotian monarch. "They are making a direct link between the king and the current leadership," notes American ambassador Douglas Hartwick.[35] In Cambodia, the *Washington Post* reports, "Princess Norodom Vacheahra is emerging as the most outspoken royal with her criticism of the prime minister [and dictator] Hun Sen."[36]

Among the constitutional monarchs of Europe, King Juan Carlos played a fundamental role in the initial transition to democracy in Spain and also in facing down an early threat to its consolidation. Spain is an outstanding example of a nation that put repressive rule behind it and since has exploded with economic and social growth, narrowing a huge gap with other European states in an extraordinarily short time. King Juan Carlos's nation is historically and currently connected to North Africa and the Middle East. He has a friendly relationship with many of the Middle East's monarchs, and might take the lead in organizing a group to consider their relationship to the modern state.

The young kings of Morocco and Jordan offer particularly interesting early partners for such a dialogue, because, as noted, these countries are already rated Partly Free by Freedom House and both men are clearly thinking about ways to reform. The sheiks governing Kuwait, Qatar, and Bahrain also are good early partners for dialogue. Bahrain's monarch already has said he is a constitutional monarch, although he has a way to go. Qatar has shown keen interest in the Community of Democracies, including hosting meetings on democracy with the community. Oman, the UAE, and Saudi Arabia represent larger challenges, but even in these countries there are some royals with whom a dialogue might be initiated. Asian constitutional monarchs—including the crown prince of Japan and his wife, a former diplomat—could meet with the Brunei and Bhutan monarchs. The Thai king might take the lead in the discussion. Swaziland must be part of the larger dialogue as there are no obvious regional interlocutors.

The argument for constitutional monarchy is compelling. Across the globe, in the most diverse of cultures and circumstances, such monarchs have been able to preserve their property, their prestige, and their families' continuance as monarchs by cooperating in a transition. The choice is to a certain extent between the violent end of the French and Russian royal families and the continuing roles of monarchs in Japan, Thailand, Nepal, Great Britain, the Scandinavian countries, Spain, and many more. There are various possible routes and outcomes, some not even conceivable today. Some experts on the Middle East believe that several of the Gulf's sheikhs and the kings of Jordan and Morocco could be elected to office in free and fair elections, as was King Simeon in Bulgaria. On balance this seems a bad approach, as it is the essence of democracy that leaders be elected out of as well as into office—constitutional monarchs want to and can stay. Of course the transitions need to be handled with care. Islamist political groups that refuse to respect the rules of democracy, including tolerance of diversity, would have to be kept out of power until they transformed themselves. This is an arena in which Turkey's experience can be of some help. We know that Muslims can be good democrats—over half the Muslims in the world today live in, and play an active political role in, democracies. Given the choice of voting for extremist Islamist parties or for more moderate parties, Muslims have voted overwhelmingly for moderates. The transition to constitutional monarchy can only be successful if the larger struggle for moderate hearts and minds among the Middle East's Muslims is also being won. But this larger struggle itself cannot be won without a vision for the future of these monarchies and concrete progress toward realizing it.

Even democracies without monarchical experience can play a role. First, to launch such a dialogue the United States and others would need to approach the Spanish government and King Juan Carlos and other constitutional monarchs and persuade them to take the lead. Second, we would have to add our substantial influence with the Middle Eastern and other monarchs to get them to take the exercise seriously. Third, in all of the areas for specific work—from writing constitutions to the rule of law to civic education—we have some of the leading experts and organizations in the world. Of course there are many sources of expertise, including Muslims living in democracies.

Palestine and Lebanon

Moving from monarchs and the Gulf toward the Mediterranean, we see a Not Free Palestine and a Not Free Lebanon. Both deserve special attention in terms of political development. A central reason innumerable Israeli govern-ments have been unable to achieve a compromise agreement with Palestine is that Palestine Liberation Organization leader Yasser Arafat is no George Washington. He has lost whatever democratic credentials he had by acting like a dictator and terrorist. Thus he does not have the credibility of a demo-cratic leader to make and deliver on compromises. One of my guides in this is Natan Sharansky, himself a hero of the nonviolent struggle for democracy in the Soviet Union. He served twelve years in a Soviet prison for his belief in democracy. He has long stressed that Israel's security problem is the lack of democracy within Arab ranks. In the case of Palestine, this failing is clearly not due to the lack of democratic instinct or desire on the part of Palestini-ans. It is due to Arafat's own venality and desire to hold on to personal power at all costs. He has not allowed his own parliament to function freely nor allowed independent electronic media. The most important step the Com-munity of Democracies could take in this region is to insist upon and help in-troduce full-scale democracy into Palestine.

The Lebanese also richly deserve to be able to elect their own leaders and regain sovereignty. No one who has experienced it has forgotten the sophistica-tion and sparkle of Beirut before the civil war and Syrian occupation (both start-ing in the mid-1970s). Any recent visitor to the country can feel the potential for democracy and the hatred of the occupying Syrian troops and all-too-obvious Syrian secret police. One meets them at the Beirut airport and sees them all over the city. The challenge is to keep pressing ahead with recent democratic gains secured even in the face of Syrian counterpressure and to increase pressure on the Syrians to get out—as the Israelis have done from south Lebanon. The will to freedom and democracy is clearly present within the body politic of Lebanon. With Syria out, both politics and the economy should bloom again. Of course a democratic Lebanon would be a vastly better neighbor for Israel.

Egypt

At the very heart of the Arab world geographically, Egypt historically also has been its soul. But, while slightly less oppressive than some other dictatorships, Egypt is far from free under former general Hosni Mubarak, who has been president since 1981. Bringing Egypt into the ranks of democracies could have the same dramatic effect throughout the Arab world that Poland crossing the divide had within central and eastern Europe. It has the largest Arab popula-tion and the greatest influence. It also has a well-developed intelligentsia and middle class.

This is a classic situation of a dictator long in office who hides behind the hoary "après moi le deluge" excuse that the only alternatives to him are violent

Muslim extremists. He has persuaded many democratic governments to go along with this rationale. But in fact popular support in Egypt for Islamic militants has eroded as a result of their greater emphasis on violence.

Under Mubarak, the ruling National Democratic Party continues to dominate a tightly controlled political system, running presidential elections with Mubarak as the sole candidate, fraudulent elections for parliament, and vetoed requests to form new and independent political parties. Mubarak uses his secret police throughout the society. In May 2001, he jailed the leading moderate democrat in the country, Saad Ibrahim, and his Ibn Khaldun Center staff; Ibrahim's seven-year sentence was reaffirmed in July 2002 by a special security court under Mubarak's control, before he was released on appeal under international pressure. The dictator's proximate reason for repressing Ibrahim was an article that he wrote opposing Mubarak's efforts to position his son as his successor—yet another example of dictator dynasty building, or hereditary dictatorship.

The democratic nations, and particularly the United States, have enormous leverage on Mubarak, but it is largely focused on keeping him from reversing the moderate stance on Israel set by Anwar al-Sadat. In fact, Egypt will only be a durable good neighbor for Israel when it joins Israel in the democratic camp. The democracies need to change their policy toward Egypt. Once again a discreet dialogue is needed with Mubarak. And once again, the full range of strategic nonviolent tools need to be deployed to bring about free elections, an independent press, and the other accoutrements of full democracy.

A powerful, visible action would be to take $100 million from the $2 billion annual aid for Egypt and create an Egyptian Democracy Fund with it. Unlike the current aid, which runs through the Egyptian government, the Democracy Fund should be openly declared to be for direct assistance to democrats. As *Washington Post* columnist Jackson Diehl pointed out: "The Ibn Khaldun Center never benefited from the billions USAID [U.S. Agency for International Development] poured into Egypt. Nor has the Egyptian Organization for Human Rights, another group perpetually under pressure from Mubarak's police. The Center for Legal Studies on Human Rights had to close down for lack of funds. . . . [USAID money has gone to] the very kangaroo court system Mubarak used to throw Ibrahim and a host of other democracy advocates in prison."[37]

The Bush administration's announcement in August 2002, that it would not give Egypt "additional" aid above the $2 billion, owing to the rejection of Ibrahim's appeal, was the first time in the Middle East that we have used aid leverage with our mislabeled "allies" to promote democracy. So it was welcome as a first step, but it is not as effective as increasing funding for the local democrats. In fact, the instinct to withhold or withdraw is basically wrong—in the face of negative developments we should engage more, we should go on the offensive by providing greater assistance directly to democrats. Mubarak played the Bush decision as denying much-needed aid to the Egyptian people, and at a time when we were proposing to increase aid to Israel.

Algeria

Yet another country caught up in the wave of raised expectations and democratic progress in that excellent vintage year, Algeria's previous one-party regime was reformed in 1989. Antigovernment sentiment stemming from corruption, housing shortages, unemployment, and other severe economic and social problems boosted the Islamic Salvation Front, despite the party's avowed commitment to theocratic rule under sharia (Islamic law). The army canceled the second round of 1992 legislative elections in which the Islamic Salvation Front had achieved a commanding lead and barred the party, setting off a civil conflict marked by frequent random violence that has claimed some hundred thousand lives.

France, the United States, and other democracies with substantial influence over dictator Abdelaziz Bouteflika and the Algerian army's high command endorsed this refusal to honor the legitimate expression of the Algerian people's will.[38] No one can say how an Islamic-led government would have governed, whether it would have built the institutions of democracy or gone the way of the Iranian mullahs. But the outcome could have been a democracy. In preempting the election and fostering a dictator, the democracies made a tragic mistake.

Now there is once again an opportunity for a breakthrough if Algerian democrats and democratic governments and democrats worldwide join hands. Algeria is a tailor-made opportunity for a Community of Democracies priority project.

Sub-Saharan Africa

"Africa has been traumatized by human rights violations of historic proportions over the last five centuries," writes professor of law Makau Mutwa, chair of the Kenya Human Rights Commission. "The recent chapter in that long history of abuses is still being authored. But the people of Africa, like the people elsewhere, have never stopped struggling for better conditions of life and especially for more enlightened and accountable political societies.

The popular repudiation of one-party and undemocratic states over the past decade" is striking.[39]

Africa too was caught up in the wave of dramatic democratic progress in the 1990s. It is clear that success breeds success and that sustaining this momentum globally through to completion by 2025 will be helpful in each region and in each country where a dictator still exists. As dictators become fewer and fewer, those remaining will have a harder and harder time retaining their legitimacy and hold on power. People will rise to oust their oppressor when all their neighbors are moving ahead in freedom.

But to keep momentum building, it is necessary for African democracies to make themselves heard and break ranks from the calls for African, rather than democratic, solidarity. The joke about "one man, one vote, one time" in Africa is often sadly accurate, with elected leaders often allowing only one honest election and then staying in power through subsequent rigged elections, constitutional changes, trumped-up regional rivalries, and the like.

This recently occurred in Zimbabwe, with little protest from the neighbors. The blatant intimidation of the opposition in the March 2002 Zimbabwean presidential elections did not prevent Nigerian and South African observers from endorsing the skewed result for Robert Mugabe.[40] Only the Southern African Development Community's Parliamentary Forum observer mission, headed by Botswanan legislator Duke Lefhoko, bucked this trend with a stinging report on the electoral environment. "There's this peddling of this 'hear no evil, see no evil, speak no evil' in the name of African brotherhood-sisterhood solidarity," he noted, describing how he had been pressured by colleagues to temper his report. Lefhoko blasted the use of state authorities to support the incumbent, intimidate opposition members, and stifle the vote in pro-opposition urban areas. Defending his criticism of an African neighbor for violating democratic and human rights principles, Lefhoko said, "Look, someone has got to stand up for Africa. . . . For how long are we going to condone negatives as if they were positives?"[41]

There are other African voices like his, but very few at the apex of power, even among the few full-fledged African democracies. This has to change if democracy is to retain the hold it has now in Africa, much less broaden its grip. Democratically elected leaders in Africa do their people and their neighbors no service by choosing to be Africans first and democrats second. A majority of Zimbabweans have bravely proven there is no choice at all.

The world's established democracies in the West, or the North as Africans frequently call it, have a self-inflicted credibility problem in promoting democracy in Africa that only a newly consistent and principled practice can help them live it down. The legacy of colonialism still resonates, allowing the strongmen to justify their dictatorship in terms of resisting white recolonization.[42] This factor is exacerbated by the reality that in the postcolonial period, through the cold war and to the present day, Western powers supported a host of vile, venal, and repressive dictators. Dictators like Mobutu Sese Seko in Zaire—now the so-called Democratic Republic of the Congo—could not have gained or retained power without strong relationships with the West. Even the pro-democracy policies that have been adopted often rely on rulers who won power through the gun to drive reform. President Bill Clinton's declaration of an African renaissance on his 1997 African trip highlighted this misguided approach. None of the leaders with whom the president met could be called a true democrat, and a number were outright dictators who had learned the international lingo of "good governance."[43] Admittedly, policymakers face difficult situations to which there are no readily available easy answers. Rwanda, for example, is the most difficult state to which to apply a democratization model, as it is in the aftermath of a genocide in which the majority population attempted to exterminate the minority. A longer-term process to blur the distinction between Tutsi and Hutu and forge a Rwandan identity makes sense, and this is the path that dictator Paul Kagame appears to be following. Other African countries, like Uganda, also face problems born of past political use of ethnicity, although to a lesser degree.

The answer is to build and coordinate among the democracies policies focused on processes rather than individuals. In the words of astute Africa observer Bill Berkeley, "The truly radical thing for the United States to do is invest its resources and credibility not in individual leaders but in the fledgling attempts across the continent to build institutions of law and accountability; in the end, these represent the only real hope for lasting positive change in Africa."[44] The principle applies equally to all democracies. If we want to help Africans turn the continent around, we have to banish ideas of "one-stop shopping" with dictators and do our part to promote the democratic and legal institutions that can sustain progress over the long haul.

In sub-Saharan Africa as of this writing there are twenty-nine Free or Partly Free nations and eleven Not Free countries run by dictators. The eleven Free countries—Benin, Botswana, Cape Verde, Ghana, Lesotho, Mali, Mauritius, Namibia, São Tomé and Principe, Senegal, and South Africa—are distributed throughout the continent and provide a potential core of leaders who, working together and with non-African democracies, can help sustain the momentum. They should be encouraged to embrace this pathfinding role.

Nearly half of sub-Saharan Africa's states, eighteen in all, fall into the Partly Free category, which itself is a spectrum of countries advancing toward full democracy and others where democratic practice is receding. These democracies are still partial, fragile, and there has been, and will continue to be, some backsliding. The job is not yet done with them. Focused monitoring of their progress, as well as assistance to citizens pushing for full freedom, is imperative on the part of the world's democracies, and especially Africa's own. We must recognize the enormous strides made in Africa. Compared to the hundreds of years of horrors, the past decade is an extraordinary period of progress. A fundamental breakthrough has been achieved. Unlike in the Greater Middle East, the balance of power in Africa has shifted from the dictators to the democrats.

But the remaining eleven dictators still commit atrocities of such appalling savagery and scale that democrats everywhere must substantially increase the effort to finish the job in Africa. The 1994 genocide in Rwanda, the deaths and displacement of millions of Tutsis and Hutus, the slaughters in the Congo, all result from the actions of dictators. Ethnic differences can be reconciled permanently only on the basis of compromise and nonviolent dispute resolution inherent in the democratic process and rules of the game. By definition, dictators rely on the use of force, which only exacerbates ethnic, tribal, and other differences. Lack of democratic good governance and accountability is the fundamental problem in Africa. No progress can be sustained without them.

As South Africa's president Thabo Mbeki stated on 9 July 2002 at the birth of the African Union: "Through our actions, let us proclaim to the world that this is a continent of democracy, a continent of good governance, where the people participate and the rule of law is upheld." The new African Union is to require its members to hold free elections and to permit opposition parties to campaign freely. It will have the right to intervene with member states to halt or deal with genocide, war crimes, or gross violations of human rights. The group, modeled on the European Union (EU), hopes to create a regional parliament, a central bank, and a standing army to prevent disputes from erupting into violence. However, as David Coltart, an opposition-party legislator in Zimbabwe noted: "We're off to a bad start [with the recent African support of Zimbabwe's dictator]. There is a significant core of African leaders who are now committed to democratic principles. The future of Africa is going to be determined by whether that faction holds sway in the African Union."[45]

Local democrats and democrats worldwide must join together to deploy the full range of strategy and tactics, programs and actions to achieve democracy.

- We must create within the Community of Democracies an Africa caucus so that the group of twenty-nine Free and Partly Free countries, with the assistance of non-African participants in the Community of Democracies, can help with still fragile transitions (and incipient backsliding) among their members and also realize their collective strength by insisting that the last eleven dictators leave power. Just a list of the names of the twenty-nine countries is impressive: Benin, Botswana, Burkina Faso, Cape Verde, Central African Republic, Comoros, Congo (Brazzaville), Cote d'Ivoire, Gabon, Ghana, Guinea-Bissau, Kenya, Lesotho, Madagascar, Malawi, Mali, Mauritius, Mozambique, Namibia, Niger, Nigeria, São Tomé and Principe, Senegal, Seychelles, Sierra Leone, South Africa, Tanzania, Uganda, and Zambia.

- We need to create new special tribunals like the International Criminal Tribunal for Rwanda, which is trying cases from the genocide. These ad hoc tribunals can focus on the violations of international law by the remaining eleven dictators and call them to account, or find another judicial mechanism. It must be made clear that all dictators, including those who take their country backwards from Partly Free to Not Free, as President Mugabe has done with Zimbabwe, will be tried and brought to justice either by an international tribunal or a local one. The existing African Court on Human and Peoples' Rights established in June 1998 is too anemic for this task.[46]

- Nations with particular histories in Africa need to revise their priorities and play a more aggressive role in ousting "the Last Eleven" dictators. French policy is in particular need of a radical shake-up. The nation of *liberté, égalité,* and *fraternité* has too often been on the wrong side of history in Africa, sustaining dictator after dictator in the postcolonial era. Sadly, France has not been alone. Britain, Portugal, Belgium, Germany, Spain, the United States, and others all have such special histories and relationships, and therefore responsibilities.

- Perhaps most fundamental is for non-African nations and Africans themselves to begin to believe that Africans have just as much right to, and reason and capacity for, democracy as any people. There is a terribly enervating condescension among many non-Africans, an idea that we must treat Africa as a sort of child, a patient, a charity case. There is a not-so-hidden racism inherent in this view. The result is toleration of dictators, a focus not on the cause but on the effect, not on getting the right governance but on debt forgiveness, or refugee relief, or conflict prevention. We should be promoting nonviolent conflict to remove these dictators who are holding back their countries, dictators who are promoting violent conflict within their own nations and with their neighbors.

Secretary of State Colin Powell, the first African U.S. secretary of state and the first foreign minister of African descent from any non-African nation, got it right on his first official trip to Africa in May 2001. He began his trip in Mali, one of Africa's eleven Free nations, which he praised for its democracy, pledging to promote all aspects of our relations.[47] He traveled next to another Free country, South Africa. There he publicly called upon President Robert Mugabe of neighboring Zimbabwe to allow full, free, and fair elections and to leave power.[48] He went on to a then Not Free Kenya and gave the same message eye-to-eye privately with President Daniel arap Moi and then publicly as well.[49] Moi, who had been in office since 1978, claimed that only with a decade of experience can an African leader adequately guide his nation. He also responded to Secretary Powell's call for him to retire by publicly stating, "Africa's people should make their own decisions about their leaders."[50] Of course that is the point Secretary Powell—and this book—was trying to make. And when they finally had a chance in 2002 with a united opposition, Kenya's people soundly defeated Moi's proxy. Moi was chased from the inauguration of his successor by loud cries of "thief."

Zimbabwe

Mugabe's Zimbabwe exemplifies the Chinese proverb A fish rots from the head. Land seizures and political repression are spearheaded by Mugabe through his youth militia thugs (a terrifying *Lord of the Flies* model also employed in Liberia) along with the army and police. Zimbabwe stands on the brink of social and economic collapse, a situation that perversely suits the dictator. He apparently believes that his people will be consumed by the struggle for mere survival rather than for freedom. Opposition Movement for Democratic Change (MDC) leader Morgan Tsvangirai said in August 2002: "Time is running out for this country. . . . If it goes beyond a year, the government will have destroyed the infrastructure of this nation and the spirit of its people. It will mean the subsistence and informal sectors dominating and no investment. It's another African basket case; that's what it will mean."[51]

The MDC is cautiously looking toward a campaign of mass nonviolent action to oust Mugabe. Local elections are scheduled, but with 2000 and 2002 election frauds in mind, the MDC is fighting them in court. The MDC needs to be convinced that this time the democracies will really stand with Zimbabwe's democrats and ensure genuine elections and, if they are fraudulent once again, that Mugabe will be tried in The Hague and physically brought to justice. An election provides the best opportunity to organize. A boycott of elections by the MDC would make it easier for timorous African democrats to hide behind the MDC's reluctance to contest.

International support is imperative for mass mobilization. Training activists, mounting demonstrations, and printing campaign materials have upfront costs. A campaign like the one mounted by Otpor in Serbia, replete with posters, matchbooks, and calendars lampooning the regime, will help deflate

Mugabe's current appearance of omnipotence. If the local election campaign is to be effective, international monitors are key, and on a much larger scale and more forcefully than in the past. The March 2002 presidential election had far too few observers, and many of those involved were obviously predisposed toward ratifying a Mugabe victory. The parliamentary delegation from the Southern African Development Community was an African exception and should be repeated. Intimidation and violence by police, army, and militia stymied domestic election monitoring in the last election. This makes it even more critical to mobilize a professional and dedicated domestic observation of upcoming local elections.

With the independent media largely silenced by the regime, international broadcasting is a critical source of news to the population. The BBC in particular is important. The regime has essentially decided to treat the cities—which overwhelmingly supported the MDC—as occupied territory and has made the countryside its base of ill-informed support. Assuring that broadcasts can be heard throughout Zimbabwe during a campaign and vote count is essential. Gaining support of neighboring democracies—South Africa and Mozambique in particular—will be important in making sure territorial coverage is complete.

Democratic embassies need to coordinate their efforts in Harare and in the hinterland. Civic activists in Bulawayo, Zimbabwe's "second city" and capital of the Matebeleland region, have noted that few American diplomats visit the city and surrounding region, and when they do, they do not stay long. Diplomats from the democracies need to be out and visible to both the people and the servants of the regime, particularly in the most troubled regions. In addition to diplomats being highly visible and active throughout Zimbabwe, the embassies themselves need to be safe houses for those anti-Mugabe activists who feel they have no choice but to seek refuge. The embassies also should manifest their support for the Zimbabwean people in visible, audible, and imaginative ways.

Mugabe has used the food crisis to divert attention from his repression, and democracies cannot fall prey to seeing the two as disconnected. An early pan-democracy initiative—by food exporters and African democracies alike—is to assure that food gets to those who need it. Zimbabwean democrats have advised that food aid donated through the UN's World Food Program would be very difficult to reject, even with strings attached. Controlling distribution of food is crucial; leaving it in the hands of the government assures that it will be employed selectively and corruptly. This approach would rekindle flagging confidence among Zimbabweans that the world does not embrace the Mugabe regime, a claim he frequently makes, especially with regard to the United Nations.

The current panoply of "smart sanctions" has been inconsistently applied and has had little effect thus far. Allowed to attend a conference at UN headquarters in New York, Mugabe thumbed his nose at the travel ban. The Community of Democracies needs to initiate a coherent smart-sanctions policy, freezing personal assets of regime members and associates well before announcing the action. The size and locations of assets netted should be broadcast back to the Zimbabwean people, to illustrate what they already suspect: that Mugabe has profited from their deepening misery.

The regime's security forces need to know that they will be held accountable for violence against nonviolent civilians. Relationships built during Britain's training of Zimbabwean army officers in the 1980s should be used to convey this message through back channels. Officers who order their troops to fire on demonstrators, who employ torture, or who do not prevent such outrages must know that they will be pursued wherever they may try to flee and held accountable legally. South Africa, whose security forces include a number of former African National Conference (ANC) armed-wing members with strong ties to Zimbabwe, needs to play a role by making clear they are watching individuals and their activities.

Nelson Mandela could undermine Mugabe and his stature in Africa. Mugabe is now the oldest and longest-serving postcolonial African leader. According to Zimbabwean democrats, this is a major impediment to persuading Africa's democratic leaders to call for his departure. Mandela's distaste for Robert Mugabe is widely known. As part of a larger campaign, Mandela must call publicly for Mugabe to step down; this just might sink the solidarity boat keeping Mugabe afloat.

Early in 2003 there were reports that the opposition MDC was meeting with officials from Zimbabwe's governing party's most powerful figures and working on a deal for a new power-sharing government, which would call for Mugabe to step down.[52] But Mugabe is a master at survival and will only go under concerted pressure.

Congo-Kinshasa

Despite high hopes following the 1997 demise of Zaire's dictator, Mobutu Sese Seko, finally cut off from American support, the Democratic Republic of the Congo remains a democracy in name only. Guerrilla-leader-cum-president Laurent Kabila, who rode in at the head of a Rwandan-supported lightning offensive on Kinshasa, initially received a great deal of support, especially from America. It soon became apparent that his ambitions were as kleptocratic and dictatorial as Mobutu's, and he began to employ anti-Tutsi rhetoric to build support in the western Congo once he established control there.[53] In 1998, a new war began, drawing in Angola, Namibia, and Zimbabwe on the side of Kabila's government; and Rwanda, Burundi, and

Uganda, along with an ever-growing panoply of local militias and proxies, fighting against the Kinshasa authorities. This war, still ongoing after almost four years, is estimated to have claimed *over three million lives* in eastern Congo alone.[54] Incredibly, this monumental death toll receives relatively little attention. It is the highest death toll in a single conflict since the Second World War. The foreign forces are now primarily engaged in an extractive relationship with Congo, being given, or simply taking, concessions for mining gold or diamonds or for logging, as is the case of the Zimbabwean army in central Congo.[55] Hopes that this situation would improve with the 2000 assassination of Laurent Kabila and his replacement by his son Joseph have not been realized, although there has been some improvement. For the time being, Congo is the world's largest failed state.

Congo is not an obvious candidate for democratization considering its massive woes and the ongoing war. It lacks centralized governance. The international rape of Congo by its African neighbors continues, impeding any progress toward democracy in these countries and subverting it in Namibia, the only democracy worthy of the name among them. Congo has never had any approximation of democratic governance, and it now has almost no state infrastructure.

With all its obvious downsides, however, this situation does have some possibilities for promoting a democratic solution. The new Anglo-French commitment to addressing "Africa's world war," as exhibited by the joint visit of Foreign Ministers Jack Straw and Hubert Vedrine in January 2002, could mark a critical shift, for the policies of Whitehall and the Quai d'Orsay have traditionally been at odds in Africa, particularly with respect to France's fixation on preserving *la Francophonie*.[56] South Africa also is demonstrating some new leadership. A common front built around this new axis of democracies could limit the intervening states' room to maneuver, which all have employed since the war began.

One promising sign is an accord signed on 17 December 2002 in Pretoria, South Africa. It prescribes a power-sharing arrangement that would allow President Kabila to remain in office for at least two years, until democratic elections can be held. Four vice presidents would be appointed, one each from Kabila's government, the political opposition, and two armed rebel groups: the Rwandan-backed Rally for Congolese Democracy and the Ugandan-backed Congolese Liberation Movement. Unfortunately, some fighting continues, and much remains to be done to turn this or future accords into reality.[57]

First among the implementing policies that should be pressed from all democratic states, including African ones like South Africa and Namibia, is to complete and sustain the withdrawal from Congo of all foreign forces, including logistical support elements for proxy factions. If forces are not withdrawn or return, personal, regime-targeted sanctions should be imposed on neighboring dictators, and their assets should be identified, tracked, and frozen. Blacklists on regime figures, including spouses and children, and denial of visas and travel privileges also must be applied. They can be rescinded when the withdrawal is complete to the satisfaction of the democracies. In addition, corporate interests involved in this extractive business, including those from within the democratic world, must be targeted and told either to support the Business Community for Democracy's code of conduct or face sanctions themselves. These policies should be trumpeted on international broadcast media, so that the people of Congo and the combatant countries are made aware of the policy. Drawing public attention to European shopping sprees by dictators' families—including their bills—could be particularly useful in confirming what most of their benighted citizens already suspect, that they are robbing their countries blind.

The permanent withdrawal of foreign forces is absolutely essential to making the accord work. But it is not in itself sufficient. Local forces are well versed in plunder and exploitation of the population and would easily fill the vacuum left by foreign forces if allowed. Some investigative journalism has asserted that there are strong links between Congo's resources and international terrorist organizations, such as Hamas, Hizbollah, and al-Qaeda.[58] The democratic world, including the United States, needs to provide the necessary resources to fill this vacuum with UN forces (an expanded mandate, with the forces necessary, for the UN force in Congo, or MONUC) to buttress the fragile peace process and to protect mines and forests that have provided plunder to the militias. No contracts or concessions made on these resources should be recognized by the democratic world, even though a number of outside interests have profited from them. Disposition of the resources should be frozen until such time as a legitimate, and popularly chosen, Congolese democratic government comes into being and is internationally recognized. Enforcement of "blood diamond" bans need to be more rigorous, and the concept should be expanded to other traceable illicit resources emanating from the Congo, as in Liberia and Sierra Leone, where the focus on "conflict diamonds" began. Maintaining control over these areas is one of the most important things the democratic world can do to promote a democratic—and therefore sustainable—end to the Congo war.

In their diplomatic presence in Kinshasa and beyond, the democracies need to coordinate their approaches. This will break radically from past practice. The Straw-Vedrine mission points to the possibilities of ending this postcolonial (and, in many ways, colonial) division. Where ambassadorial personal relations are simply too strained to allow constructive interaction and substantive coordination, the ambassadors need to be replaced with individuals who will work toward the common democratic goal. This coordination should be consistent within the EU and between the EU and the United States. Britain should carry this policy into the commonwealth with other democracies. Perhaps hardest of all will be getting African democracies to coordinate with "Northern" democracies. Building support within the Congo will be a major factor in getting African democracies to compel their undemocratic neighbors to cease making things worse and to move in a democratic direction. Despite South Africa's own role, the Southern African Development Community has been less than effective in promoting an end to the war. Until African democracies are willing to take their undemocratic neighbors to task, thus breaking the postcolonial taboo of criticizing fellow Africans in public, it will be difficult to build the necessary common front to achieve a lasting cease-fire.

Despite years of exploitation and mismanagement (and lack of any governance since the late Mobutu period) Congo is not devoid of intellectual capital and talent. For example, Democratic leader Etienne Tshisekedi, a fixture on the Congolese political scene, was sidelined immediately by Laurent Kabila as a potential threat. As with many societies ravaged by war, the Congo has a reservoir of educated talent outside the country that could be encouraged to return with some incentives. In addition, many of those who remain in Congo could take a greater role in helping determine the county's future. The accord includes such figures, and the international democratic community needs to insist that the outcome is not a division of spoils among armed groups. Here, again, control of the resource base will be a critical bargaining chip. The embassies of the democracies need to engage such figures openly and give promising individuals new visibility. Congolese are known for keeping on top of the news, and one of the benefits of the anarchy is the possibility of a relatively unregulated press. Showing interest in promising *democratic* Congolese leaders (with potential broad-based appeal) and political parties could have a major effect.

The increased international humanitarian presence, especially in the eastern Congo, provides an opportunity to promote democracy at a grassroots level. While food and medical relief are indeed urgently needed to stabilize a ravaged population, a shift as soon as possible to promoting local agricultural production and self-governance would be especially useful in helping build the basis for a more prosperous and democratic Congo. For example, it is crucial not to allow the local militia to handle aid distribution but instead to use local (vetted) humanitarian organizations to oversee distribution. Experimental programs pioneered in other African conflicts, like the STAR Program in southern Sudan, which uses the contact created by humanitarian aid to help build local democratic governing capacity, should be considered for eastern Congo, which really needs to start from scratch. When 30 percent of the east Congo city of Goma was destroyed and 80 percent of the homes were damaged by a volcanic eruption on 24 January 2002, hundreds died and thousands were made homeless. But Goma's citizens rallied, did not flee, and worked together to recover. The civic-mindedness and attachment to home shown by the volcano victims in Goma, eastern Congo, suggests that there are great untapped possibilities for building democracy there from the ground up. It also, sadly, illustrated what a low priority the world has given Congo's woes. It took a volcano that killed a few hundred people and rendered inhabitants of a town homeless to draw attention to a region ravaged consistently by war with millions of deaths since the Rwanda genocide in 1994.[59]

Afghanistan has demonstrated that even after decades of warfare a nation can make a fresh, if still problematic, start when there is enough positive international engagement. Few would have predicted that a provisional secular government would be sitting in Kabul in 2002. Congo is in a somewhat similar situation. Long chaotic, embroiled in warfare that has split the country into fiefdoms, it can still be moved toward democracy. Concerted and determined international involvement, including a relatively small but critical military component, as in Afghanistan, could help set the country on a path to democratic self-rule. Democracies are not built overnight, and Congo faces a long road even after the neighbors' forces withdraw, the accord is a success, and a provisional government is seated with elections slated. But the democratic world could, with an implementation strategy and some exertion, help get it to that stage.

The Last Dictators in Europe and the Americas

Belarus, Cuba, and Haiti are the last nations in Europe and the Americas still suffering under dictators. We set forth some ideas here on how to liberate the first two.

Belarus

The situation in the former Soviet republic of Belarus, after a brief spring of democracy in the early 1990s, has been on a steady downward trajectory since Aleksandr Lukashenko was elected president in 1994. Since then, he has consolidated his powers, dismissed the legal legislature, and stifled dissent with increasingly repressive laws and decrees. The most recent presidential elections, held in September 2001, were fraudulent.

In addition, the Lukashenko regime has kept some very shady company, including rogue states like Iraq, which has had air defense personnel trained in Belarus. Having a large stockpile of modern Soviet weaponry, Belarus has emerged as a major player in the international arms trade, from small arms to sophisticated antiaircraft missiles.[60] While its neighbors to the west—the Baltic states and Poland—are either already members of NATO or soon will be and have made rapid economic progress, Belarus remains an economic backwater, drawing little foreign investment and giving Belarusians little confidence in a better future.

Belarus also seems to be a backwater for cutting-edge democracy promotion as well, especially at the policy level. The last presidential election should have made clear to all that the Lukashenko regime was so control oriented in the Soviet style that it would not allow the already stacked process to go forward without interference and secrecy. But already cracks in the common front between the European Union and the United States are beginning to emerge. In February 2002 the U.S. assistant secretary of state for democracy, human rights, and labor, Lorne Craner, took the important step of decrying an ongoing crackdown on the Belarusian independent media.[61] Alas, his voice seems a lonely one. Some European parliamentarians and ministries have given invitations to their counterparts in Belarus, without making clear that these officials are illegitimate.

The United States has an active ambassador in Minsk, Michael Kozak, who has engaged with members of Belarusian civil society. This is an anomaly among the diplomatic corps there, which mostly sticks to the "client-centered" old-school approach, which does little but prop up dictators.

What is to be done? First, the world must recognize the incredible courage, tenacity, and creativity of the ongoing nonviolent campaign for democracy being waged by Belarussians. Groups like Zubr, Charter 97, and others are conducting nearly daily protests and other actions. In the face of beatings and jailings, they persist.

A democracy-promotion strategy for Belarus necessarily requires common purpose among the North American and European policy actors, both in their national capitals and in Minsk. Without this common front, represented by international institutions such as the OSCE, the EU, NATO, the Council of Europe, the United Nations, and others, the Lukashenko regime will be able to divide the democracies and continue repression. To gain broad policy unity, high-level leadership is needed. Institutions traditionally guard their prerogatives and independence jealously and commonly refuse to coordinate. Unless Belarus is addressed at and between the highest levels of governments, Lukashenko will continue to have more than enough room to maneuver. It appears that such leadership needs to come from Washington. OSCE's mission in Belarus was relatively aggressive, but after the mission was closed by Lukashenko, the OSCE descended into its lowest-common-denominator mode, with mealy-mouthed pronouncements of "optimism" despite the continuing crackdown on the independent print media and other elements of civil society.

President Bush, Prime Minister Tony Blair, and Chancellor Gerhard Schroeder, along with EU figures like Javier Solana and Chris Patten, need to articulate clearly that despite years of relatively muted protest, the Western democracies have not forsaken the Belarusian people and will work to help them realize their hope for prosperity and democratic rule. They should make clear that they want to visit Belarus, putting the regime on the spot. As President Bush did in China, democratic leaders should ask for live television coverage of a speech followed by a question-and-answer session. Most important, they should meet with the democrats. It should be made clear that Euro-Atlantic institutions remain open to Belarus once it attains democracy and that the democratic world would like to help bring this about.

A good step toward delegitimizing Lukashenko was taken in November 2002 when every member of the EU (except Portugal) imposed a travel ban on Lukashenko and seven of his officials over human rights violations; the EU had earlier banned travel by the dictators of Burma and Zimbabwe. This helped foil Lukashenko's attempt to attend the NATO summit in Prague that month, to which in any case he had not been invited.

Addressing Minsk's pernicious role in the international arms trade is critical. Sanctions on this front, if targeted against the regime, would be appropriate. Lukashenko's complicity in arming Saddam Hussein's forces, warlords in Africa, and other unsavory characters is gaining recognition. As with all targeted sanctions, building a broad front among democracies with simultaneous imposition is the way forward.

Democratic capitals in Europe and North America also need to present a common approach toward Russia, Lukashenko's most important patron. President Vladimir Putin has been supportive of Lukashenko but has kept his distance at some junctures. For example, on 17 June 2002 he issued a a stiff public rebuff of Lukashenko's pushing for a Soviet-style union on his own terms.[62] Lukashenko seemed to cool to the idea of union subsequently. As with many of Moscow's other relationships, the one with Lukashenko calls into doubt Putin's commitment to democracy in the neighborhood. While drawing closer to the United States after 11 September, Russia maintains a relationship with a regime in Minsk that clearly supports tyranny, and possibly terrorism, abroad. The established democracies need to make this an issue. If Russia, now with its new relationship with NATO and trying to draw closer to the EU, is going to portray itself as a democracy, its relationships should reflect this policy.

Russia's influence—potentially for the good—is strong in Belarus. Lukashenko is totally dependent on Russian oil and gas at low prices. If this power-sustaining subsidy were removed or even threatened, Lukashenko could be ousted within months if not weeks. Another huge Russian lever is television. Russian television is widely preferred by Belarusians to local television for both entertainment and news. Putin's recent crackdown on independent broadcast media has therefore hit not only Russian viewers but also ten million Belarusians as well. Western democracies should purchase air time on Russian "independent" television for Belarus-oriented programming (run by Belarusians working in Russia) and also give Russian independent journalists a chance to broadcast on Russian television once again. For Putin to go on television and call upon Belarusians to hold genuine elections and rid themselves of Lukashenko would finish the dictator.

All high-level visitors should go to sites of popular significance, especially the Kurapaty memorial site for victims of Joseph Stalin (threatened by road expansion by Lukashenko) and the Gomel region, which was most affected by the 1986 Chernobyl nuclear disaster, which remains a public health nightmare, especially for children.[63] Visitors need to be seen and heard at these sites and others of popular significance to build a rapport with the general population. Visitors should meet publicly with Zubr, Charter 97, and other major democratic opposition groups.

The embassies of the democracies must be oases of unfiltered thought and discourse, open to the general population, especially youth. As mentioned earlier, a free Internet café and reading room would be popular and useful.

Ambassadors and their staffs need to make a concerted effort to see the country, meet with locals inside and outside the capital, and give Belarusian democratic and independent figures a constant hearing and visibility. If the goal is to promote democracy, it is at least as important to meet with the Belarusians who share those values as it is to meet with officials who fear them. While some will interpret the security consciousness bolstered by the 11 September attack on the United States as a reason to stick to traditional duties and stay within compound walls, this is poison to promoting a democratic Belarus.

The democratic ambassadors need to share regularly what they are hearing from their sources and discuss what initiatives need to be undertaken on a tactical level to support the overarching democracy strategy. Internal embassy democracy working groups would need to both precede and follow such meetings to assure that all sections are on board in the effort.

The independent sector must also do its part. American programmatic organizations such as the National Democratic Institute, the International Republican Institute, the National Endowment for Democracy, and Freedom House have ongoing programs focused on Belarus. But none of these organizations has a constant on-the-ground presence. Rather, they operate from neighboring Poland or Lithuania. Without constant contact with the local situation, efforts to assist local democrats are hamstrung. There is no substitute for finding a way in, difficult though it may be.

Foreign NGOs from the democratic world can help train local democrats. Political party training is a necessity. Belarus's democrats did manage to largely unite around trade union leader Vladimir Goncharik in the September 2001 presidential election, but much potential momentum was lost through ego rivalry among opposition politicians—and the fear that a declared common candidate would be barred from the ballot. But had there been a more cohesive common democratic front, built around three or four core issues, the democrats would have been better able to confront the formidable obstacles that faced them in propagating their message.

The American Bar Association's Central and East European Law Initiative in the months before the presidential election ran what they called a "street law" program to teach Belarusians their rights under the Belarusian legal code.[64] The idea is that they could better withstand intimidation by authorities if they knew their rights. Programs like this have an added benefit of exposing further the lawlessness of the regime, which relies on raw power and intimidation as much as it does on undemocratically passed or decreed laws. The laws on the books do, in theory, guarantee rights and freedoms that citizens do not enjoy in practice.

Training in nonviolent organization and resistance techniques is of paramount importance. Belarus has a number of determined young people involved in the Zubr (Bison) youth movement, among other civic groups.[65] They have received some training by Gene Sharp and his colleagues and are conducting a remarkably skillful and courageous ongoing campaign of nonviolent resistance—one of the best in any of the remaining dictatorships. But more training and assistance are needed. In Serbia, some of the most effective actors in assisting civil society and political organization were from new democracies like Slovakia. In Belarus, Poles, Lithuanians, Serbs, and Slovaks have already played an important role.

Belarus has too long been written off as a country too poor and too close to Russia to save. But it clearly has enough dissatisfied people hungry for change to make the dictator protect his power with blatant fraud and repression. This alone should convince policymakers of the need to help these people wrest power from their illegitimate ruler. The fact that Belarus's descent into dictatorship has encountered so little resistance from the democratic world has led regimes in larger, more strategic countries such as Ukraine to conclude that they can pursue a similar path. Helping bring Belarus back from the brink would send a signal to the citizens and governments of other post-Soviet tyrannies: the democracies do not recognize democracy-free zones, and we are beginning to act.

Cuba

Fidel Castro is the world's longest-ruling dictator. Coming to power with a groundswell of popular backing in 1959 after helping overthrow rightist dictator Fulgencio Batista, Castro quickly displayed his own caudillo pretensions with repression, imprisonment, and killing of political rivals from the revolution. Castro soon aligned himself with the USSR in the raging cold war. Following the ill-fated 1961 Bay of Pigs attempt to overthrow the Castro regime and the Cuban missile crisis the following year, the relationship between Washington and Havana became one of the world's most poisonous and neuralgic. The United States imposed a total trade and investment embargo on Cuba in its effort to undercut the Castro regime, but with massive Soviet subsidies during the cold war, these had little effect. Contrary to predictions that the regime would rapidly crumble with the retrenchment of its erstwhile patron in Moscow, the Castro regime carries on more than a decade after the dissolution of the Soviet Union.

Cuba's current situation places it firmly in stage 1 of the continuum of democratization outlined in chapter 5. There are dissidents who are repressed, imprisoned, and socially marginalized. Castro has allowed some foreign investment and is attracting tourists to Cuba's beaches, gaining foreign exchange. Cuban culture remains vibrant, with international recognition of Cuban music enjoying a renaissance. Musicians are among the few who travel without much difficulty. But despite these nuances, Cuba remains a full-blooded dictatorship, one of just two remaining in an overwhelmingly free hemisphere (Haiti is the only other Not Free country in the Americas).

Clearly, the American trade and investment embargo against Cuba has not had—and will not have—its desired effect. Other investors from Europe, Canada, Mexico, and beyond have been more than happy to avail themselves of the opportunities Castro opens (and sometimes closes) in Cuba. However, these investors, with their new access, have done little to further the cause of freedom. In the meantime, the continuation of the embargo has become a matter of principle for portions of the powerful Cuban American community. Support for the embargo has become a yardstick of how anti-Castro a politician is. The understandably emotional issue has dampened rational debate on what policies can best advance the cause of establishing democracy in Cuba. It also has provided Castro with a convenient tool for appealing to Cuban nationalism, standing up to the "imperialist" giant to the north. Indeed, I have long believed that if the United States had pursued a different policy (but not just ending the embargo), Castro would long ago have been overthrown. And this ongoing policy has been a barrier to consensus with other democracies on the real problem, Castro's dictatorship.

A major revolution in thinking on Cuba by American and other democrats could help catalyze meaningful change in the country. The United States should resolutely engage the Cuban people in order to achieve the goal the vast majority of Americans, Cubans, and others hold dear: to see the Cuban people choose their own leaders without coercion. By deciding to embark on a path of democratic engagement—within self-imposed and agreed limits— the United States can build a critical mass among the democracies behind a more principled approach. For just as surely as the American policy of unilateral isolation has failed to promote change in Cuba, so will a policy of value-neutral engagement for profit's sake. By making a radical shift with a strategic democracy plan, the United States can seize the initiative for democracy in a potentially ripe situation.

The year 2002 witnessed a new level in the fight for democracy on the ground inside Cuba. In the most important single development in many years, 11,200 Cubans signed a petition calling for a referendum on the need to guarantee the rights of free expression and association, an amnesty for political prisoners, more opportunities for private business, a new electoral law, and a general election. It was presented to the National Assembly on 10 May 2002. In accordance with the Cuban Constitution, the National Assembly must consider and vote on any measure brought to it by at least 10,000 registered voters. As Oswaldo Paya, the leader of this effort, called the Varela Project, stated: "It is a myth that this regime is eternal and invincible; the people can displace it. . . . In a culture of fear, change begins when people overcome their fear. These 11,200 people are the vanguard. The fact that 11,200 people have demanded change is a change in itself."[66] By early 2003, more than thirty thousand Cubans had signed.

During his visit to Cuba, former president Jimmy Carter, in a televised address to the Cuban people on 14 May 2002, specifically mentioned the Varela Project, as did President Bush in his 20 May 2002 address on policy toward Cuba.

President Carter and President Bush vigorously supported democracy and democrats in Cuba. President Carter's public appeals for democracy were the clearest and strongest ever made by a Western statesman on Cuban soil, although he was gentle toward Castro, calling pre-1959 leader Batista a dictator but mostly praising Castro's supposed accomplishments. President Bush announced a new program of scholarships for Cubans to study in the United States and increased assistance to American NGOs helping the Cuban people.

But the stalemate on overall policy continued. President Carter called for dropping the U.S. embargo on travel and trade, without putting any sanctions on Castro in their place. President Bush strongly reaffirmed his commitment to the embargoes, offering only a vague promise to do something about them after Castro granted nearly complete freedoms to the Cuban people within a single year—by the time of the 2003 elections to the Cuban National Assembly. This standoff made it that much easier for Castro to respond to Carter, Bush, and the Varela Project by carrying out a charade of consultation with the Cuban people and claiming that 99 percent had signed a document making the present socialist system "untouchable and eternal."[67]

A bold new approach is needed. It could begin with the United States, Mexico, and other leading democracies reaching agreement on and announcing the following Contract with the Cuban People:

- Development of a democracy action program for Cuba. The initial stage would be devoted to a dialogue with Cuban democrats inside and outside and with the regime. The objective would be to reach agreement on and to commence a democracy plan and program to introduce in Cuba the full range of democratic institutions—a free press, trade unions, political parties, and full and free elections.
- Removal of Castro by other means, if necessary. If Castro refused to cooperate, the democratic community would turn to his removal from power through other means. This would involve aggressively helping democratic forces in Cuba to organize a nonviolent campaign to achieve democracy and instituting a special tribunal to bring Castro to international justice.
- An appropriately funded program of support for democratic groups and the new democratic institutions.
- An economic assistance program run through the Catholic Church and other legitimate institutions of civil society.
- The removal of all trade and investment restrictions by the United States, and in their place a set of political and economic sanctions directed at Castro and his pillars of support.

The way forward will have to start at the presidential level, for there is a lot of convincing to do, beginning, of course, with President Bush himself. A majority of the Congress and of the American public favors lifting the travel and trade sanctions, but support needs to be built for a package of smart sanctions and programs to engage Cubans, oust Castro, and institute democracy. Equally, unless those who have fought most ardently to maintain the embargo and such accessories as the extraterritorial Helms-Burton law are present at the creation and convinced of the administration's and Congress's commitment to adhere to the goal of promoting a democratic future for Cuba in the near term, there will be no chance for a meaningful policy shift. With early, open, and honest dialogue about lifting the embargo as part of a package that includes new democracy-promoting initiatives and sanctions, a meeting of minds is not only possible but likely. Once the administration, Congress, and civic leaders have consulted sufficiently to build critical mass behind the new approach, the president, along with congressional leaders, should work with Mexico and other key democracies in this hemisphere and beyond within the Community of Democracies to bring as many on board as possible.

As a corollary to allowing U.S. corporations and individuals to enter the Cuban market, all those entering should be prevailed upon to sign on to a code of conduct. The code of conduct would publicly commit firms and individuals to adhere to internationally recognized labor standards, including the right to organize independent trade unions, and to agree to the use of facilities after hours as satellite "freedom houses." For far too long, Castro has successfully split the democracies. Many democracies—and their publics—have averted their eyes from Castro's brutal rule. As the Contract with the Cuban People is internationalized, the president should encourage countries that are home to firms with significant investment in Cuba to sign similar codes of conduct.

Most important, the international contract should enumerate what the democracies will do to help Cubans both to make their democratic breakthrough and thereafter. This "democracy dividend" needs to include support from international financial institutions, grants, and other forms of economic assistance. Major donors should announce a provisional quick-start escrow account to help consolidate a transition. In addition, potential foreign investors should make clear their intent to invest in Cuba once the country makes its turn. Only Castro and his lawless rule stand between them and a prosperous Cuba.

Critically, the contract must commit the Community of Democracies, and especially the Organization of American States, to help those fighting for democracy in Cuba *now*. Latin American democracies need to play a prominent role. Most have had to drive out their own caudillos of various stripes over the past two decades and can offer valuable lessons on strategy and tactics. But they will need to be persuaded that the United States is serious about a more nuanced policy; in 2003, the Latin American caucus within the United Nations again elected Castro's Cuba to a seat on the UN Human Rights Commission. Their being at least as vocal as the United States on a common new approach would have a powerful impact.

Within Cuba, democratic embassies need to actively pursue a strategy of engagement with the people. The new approach demands visibility and audacity to show the Cubans that this is a quantum leap to helping them achieve democracy. Dispelling the oft repeated official shibboleth that the Cuban American community is waiting to purchase the country from underneath them and undo the few popular advances of the past forty years—in education and health care—is crucial.

A Cuban American democratic activist should be appointed as the next head of the massive U.S. interests section in Havana. The section now has about fifty Americans and over a hundred Cubans. Under the last two heads of section, it has finally begun to be more active and open, fitting the recommended new policy. The current head, James Cason, "has opened his offices and his home to Castro's . . . opponents. He has attended dissidents' meetings across the country, hailing them as Cuba's future leaders. A rattled Mr. Castro called Mr. Cason a 'bully with diplomatic immunity.'"[68] His predecessor, Vicki Huddleston, distributed radios to make it easier for Cubans to listen to U.S.-funded Radio Marti.[69] As in other dictatorships, coordination among democratic ambassadors is imperative. Latin Americans and Europeans, who have strong presence or standing in Havana, will have access that others will not. The democratic embassies need a common strategy playing to their comparative advantages. Assisting Cuba's repressed dissidents and democracy activists requires aid in strategy, planning, and protection. Latin American and European democracy activists must play leading roles in this effort as diplomats, tourists, teachers, and businesspeople.

All democratic embassies need open and vibrant cultural sections, complete with a free Internet café and safe room for meetings. *Casa America,* as this section should be called, needs analogues in all democratic embassies. When necessary, embassies need to have an open-door policy to protect those pursued by the secret police. News tickers of the sort placed above the Berlin Wall should be prominently mounted on embassy grounds and the premises of foreign firms. While Castro's state apparatus is pervasive, it should be stretched as thin as possible. Cracks, already evident, will begin to widen.

There is an urgent need to train young Cubans in nonviolent organization and confrontation techniques. This can be accomplished both outside and inside Cuba. Exit visas are more easily had for academic study in Latin America, so Latin American countries should, in conjunction with the Community of Democracies, create programs for this purpose. Cultural, academic, and professional exchanges give expanded access to Cuban society and potential new leaders and should be significantly increased. The isolation wrought by the Castro dictatorship, while never as complete as North Korea's, has not only set the country apart from its natural economic partners but has also put a damper on Cuba's cultural and social interchange with the world. Poking holes in this wall can only help accelerate Cuba's democratization.

The Varela Project and the willingness of more than thirty thousand Cubans to take the risk of signing shows the way forward. Just think what would have happened had millions of Cubans signed it instead of fearfully going along with Castro's subsequent charade. Vladimiro Roca, a dissident released from prison in May 2002 after serving nearly five years in prison for criticizing the Castro regime, said people are starting to come to his door: "Some come ashamed of having signed the other [Castro's petition]. They are asking about Varela and want to sign it. Little by little people have less fear of speaking out against the government."[70] This same easing of fear, so palpable to those of us living in eastern Europe in the late 1980s, was the beginning of the end for other communist regimes. On International Human Rights Day, 10 December 2002, Martha Beatriz Roque courageously hosted seventy democrats in her Havana home and reported similar meetings in all fourteen provinces. She heads the Assembly to Promote Civil Society, an umbrella organization of three hundred small groups preparing for a transition to democracy in a post-Castro Cuba.[71] Once the cement of fear begins to crack, a dictator's days are numbered.

Fissures in the security services, the Communist Party, and the military need to be exploited. All dictatorships in their terminal phases see senior-level defections, either overt or through inaction at critical moments. Since the end of the cold war, Castro has purged senior officers in the army, especially those who commanded expeditionary forces in Africa.[72] Resentment in the ranks certainly exists. Ensuring that the army will not use arms against the people when the regime begins to fall is of paramount importance. The army, or elements thereof, may be forced to counterbalance and even act against more rabid forces of the militia or secret police. Inroads into the security forces by the democracies and pro-democracy Cubans can also help identify plans to seize power to prevent democracy from succeeding Castro. In any event, it is doubtful such a measure could hold for long, given the long-standing thirst for freedom of the Cuban people.

As with Iraq and some other closed societies, division among democracies on the proper terms of engagement has been a trump card in the otherwise weak hand of the Cuban dictator. By making a principled and strategic decision to work to promote regime change in Cuba through engagement with its people and increased pressure on the dictator himself, the United States and other democracies and democrats can seize the momentum and catalyze a completely new—and certainly successful—approach to end Castro's record-long despotism.

Epilogue and Action Agenda

The only thing necessary for the triumph of evil is for good men to stand by and do nothing.

—Edmund Burke

We have talked here of how humanity might rid itself of the last few dozen dictators still in power by the year 2025. Indeed, there seems no positive alternative to their removal. History almost guarantees that any dictators left standing will render this century even bloodier than the last, for dictatorships, as we have seen, are naturally destructive; murder, intimidation, and oppression are their business. They are likewise destructive of economic success. While tyrants raise grand palaces in orgies of self-praise, their people live in poverty, able to watch—but unable to touch—the prosperity that flows naturally from peace and freedom.

It is our task to transform the general wish for full democracy into the conviction that it can be achieved within a reasonable time; 2025 is where we set the bar. This means that our concepts of international power must now discover a political architecture that fosters democracy at every level and brands dictators as criminals and pariahs.

Closed societies must be opened to the light of democratizing possibilities, which means that they must be engaged and their democrats nurtured. Without abolishing diplomatic conventions, the embassies of democratic nations must become freedom houses and their ambassadors, freedom fighters. Dictators must be seen and treated as individuals, not manifestations of a regime or culture. Thus armed, humanity can formulate more particular plans that will bring the tyrants down, one by one.

In preparing this blueprint for achieving full democracy by 2025, I have drawn heavily on my experience as a diplomat and entrepreneur inside dictatorships and in areas where democracy has newly taken root. But one of the chief guiding lessons of my life was learned much earlier.

When I was ten, my family lived in Alexandria, Virginia, an old Potomac River port across from Washington, D.C. My father was then a U.S. Navy captain assigned to the Joint Chiefs of Staff at the Pentagon. I was learning the ways of the business world on a newspaper route, delivering copies of the *Alexandria Gazette* door-to-door. This was in the early 1950s, when Alexandria was still a southern town that had seen better days; its renaissance as an affluent suburb still lay in the future. Not surprisingly, many of my customers were inclined to delay payment for their subscription, sometimes for months, sometimes with threats of violence to the nagging paperboy. The *Gazette*, however, wanted payment for the papers I received from them, putting me in a financial hole that deepened, week by week. In desperation, I turned to my father for advice. As one would expect, this took the form of action.

Next time I went collecting, I had a companion: a large, stern fellow in the winter blues of a U.S. naval officer, with a captain's four gold stripes on the sleeves and a chest covered with ribbons. As I went from one delinquent customer to another, my father stayed at my side. He never said a word but looked on with the cold visage of the submariner he was. Everyone we visited was suddenly able to pay.

On that winter day in Alexandria, long before I marched for civil rights or for democracy in communist Hungary or for China's Falun Gong, I learned what could be achieved if the powerful and free stood beside the disenfranchised and oppressed. Years later, Polish workers in Gdansk gave us a word for it: solidarity.

The term—the idea of standing together—has taken on a life of its own. Cuban democrat Oswaldo Paya received an exit visa from the Castro government not because of some relaxation of the regime's iron grip upon its people but because Paya had been awarded the European Parliament's Andrei Sakharov Prize in 2002 and had to claim it in Europe. "In the past few weeks," wrote *Washington Post* columnist Jackson Diehl, "he has met with European prime ministers, the pope and Secretary of State Powell. They all have asked what they can do to help. 'Solidarity' is Paya's simple answer."[1]

In January 2003, a Chinese court sentenced Wang Bingzhang to life imprisonment for allegedly leading a terrorist group; his actual crime: promoting free trade unions and multiparty democracy in China. His American colleagues acted quickly to focus the spotlight of international attention on this appalling miscarriage of Chinese justice.[2] With any luck, such solidarity will win his release.

Although it has become fashionable to give NATO bombers no credit for the collapse of the cruel Milosevic regime, few actions carry more weight than the willingness to go to war on behalf of another nation's people. Often the mere presence of a mature and powerful player standing shoulder to shoulder with thwarted aspirants to freedom is enough to tip the scales toward democracy. Sometimes, as I learned half a century ago, you need to bring a grown-up, and it helps if that grown-up is a navy captain.

But such solidarity must be active and also based on an understanding that, most often, local democrats have gained freedom through the application of the full range of nonviolent force—organization underground and eventual taking of the streets and power. Our support for these nonviolent movements and campaigns is key to success.

Indeed, it was just this combination of military strength and our shared willingness to stand up for certain inalienable rights and become actively involved on the side of local democrats that saw the world through the cold war and opened the way to democracy in central and eastern Europe. The history of democracy is a history of such solidarity between the mighty and the weak, the developed and the developing, the rich and the poor. Now that evolutionary process demands another quantum step: a bold, new moral vision based on the proposition that dictatorships have run their course and that full democracy is at hand. Throughout the cold war we had such a common and simple understanding of the main danger and opportunity. Now the goal of ousting those who still threaten our security and building a universally democratic world can provide renewed energy and unity.

With such unity, nothing can stop the democracies and democrats. One can already read a good deal of prophetic handwriting on the crumbling walls of tyranny. In 2002 alone, according to Freedom House findings, gains for democracy were recorded in twenty-nine countries, nearly three times the number of nations in which freedom suffered setbacks. Even Kenya's immovable dictator Daniel arap Moi was finally put out to pasture. And Saddam Hussein has been ousted thanks to the United States and its coalition of partners.

In Saudi Arabia, one of the nine most repressive dictatorships in the world, 104 Saudi business leaders, professors, and intellectuals signed "A Vision for the Present and Future of the Country" in January 2003. It called for a Saudi parliament, free elections, a fairer distribution of wealth, a crackdown on corruption, and more rights for women. Crown Prince Abdullah met with the signers.[3]

Nor do the dictatorships have any economic wind behind them. In 2002, the total gross domestic product of the Free countries stood at $26.8 trillion, as against only $1.7 trillion for the Not Free countries.

Thus the time is right for the free people of the world to help the oppressed find democracy. What steps can we take? This book lays out a road map. It attempts to show how to oust the remaining dictators. We summarize this action agenda here.

Action Agenda

The twenty-first century presents us with two possible scenarios: with and without dictators. We need to:

√ Increase understanding that dictators could make the twenty-first century even bloodier than they made the twentieth century.
√ Dramatize the benefits for peace, prosperity, and freedom of a world without dictators.

We must achieve a conceptual breakthrough—a conviction that all dictators can be ousted within one more generation.

√ Educate the entire world about the huge number of dictators ousted over the last generation and the methods used.
√ Redefine national security/power as spread of democracy and alliances among democracies.
√ Set goal of ousting all dictators by 2025.

A new architecture of international power should be built to achieve this goal.

√ The Community of Democracies and NATO need to be transformed into a global democratic alliance, with on-call forces, regional programs, and caucuses within existing international organizations.
√ Dictatorship must be declared a crime against humanity and remaining dictators prosecuted before international tribunals.
√ Nongovernmental democrats inside dictatorships must be organized and recognized as the legitimate voice of their peoples.

Opening up, not walling off, closed societies is a key to success.

√ New policy and budget priority should be given to opening and dictator-ousting programs.

√ The classic opening programs should be refocused and new programs created, for example an independent television and radio fund.
√ Private foundations and businesses need a much bolder focus on democracy promotion.

In a major innovation, we should institute democracy development plans and programs for each of the remaining dictatorships. The plans should include:

√ Ensuring they complete three stages of democratic growth by an agreed date.
√ Creating an autonomous International Dictatorship-to-Democracy Center under the Community of Democracy and United Nations sponsorship to conduct these programs.
√ Making indigenous democrats central players through roundtables and other devices.

A democracy-centered diplomacy transforms its embassies into freedom houses and its ambassadors into freedom fighters by

√ Visibly supporting the democrats—meetings with them, symbolic events, marches, campaign buttons, electronic billboards.
√ Holding regular fireside chats with each subject people via radio, television, Internet by ambassadors, presidents/prime ministers/parliamentarians.
√ Pursuing dialogue with the dictator and regime about transition and exit.

While force is sometimes needed, we must enhance understanding of the nature and power of nonviolent conflict in ousting dictators.

√ The track record is impressive; the skills can be taught.
√ Teach the strategy and tactics for a two-stage nonviolent campaign to oust a dictator.
√ Emphasize the critical role for outsiders to play.

It is important to focus attention on each of the Last Forty-five as an individual dictator; dictators should not be allowed to hide behind a regime or culture or country.

√ Do an annual report on each of the Least Wanted and publicize widely, in key languages.
√ Develop and keep updated a criminal indictment for each.

Develop a comprehensive action plan for every one of the regions and countries still suffering from dictators combining all of the elements recommended in this book.

√ Recognize that highest priorities should be given to the largest remaining problems: the Greater Middle East and China.
√ Work with varying coalitions of interested democratic nations and democrats.
√ Focus sanctions on the dictators, not the peoples.

The Community of Democracies must adopt this common goal: All Dictators Out by 2025. It must then use its majority within the United Nations to have this goal and program adopted as a matter of binding international policy and law. Ousting dictators must be brought from the fringes to the center of national-security and foreign policy. Progress over the last generation is encouraging. Now let us decide to finish the job.

"I must tell you that initially I thought getting rid of all the world's dictators was a quixotic notion that had as much chance of succeeding as me flapping my wings and flying," longtime *Washington Post* correspondent Stuart Auerbach wrote to me. "After reading [this] book, however, I realized that stating that aim and setting a program to achieve it are important—even if success desn't come as quickly as we would like." I hope you agree.

It is not enough to be outraged by the deaths of two million North Koreans, starved by a dictator's thirst for opulence and eternal power; the dictator must be forced to step down. We cannot accept as legitimate a dictator who ordered the deaths of thousands whose only "crime" was practicing China's oldest form of spiritual and physical exercise. We cannot stand idly by as dictators develop weapons of mass destruction and share them with other dictators, and fuel and support terrorism—which they will do for as long as they remain in power. It is time that these dangerous political relics went extinct. We must finally say enough is enough—and mean it. We must join together the world's democracies and democrats to oust the last dictators and build universal democracy.

Afterword

If the world's democracies make liberty the priority of their policy, the days of the dictators are numbered . . . The winds of freedom that swept across the Black Sea (from Georgia) to Ukraine now rush across the Central Asian steppes and stir the cedars of Lebanon.

—President Mikheil Saakashvili
Republic of Georgia
May 2005

The world is entranced with rose, orange, tulip, and cedar revolutions. Free elections are held in Afghanistan, Iraq, Palestine, and Lebanon. People's power moves from an academic subject to the front pages of the world's newspapers. President George W. Bush states "We are determined to seek and support the growth of democratic movements and institutions in every nation and culture, with the ultimate goal of ending tyranny in our world." United Nations Secretary General Kofi Annan proposes abolishing the discredited UN Commission on Human Rights and creating a Human Rights Council made up solely of nations committed to human rights. The Action Agenda of this book becomes the centerpiece of legislation sponsored by the leading promoters of democracy in the United States Congress, and some of its individual proposals already are becoming reality.

The period since I wrote this book also has witnessed some negative developments. Russia passed back across the line from Partly Free to Not Free nations, for the first time in over a decade. Dictators continued to wreak havoc on their own people, their neighbors, and the world. Robert Mugabe stole yet another election and drove Zimbabweans into even greater hunger and want. North Korea's Kim Jong Il and Iran's Supreme Leader

Seyyid Ali Khamenei brought their nuclear ambitions to the forefront of threats to international security. China's newest dictator Hu Jintao continued the repressive policies of his predecessors and threatened to use force against Taiwan. The Real Axis of Evil, the de facto alliance among these dozens of dictators, has been dramatically illustrated by revelations of nuclear weapons and launch vehicle designs passing from China and North Korea to Pakistan and on to Libya and Iran—all ruled by tyrants. As Nicholas Kristof reported in the *Washington Post* May 17, 2005, "Chinese intellectuals were horrified when Mr. Hu issued an internal statement saying that while North Korea had made economic mistakes, it had the right ideas politically." Dictators approve of one another's use of force to stay in power, and they remain the central threat to international peace, justice, and freedom.

But a net assessment comparing the world in 2003 and 2005 must conclude that the forces of freedom are growing stronger. In its most recent annual report, Freedom House notes that 26 countries registered gains and eleven showed setbacks in 2004. Liberia, in 2003 one of the world's most repressive nations and gravest causes of regional slaughter and suffering, crossed the line from Not Free to Partly Free with the ouster of Charles Taylor. Breakthroughs towards democracy in certain former Soviet and Middle Eastern nations raised questions of whether this "contagion" could spread throughout these regions and even to Asia and Africa.

From Georgia in 2003, to Ukraine a year later, to Kyrgyzstan and Lebanon in 2005, people power spread and triumphed. The *New York Times* stated on March 25, 2005, "What is most surprising is how quickly those governments fell when faced by protesters asserting the rights they had been promised . . . for opposition leaders and even for some of those (still) in power in other republics, the events . . . have come like a contagion, spreading in fast and unpredictable ways." As I noted earlier in this book, "surprise" universally describes the reaction of the press, diplomats, and academics to the now many dozens of cases of nonviolent movements' removal of dictators. It remains quite extraordinary to me how little learning there has been from earlier cases of "contagion." Latin America, Africa, Europe, and Asia all have had concentrated bursts of progress towards democracy.

Let us look briefly at the four remaining areas of the world (former Soviet Union, Middle East, Asia, and Africa) where there are still a significant number of dictators and therefore a substantial democracy deficit and ask whether events and trends over the past two years have made "contagion" and peaceful regime change more or less likely.

In Central and Eastern Europe and the former Soviet Union, twelve countries are Free, seven are Partly Free, and eight are Not Free. In seven of these last eight dictatorships there is some semblance of civil society, some brave individuals and groups which could form the sort of broadly-based coalition which typically is required for a people power movement to succeed. Only Turkmenistan's Great Leader has managed to stamp out any semblance of independent civil society, and even there I am confident just beneath the surface lie people of vision and courage who eventually will come together. The strident reaction of this region's last dictators to the events in Georgia, Ukraine, and Kyrgyzstan is one indication of how seriously they assess the potential for a people power movement in their own countries. Alexander Lukashenko in Belarus faces a persistent internal resistance with growing international recognition and support. Russia's Valdimir Putin faces declining popularity and the beginnings of serious opponents going into Presidential elections in 2008, when he is barred by law from running in but undoubtedly will try to find a way to remain in power. The world's growing willingness to show support for Russians who are struggling against Putin's repression was illustrated on May 10, 2005 when President Bush met in Moscow with eighteen representatives of media and advocacy groups.

A widespread view holds that this region's remaining dictators have learned the lesson that you must use force or be swept aside, and that therefore they will use force and will remain in power. The problem with this argument is that virtually all of those who have been swept aside wanted to use force but were prevented from doing so by divisions within their own security services and/or these services ultimate unwillingness to shoot large numbers of unarmed students, women, even children peacefully demonstrating for a better future for their nation. In a striking investigative piece of journalism of January 17, 2005 entitled "How Top Spies in Ukraine Changed the Nation's Path," the *New York Times* reported that the SBU (the Ukrainian equivalent of the KGB) prevented the Interior Ministry's forces from implementing orders they had received from top leadership to move against the peaceful demonstrators.

In Georgia, President Eduard Shevardnadze's orders to the police to use force also were ignored. And in Lebanon, as the Associated Press reported on February 28, 2005, "throughout the day protesters handed out red roses to soldiers and police . . . Some soldiers and police even sympathized with the protesters and were seen advising newcomers on how to evade the cordon." The peaceful and successful outcomes in Georgia, Ukraine, Lebanon, and elsewhere in part were the result of training/experience sharing by Serbs, Croats, Romanians, Slovaks, and others in how to "control the temperature" of protesting crowds and establish connections with the militia and other security forces. By contrast, when demonstrators in Uzbekistan in May 2005 used force against the authorities, the police opened fire, killed many and the protest was quashed.

In the greater Middle East, the political context and discourse are substantially different than one to two years ago. Along with a continuing focus on the Palestine-Israeli issue and the violence in Iraq, the other central focus has become bringing democracy to these universally politically retarded states. The United Nations-sponsored third Arab Human Development Report released on April 5, 2005 and written by thirty nine Arab scholars and intellectuals, states that "there is a near-complete consensus that there is a serious failing in the Arab world and that this is located in the political sphere . . . There is a rational and understandable thirst among Arabs to be rid of despots and to enjoy democratic governance."

Dramatic events have burst forth in every corner of the Arab world. In addition to the elections cited above in four countries, even the Saudi monarchy has been forced to allow municipal elections and President Hosni Mubarak to allow multicandidate presidential elections. While both reforms are limited, Saudis and Egyptians are pushing for bigger reforms. For example, the "enough" movement in Egypt, joined by such prestigious groups as the country's young actors, is calling on Mubarak not to run again and to allow truly free and fair elections. Freedom House reported that "In 2004 some potentially positive steps forward took place in the Middle East and North Africa, especially in the areas of women's rights and increased civic activism." Despite orders from the Syrian-controlled government banning demonstrations, Muslim and Christian Lebanese joined together and occupied Beirut's Martyrs Square for weeks, tore down the huge billboards with photos of Syrian dictator/foreign occupier Bashar al-Assad and pushed his occupying forces out of the country. In Syria itself the winds of change are blowing, al-Assad has been forced to legalize multiple political parties and pressures for real democracy are growing.

As President Bush noted on March 9, 2005, "The chances of democratic progress in the broader Middle East have seemed frozen in place for decades. Yet, at last, clearly and suddenly, the thaw has begun."

Whatever an individual's personal beliefs and aspirations, they will be better protected and fostered within a system in which the government is controlled by the people and not the other way around. A growing number of Muslims are recognizing that the greatest oppression of their religion occurs in dictatorships. Uighurs in Communist China, Chechens in Putin's Russia, Shiites in absolutist monarchial Saudi Arabia, Uzbeks in Karimov's despotism all are oppressed, even slaughtered. Those who truly care about Islam should be the strongest promoters of a democratic world. Muslims living in democracies, which over half of them do, are free to practice their faith. Christians,

Buddhists, Falun Gong, Jews, and many other faiths and spiritual practices are oppressed in these very same dictatorships, while they too flourish in democracies.

In Asia, the past two years also have witnessed progress towards the preconditions for breakthroughs to freedom, though it is sometimes less visible on the surface. In perhaps the most "frozen" country of all, North Korea, cracks in the ice have begun to appear. Kim Jong Il's devastatingly failed economic policy has forced him to begin a modicum of market reform. High level defections and refugee flows persist. Cell phones and radios capable of receiving and communicating with the outside world are increasing. Vietnam and the other dictatorships of Southeast Asia also are opening up—cautiously but clearly.

Dramatic changes in Chinese society continue at an accelerating pace. Outrage over growing corruption has burst into growing numbers of spontaneous protests by workers, farmers and others across the country—literally thousands in 2004. As more Chinese travel and see democratic societies first hand, and information spreads internally despite massive censorship, resentment at the Communist Party's monopoly on power also spreads. The transfer of the dictator's mantle from Jiang Zemin to Hu Jintao, without a competitive fair and free election, to date has not resulted in any change in repression. Journalists, writers, students, religious practitioners—the elite of China's youth, the people's consciences—continue to be jailed and tortured in large numbers. The people of Hong Kong are even denied by Beijing the right to vote for their own mayor. Thus, the contrast and tension between a rapidly modernizing, educated, information-hungry twenty first century society and an Internet controlling, SARS-concealing, fearful-of-change, corrupt and corrupting dictatorship grows starker and less unsustainable over time. The base and the super-structure are diverging.

As Freedom House reported, sub-Saharan Africa has eleven Free countries, twenty one Partly Free, and sixteen Not Free. In 2004, Liberia moved from Not Free to Partly Free as a result of greater political freedom that developed through the establishment of a broad-based, transitional government. Zimbabwe's political rights declined further due to increased government repression of the political opposition, and Cote d'Ivoire's civil liberties declined because of an upsurge in violence emanating from an unresolved civil conflict.

In a struggle still unresolved as of this writing, following the death of Africa's longest-ruling dictator, Togo's Gnassingbe Eyadema on February 5, 2005, his son supported by the army staged yet another hereditary dictator transition/coup. In one of the most encouraging developments of this period, neighboring governments reacted strongly and insisted upon elections. Unfortunately this example of solidarity by neighboring African democracies is the exception. Mugabe continues to enjoy excessive tolerance from South Africa's Thabo Mbeki and other regional leaders. At the same time there is a growing consensus among Africans, aid donors and agencies that there is a direct relationship between good governance, importantly including democratically elected governments and functioning systems of checks and balances, and economic development.

Across all regions, the tolerance for dictators narrowed over the past two years. As Secretary of State Condoleezza Rice stated during the Third Ministerial Conference of the Community of Democracies in Santiago, Chile April 28–30, 2005, "Tyranny is a crime of man, not a fact of nature. Our goal must always be the elimination of tyranny in our world." And in his second Inaugural Address President Bush stated "Those who deny freedom to others deserve it not for themselves . . . and cannot long retain it." In concept and in practice, the political landscape is moving towards acceptance of a central recommendation in my book—that there is a "crime of dictatorship" within the overall construct of crimes against humanity. This specific crime is the violation of civil and political rights guaranteed under the domestic laws and constitutions of even not-free countries and the international conventions to which they have adhered. On these grounds alone its practitioners should be considered criminals, evidence gathered, trials held and justice delivered. A group of American lawyers and jurists is developing the "crime of dictatorship" in greater detail, including how it might be introduced into international law and practice. Of course dictators typically also commit other crimes—corruption, murder, and not infrequently war crimes.

Over the past two years Charles Taylor of Liberia has been indicted by a UN mandated court and an Interpol warrant has been issued for his arrest. On July 23, 2004, President Bush froze the assets of Taylor, his family and top aids, accusing them of undermining "Liberia's transition to democracy and the orderly development of its political, administrative, and economic institutions." Iraq's Saddam Hussein also is facing trial for his many crimes. The trial of Slobodan Milosevic continues in The Hague. The Chilean courts continue their efforts to bring Augusto Pinochet to justice, and his former American bankers the Allbrittons and Riggs have been compelled to compensate some of his victims. The not-yet-passed ADVANCE Democracy Act of 2005, which contains many of this book's Action Agenda recommendations, provides for the first systematic collection of information by the U.S. government about the crimes of dictators.

Some key pillars of the infrastructure for the promotion of democracy have progressed over this period as well. The United Nations Democracy Fund, designed to help countries establish or strengthen democracy, which was proposed by President Bush in September 2004, has been endorsed by Secretary General Kofi Annan and is supported by a growing number of democratic states. The Community of Democracies proposed caucus of democracies began to function under Chile's leadership within the UN system. The Ministerial meeting of the Community of Democracies endorsed Hungary's proposed Democracy Transition Center. And as noted previously, Secretary General Annan has proposed replacing the discredited UN Commission on Human Rights with a new Human Rights Council whose members would pledge to abide by the highest human rights standards.

We have seen numerous recent examples where domestic and international election observers and trainers in the strategy and tactics of nonviolent regime change have made a central difference in bringing democracy. In 2004 alone, the United Nations supported elections in more than twenty countries, including Afghanistan, Palestine, Iraq, and Burundi. Student groups like Pora, which played a critical leadership role in bringing freedom out of election fraud in Ukraine, were trained by young Serbs, Georgians, and others, and in turn have committed themselves to training their counterparts in Belarus, Russia, and Central Asia. They were taught and are teaching techniques for organizing, conducting street theater, poking fun at leaders to reduce fear of them among the general population, and establishing connections with the security services.

Diplomats also have begun to play a more forthright role. Secretary Rice's public decision to postpone a visit to Egypt until a candidate for the Presidency was released from prison sent a strong message that the United States is not prepared to continue to support the Middle East's dictators. In Kiev, during the critical moments of the orange revolution, young French and Japanese diplomats played key roles in protecting the protesters. French and American diplomacy joined together to push for the emergence of an independent and democratic Lebanon.

The world's democracies outnumber the dictatorships by some 120 to 45, and the world's democrats outnumber the declining species of just 45 despots by over six billion people. Working together, there is nothing that can stop the world's democracies and democrats from achieving universal freedom. The Community of Democracies Ministers stated on April 30, 2005, "We believe that increasing the number of democratic nations and supporting the development and strengthening of emerging democracies helps to build a safer world in which individuals, women and men equally, can live freely and in an environment of peace, stability and well-being characterized by respect for the rule of law . . . all members States of the UN have pledged to strengthen their capacity to implement the principles and practices of democracy."

This book opens with a dedication "To all those with the vision and courage to oust their oppressors." Over the past two years, men and women of courage and vision have appeared in every one of the remaining dictatorships. It is our task to support them as they insist that national and international commitments to democracy matter.

Notes

Introduction

1. Alessandra Stanley, "Pope Finds a Hard Road," *New York Times*, 25 June 2001.

Chapter 1

1. Hubert Vedrine, "France Criticizes 'Simplistic' US Policy," *BBC News*, 7 February 2002, http://news.bbc.co.uk/hi/english/world/europe/newsid_1805000/1805341.stm.

2. Michael Rubin, "Sulaymaniyah Dispatch: Food Fight," *New Republic*, 18 June 2001, www.tnr.com/061801/rubin061801.html.

3. Probably some 2 million to 3 million civilians were killed in the North and South, and many more were turned into refugees. There were 33,629 U.S. battle deaths, plus 20,617 from other causes, and an estimated 400,000 South Korean military fatalities. Possibly 1 million to 2 million communist troops perished. All together the Korean War death range is 3.4 million–5.4 million. See Rosemary Foot, *A Substitute for Victory: The Politics of Peacemaking at the Korean Armistice Talks* (Ithaca, N.Y.: Cornell University Press, 1990).

4. International Institute for Strategic Studies, *The Military Balance, 2000–2001* (Oxford: Oxford University Press, 2000).

5. "The Iran/Iraq war resulted in an estimated 400,000 deaths (roughly 1/4 Iraqi and 3/4 Iranian), and around 750,000 people were injured." "Iraq: A History of Conflict," from "Road to the Brink," *BBC News*, 12 November 1997, http://news6.thdo.bbc.co.uk/hi/english/events/crisis_in_the_gulf/road_to_the_brink/newsid_29000/29099.stm.

6. "The One-China Plot Thickens in Pyongyang," Stratfor.com, 7 March 2000.

7. "Containment Plan Is Resisted in Asia," *Washington Post*, 31 December 2002.

8. "China Arrests Noted Businesswoman in Crackdown in Muslim Region," *Wall Street Journal*, 18 August 1999.

9. U.S. Department of State, *Patterns of Global Terrorism, 2001: Overview of State-Sponsored Terrorism*, 2001, www.state.gov/s/ct/rls/pgtrpt/2001/html/ 10249.htm. There is evidence of China's close arms-trade relationships with these countries. For example, support for the war in southern Sudan: "Oil Linked to Sudan Abuses," *BBC News*, 15 March 2001. Air-defense construction in Iraq: "Iraq Denies China Air Defense Link," *BBC News*, 21 February 2001. See also "Analysis: Capabilities of US 'Rogue States,'" *BBC News*, 15 May 2002, http://news.bbc.co.uk/hi/english/world/americas/newsid_1988000/ 1988810.stm; "Iran 'Pursuing Nuclear Programme," *BBC News*, 8 September 2001, http://news.bbc.co.uk/hi/english/world/middle_east/newsid_1531000/ 1531953.stm.

10. "Iraq Voices Readiness to Develop Ties with China," *People's Daily*, 26 June 2000. *People's Daily* is unwittingly a rich source of documentation on dictators' mutual support, including wide coverage of dictator cooperation not directly involving China. The Communist Party mouthpiece's extensive coverage of other dictators cooperating in thumbing their noses at world democracies is itself another example of Beijing's consistent support of the dictators' club. Its English-language internet address is http://english.peopledaily.com. cn.

11. "Iran Pursuing Nuclear Programme," *BBC News*, 8 September 2001, http://news.bbc.co.uk/hi/english/world/middle_east/newsid_1531000/153195 3.stm.

12. "Jiang Urges Unity in Terrorism Fight," *South China Morning Post*, 15 September 2001.

13. American Foreign Policy Council, *China Reform Monitor*, 21 October 2001.

14. American Foreign Policy Council, *China Reform Monitor*, 21 October 2001.

15. "Lukashenko Pleased at China's Win at UN Human Rights Session," *People's Daily*, 22 April 2001.

16. "Chinese President Holds Talks with Belarussian President," *People's Daily*, 20 July 2001.

17. "Chinese President Holds Talks with Belarussian President."

18. "China Donates Agricultural Equipment to Zimbabwe," *People's Daily*, 10 April 2001.

19. "Zimbabwe Sticks to One China Policy," *People's Daily*, 6 July 2001, and "Chinese, Zimbabwean Parliament Leaders Meet in Beijing," *People's Daily*, 23 October 2001.

20. "Li Peng Condemns Hegemony," *People's Daily*, 14 June 2000.

21. "Iraq, Yugoslavia to Establish Strategic Relations," *People's Daily*, 27 July 2000.

22. "Khamenei, Castro Meet, Reject US Hegemony," *People's Daily*, 10 May 2001.

23. "Khamenei, Castro Meet."

24. Douglas Farah, "An 'Axis' Connected to Gaddafi: Leaders Trained in Libya Have Used War to Safeguard Wealth," *Washington Post*, 2 November 2001.

25. Douglas Farah, "Al Qaeda Cash Tied to Diamond Trade: Sale of Gems From Sierra Leone Rebels Raised Millions, Sources Say," *Washington Post*, 2 November 2001

26. Farah, "Al Qaeda."

27. "Zimbabwe's Resource Colonialism in the DRC," Global Witness, 26 August 2001, www.oneworld.org/globalwitness.

28. "How Loyal is Zimbabwe's Army?" *BBC News*, 10 January 2002, http://news.bbc.co.uk/hi/english/world/africa/newsid_1754000/1754063.stm.

29. A book remains to be written on the bizarre world of Pyongyang's engagement with—usually the worst of—Africa. North Korean forces trained the Zimbabwean Fifth Brigade, implicated in atrocities against Zimbabwe's Ndbele people in the early 1980s. In addition, North Koreans have trained thousands of military and internal security personnel throughout the continent. A few articles give a flavor of this underreported phenomenon. Aidan Foster-Carter in his article "Pyongyang Watch: Out of Africa," in *Asia Times Online*, 9 June 2001, www.aitimes.com/koreas/CF09Dg01.html reported that the North Korean regime's diplomats have built up a legendary reputation for criminality, supposedly because each diplomatic mission has to self-finance. Danna Herman in the *Christian Science Monitor* reported on 2 July 2001 that North Korean diplomats have been among the most egregious traders in ivory (www.save-the-elephants.org/Elephant%20News%20items/former_straydogs_join_fight_to.htm).

30. Stjepan Mesic, "The Road to War," in *The War in Croatia and Bosnia-Herzegovina, 1991–1995*, ed. Branka Magas and Ivo Zanic (London: Frank Cass, 2001), 11–12. The author of this article is now the democratically elected president of Croatia.

31. Amartya Sen, *The Political Economy of Hunger* (Oxford: Clarendon Press, 1990).

32. John Norton Moore, "Beyond the Democratic Peace" (unpublished paper, 2001). Also John Norton Moore, "Toward a New Paradigm," *37 Virginia Journal of International Law 814* (1997).

33. James Gwartney and Robert Lawson, *Economic Freedom of the World* (Vancouver: Fraser Institute, 1997).

34. *Transparency International Corruption Perceptions Index 2002* (Berlin: Transparency International, 2002).

35. Rudy J. Rummel, *Death by Government* (Somerset, N.J.: Transaction Publishers, 1994).

36. Moore, "Beyond the Democratic Peace."

37. Rummel, *Death by Government.*

38. Moore, "Beyond the Democratic Peace."

39. "In the President's Words: 'Free People Will Keep the Peace of the World,'" *New York Times*, 27 February 2003.

40. Imports measured in barrels per day. U.S. Department of Energy, Energy Information Administration, *Petroleum Supply Annual 2000*, 1:70, table 29. Cross-referenced with Freedom House's 2000 country survey.

41. Natan Sharansky, "Democracy for Peace," *Essential Essays No. 1* (Washington, D.C.: American Enterprise Institute, 2002).

42. "China Denies Its Warships Off Spratlys," *BBC News*, 26 June 2001, http://news.bbc.co.uk/hi/english/world/asia-pacific/newsid_1408000/1408519.stm.

43. "Kabul's Women Come Out of Hiding," *Washington Post*, 9 December 2001.

Chapter 2

1. For an explanation of the methodology used in these ratings, see *Freedom in the World, 2001–2002* (New York: Freedom House, 2002).

2. The Universal Declaration of Human Rights is available on the United Nations website, www.un.org/Overview/rights.html.

3. Operation Ajax remains a neuralgic irritant to Iranian perceptions of the United States. See Sussan Siavoshi, *Liberal Nationalism in Iran: The Failure of a Movement* (Boulder, Colo.: Westview Press, 1990).

4. *First Line of Defense: Ambassadors, Embassies, and American Interests Abroad* (Washington, D.C.: American Academy of Diplomacy, 2000).

5. *Global Trends 2015: A Dialogue about the Future with Nongovernment Experts*, National Intelligence Council, NIC 2000-12, December 2000 (Washington, D.C.: U.S. Government Printing Office, 2000).

6. Peter Finn, "Police in Hamburg Detain 7," *Washington Post*, 4 July 2002.

7. Ross Terrill, "China the Uncertain Ally," *New York Times*, 19 February 2002.

8. Remarks by Polish foreign minister Wlodzimiercz Cimoszewicz, at Freedom House, Washington, D.C., 10 September 2002.

9. *The Collected Works of Mahatma Gandhi* (Ahmedabad, India: Navajivan Publishing House), 10:41.

10. The Toledo anecdote is from personal conversations the author had at the time.

11. William Schulz, *In Our Own Best Interest: How Defending Human Rights Benefits Us All* (Boston: Beacon Press, 2001).

12. Adrienne Rich, *On Lies, Secrets, and Silence: Selected Prose, 1966–1978* (New York: Norton, 1979).

13. Rupert Murdoch, in speech delivered on 23 May 2000, cited in Danny Schechter, *Falun Gong's Challenge to China—Spiritual Practice or "Evil Cult?"* (New York: Akashic Books, 2000).

14. Elisabeth Rosenthal, "China's Sparkle Bedazzles a Visiting Castro," *New York Times*, 28 February 2003.

15. "Mugabe and the Red Carpet," *European Press Review*, BBC *Monitoring*, 7 March 2001, www.bbc.co.uk/1/hi/world/europe/1206598.stm.

16. Jackson Diehl, "The Silence Signal," *Washington Post*, 5 August 2002.

17. "Secretary Albright Pushes Human Rights," *Washington Post*, 17 March 2000.

18. Richard Holbrooke, *To End a War* (New York: Random House, 1998).

19. Zhang Liang, with Andrew J. Nathan and Perry Link, eds., *The Tiananmen Papers* (New York: Public Affairs, 2001).

20. Georgie Anne Geyer, "Cuba's Castro Keeps on Ticking," *Washington Times*, 29 January 2002.

21. "Zimbabwe Leaders Face Financial Probe," *BBC News*, 23 January 2002.

22. Schulz, *In Our Own Best Interest*.

Chapter 3

1. Jackson Diehl, "Democracy Drowned Out," *Washington Post*, 18 November 2002.

2. Richard Mintner, "Another Cold War?" *Wall Street Journal Europe*, 30 June 2000.

3. William Safire, "Needed: Freedom's Caucus," *New York Times*, 31 May 2001.

4. Diehl, "Democracy Drowned Out."

5. David J. Scheffer, "Try Him for His Crimes," *Washington Post*, 12 September 2002.

6. E. J. Dionne Jr., "Pelosi: Good News for Human Rights," *Washington Post*, 19 November 2002.

Chapter 4

1. Leonid Romankov, "Opening Totalitarian Societies to the Outside World: A View from Russia," in *Realizing Human Rights*, ed. Samantha Power and Graham Allison (New York: St. Martin's Press, 2000).

2. Robert G. Herman and Theodore J. Piccone, eds., *Defending Democracy: A Global Survey of Foreign Policy Trends, 1992–2002* (Washington, D.C.: Democracy Coalition Project Inc., 2002).

3. Conversation with John Fox, November 2001.

4. Conversation with Ken Wollack, December 2001.

5. Mary McGrory, "Helping to Plow New Fields," *Washington Post*, 29 July 1989.

6. Jackson Diehl, "Casey Kasem or Freedom," *Washington Post*, 16 December 2002.

7. Steve York's brilliant film *Bringing Down a Dictator* shows the importance of Radio B-92 and ANEM in the struggle against Milosevic. In addition, a new book by Matthew Collin, *Guerrilla Radio: Rock 'n' Roll Radio and Serbia's Underground Resistance* (New York: Thunder's Mouth Press/Nation Books, 2002), examines the B-92 and ANEM story in detail.

Chapter 5

1. The Universal Declaration of Human Rights has been reprinted in numerous reference works and can be accessed online through the UN's website at www.un.org/Overview.rights.html.

2. Arie Bloed, ed., *From Helsinki to Vienna: Basic Documents of the Helsinki Process* (Utrecht, Netherlands: Martinus Nijhoff, 1990).

3. John Keane, *Vaclav Havel: A Political Tragedy in Six Acts* (New York: Basic Books, 2000).

4. Keane, *Vaclav Havel.*

Chapter 6

1. Discussions by the author and research associate with Czech diplomats and Freedom House staff, February 2002.

2. "Laos Sentences European Activists," *BBC News*, 9 November 2001, http://news.bbc.co.uk/1/hi/world/asia-pacific/1646407.stm.

3. Smith Hempstone, *Rogue Ambassador* (Sewanee, Tenn.: University of the South Press, 1997).

4. Mary McGrory, "Helping to Plow New Fields," *Washington Post*, 29 July 1989.

5. Piers Brandon, "Time Traveler," *Columbia Journalism Review* (January/February 1997).

6. Gene Sharp, *From Dictatorship to Democracy* (Boston: Albert Einstein Institution, 2002).

7. Rachel L. Swarns, "Look at Him Now," *New York Times*, 31 January 2002.

8. Cullen Murphy, "The Last Resort," *New Yorker*, April 1992.

9. Jane Perlez, "Iraq's Neighbors," *New York Times*, 8 October 2002.

10. Zhang Liang, with Andrew J. Nathan and Perry Link, eds., *The Tiananmen Papers* (New York: Public Affairs, 2001).

11. Hempstone, *Rogue Ambassador*.

12. Hempstone, *Rogue Ambassador*.

13. The Chile story is drawn from the following three sources: George P. Shultz, *Turmoil and Triumph: My Years as Secretary of State* (New York: Charles Scribners's Sons, 1993); George F. Jones, 1996 interview, in *Frontline Democracy: The U.S. Foreign Affairs Oral History Collection* (Arlington, Va.: Association for Diplomatic Studies and Training, 2000); and Harry G. Barnes Jr., "U.S. Human Rights Policies and Chile," monograph for U.S. Institute of Peace Human Rights Implementation Project, Washington, D.C., 2001.

14. Barnes, "U.S. Human Rights Policies in Chile."

15. Peter Ackerman and Jack Du Vall, *A Force More Powerful* (New York: Palgrave, 2000).

16. Ackerman and Du Vall, *A Force More Powerful*.

17. Dusko Doder and Louise Branson, *Milosevic: Portrait of a Tyrant* (New York: Free Press, 1999).

18. Hempstone, *Rogue Ambassador*. Supplemented by conversations with Ambassador Hempstone in 2002.

Chapter 7

1. Gene Sharp, *The Politics of Nonviolent Action* (Boston: Porter Sargent Publishers, 1973).

2. Peter Ackerman and Jack Du Vall, *A Force More Powerful* (New York: Palgrave, 2000).

3. Reprinted with permission from Czelaw Bielecki, ed., *The Little Conspirator* (Warsaw, 1982).

4. Arch Puddington, *Broadcasting Freedom: The Cold War Triumph of Radio Free Europe and Radio Liberty* (Lexington: University Press of Kentucky, 2000).

5. George P. Shultz, *Turmoil and Triumph: My Years as Secretary of State* (New York: Charles Scribners's Sons, 1993).

6. Congressman Steve Solarz, interview by author, 11 December 2001. Ambassador Mike Armacost, telephone interview by author, 19 November 2001. Ambassador Mort Abramowitz, interview by Kurt Bassuener, 27 November 2001. Ambassador Steve Bosworth, telephone interview by author, 4 December 2001. Ambassador Robert G. Rich, interview by Thomas Dunnigan, January 1994, in *Frontline Diplomacy: The U.S. Foreign Affairs Oral History Collection* (Arlington, Va.: Association for Diplomatic Studies and Training, 2000). Ulrich A. Strauss, interview by Charles Stuart Kennedy, 11 December 1992, in *Frontline*

Diplomacy. Richard B. Finn, interview by Charles Stuart Kennedy, 8 April 1991, in *Frontline Diplomacy*. Gaston Sigur, interview by Charles Stuart Kennedy, 24 April 1990, in *Frontline of Diplomacy*. Frederick Z. Brown, interview by Charles Stuart Kennedy, 2 February 1990, in *Frontline of Diplomacy*.

7. Wayne Merry, interview by Kurt Bassuener, 30 December 2001.

Chapter 8

The profiles of the forty-five dictators were drawn from the sources listed below. My colleagues, Charles Graybow and Kristin Guida, and I did not believe it was necessary or practical to provide individual footnotes for each profile, most of which are brief. Also we relied in significant part on our own knowledge of these countries and dictators. The author would be pleased to answer any questions about individual profiles.

Amnesty International (London).

Aburish, Said K. *Saddam Hussein: The Politics of Revenge*. New York: Bloomsbury, 2000.

Al-Kattan, Mohammed. "The Mysterious Amman Massacre May be Linked to Funds Embezzled by Saddam's Murdered Sons-in-Law." *Washington Report on Middle East Affairs* (April 1998).

Anderson, Frank. "Qadhafi's Libya: The Limits of Optimism." *Middle East Policy* 1, no. 4 (June 1999).

Associated Press.

Ayittey, George. *Africa in Chaos*. New York: St. Martin's Press, 1998.

Barrouhi, Abdelaziz. "Qadhafi Switches His Bets to Black." *Middle East Times* (September 1998).

Burr, J. Millard, and Robert O. Collins. *Requiem for the Sudan: War, Drought, and Disaster Relief on the Nile*. Boulder: Westview Press, 1995.

Daily Telegraph (London).

The Economist (London).

Far Eastern Economic Review (Hong Kong).

Fekry, Ahmed. "Exaggerated Birthday Coverage for Mubarak Makes Many Cringe." *Middle East Times* (Issue 2001-19).

Goldman, Merle. *Sowing the Seeds of Democracy in China: Political Reform in the Deng Xiaoping Era*. Cambridge: Harvard University Press, 1994.

Haggard, Stephan, and Robert R. Kaufman. *The Political Economy of Democratic Transitions*. Princeton: Princeton University Press, 1995.

Hindawi, Hussain. "Libya's Love Affair with Africa." *Middle East Times* (3 August 2001).

Human Rights Watch (New York).

Linz, Juan J., and Alfred Stepan. *Problems of Democratic Transition and Consolidation*. Baltimore: The Johns Hopkins University Press, 1996.

Jones-Luong, Pauline, Yale University, New Haven, Connecticut.

Kangas, Roger. *Uzbekistan in the Twentieth Century: Political Development and the Evolution of Power.* New York: St. Martin's Press, 1994.

Makiya, Kanan. *Republic of Fear: The Politics of Modern Iraq.* Berkeley: University of California Press, 1989.

McBride, Edward. "Monuments to Self: Baghdad's Grand Projects in the Age of Saddam Hussein." *Metropolis* (June 1999).

Miller, Judith. *God Has Ninety-Nine Names: Reporting from a Militant Middle East.* New York: Simon & Schuster, 1996.

Miller, Judith, and Laurie Mylroie. *Saddam Hussein and the Crisis in the Gulf.* New York: Times Books, 1990.

Petterson, Donald. *Inside Sudan: Political Islam, Conflict, and Catastrophe.* Boulder: Westview Press, 1999.

Post, Dr. Jerrold. Statement before House Armed Services Committee on Psychology of Saddam Hussein (December 1990).

Reno, William. *Warlord Politics and African States.* Boulder: Lynne Rienner Publishers, 1998.

Reuters.

Schell, Orville. *Mandate of Heaven: A New Generation of Entrepreneurs, Dissidents, Bohemians, and Technocrats Lay Claim to China's Future.* New York: Simon & Schuster, 1994.

Sherbiny, Naiem. "Mr. Mubarak Comes to Washington." In *Civil Society: Democratization in the Arab World* 8, no. 91 (Cairo: July 1999)—monthly publication of the Ibn Khaldun Center for Development Studies.

"Sudan Pushes Polygamy." *BBC News.* 15 August, 2001.

Tremlett, George. *Gadaffi: The Desert Mystic.* New York: Carroll & Graf, 1993.

U.S. State Department Country Reports on Human Rights Practices (Washington, D.C.).

Chapter 9

1. Ross Terrill, "China, the Uncertain Ally," *New York Times*, 19 February 2002.

2. Gordon G. Chang, *The Coming Collapse of China* (New York: Random House, 2001).

3. Zhang Liang, with Andrew J. Nathan and Perry Link, eds., *The Tiananmen Papers* (New York: Public Affairs, 2001).

4. Liang, *Tiananmen Papers.*

5. Danny Schechter, *Falun Gong's Challenge to China: Spiritual Practice or "Evil Cult"?* (New York: Akashic Books, 2000).

6. Schechter, *Falun Gong's Challenge.*

7. Chang, *Coming Collapse.*

8. Schechter, *Falun Gong's Challenge.*

9. "China's Old Habits Die Hard," *BBC News*, 16 November 2002.

10. Bette Bao Lord, telephone interview by author, 11 February 2002.

11. Michael Ledeen, telephone interview by author, 11 February 2002.

12. Chris Buckley, "Ex-Aide to Mao Urges China to Move toward Democracy," *New York Times*, 7 January 2003.

13. Elizabeth Rosenthal, "Chinese Leader Gives Up a Job but Not His Power," *New York Times*, 16 November 2002.

14. Elizabeth Bumiller, "In China Speech, President Bush Calls for More Religious Freedom," *New York Times*, 22 February 2002.

15. Liang, *Tiananmen Papers*.

16. Philip Pan and John Pomfret, "Critics Scoff as Chinese Premier Defends Record," *Washington Post*, 16 March 2002.

17. "Pyongyang, I Love You," *BBC News*. Text of South Korean President Kim Dae Jung's speech upon arrival in Pyongyang, 13 June 2000, http://news.bbc.co.uk/1/hi/world/asia-pacific/788682.stm.

18. A long dance of invitations from Seoul and promises from Pyongyang to come later ensued, but no Kim Jong Il trip south ever came to pass. "Kim Jong-il to Go South 'in Spring,'" *BBC News*, 13 September 2000, http://news.bbc.co.uk/1/hi/world/asia-pacific/923016.stm. "S Korea Calls for New Summit," *BBC News*, 6 June 2001, http://news.bbc.co.uk/1/hi/world/asia-pacific/1372722.stm.

19. Mike Allen, "North Korea Urged to Pull Back Arms," *Washington Post*, 17 February 2002.

20. Allen, "North Korea Urged to Pull Back Arms," 17 February 2002.

21. Debbie Liang-Fenton, executive director of the Committee for Human Rights in North Korea, telephone interview by author, 13 February 2002.

22. The Korean diaspora in Japan, numbering some 700,000, is a major source of foreign currency for the strapped Kim Jong Il regime in Pyongyang, though estimates vary extremely widely as to exactly how much money is sent back. In 1996 estimates varied from $100 million to $600 million per year. *Washington Post*, 7 June 1996.

23. Klaus-Dieter Frankenberger, "Views from Abroad," *Washington Post*, 15 March 2002.

24. "No Exceptions," *Washington Post*, 29 December 2002.

25. Reuel Marc Gerecht, "An Iraq War Won't Destabilize the Middle East," *New York Times*, 26 November 2002.

26. Owen Bennett-Jones, "A Sacking and a Coup," *BBC News*, 20 October 1999, http://news.bbc.co.uk/1/hi/world/from_our_own_correspondent/480306.stm.

27. James Burns, "Pakistan's Military Ruler Declares Himself President," *New York Times*, 20 June 2001.

28. "Means of Influence," editorial, *Washington Post*, 15 October 2002.

29. Franklin Foer, "Reza Pahlavi's Next Revolution—Successor Story," *New Republic*, 14 January 2002.

30. Tehran residents were prevented from staging a vigil in the town center by police and Islamist militia, who were assiduously enforcing a ban on public gatherings. See "Islamic World Deplores US Losses," *BBC News*, 14 September 2001, http://news.bbc.co.uk/1/hi/world/americas/1544955.stm.

31. Full text: State of the Union address, *BBC News*, 30 January 2002, http://news.bbc.co.uk/1/hi/world/americas/1790537.stm.

32. Walter Pincus, "U.S. Officials Talk of Peaceful Change," *Washington Post*, 8 April 2003.

33. "Kurds Map-out Post-Saddam Future," *BBC News*, 22 July 2002, http://news.bbc.co.uk/1/hi/world/middle_east/2144063.stm.

34. "A Survey of Thailand," *Economist*, 2 March 2002.

35. Seth Mydans, "Communists in Laos Dust Off the Nation's Royal Past," *New York Times*, 5 January 2003.

36. Nora Boustany, "A Royal Critic of 'Democracy' in Cambodia," *Washington Post*, 7 March 2003.

37. Jackson Diehl, "AID's Egyptian Disgrace," *Washington Post*, 2 September 2002.

38. "Algeria's Decade of Bloody Conflict," *BBC News*, 11 January 2002, http://news.bbc.co.uk/2/hi/middle_east/1755099.stm.

39. Samantha Power and Graham Allison, eds., *Realizing Human Rights* (New York: St. Martin's Press, 2000).

40. "Analysis: How Free and Fair Was the Poll?" *BBC News*, 14 March 2002, http://news.bbc.co.uk/2/hi/africa/1870970.stm.

41. Jon Jeter, "U.S., Opposition Reject Claim of Mugabe Victory," *Washington Post*, 14 March 2002.

42. Zimbabwe's dictator, Robert Mugabe, does this with alacrity. See "Zimbabwe Attacks UK 'Colonialism,'" *BBC News*, 3 March 2002, http://news.bbc.co.uk/2/hi/uk_politics/1852053.stm.

43. On Clinton's trip and the hype surrounding it, see *Washington Post*, 27 October 1998 and "Itinerary and Guide to Clinton's Visit," *BBC News*, 3 March 1998, http://news.bbc.co.uk/2/special_report/1998/03/98/africa/68674.stm.

44. Bill Berkeley, *The Graves Are Not Yet Full: Race, Tribe, and Power in the Heart of Africa* (New York: Basic Books, 2001).

45. Rachel Swarms, "Role in Group Enhances Mbeki's Image," *New York Times*, 10 July 2002.

46. Powers, *Realizing Human Rights*.

47. "Press Availability with Malian Foreign Minister Madibo Sidibe following Meeting with President Konare," U.S. Department of State, 23 May 2001, http://www.state.gov/secretary/rm/2001/3013.htm.

48. "Powell Condemns Mugabe," *BBC News*, 25 May 2001, http://news.bbc.co.uk/2/hi/world/africa/1352238.stm.

49. "Remarks with Kenyan President Daniel arap Moi following Their Meeting," U.S. Department of State, 26 May 2001, http://www.state.gov/secretary/rm/2001/3110.stm.

50. "Powell Presses Kenya on Reform," *BBC News*, 26 May 2001, http://news.bbc.co.uk/2/hi/world/africa/1352918.stm.

51. *Washington Times*, 12 August 2002.

52. "Zimbabwe Plan Said to Include an Exit Strategy for Mugabe," *New York Times*, 12 January 2003.

53. A series of articles in the *Washington Post* by veteran war correspondent John Pomfret in 1997 showed Kabila's dark side early on. See "Rwandans Led Revolt in Congo—Defense Minister Says Arms, Troops Supplied for Anti-Mobutu Drive," *Washington Post*, 9 July 1997; and "Massacres Were a Weapon in Congo's Civil War—Evidence Mounts of Atrocities by Kabila's Forces," *Washington Post*, 11 June 1997.

54. The International Rescue Committee's epidemiologist, Les Roberts, has done pioneering research into the human toll of the ongoing Congo war. See "Mortality Study, Eastern Democratic Republic of Congo," February–April 2001, on the International Rescue Committee's website, http://news.bbc.co.uk/2/hi/special_report/1998/12/98/french_in_africa/235589.stm.

55. A number of studies have been issued about extraction by all foreign forces operating in the Congo. See Justin Pearce, "Mugabe's Costly Congo Venture," *BBC News*, 25 July 2000, http://news.bbc.co.uk/2/hi/world/africa/611898.stm.

56. "Analysis: Allies in Africa," *BBC News*, 23 January 2002, http://news.bbc.co.uk/2/hi/world/europe/1776025.stm. On French Africa policy, see also Lucy Ash, "France: Superpower or Sugar Daddy?" from BBC Radio 4's two-part special report "A Mission to Civilise? The French in Africa," *BBC News*, 23 December 1998, http://news.bbc.co.uk/2/hi/special_report/1998/12/98/french_in_africa/235589.stm.

57. Emily Wax, "Congo, Rebels Reach Accord," *Washington Post*, 18 December 2002.

58. Douglas Farah, "Digging Up Congo's Dirty Gems," *Washington Post*, 30 December 2001.

59. Mark Dummett, "DR Congo's Endless Suffering," *BBC News*, 24 January 2002, http://news.bbc.co.uk/2/hi/world/africa/1780540.stm.

60. Mark Lonzi, "Europe's Armory for Terrorism," *Washington Post*, 3 January 2002.

61. Since this statement, two of the members of the delegation have been arrested and imprisoned in a work camp for "libel." See Valentinas Mite, "Journalists Sentenced for Libeling Lukashenko," *RFE/RL Poland, Belarus, and Ukraine Report*, 2 July 2002, www.rferl.org/pbureport/2002/07/26-020702.html. The statement by Assistant Secretary Lorne Craner from 8 February 2002 can be found at www.state.gov/r/pa/prs/ps/2002/7915.htm.

62. "Putin Pours Cold Water on Lukashenko's Merger Plans," *RFE/RL Poland, Belarus, and Ukraine Report*, 18 June 2002, www.rferl.org/pbureport/2002/06/24-180602.html.

63. On the Kurapaty memorial and Lukashenko's efforts to pave it over, see "Activists Petition Government to Protect Kurapaty Site," RFE/RL, 12 June 2002, www.rferl.org/ucs/2002/06/24-120602.html.

64. ABA CEELI briefing, Washington, D.C., August 2001.

65. Zubr's website can be visited at www.zubr-belarus.com. The group maintains an active international network and sends regular updates, as does the Charter 97 Civic Initiative (www.charter97.org) Zubr members are routinely harassed and arrested for their demonstrations.

66. Kevin Sullivan, "Anti-Castro Forces Mount Petition Drive," *Washington Post*, 28 April 2002.

67. Mary Jordan, "Castro Takes a Page from Foes' Playbook," *Washington Post*, 25 July 2002.

68. "An American Envoy Tugs Castro's Beard," *Economist*, 22 March 2003.

69. Fred Bernstein, "Lighting Matches in Cuba on the 4th," *New York Times*, 4 July 2002.

70. Jordan, "Castro Takes a Page," *Washington Post*, 25 July 2002.

71. "Cuban Dissidents Gather as Police Look On," *New York Times*, 11 December 2002.

72. Ernesto F. Betancourt, "Cuba's Balance of Payments Gap, the Remittances Scam, Drug Trafficking, and Money Laundering, from Cuba in Transition," *ASCE 2000*, 3 February 2003, http://lanic.utexas.edu/la/cb/cuba/asce/cuba10/betancourt.pdf.

Epilogue and Action Agenda

1. Jackson Diehl, "Solidarity, Cuban-Style," *Washington Post*, 13 January 2003.

2. Elizabeth Rosenthal, "China Orders Life Sentence for Dissident with U.S. Tie," *New York Times*, 10 February 2003.

3. Michael Dobbs, "Reform with an Islamic Slant," *Washington Post*, 9 March 2003.

Index